THE
BIRD

MASTER
OF FLIGHT

COLIN HARRISON
HOWARD LOXTON

Consulting Editor
Matthew M. Vriends, PhD

BARRON'S

in association with
David Bateman

First U.S. edition published 1993 by Barron's Educational Series, Inc., in association with David Bateman Ltd, 'Golden Heights', 32–34 View Road, Glenfield, Auckland, New Zealand

All inquiries should be addressed to:
Barron's Educational Series, Inc.
250 Wireless Boulevard
Hauppauge, New York 11788

Library of Congress Catalog Card No. 92-44566

International Standard Book No. 0-8120-6325-2

Library of Congress Cataloging in Publication Data

Harrison, Colin James Oliver.
    The bird: master of flight/Colin Harrison and Howard Loxton.
        p. cm.
    Includes bibliographical references and index.
    ISBN 0-8120-6325-2
    1. Birds. I. Loxton, Howard. II. Title.
QL673.H289 1993   92-44566
598--dc20   CIP

PRINTED IN HONG KONG

Design: Errol McLeary
Production: Paul Bateman
Copy editing and index: Margaret Forde
Typesetting: Typocrafters, Auckland, New Zealand
Printed in Hong Kong by Everbest Printing Co. Ltd

"And I beheld the birds in the bushes building their nests, which no man, with all his wits, could ever make. And I marvelled to know who taught the magpie to place the sticks in which to lay her eggs and to breed her young; for no craftsman could make such a nest hold together, and it would be a wonderful mason who could construct a mould for it! And yet I wondered still more at other birds — how they concealed and covered their eggs secretly on moors and marshlands, so that men should never find them; and how they hid them more carefully still when they went away, for fear of the birds of prey and of wild beasts. And there were some birds, I noticed, that trod their mates in the trees, and brought forth their young high up above the ground; while others conceived at their beaks through the act of breathing. And I noted carefully the way that peacocks breed. And when I saw all these things I wondered what master they had."

from *The Vision concerning Piers the Plowman*, written *ca.* 1367 by William Langland, rendered into modern English.

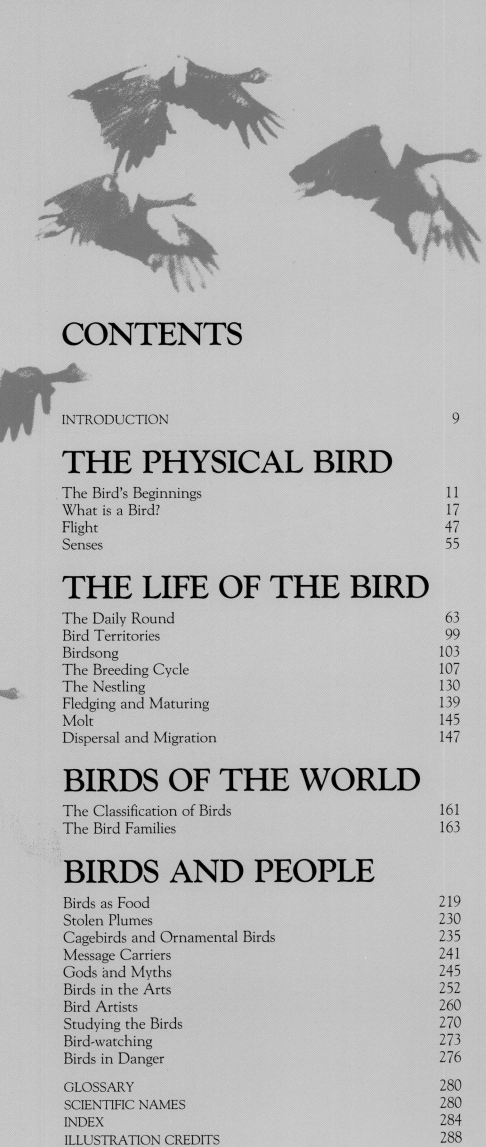

CONTENTS

INTRODUCTION

Everywhere that we may go on this Earth we are likely to find birds: in the valleys, on the mountain tops and winging their way across the oceans. People have fed on them, been inspired by them, and found them a lasting source of fascination. Although our ancestors linked them with the gods, today's scientists seek to understand their mysteries and bird-watching has become an engrossing pursuit of millions of people.

Many people get great satisfaction from being able to identify the different birds that they see, and there are numerous regional field guides available to aid their recognition of bird species. In this book we have taken a wider view, attempting to encompass the whole Avian Order and give the reader an understanding of the characteristics that make a bird a bird and an appreciation of the great diversity of birds and their different ways of life. It is not designed to be pushed into your pocket for quick consultation but to be read at leisure, when you can enjoy the photographs taken by some of the world's best bird photographers and other fine illustrations that we have been able to assemble.

We have based the information about bird life on the latest research available and the presentation of the bird families follows the taxonomic classification using DNA analysis that was introduced by C. G. Sibley and J. E. Ahlquist while the book was being written. We have not, however, adopted any hypotheses that have not been proven, and have clearly distinguished conjecture from established fact. Mainly common names for species are used in the text, with scientific names also given in captions. The index gives scientific names with the common name and there is a separate cross reference listing of scientific names so that birds can be found under either. The index also indicates the bird family or part of a family to which each bird belongs by reference to the number given to it in the "Birds of the World" section of the book.

The latter part of the book presents something of the relationship between birds and ourselves, tracing the way attitudes have changed from worship to exploitation and to a growing contemporary awareness of the need to respect the natural world and conserve it. The roles that birds play in our culture and our imagination thus complement their natural diversity.

If you are a bird enthusiast already, we hope that this book will deepen and extend your understanding of these fascinating creatures. If you are new to the subject, we are confident that it will make you an enthusiast in the future.

THE PHYSICAL BIRD

THE BIRD'S BEGINNINGS

The flying reptile

A bird's appearance is very deceptive. The image we usually see is of a beautifully smooth-feathered creature, its rounded outline tapering to wings and tail. Strip away this cover and a creature is revealed with thin forelimbs, spindly legs and a short squat body with a bony stub to support the tail. Its thin neck carries a head that has a bulging cranium, large eyes and a projecting bony bill. Birds are rarely seen like this except when they are naked nestlings or when fowl have been plucked ready for cooking, but this image of the bird makes it easier to comprehend the origins and evolution of the whole Avian Order.

Snow Geese (Anser caerulescens). *Birds have evolved with the ability to maintain balance in the air, produce the power to fly and offer an aerodynamic shape to enable them to stay airborne. They have developed a bone structure to make them lighter in the air and organic functions and life cycles are both affected by the demands of flight.*

A useful clue to the origins of birds is the scaly covering of their legs and feet: it is a sign that birds evolved from reptiles. This might seem difficult to prove but fortunately strong evidence survives. About 150,000,000 years ago a few individuals of a creature that we now call *Archaeopteryx* fell and died in the fine mud of lagoons in what is now a part of Germany. Soft silt rapidly covered them, hiding them from predators and preserving much of the detail of their structure when it hardened around them. Their well-preserved fossilized remains clearly show reptilian characteristics. These include a long and slender bony tail, a tapering muzzle, its jaws set with small teeth, and other features of a reptile skeleton.

In some respects however these fossils are not reptilian. The forelimbs are modified to carry what is unmistakably the full set of flight feathers that make up a bird's wing, feathers that are still visible as impressions in the stony fossil matrix. However, the forelimb digits are not completely fused together (as they would be in a modern bird); the ends are still free and equipped with claws. Another row of large flight feathers fringes either side of the long tail. This animal, though not necessarily a direct ancestor of modern birds, clearly shows the way in which evolutionary change was occurring.

Archaeopteryx was certainly not the first bird. It occurred in the Jurassic geological period, and evidence is now being found that suggests that birds were recognizably evolving from reptiles in the Late Triassic, about 220,000,000 years ago, the time at which mammals also evolved. *Archaeopteryx* came some 70,000,000 years later in the scheme of things and, while it helps to demonstrate the process of change, we do not know how it relates to other possible lines of bird evolution at this period.

Evolving feathers

It would seem that the reptile ancestors were producing new forms that were warm-blooded — able to control their body temperature — an advantage because they could then be active for much longer periods. Bare skin was vulnerable to external conditions, so the next stage in controlling body temperature was to evolve insulation from the climate outside the body to prevent valuable heat being lost and to conserve energy.

Mammals produced fur, an overlapping mass of fine slender structures covering the body that could be raised or lowered to adjust the thickness of the layer. The fossils of some flying reptiles, the pterosaurs, show evidence that they too had a furry body covering.

Birds evolved a use of the same material — keratin — in a different form, producing flat outgrowths of the skin layer: feathers. These feathers are thought to be derived from reptilian scales, increased in size, overlapping and finely split to provide flexibility. They could be raised to hold air between them, creating a thick protective and insulating layer, and in hot conditions they could be sleeked against the body.

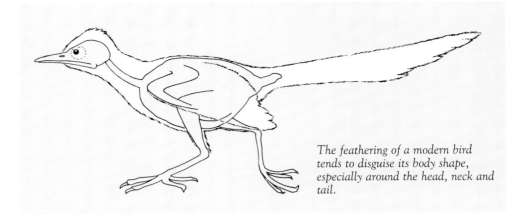

The feathering of a modern bird tends to disguise its body shape, especially around the head, neck and tail.

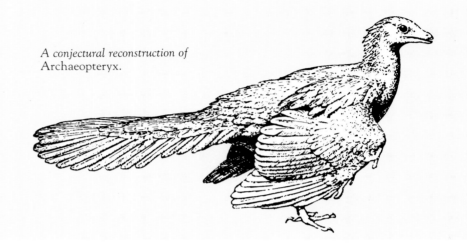

A conjectural reconstruction of Archaeopteryx.

On the thin bony limbs and tail insulation would be less important and they could be lost (on legs) or become larger and more exaggerated in shape and structure, so producing the larger and longer feathers now used in flight.

Why did flight evolve?

Why, even under these circumstances, did flight evolve? It is a convenient method of moving from place to place and for overcoming terrestrial barriers, but this alone would not seem to provide the pressure for evolutionary change. Modern birds of various species have lost their powers of flight. This usually occurs

The chick of the modern Hoatzin has moveable claws on each wing, which it can use to grip onto twigs and plants. As the bird matures these wing claws are lost, but they are reminiscent of the hooks on the wings of Archaeopteryx.

A fossil of Archaeopteryx discovered in the Jurassic limestone of Bavaria. This animal had basically reptilian features but was more than halfway to being a bird. It has the structure of a running lizard but with a bird's wing of flight feathers and more large feathers bordering the tail. In addition, it shows the early stages of a skeletal structure adapted to flight.

Compsognathus (top), a dinosaur that ran on its hind feet, lived 150,000,000 years ago at the same time and in the same territory as Archaeopteryx (above), and was of a similar size and superficially very similar in structure. Its foot bones were fused together to form a bird-like lower leg bone with three toes pointing forward and one tiny one pointing back — a foot designed for running. The fact that birds have a similar leg and foot structure may be a clue to a running reptile ancestry.

where they are not threatened by predators, so one may suspect that the need to escape predation has played a vital part in the evolution and retention of flight in birds.

Two different ideas are often put forward as possible ways in which bird-flight evolved. One suggests that the reptile-type ancestors climbed trees and developed wing and tail feathers in order to glide between branches or to the ground, and later to fly for longer distances. The claws present on the wings of *Archaeopteryx* are cited as evidence that it climbed, but this ignores the need to protect its feathers from abrasion and damage caused by contact with hard surfaces. The climbing and gliding animals that we know, such as the Flying Squirrel,

incorporate all four limbs in the structure that aids gliding and flight. They do not develop the larger hind limbs that *Archaeopteryx* had and that lacked flight feathers.

Evolution from a reptile adapted for running seems more likely. Similarities of structure can be seen in the coelurosaurs. These were small carnivorous dinosaurs that stood and walked on well-developed hind legs, the smaller forelimbs probably being used mainly in catching prey and feeding. They resembled birds in having a light skeleton with hollow bones and their forelimb digits were reduced to three, as in *Archaeopteryx*.

Archaeopteryx had the structure of a running lizard, but with a bird's wing of flight feathers on the forelimbs and feathers bordering the tail. If it raised and spread them when running they would have provided both lift and stability to aid its progress. It also showed the early stages of skeletal structure used in flight: a big crested humerus and a fused furcula and, it is now believed, *Archaeopteryx* had a very small flanged breastbone.

If it could move through the air, even if only in descent and with clumsy fluttering, it would have achieved a wonderful new advantage. If, when pursued, it could mount up by running jumps through twigs and branches or onto rocks and then launch itself from a raised site, its escape was likely. Nothing baffles a predator more than the disappearance of its prey from the spot where it had hoped to catch it. If prey has not moved far the pursuit might be resumed, so there is strong survival value in traveling as far as possible through the air and a strong selective pressure for the evolution of effective long-distance flight.

The evidence makes it reasonably certain that birds evolved from the early reptiles, probably in parallel with mammals, and by the Late Jurassic there is evidence that powered flight existed. Unfortunately there is no continuity of known fossil evidence. If *Archaeopteryx* represents a typical Late Jurassic stage, what were birds and other flying forms like in their first 70 million years of evolution before *Archaeopteryx*? Though other reptiles went on to develop flying forms, such as the pterosaurs, only fragmentary evidence has been found for the development of birds. This material suggests that they evolved highly specialized forms that later became extinct, to be replaced by similar forms at later periods. We have little idea of the typical intervening stages between the early forms and the perfection of flight that can be seen in modern birds.

Flight has given birds huge advantages in terms of both short- and long-distance movement through the air and enabled them to use specialized feeding methods and to breed on sites that are difficult to reach by other means. However, flight also inhibits birds. It has imposed limitations on them and forced some adaptations. A flying creature is dependent on feathers and its postures and movements are determined by the need to look after those feathers. The use of forelimbs as wings means that feeding must usually be done with the bill alone (though some birds have learned to use their claws) enforcing a range of specializations. Possession of plumage also affects how and where breeding can occur for allowance must be made for replacing feathers. As in most aspects of evolution, gains from adaptation are to some degree accompanied by losses in some other respect; the overall benefit is what ensures survival.

The earliest birds

Information on and material relating to the earliest birds is fragmentary in the extreme. Some apparently avian bones exist from the Late Triassic, about 220 million years ago; then a few specimens of *Archaeopteryx*, assigned to a subclass, Archaeornithes, were found in Late Jurassic rocks from about 150 million years ago. Another 25 million years on, in the early Cretaceous, there is evidence of three more groups of birds, also given the status of subclasses.

One of these was discovered only recently and separated from the known birds as the Enantiornithes (the "Other Birds"). Evidence of its existence is widespread — in Europe, Mongolia, Central and South America and probably Australia. These birds seem to have been varied in structure, but we have little real idea of what they looked like.

Another subclass is that of the Odontornithes (the "Toothed Birds"). They were very like the present birds in structure, but differed in possessing small sharp teeth set in sockets in the jawbones. This subclass divided early in the Cretaceous period into two distinct lines. The less extreme line is represented by genera such as *Ichthyornis* and only known from the Late Cretaceous. They had a well-developed keel to the breastbone, to accommodate the flight muscle, and were somewhat like the present-day terns in general proportions.

The other line of toothed birds is known from both Early and Late Cretaceous. It com-

prises species that had become much more specialized. They were something like the present-day divers, or loons, *Gavia* species. They were aquatic and flightless, long-bodied with swimming legs and feet well to the rear of the body for propulsion, longish neck and tapering bill, and wings reduced to single small vestigial bones. They must have bred on low shores, close by the water. *Hesperornis regalis* is the best known of the species.

The Cretaceous period extended from 136 to 65 million years ago. The Enantiornithes and Odontornithes seem to have occurred through most of the period but, like the dinosaurs, had disappeared at the end of it. There seems no obvious reason to link their disappearance with the fate of the dinosaurs. These birds may simply have failed to compete successfully with the third new subclass — the Neornithes (the "Recent Birds"), which includes all those that we know today.

Recent birds

There is some disagreement about when this final subclass began to make its presence felt. In the DNA–DNA hybridization classification (page 163), a timescale calculation has been included that suggests that these birds originated near the beginning of the Cretaceous, with the ratites diverging from the rest as early as about 130 million years ago and the waterfowl and gamebirds separating off soon afterwards. It is suggested that most of the main orders would have originated about 124 to 95 million years ago. The main adaptive radiation that produced the waterbirds and seabirds seems to have occurred at around the time of change from Cretaceous to Tertiary faunas.

The fossil evidence from Cretaceous times is too scarce to tell anything significant about Recent Birds at this period. For the subsequent Tertiary period, the last 65 million years, much more information is available.

Most of the main bird forms that occur today seem already to be apparent in some form as far back as the early Tertiary. Although the songbirds are a dominant part of the world's birdlife now, there appear to have been only a very few species present then, and their massive adaptive radiation occurred later. When they were absent during this earlier period the ecological niches that they occupy today as eaters of small creatures and seeds seem to have been filled by species from nonpasserine groups, smaller than those existing in the families at present, such as tiny raptors and gamebirds.

Some forms existing in the early Tertiary became extinct. One group that persisted for

The appearances of prehistoric birds can only be guessed at from the sometimes fragmentary fossil evidence that survives and reconstructions depend as much upon the intelligent use of the imagination as scientific fact. These artist's constructions are only conjectural but do give some idea of the diversity of early birds.
1. Ichthyornis 2. Hesperornis
3. A pelagornithiform
4. A plotopterid 5. Diatrymid.

a long time was the "Bony-toothed Birds," Pelagornithiformes. These were large to very large, gliding, albatross-like seabirds, some with a wingspan of over 15 feet (6 m). However, the body was short and heavy, the head small and the bill very long. The effect was pelican-like but with a stouter and more rounded bill, along the jaw edges of which were a row of sharp bony spikes, extensions of the jawbone. The bill ended in a hook. They were cosmopolitan birds of the oceans that already showed adaptive radiation to produce varied species in the Palaeocene and lower Eocene of Europe, over 55 million years ago, and were last known from New Zealand in the Pliocene 50 million years later. The worsening weather of the coming Ice Ages may have finally destroyed them.

One noticeable feature of past avifaunas is the way in which certain types of birds are repeatedly evolved, but from different groups. The penguins produced giant forms in Oligocene and Miocene times, when the huge penguin-like Plotopterids were also evolved from pelicanid birds, with wings reduced to flippers. Later, large flightless auks were evolved in late Miocene to Pleistocene times off California and in recent times in the North Atlantic.

In addition to our present ratites, large cursorial (running) flightless birds evolved from time to time. Big, large-headed Diatrymids roamed North America and Europe in the Palaeocene, a range of various-sized Phorusrachids apparently used a vacant niche for large predators in South America from the Oligocene to the Pleistocene, and there were emu-like Dromornithids in Australia from Miocene to

The Cactus Ground-Finch (Geospiza conirostris), a recent island species developed on the Galapagos Islands in the last million years. The Galapagos Islands are famous for the inspiration that they gave Charles Darwin, who noted how the finches had evolved from a common ancestor to use the available resources. This species feeds on cactus, widely available on the islands.

Right *Galapagos Hawk (Buteo galapagoensis).*

Pleistocene. These last two groups went out with the Ice Ages; but possibly the massive Elephant-birds, Aepyornithids, of Madagascar and Africa, and certainly the range of Moas of New Zealand, should be regarded as recent species helped to extermination by man.

Although people tend to think of birds as a group increasing through time, in the mid-Tertiary there appears to have been an active period of adaptive radiation in which birds took advantage of the different habitats and formed new species (speciation), and a probable decrease during the climatic fluctuations of the last two million years. More recent bursts of speciation on some islands, and in areas where populations were isolated by climatic change, show the potential for alteration in numbers of species over relatively short periods of the geological timescale. The Honeycreepers of the Hawaiian Islands and the finches of the Galapagos Islands are examples of this.

WHAT IS A BIRD?

Few people would have any difficulty in identifying a bird. Whereas other animals may seem to come in a bewildering variety of forms, a bird is easily recognizable. The basic form is the same irrespective of size, which can vary from one tiny species with a body little more than 1 inch (2.5 cm) long to birds more than 100 times as big, and in spite of elaborations of plumage and individual characteristics developed by different species to cope with a wide range of ways of living.

What sets them apart from all other creatures and makes them recognizable as birds is that they have feathers: small ones that cover the body and larger ones that form wings and tail. Feathers make flight possible for birds, and feathers, together with other adaptations necessary for efficient flight and to guard against feather damage, have helped to shape the bird as a different and distinct kind of creature. Feathers separate the birds from all other groups of animals, backboned or invertebrate, making them different even from other flying creatures and their own reptile ancestors.

The skeleton

The shape of the bird's body, and of the skeleton on which it is based, is a result of adaptation for flight. Ground-living animals find an elongated and flexible body an advantage in moving through vegetation, for swimming, for walking and for running on four legs. Flexure of the body is a disadvantage for a creature that needs to maintain balance while moving through the air, so the bird body has become short and compact.

Because a bird must be as light as possible in ratio to its flying strength, it has evolved a comparatively lighter skeleton than that of other animals. This has partly been achieved by the fusion of some bones, reducing their number, especially in the lower spine, which in turn reduces the weight of muscle and ligament required. It has also been lightened by the shortening of the body, the reduction in the length of the tail and the loss of heavy jaw bones and teeth.

An even more important modification of the skeleton is not so obvious: the bones themselves are often hollow, not solid as in most animal skeletons, though with internal supports to strengthen them. The larger the bird, the more air space there is within the bone.

The legs must be strong and springy, to absorb some of the force of landing and give a push at takeoff. With perching birds this is carried over to the hopping mode of progress, but terrestrial birds are adapted for walking and running. The legs must be centrally placed to be near the center of gravity since they are the only support. They lift the body and its plumage clear of the ground and help to avoid damage to the feathers.

The lower leg is a thin structure of bone and sinew, inherited from the running reptiles, and it originates mainly from foot bones fused together to form a simpler structure.

The legs form the only motive power when the bird is on the ground. The forelimbs have become wings, structures designed only to carry the feathers needed for flight. They are composed mainly of bones and tendons, with relatively little muscle. The wings must propel the bird through the air and a strong attachment is needed where they join the body.

The forelimbs can be extended outwards to either side, and as they stretch out, the fans of overlapping feathers spread to form the

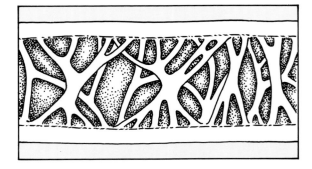

wing. When folded back against the body the humerus projects backwards, radius and ulna forward beneath it, and the digits back between them. As the wing closes against the body, the feather fans close and overlap, secondaries over

Many of a bird's bones are hollow tubes, crisscrossed with internal struts to give them strength: a feature that helps reduce weight for flying.

The Avian Order embraces birds of hugely different size, but bird skeletons vary only in minute details: differences in toes and the number of neck vertebrae.

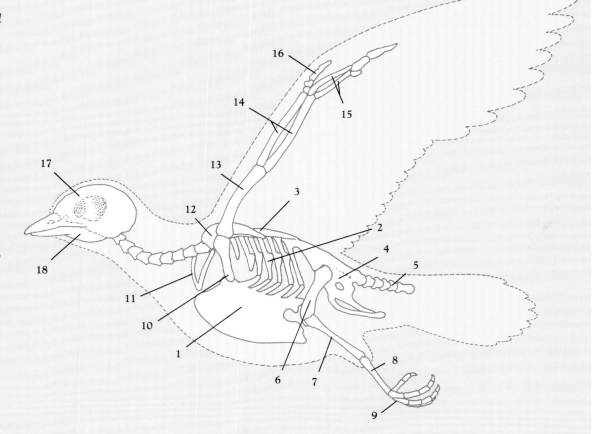

1. *The breastbone, the sternum, is a curved bony shield with a central keel projecting below to which are attached the big muscles that power the wings.*

2. *The ribs attach the sternum to the backbone. Relatively short and stout, they have a joint that allows some flexing between sternum and backbone but otherwise form a fairly compact cage. A projection on each rib overlapping the next aids solidity.*

3. *The backbone, flexible at neck and tail, is solid where it carries the body. Forward vertebrae are large, with interlocking projections. Bonding muscles and ossified tendons hold the whole together. Rear body vertebrae are fused together to form a bony rod, the synsacrum.*

4. *The pelvic bones are fused to form thin curved plates that project on either side to form another shieldlike structure that protects the organs of the hinder part of the body.*

5. *At the rear of the tail a series of greatly reduced vertebrae form a small movable support for the fan of large tail feathers.*

6. *The legs articulate in ball-and-socket joints on either side towards the anterior of the pelvis. The upper leg bone, the femur, is relatively short and with the knee joint is hidden in the muscular upper leg.*

7. *The tibia and fibula of the lower legs of reptiles and mammals are here fused together and they are fused to the upper foot bones to form the tibiotarsus, the upper bone of the visible leg of birds. It has a well-developed joint articulation at its lower end.*

8. *The apparent lower leg bone of birds, the tarsometatarsus, is formed of fused bones and joins the tibiotarsus in a backward-projecting joint.*

9. *Three rounded projections at the lower end of the tibiotarsus and a small bone, the metatarsal, attached at the rear are jointed to three jointed bones in front and a backward-pointing toe on the metatarsal. Each has a claw. Strong tendons that control the toes pass over the back of the leg joint, through a series of special holes or channels.*

10. *A pair of coracoid bones, projecting upward, forward and slightly outward from the front edge of the breastbone, join the strap-shaped shoulder blades, or scapulas, which lie along either side of the backbone, bound in place by muscle layers.*

11. *The V-shaped wishbone, or furcula, lies between these scapulas and coracoids, attached at its base to the front of the breastbone, forming a flexible support for the whole.*

12. *The scapulas, that with the coracoid bones and wishbone form a complex support and attachment for the upper arm bone, the humerus.*

13. *The humerus is often the biggest and strongest bone of the body, since it carries the wings at one end and the attachment for the powerful flight muscles at the other. The inner end is enlarged and flattened and at its tip has a smooth surface for a moving joint with the body bones. It is to this*

inner end that the big muscles for the wingbeats are attached.

14. *The paired forearm bones, the radius and ulna, are like those of reptiles and mammals, but in birds only serve to carry the inner half of the wing's flight feathers, the secondaries.*

15. *At the joint of the wing there are two small wrist bones that give some flexibility; but the hand has been reduced to two fused digits forming the carepometacarpus, with three small bones beyond. These form a rigid spike of bone that carries the outer half of the wing feathers, the primaries.*

16. *A projecting bony spike at the inner end of the carpometacarpus, just on the angle of the wing joint, is the relic of another digit. It carries its own tiny feather tuft, like a miniature wing. This little bone, the bastard wing or alula, can be raised forwards, projecting like a minute*

thumb, and plays a part in some kinds of flight movements.

17. *The skull is rounded and sometimes slightly domed at the back. This part houses the brain. The external openings of the ears are low down at the sides and toward the back. The eye sockets are just in front of the cranium. Sight is of primary importance in birds and the great rounded cavities that house the eye extend into the skull, separated along the midline only by a thin sheet of bone.*

18. *The long V-shaped lower jaw bone articulates with the skull well back on the lower side just at the rear of the eye sockets. Each side of the jaw articulates with a small separate bone, the quadrate, which in turn binds onto the skull. This allows some small flexibility in the jaw movements. In some birds the upper rostrum has limited movement where it joins the skull.*

and walk, accommodating two kinds of movement demands a compromise. To bring their center of gravity to the optimum position for both walking and flying, birds with long legs usually have to stretch them out when flying, or tuck them into the body if they are short, and when walking the body is tilted upwards so that the weight is centered over the legs.

In a rough comparison with the human body the bird's "knee" is placed high up against the side of the body, acting rather as the hip joint does in humans, with the "ankle" providing the flexion that is given by your knee. The "foot" is carried above the ground and the weight distributed instead through the toes, which are splayed out to form a more stable base over a larger area. Birds that spend most of their lives on or in water have further differences and many of these species have very poor balance when they try to walk on land — they can only waddle or shuffle along.

Some birds have evolved the ability to use the feet when feeding, but for most species the

The Ostrich (Struthio camelus) is the largest of all modern birds: males can stand 8 feet (2.4 m) tall and weigh over 330 pounds (136 kg); females are only slightly smaller. They lay the largest egg of any living bird, though it is comparatively small in relation to the female's size — only 1 percent of her weight. Ostriches belong to an ancient family with fossils known from 60 million years ago. These recently hatched young, with their striped plumage, were already nearly 1 foot (30 cm) tall when they came out of the egg. In contrast, the smallest known bird, the tiny Bee Hummingbird (Mellisuga helenae) is smaller than this Ostrich's eye.

Right *The spread wings of a Blue-footed Booby (Sula nebouxii) in one of its display postures show the sections of the wing and the way the wing feathers relate to the bones. The webs on the bright blue feet extend to the inward-bent hind toes.*

longer primaries, and the primary tips rest on top of the tail.

The ideal center of gravity for a moving body is between the limbs but, since birds both fly

When in the air, long-legged, long-necked birds such as this Great Egret (Casmerodius albus) stretch out their legs and draw in their necks to keep their center of gravity in an optimum position for flight.

and wings, the muscles seem small and slender. Movement is mostly controlled by strong thin tendons replacing muscles and attached to bone projections, rather like the strings that work a marionette. On the legs the big muscles are at the upper end, above the knee joint, and they find the big area of body attachment that they need on the flat lateral surfaces of the big broad pelvis. When the bird is standing they are usually at about the center of gravity. However, in birds that spend much of their lives using their feet for swimming, the legs and their muscles are towards the rear end of a longish body, where propulsion is most needed. This makes balance more awkward and such birds may have difficulty in moving on land, as in grebes and loons, or divers. Birds such as auks and penguins, which swim with their wings, also have legs and feet towards the rear and these birds rest upright on land.

The other big mass of muscles is needed to provide wing movement. Muscles work in pairs, pulling against each other. A pair of major muscles is needed on each side, one to raise the wing, the other to pull it down. The projecting keel of the breastbone provides the necessary large attachment surface for these muscles. In flightless birds both keel and muscles are greatly reduced.

The big breast muscles, apparent on most birds and placed on each side of the keel, consist of a smaller inner muscle and a much larger outer one. The inner one raises the wing, needing less force to lift a partly folded wing. It is larger in birds using wings to swim under water. The larger outer muscle must exert the greater downward pull, forcing the spread wing down against the air, raising the body and making powered flight possible. Both muscles are attached to the inner wing bone, the humerus, on its enlarged inner end. The breast muscles are below the wing and in order to raise the wing the inner supracoracoidal muscle must pull upwards over some raised support. This support is provided by the upper end of the coracoid bone projecting at the front of the breastbone. The muscle tapers forwards and upwards through a deep hollow in the upper coracoid, partly supported and enclosed by the narrow shoulder blade, the scapula, and the wishbone to form a hole through which the muscle can pass, resting on the edge like a rope on a pulley as it raises the humerus and hence the wing. For the great downward pull the big outer pectoral muscle goes directly to the broad, elongated deltoid crest along the inner humerus and pulls the wing down as it contracts.

Bird locomotion makes considerable demands on these muscles. Even though a flying bird may alternate wing beats with swoops or glides, the activity of flying may continue at times for hours or even days. One group of birds, embracing most of the swifts, flies for the greater part of their lifetime, seemingly coming to ground or perch only when nesting.

Two types of muscle can be recognized in birds. Broad white muscle fibers are fueled by a stored carbohydrate, glycogen. They provide vigorous bursts of activity for limited duration

legs and feet are just the means by which they move on land or in water; the wings are only used during flight. Feeding must be done by the head alone, so the mouth must reach out to take food and be able to reach the ground. As a result there is often some correlation between leg length and neck length, as in ostriches and flamingos.

The other thing that a bird must do with its head is to reach all parts of the plumage, from wing tips to tail, in order to clean and preen the feathers.

To enable the bill to take food and to preen without help from the limbs, the bird needs a reasonably long and flexible neck, which tends to loop downwards and rise under the back of the head. The foremost of the vertebrae of the backbone are reduced to narrow rings on which the head can easily rotate. The neck that is usually visible from the outside is a concealing sheath of loose skin and feathers that looks shorter than the long neck that it hides. It is only when the bird is very active that the full flexibility of its structure is revealed.

The muscles

Birds must compromise between the need for muscles to provide motive power and the problems of economy and distribution of weight. Although muscles occur in fairly thin layers on much of the body, they are widely distributed and even the erection of feathers needs some small muscular traction.

The neck has a long and elaborate system of small, paired, overlapping muscles that permit complex movements of head and neck, but the main muscle masses are associated with the bird's locomotion. Towards the end of the legs

Left An Anhinga (Anhinga anhinga) dries its plumage and preens, its long neck helping it to reach almost all of its body except its head. All birds' necks are longer than they look when not extended.

Top right A Kaka Parrot (Nestor meridionalis) feeding. It has a strong grip with two toes in each direction. Parrots are among the few birds that raise the foot to the bill.

Right The burst crop of a shot pigeon shows how much barley it contained, eaten quickly for slow digestion later.

Far right A Wood-Pigeon (Columba palumbus) holds the base of the bill of its young, encouraging it to take the "pigeon's milk" that the parent has brought up from its crop. For this older nestling, the milk may be mixed with seeds.

Following pages The Blackcap (Sylvia atricapilla) is a bird of treetop foliage, though it rests at lower levels and nests in low shrub. It has a rich warbling song, one of the finest of a genus of fine singers.

and are apparent in muscles such as those of the breasts of gamebirds, where they enable these birds to suddenly irrupt into short but vigorous flight. Narrow red muscle fibers use the oxygen from the blood supply to burn stored fat and can continue to do so for a much longer period. There are also fibers of intermediate type that use a combination of both processes to provide energy and power.

Digestion

A bird needs plenty of energy and muscle power to fly but it cannot afford to carry any unnecessary weight. It must therefore digest food rapidly and make the utmost use of it. It does not pass great quantities of water through the body but retains liquid, absorbing it from the feces before defecation, recycling it through the system so that a comparatively small amount is carried in the gut. Diet also tends to avoid bulky green vegetation that contains a great deal of cellulose and takes a long time to digest, though some of the more terrestrial birds do eat leaves. Although some birds take in large quantities, from which nutrients are extracted rather inefficiently, the food passes through very quickly.

Despite the need to keep down weight, many birds, ranging from seed eaters to birds of prey, are able to store large quantities of food at the very beginning of the digestive system in an extension of the esophagus called the crop. When concentrating on feeding in the open, birds are vulnerable to their enemies. The crop enables them to eat quickly and then retire to the shelter of a bush or other safe place to digest what they have eaten.

In many birds the crop also provides a temporary storage place for food collected far from the nest that has to be carried back to the young. Seabirds, especially, may have to fly long distances from their feeding areas to the nest, too far to carry back fish in the bill. More efficiently they swallow food and hold it in the crop, regurgitating it when they get back to their chicks. In pigeons and flamingos, parts of the crop wall become thicker during the nesting period and are shed to form a substance, frequently known as pigeon's milk, which is fed to the young.

White-fronted Terns (Sterna striata) copulating. The male must bring his tail end around and under that of the female.

Carnivorous birds, whether they eat insects, fish, land animals or other birds, rely on powerful stomach acids to break down and digest food, but those that eat vegetation must first break it down into finer particles. They have no teeth to chew it up but instead swallow grit that accumulates in the secondary part of the stomach. This part of the gut, the gizzard, has thick, hard muscular walls and here, churned by muscular contractions, the grit grinds up food. Since the grit itself is also ground down it must be continually replenished. Carrying the weight of grit around may seem to cancel out the weight loss obtained by not having teeth and heavy jaws but because it is carried much nearer to the center of gravity of the bird it does not cause such a problem in flight.

Food passes through the usual animal digestive processes. Saliva, which coats the food in the mouth, helps it to pass down the gullet and through the crop to the stomach. Beyond the stomach, food passes through the duodenum where secretions from the pancreas break down fat and protein and turn starch to body sugar. Some of the output from the liver is fed in at this point and also helps digestion, though much of it is waste. As the food passes through the next section of the system, the intestine, the products that the body needs are absorbed through the duodenum's lining. Finally unabsorbed food, and wastes, including those discharged by the kidneys, pass out through the rectum, where much of the water is reabsorbed into the body, to be discharged through the cloaca, the bird's only excretory orifice.

Reproduction

In birds the reproductive organs are usually internal in both sexes, ducts opening into the cloaca. In males the end of the ducts may have some erectile tissue within the cloaca. An external penis-like structure is apparent in the Ostrich and in waterfowl. In the latter it may assist copulation, which takes place in the water. In the Ostrich its function is less obvious, other than as an object of display.

The organs of reproduction are present in the upper part of the body cavity, near the kidneys. The male has a pair of testes with ducts to the cloaca. These are tiny in nonbreeding birds but greatly enlarged when breeding. In the female only one ovary develops, normally on the left side. This contains all the minute egg cells that the bird will need in its lifetime. There is a simple oviduct leading to the cloaca, with a funnel-shaped opening at the oviduct end.

In the breeding season, the sperm from the male's testes is stored in sacs near the cloaca.

Mating often appears to be a precarious affair with the female crouching and the male balancing on her back, often with fluttering wings to steady himself. He lowers his body, twisting his tail under hers to bring the two cloacas together so that the sperm can be ejected into the female.

Circulation

The circulatory system of the bird retains some evidence of its reptilian origin. In both amphibians and reptiles, however, the blood flow to and from the lungs is incompletely separated as it is pumped through the heart and can mix, reducing its effectiveness. Birds resemble mammals in having evolved a four-chambered heart in which the circulation of blood to the lungs for oxygenation, and to the body requiring oxygen, is separated into entering and leaving and produces a more efficient oxygen supply. The red blood corpuscles of birds carry large amounts of a type of hemoglobin that can make oxygen rapidly available in circumstances of sudden need.

The blood carries both the nutrients required by the body and the oxygen that can turn carbohydrates into heat and energy. To provide the energy needed for flight, the supply of oxygen and removal of burned up materials must be rapid and this requires a powerful heart. By comparison with ourselves, the bird has a proportionally much larger heart: in humans it is about 0.42 percent of body weight, in a House Sparrow 1.68 and in smaller birds even more — the heart of the tiny Ruby-throated Hummingbird accounts for 2.37 percent of its weight. Pulse rates are also generally much more rapid: in sparrows, more than six times faster than in the human heart, and 14.5 times faster in the hummingbird.

There are differences in the arrangement of the circulation too. In the neck, for instance, there is a linking vein so that if the neck is twisted to constrict the jugular on one side it can flow across and return on the other, a refinement especially useful in long-necked birds such as swans and cranes. Blood from the rear regions of the body is returned particularly quickly, making a larger supply available to the muscles that power the wings.

Feathers are an efficient form of insulation, but where they do not cover the legs, heat is much more easily lost. This could cause serious problems, especially in the long-legged waterbirds, but since there aren't very big muscles in the lower leg, the blood supply is reduced and the feet and legs kept at much lower temperatures than the rest of the body. Cooling, even in this supply, is countered by breaking it down into a fine capillary system that delivers blood in the lower leg. The arteries that feed these capillaries run close to the veins carrying the returning blood, passing much of the heat directly across and back to the main part of the body so that the blood that does reach the exposed legs is itself at a lower temperature, and has much less heat to lose to the atmosphere.

The Pied Stilt (Himantopus leucocephalus), *like other long-legged waders, would find heavily feathered legs a nuisance. Lacking the insulation feathers would provide, their legs have a reduced blood supply to reduce heat loss.*

Respiration

To fuel the energy that flight demands requires not only a regular supply of food but plenty of oxygen to react with it. Flight can demand as much as ten times the amount of energy that the bird uses at rest, so oxygen must be available not only in volume but at speed — and at the same time the carbon dioxide produced by the combustion process that creates energy must be got rid of in similar quantities and just as efficiently.

Surprisingly, perhaps, this is not achieved by having particularly large lungs. Compared with your own lungs, which take up about 5 percent of your body volume, a bird's lungs are relatively small — in a Mallard, for instance, only about 2 percent.

A skein of migrating Pink-footed Geese (Anser brachyrhynchus). *Some birds fly very high, especially when migrating, sometimes at altitudes of as much as 20,000 feet (6,000 m) where the more rarified air demands a very efficient respiratory system.*

Bottom *Whooper, Bewick's and Mute Swans (Cygnus cygnus, C. bewickii and C. olor) with Tufted Ducks (Aythya fuligula), Pochards (A. ferina) and Coots (Fulica atra). The yellow-billed Whooper and Bewick's Swans have a longer trachea than the red-billed Mute Swans, enabling them to produce their whooping calls. Ducks have a swollen bulla at the base of the trachea to help them produce their calls. One swan on the left still has the dark plumage of the immature bird.*

Below *A cock Yellowhammer (Emberiza citrinella) singing its phrase, which has long been represented as "little-bit-of-bread-and-no-cheese" with the last note extended.*

Birds collect and store air not only in the lungs but in air sacs that are spread through the body cavities and even in the hollow interiors of their bones. The volume of this extra air space provides an increase from the lungs' 2 percent to about 18 percent of the Mallard's volume.

When birds breathe, the extensions of the lungs are not directly involved in the transfer of oxygen to the blood or of carbon dioxide from it. This is achieved in the lungs themselves, where the tiny blood vessels and air tubes between which the exchanges of gas take place are very much smaller and more efficient than in mammals. However, the various air sacs have an important influence on the flow of air that also increases the efficiency of the exchange. Blood that is low in oxygen will absorb it much more rapidly than when it is already present in quantity and in the other direction it will most readily shed carbon dioxide when it is heavily loaded with it and the air is not. The air sacs promote a one-way flow of air, unlike the in-out system by which you breathe, first filling and then deflating the lungs.

Inspiration and expiration is achieved by movement of the sternum and the ribs; the bird does not have a diaphragm to push against its lungs. As the body cavity enlarges, air rushes in through the nostrils (which in most birds are located at the top of the upper mandible) to fill the abdominal sacs, with some air also going to other posterior sacs. Contraction of the cavity pushes air out of these sacs into the lung. The next intake pushes the air further on and into the anterior sacs before it is exhaled.

This system is particularly efficient because when entering the lung from the rear, the oxygen-charged air first meets blood that has already passed through the lungs and already carries quite a lot of oxygen but little carbon dioxide so that the carbon dioxide transfer is great, the oxygen transfer small. As it passes through the lung, this balance changes in both the blood it meets and the composition of the air. As it leaves the lung and flows into the forward or interclavicular air sac, the oxygen-starved blood is still able to take up the depleted remains of oxygen in the lung and, although the air already carries carbon dioxide, there is so much more in the blood that it still transfers.

The advantages of this system are not particularly noticeable at ground level, where many animals, ourselves included if our lungs have not been damaged by smoking and pollution, can supply the oxygen required for exertions such as running fast. Bats, which are mammals with lungs like ours, succeed in flying without problems. However, unlike birds, they do not fly to great heights. It is at high altitudes, where the air is thin and oxygen scarce, that birds gain the greatest advantage. It is of particular importance to those that migrate over great distances and often at altitudes as high as 30,000 feet (9,000 m) above the earth.

Vocal apparatus

Birds do not have vocal chords at the upper end of the windpipe (trachea) as we do. The majority of the vocal sounds that birds make are produced in the syrinx, a "voice box" that is situated at the lower end of the trachea at the junction of the bronchi, the two tubes that carry air from the trachea to the lungs. The bronchial tubes are constructed from rings of cartilage linked by connecting tissue and it is some of this tissue that has been modified to form fine membranes that vibrate to produce sound, the pitch being related to the tension of the membrane. The syrinx is enveloped by an air sac that sets the membranes vibrating and can modify the tone produced. In some birds with more complex development, further modifications are controlled by the bill and tongue and the mouth cavity.

There are considerable differences between the vocal apparatus of the songbirds, especially those such as the Eurasian Blackbird and the Nightingale, which have melodious songs, and the nonpasserines, though more properly they are divided on the basis of the syrinx musculature into Oscines (which have more muscles) and Nonoscines, some of which have as few as three, capable only of producing honks, caws and rattling noises.

Some calls, such as those made by the Whooper Swan, are not formed by the syrinx but by convolutions in the trachea itself, which, in that species, produce its characteristic whooping call. In whooping swans and some cranes, the trachea is so long that a loop of it is accommodated in a special cavity at the front of the breastbone. Warbling calls may be produced by complex modifications not yet understood and it seems likely that in songs that fall into two parts, such as that of the Chaffinch, the parts are produced separately, each by one of the bronchi only.

Legs and feet

There is considerable variation in the length of birds' legs in relation to their body size, although all share the same structure. The bone from the "knee" to the "ankle" (the tibiotarsus) and that from the "ankle" to the "heel" (the tarsometatarsus) are of about equal length, a proportion maintained in all birds, however long the actual leg, which helps to keep the center of gravity of the bird above the feet whether straight or bent. However, there is an exception to this in swimming birds, in which the feet are well back on the body for propulsion or steering. On land the body is more upright. Grebes and loons (divers) move awkwardly for short distances in a crouching stance as do many petrels and shearwaters. Birds that swim with wings, like auks and penguins, have an upright posture and may walk well; foot-propelled swimmers such as ducks and cormorants have wide-spaced feet and a waddling gait.

The wading birds, such as cranes and herons, which feed standing in water close to shore or in marshes, have long, stilt-like legs, as do those that live in open country and need to run efficiently. Birds that need to move easily about in trees, or in grass and low undergrowth, have short legs. The long-legged birds, and many others, mainly those that spend most of their time on the ground, walk by lifting and bending each leg in turn. For those that spend most of their lives in trees, hopping is an easier form of locomotion, often half flying and half jumping and always landing on both feet. Most of them move in the same way on the ground. Walking (and running) seems to be a later evolutionary development: in some species, including the Raven and the Skylark, young birds that have just left the nest will hop for the first few days and then begin to walk as mature birds do.

In most species adult birds stick to one form of locomotion but there are a few, such as the Northern Hemisphere Magpie, that walk when moving slowly but bound along with long hops when they want to move more rapidly.

Although birds probably evolved from a running ancestor, the legs and pelvis-shape of most birds, and the convenience of the double leg push in takeoff and landing appear to fit better with hopping as a later locomotion. In birds, hopping is a short jump using both legs simultaneously. It occurs most typically in perching birds that move among twigs and branches, hopping forwards or sideways and sometimes using a little help from wings and

Jacanas, such as this African Jacana (Actophilornis africanus), *have long legs and long splayed toes that spread the weight, allowing them to walk on floating water plants.*

tail if the gap between twigs is large. Some species that have evolved from groups of perching birds have become mainly terrestrial but still move in a series of rapid hops. This can be seen in birds such as wrens and chats.

Perching and hopping birds have toes that are easily curled and their hind toe is usually well developed to aid in gripping the perch. Whereas hopping on horizontal twigs is relatively easy, birds that use slanting or vertical perches need a much stronger grip. Examples are warblers of grassland or reeds and the antbirds that follow the hunting ant columns of tropical forests. The often skulking babbler species have strong hind toes and some small babblers can somersault around a perch backwards with small shifts of strong gripping feet. Any bird-bander who handles tit species will know the pressure in the feet gripping their fingers.

Strong gripping feet are used by some birds to hold a food object down on a perch while eating it, or, as in the case of parrots, may be used to raise it to the bill. This type of foot has been put to good use by the birds of prey whose strong, stout toes with big curved claws seize the prey and may kill it as well as hold it. They can also be used to carry objects, such as prey and nest material.

Strong legs and strong gripping feet with sharp claws are used by nuthatches and sittellas to support the bird's body with tail raised from the trunk while it hunts in any direction over the larger branches and trunks of trees. However, many of the birds that clamber over trees make less use of the feet. Woodpeckers, woodcreepers and treecreepers cling to bark with large feet but always face upwards, with bodies tilted away from the tree and partly supported by the tail feathers pressing on the bark. The feathers are usually strengthened with strong spiny shafts, so that they do not wear away easily.

To ascend a trunk, the bird moves in a series of hops, gripping as it goes. To go downwards, such birds use small hops and the force of gravity.

There are various structural adaptations to the feet in perching birds. Although the typical bird's foot has three toes pointing forwards and one back (anisodactylous) this does not seem to be wholly satisfactory for some of the non-passerine perching birds and modifications have been evolved. In kingfishers and related birds, such as motmots, bee-eaters and rollers, that use the foot mainly for support while watching and waiting for prey, the toes have become fused together along the basal section to form a broader and flatter resting pad. This is called a syndactyl foot.

A more frequent modification has a toe turned backwards so that two point in each direction, possibly offering a more stable support.

An early stage in this modification, used for rather different purposes, can be seen in the Osprey, which can turn its outer toe backwards to help in holding its slippery prey. In owls too the outer toe is reversible. The zygodactyl foot, with permanently reversed outer toe, is present

in groups such as parrots, cuckoos, jacamars, barbets and woodpeckers. The trogons also have a foot of this type, but peculiar to them in that it is the inner of the three toes that is turned back (heterodactyl).

The little colies or mousebirds, which often hang from twigs but may also perch or run, have a pamprodactyl foot in which all four toes point forwards, but the outer one and the inner theoretical hind toe are reversible. The typical swifts also have a foot of this kind, but with only the hind toe reversible, and they only cling to surfaces or shuffle a short distance at nest sites.

In some of the modified forms one of the toes may be lost, as in some kingfishers and in the three-toed woodpeckers.

Some species among the perching birds that have become terrestrial walk instead of hopping. In the corvids the type of bounding hop seen in jays is replaced by a steady walk in a more upright posture in the crows. However, walking may not be fast enough and a crow in a hurry breaks into a series of clumsy bounding hops. Movements of this kind occur in other groups such as starlings and babblers, and some species occasionally use a kind of galloping hop in which one foot always touches the ground before the other.

A Black-chinned Yuhina (Yuhina nigrimenta), one of the small, strong-footed Asiatic babblers, lands on a twig with a firm grip that uses the forward-curving hind toe.

Right *A pale-breasted northern form of the Nuthatch (Sitta europaea) by the large nest hole it has partly plastered up with mud, shows its strong-footed agility as it carries off a nestling's fecal pellet, the soft dropping enclosed in a gelatinous sac. Most birds climb backwards down a trunk but the Nuthatch is able to walk straight down.*

A Green Woodpecker (Picus viridis) can grip bark firmly with its claws but uses its stiff tail to give added support.

Left *Birds that live and nest in tall grasses and reeds must have strong feet for clinging to vertical supports, like this Reed-Warbler (Acrocephalus scirpaceus) visiting its deep cup nest, hanging between upright stems.*

Below *Like many honey eaters, the Tui (Prosthemadera novaeseelandiae) has strong feet to help it climb and reach flowers to remove nectar with its brush-tipped tongue.*

A number of small songbirds — larks, wagtails and pipits — are habitual walkers. Their claws are shorter than in arboreal species and the hind claw may be straight and long, as in the longspur buntings, perhaps aiding balance in walking and running. Only a few have apparently returned to trees. The forest gamebirds — guans and curassows — walk and run along branches, the turacos run and leap on thinner branches and twigs, whereas pigeons are both arboreal and terrestrial walkers.

Ideally legs should be close together for rapid walking and running. With a wider pelvis a bird must rock from side to side as it runs, as a rear view of a running chicken will show. A narrow pelvis is an advantage and is often linked with reduction or loss of flight. The ratites, and in particular the Kiwi, show more extreme examples of this.

Running is wasteful of energy and usually occurs in short bursts for chasing prey or evading predators. It can be fast. A running Ostrich may reach about 37 mph (60 kph). Adaptations to running include slender build, long legs and small feet. Birds such as coursers have small feet with short toes and in the Ostrich the toes are not only short but have been reduced to two.

Fighting Coots (Fulica atra) show the fleshy lobes along the toes that make the feet into efficient paddles in swimming and diving but fold back when the foot moves forward through the water.

Right *Ostriches (Struthio camelus) are specialist running birds. They have lost two of their toes and one of the remaining pair is small: are their feet slowly evolving into something like the horse's hoof?*

Below *The Red-billed Whistling Duck (Dendrocygna autumnalis) has the typical swimming foot, with webbing between three toes.*

Running demands open spaces with very short or sparse vegetation. Long-legged birds that feed in shallow water or marshland move more slowly and have longer toes and more deliberate steps. The long toes help to spread the body weight over soft ground or on mud. In the jacanas or lily trotters the toes and their claws have become exceptionally long, allowing the birds to walk over the floating water plants on which they spend most of their time.

Swimming has also led to extensive adaptation of legs and feet. Floating birds propel themselves with their legs and the greater the surface area available when pushing the better the result. Moorhens seem to manage with normal long-toed legs, but the earliest stage in adaptation is usually fleshy lobes to enlarge the toes. Phalaropes and coots have narrow lobes to aid propulsion. In divers (loons) and grebes the toes are large fleshy lobes that together form a large flat surface but can be turned edge on for ease in pulling the feet forward after the propelling stroke. The most efficient way of providing strong propulsion seems to be to have a web of skin between the toes, offering a large solid surface when extended, rapidly reduced when the toes are folded together. Webs join the three front toes in birds such as waterfowl, albatrosses and shearwaters, and gulls and their relatives. The web is extended to the hind toe also in pelicans, cormorants and similar groups and this increases the area of the spread foot still further, but may make walking and perching a little more difficult.

For birds that swim at the surface, paddling with feet, webbed or unwebbed, is rather like walking. The feet thrust back alternately and a double thrust of both feet tends to be used only for acceleration at special moments, as in the aggressive display of the Mute Swan. Neverthe-

less, a number of these web-footed and lobed-footed birds are underwater divers and hunters. For swimming under water a simultaneous kick with both feet is necessary. The legs, which are set towards the rear of the body, are raised and turned outwards to a more horizontal position, so that the backward thrust is a lateral one with the feet on either side of the body. Diving ducks are buoyant birds that without a forward movement will float quickly up to the surface. In forcing themselves down and along under water they must raise the legs laterally to a point where the backward kick of the feet may occur above the level of the back.

Diving ducks that eat weed and shellfish can be heavily built and relatively slow in movement. The birds that hunt fish under water are usually streamlined, with elongated body, neck and head, the legs well to the rear and the bill often hooked to hold the prey more securely. They can move with surprising rapidity. Bird species that use the wings for swimming under water have webbed feet that may be used for steering and braking.

These various adaptations of legs and feet have evolved so that birds can make the maximum use of them. Some birds, particularly those that rely mainly on flight, may have little use for legs and feet and these may be relatively small and weak. This is true for birds such as nightjars and their relatives, and some swifts, and in the frigatebirds, which have superb mastery of flight, the legs and feet are tiny in comparison with bill, wings and tail.

Most birds use their beaks if they have to resort to violence over territory or mates, though the junglefowl, from which the domestic chicken and the fighting cock have been bred, and some other gamebirds, have developed sharp projecting spurs with bony cores on their legs. They use these to strike at their opponents.

A number of bird orders also have a modification of the claw of their third toe, giving a row of serrations on the underside that form an effective comb that makes it easier for them to preen their feathers.

Beaks and bills

With the loss of the forelimbs to form wings, birds are like humans trying to eat with their hands tied behind them. Some bird species can make limited use of their feet to hold down food while they tear at it or break it up. A few, such as the swamphens and parrots, may raise food held in the foot to feed. Apart from these, the birds must rely on a long flexible neck and the jaws, or mandibles, which form a projecting bill or beak at the front of the skull.

The main conical structure, the rostrum, which carries the upper jaws, looks like a solid extension of the skull. However, although a solid strip of bone extends from the forehead to the tip, the section in front of the big eye sockets is hollow and contains the nasal cavity, opening to the outside as a pair of nostrils and also down into the roof of the mouth. The visible nostrils may be large and obvious, as in

the Turkey Vulture, where it is possible to see through from one side to the other, or mainly hidden by feathers, as in larks and grouse, perhaps to keep out dust or cold.

Some birds have small nostrils, and in the plunge-diving Gannet they are sealed up and the bird breathes through a flange on each side of the upper jaw that can be closed by water

Compare the head of the Steppe Eagle (Aquila nipalensis) *with that of the Turkey Vulture. It has more typical smaller nostrils, embedded in a fleshy cere in birds of prey. The ear openings are hidden in the feathers and it has the more usual unspecialized tongue.*

The large nostrils of the Turkey Vulture (Cathartes aura) *are conspicuous and able to detect decaying carcasses. There are no feathers on the bare head to hide the typical ear opening. The rough surface of the tongue helps to grip the food as the bird tears at carrion.*

pressure. In the albatrosses, petrels and related seabirds, there is a double tube of varying length on top of the bill, covering the nostrils. These birds have a keen sense of smell and can detect fish-oil slicks at a distance. The nostril tubes may help them to pick up such scents.

The kiwis are oddities in that their nostrils are near the tip of the long slender bill, helping the birds to sense the worms and other creatures as they probe the soil.

In front of the nostrils is the projecting upper jaw of the bill. Although this looks solid, it is light and hollow, but very strong. At its lower sides are the strong cutting edges of the jaws and these connect with tiny bony rods that extend back to the base of the cranium where a small bone, the quadrate, joins the jaws to the skull.

This upper part of the bill appears rigid but it is often joined to the skull by thin bone layers and can be bent up slightly. In long

slender bills, such as those of shorebirds, this upward curvature is more marked. In some birds, such as the parrots, there is a bony hinge where the bill joins the skull, allowing more movement.

The lower jaw consists of two narrow strips of bony material, tightly joined but not necessarily fused together at the tip, and hinging in the region of the quadrate, well back on the skull. The bones of which the jaws are composed are often not fully fused and the structures are flexible. This is useful to birds that may try to swallow very large prey. The jaw bones that support the large throat pouch of the Pelican are thin flexible rods.

There may be sensory nerve endings towards the tips of the jaws and a thin covering of live tissue produces a strong keratin sheath. This is the shiny and sometimes colorful outer layer of the bill. In some birds, such as the tubenosed seabirds and gannets, this is composed of a series of separate plates, but in most birds it is a continuous sheath. It grows sufficiently to replace any parts or sharp edges worn away when the bill is in use. In birds like kingfishers and barbets, which make nest holes in hard earth or wood, the sheath shows extra growth when this is happening. In some auks, such as the puffins, brightly colored keratin sheaths grow to cover parts of the bill during the breeding season and then drop off.

Birds do not have teeth or the type of movable jaw that can chew. They must seize and swallow food, leaving digestion to do the rest, and bills are designed for this purpose. The basic bill would be of moderate length, narrow and pointed, like a pair of forceps, used for picking up small objects, but birds have diverged from this, some evolving long slender bills, straight or downcurved, for reaching and probing after small prey. Long straight bills usually probe into soft sand or mud and are found on a number of shorebirds. Proportionally very long bills, like those of snipe and woodcock, must probe blindly. They have flexible tips equipped with sensitive nerve endings and the birds feed by scent and touch. Such birds can feed equally well at night and shoreline feeders take advantage of night tides. Thin upcurved bills, such as those of Avocet and Terek Sandpiper, find food by sweeping from side to side in shallow water.

All these bill shapes are also present on a tiny scale in hummingbirds, in which they are adaptations for extracting nectar from variously shaped flowers.

Another bill for lateral sweeping in shallow water is the long thin one of the Spoonbill, with a flat expanded tip for extracting small creatures from the water. Ducks have similar broad flat bills for sifting fine food particles from water, but they are much shorter. They may have a series of fine ridges on the inside edges of the jaws for sieving out food. Straining devices also occur in the large broad bills of the prions that sieve the surface as they skim over the sea, and in flamingos similar structures extract minute creatures or algae from the saline waters in which they wade.

A Fork-tailed Woodnymph Hummingbird (Thalurania furcata). *Hummingbirds' long bills are adapted to match the blossoms from which they feed.*

Right *A Bar-tailed Godwit* (Limosa lapponica) *resting on one leg and yawning. Its slender jaws are very flexible and, with sensory nerves that run to the tip, can sense and seize small mollusks and worms when the bill is buried deep in mud or sand. This bird is almost in breeding plumage, unlike the winter-plumaged birds behind, sleeping with their bills buried in the feathers of their backs.*

There is specialization even between flamingos: Greater Flamingos, which stand nearly 5 feet (1.5 m) tall, have coarse filters and take mainly insect larvae and other animals that they find in mud. They feed only where they can reach the bottom. Lesser Flamingos have finer filters for algae and can feed in deeper water.

Skimmers have the lower jaws fused to form a flat upright blade projecting beyond the upper that skims the surface of the water.

Some diving birds with tapering bills catch small fish but those that seize larger and more slippery fish or squid often have a hook on the bill tip. Small insect-hunting songbirds may also have hooked bill tips, well developed in minor raptors such as shrikes and Australian butcherbirds.

Shorter, stouter bills with hooked tips can be used for tearing and these can be seen in birds of prey.

In birds that hunt on the wing, the prey must go quickly into the throat. The fly-catching perching birds have fairly short bills, usually with a small hooked tip. To increase the chance of catching prey, the bill has a broad base and a very wide gape, while projecting bristles at the sides of the bill widen the catching area still further. In the swifts and nightjars the bill looks very small, but the open gape is so large that it appears to almost split the head in half.

Birds that eat mainly fruit have bills of varied shape, but usually short enough to crush the food, and with a fairly wide gape for seizing large objects.

Some species, such as toucans, have serrations on the bill edges that might help them to hold large fruit. Both toucans and hornbills show a problem associated with long bills — that of getting food back to the throat. They hold it in the bill tip, then toss the head back, releasing the object and catching it in the throat end of the bill.

Flamingos feed with the head partly, or wholly, under water and the bill upside down. Both Greater and Lesser Flamingos can live in places unsuited to most birds, places too alkaline for ordinary plants and fish but which support the tiny shrimps essential to the flamingo's pigmentation.

end of the tongue is usually finely split to form a brush tip to pick up such food more easily.

Short stout bills tend to be used for crushing or shredding parts of plants: buds, leaves and stems or seeds. Hard seeds offer problems when used as food. Larger seed-eating birds swallow them whole and rely on the action of the gizzard to grind them up.

Small birds that feed mainly on seeds, such as finches, buntings and weavers, use the bill to remove the husk. These birds have grooves in the palate so that a seed can be held in the bill while the sharp edge shears away part of the outer husk. The tongue revolves the seed so that the husk is removed completely and the inner kernel swallowed.

Some birds use cruder ways of getting at seeds and nuts: woodpeckers and nuthatches wedge them in crevices and hammer them open with the bill, but others are more subtle. Some tits can open larger seeds and even dried stones of small fruits, by hammering at a point of weakness. The crossbills are finches that have a specialized adaptation, their crossed bill tips being used to lever apart the woody scales of pine cones to reach the hidden seeds.

The parrots have one of the most highly developed bills. In addition to their use in feeding, they are employed as a kind of third foot when the birds are clambering among branches. The upper part of the bill is strongly curved to a hooked tip and the inner palate forms a hard flat plate. The lower jaw, also curved but shorter and much blunter, fits within the upper; the upper is hinged at the skull so that the mouth can open wide if need be. The lower jaw can also be moved to press against the upper palate, sometimes with considerable force, to crack objects, and the short stout tongue moves and rotates the item being eaten.

It seems surprising that more birds do not use bill serrations. The fish-eating ducks have slender bills on which the outer sheath produces small, tooth-like projections along the jaw edges for a better grip. Although the puffins pack fish crosswise in the bill to carry back to their young, the serrations used to hold them are not on the bill but on the tongue.

The finest bills are those of small birds — hummingbirds and sunbirds — that take nectar from flowers. A number of other birds, from small parrots to white-eyes, may also take nectar and pollen. Bill shape may vary but, where this is an important part of the diet, the

A Crossbill (Loxia curvirostra) *uses its specially adapted bill to remove the seeds from a pine cone.*

Below *Ground Hornbills (Buceros leadbeateri) throw food into the air then catch it to get it to the back of their long bills.*

Plumage and scales

Feathers, scales, mammal fur and human hair are all specialized outgrowths of the skin. They are composed of an inert material called keratin. This also forms the bill sheath and claws of birds and the type of keratin found in bird feathers is the same as that which forms reptile scales. Birds also have scales, on the legs and feet. These are plates of material at times extending to form a continuous cover. Both bird scales and feathers arise from the same type of embryonic cell and the close affinity between them is indicated by the way in which feathers sometimes replace scales on the legs and feet. This usually occurs where species need extra warmth for incubation in cold climates, as in some owls, raptors and gamebirds.

The feather can be envisaged as an enlarged and flattened structure evolved from a scale. The typical feather consists of a stiff central shaft, the rachis, arising from a bare basal portion, the calamus, that is usually embedded in the skin. The rachis supports the large flat area of the feather, the vane. The vane appears solid, but the structure is split on either side of the shaft as a parallel series of tiny slanting strips, the barbs. Along either side of each barb is another projecting series of thin structures, the barbels that lock together. This hooking and interlocking creates the continuous structure of the large flat vane. The vane can split apart between any two barbs but, by running the feather through the bill, as in preening, the bird can zip them up and lock them together again.

On some feathers some barbules and barbs may have a longer smoother structure, without the interlocking devices. These form looser filamentous structures, known as down, which often tend to tangle together. On typical body feathers — contour feathers — the barbs at the base of the vane may be downy.

A contour feather may have a small secondary feather-like structure attached to the back of it at the top of the calamus. This aftershaft or afterfeather is very variable in its occurrence. In some ratites it is more developed and in the Emu is almost as large as, and of similar structure to, the main vane, producing a double feather. In most cases it is smaller and downy in structure. Where it is present it adds to the insulating properties of the plumage, but it is often small or almost absent.

Sometimes contour feathers may have the whole vane downy in structure; they are then known as semiplumes. Some are completely modified as downy structures, with rachis reduced or missing, and have an insulating function. A few feathers may be reduced to vestigial structures.

Bristles consist of a fine thin rachis and perhaps a few downy barbs at the base. They may have a sensory function. Filoplumes are bristle-like structures with a tiny tuft of barbs at the tip. They occur next to contour feathers, arising from follicles rich in nerve endings. They appear to be sensitive and to aid adjustment and maintenance of plumage.

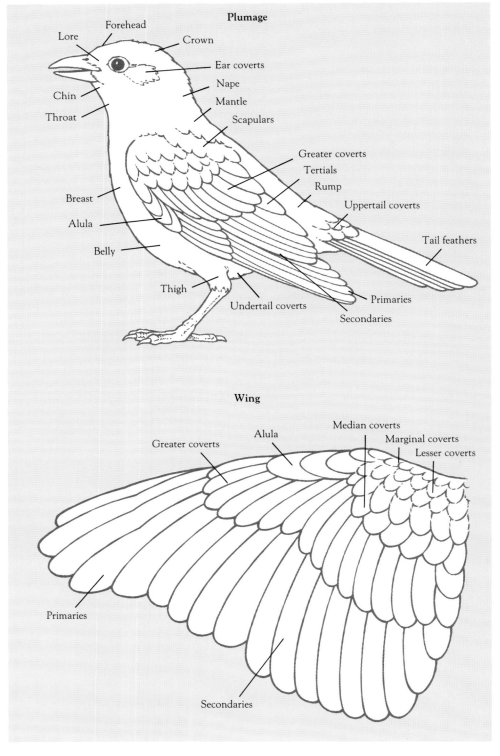

Main flight feathers and body contour feathers are all vaned. The barbs on either side of the rachis, the central shaft of a typical feather, each have a row of ridged and notched barbels on the side toward the feather base that lock into a set of hooks on the opposing face of the next barb and give the vane a solid structure. Down feathers have a smoother structure, with barbules that do not interlock, and filoplumes and bristles are specialized forms.

Left *Water droplets on the wing of a Mallard* (Anas platyrhynchos) *cannot penetrate the fine structure of the surface of the feather vanes.*

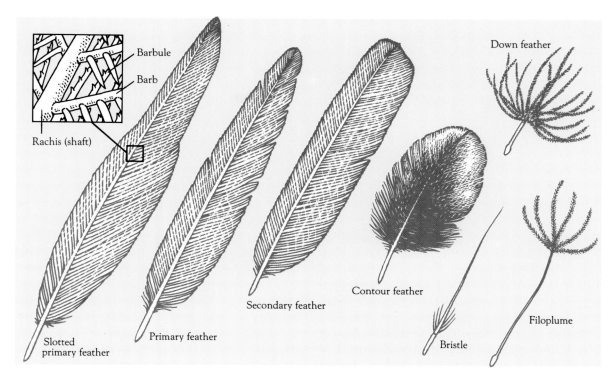

Barbule
Barb
Rachis (shaft)
Slotted primary feather
Primary feather
Secondary feather
Contour feather
Bristle
Down feather
Filoplume

Left *Plumage is not a continuous even covering. Feathers are in tracts with very narrow strips of down or bare skin between which form distinct patches of plumage with edges that touch or overlap. There are names for certain areas of feathers and for distinct patches or stripes of color that may recur on a number of species. They form a kind of "plumage map" that helps in describing a bird.*

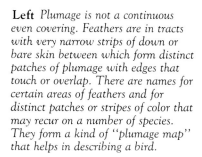

Right *The neck plumage of the Red-legged Seriema* (Cariama cristata) *shows the looser-structured and more open type of feather, and the bird has a fine forehead crest.*

The feather grows from a tiny mound of active cells on the surface of the inner, dermal layer of skin. It slants out through the outer skin layer as a thin cylindrical structure with a rounded tip. Towards its basal end is an inner pulp supplied with blood and nourishing growth. The rest consists of a thin outer protective sheath of keratin that crumbles away as growth is completed. Within this the feather itself forms as a tubular structure continually growing at its base.

The structure differentiates as it is formed. The thicker ridge that will form the rachis grows on the forward or outward side of the tube. The barbs with their barbules curve around, compressed and slanting upwards to meet at the tips and complete the tube. Towards the base of the feather, where the barbs are shorter, there is space opposite the rachis and here the aftershaft forms.

As the feather structure lengthens and dries, the outer sheath breaks away, downwards from the tip, and the released barbs straighten, the vane opening out and becoming the final feather structure, held by the central rachis.

When the growth of the feather is complete the blood supply is cut off. It remains attached to the muscles at its root but is in fact dead tissue. Since the feather is no longer growing, any damage to it cannot be regenerated. Even without injury, normal day to day activity, especially the abrasion sustained in flight, wears down the feather until it becomes inefficient at its job and must be replaced. A new feather then grows in the same follicle and pushes the old feather out — the process known as molt. Molt and renewal of plumage take place at different times according to the annual cycle and life-style of the species. Because replacing feathers during molt makes energy demands, and during the process the mobility of some species is restricted, it will usually take place when it will least conflict with the bird's other needs.

Hot and cold

The plumage of birds in hot climates is thinner, with reduced down and fewer feathers, which may have less barbs, making it appear coarser in texture. There are often bare areas of skin, usually on head and neck and between feather tracts.

In cold areas, birds tend to have more dense and downy plumage and to grow thicker plumage in winter. In arctic owls and grouse, feathering tends to extend down the legs and the Ptarmigan has feathering on the soles of the feet as well, resulting in something like a rabbit's foot.

The molt process means that the amount of plumage any bird carries will vary through the year. The number of feathers also varies greatly from species to species, but not directly related to their size. A swan in winter plumage may have over 25,000 feathers but even the tiniest hummingbird will probably have approaching 1,000. The individual feather size, however, will usually reflect the size of the bird itself.

Feather color

Bird plumage displays a dazzling variation of color from somber.hues to sparkling brightness and shining iridescences. Sometimes the colors and the patterns in which they are arranged are effective forms of camouflage, whether browns and grays to help the bird merge into the undergrowth of a Scottish wood, the bright greens and yellows of parrots in the canopy of a tropical forest, or the pure white of the Ptarmigan's winter plumage. In many species the male birds change their appearance with the coming of the mating season and produce a strikingly patterned or colored breeding plumage to attract their mates, or special features that can be used to emphasize their courtship behavior.

Like the colors on an artist's palette, the primary colors that make up the many different hues are relatively simple and few in number. It is the variation in their intensity and the different ways in which they are combined that produce the range of colors that we see.

Feathers are inert structures. The pigments that produce the color, and the peculiarities of structure that may visually modify them, become part of the feather during growth. There are some cases where the color may change, but these few are exceptions with external causes and are staining, not part of the bird's pigmentation. Iron salts in water may give a rust color on the white plumage of some waterfowl, often slight, but with Emperor Geese of arctic America may sometimes result in the white head being stained deep orange. Similar compounds turn the white plumage of the Bearded Vulture to orange buff. Preen oil may be tinted and the preen gland of the Great Indian Hornbill has a yellow color that may show on the plumage after preening.

The pigments that most frequently occur in the feathers themselves are the melanins, like the black or dark brown substances present in human hair and skin, which occur as granules and can be seen under a microscope as tiny dark specks. Although chemically similar to each other, the way in which they are genetically controlled and inherited appears to indicate three melanins: one giving black and gray tints, another producing brown to yellowish buff and a third resulting in chestnut red to pinkish tints.

For most birds, red and yellow colors and mixtures originate from fat-soluble lipochrome pigments that color the structure. Some of these appear to be derived from carotenoid plant pigments, either ingested as plants or via insects. Other red and yellow colors, such as those of some parrots, are chemically different from those of most birds.

Another pigment derived from food is the one giving a red or pink color in flamingos, and possibly other waterbirds, which is obtained from the crustaceans in their diet. Porphyrin pigments also occur in some plumages to give pinkish tints. In the turacos the bright red color of the flight feathers and the green of body feathers are both specialized pigments of this type.

The three melanins, and the red and yellow, are the basis for most plumage colors. Some important colors are added not by pigmentation but by structural specializations. The keratin structure of feathers may contain minute internal air spaces and these may affect the way in which color is seen through it. A common example occurs when black melanin is seen through a keratin layer and appears blue. Almost all blue color in bird plumage is of this type. If the underlying melanin is chestnut red, the visual color is magenta purple, as seen, for example, in some of the kingfishers. If a yellow pigment layer is superimposed on the blue structural effect, the result is green, producing the typical green plumage. Mutations in which either melanin or the yellow pigment is suppressed produce yellow or blue variant individuals, such as can be seen in domestic varieties of the Budgerigar or in Ring-necked Parakeets. However, duller olive green color, such as that of the European Greenfinch, may be the result of very minute color spots of yellow and black pigment side by side, appearing green.

Iridescent colors, only apparent at certain angles, are also the result of keratin structure modifying the effect of the underlying pigments. Such plumage may show some color change as the plumage moves relative to the light falling upon it and may show plain dark melanin color at some angles.

The angle of the feather itself also produces different effects. Short feathers growing very close together and almost straight out from the skin produce the same effect as the pile of velvet.

In some birds, such as pigeons, a breakdown of feather structure produces powder from powder down, which then covers the feathers, may give a general pale gray or blue gray tint.

In general, color is fixed when feather growth is complete but, in some birds, there may be apparent change during the lifetime of a feather when factors such as exposure to light affect its color. A fine pink flush may occur on the newly molted plumage of some terns, gulls, pelicans and ducks that very soon is lost.

Yellow pigment seems to be the most vulnerable to fading in strong light and, in hot climates, the green plumage of birds such as kingfishers and bee-eaters may turn gradually blue. The Green Magpie or Hunting Cissa of oriental tropical forests has a bright green plumage that tends to become blue if heavily exposed. In poorly fed captive birds of this species the feathers may be blue from the molt,

1. *The iridescent feathers of the Common Starling (Sturnus vulgaris) have blackish pigment but the structure of the feathers reflects colored light rays.*

2. *The Iora (Aegithina tiphia) has plain yellow pigmented plumage. The small nest is tightly bound with spiders' webs.*

3. *The green plumage of the Blue-winged Leafbird (Chloropsis cochinchinensis) is produced from black pigment modified by the feather structure to appear blue and combined with yellow pigment — the way green is usually produced in feathers. The young begin to sprout wing feathers first, since they take longest to grow; these are still partly encased in their protective sheaths.*

4. *The pink coloring of the feathers of Roseate Spoonbill (Ajaja ajaja) depends upon a diet rich in crustaceans.*

5. *The Monal Pheasant (Lophophorus impejanus) has mainly black and chestnut plumage but the back of the head and back is beautifully modified by feather structure to produce blues and purples, in places turned to green by additional yellow. The head feathers have long shafts and small terminal vanes.*

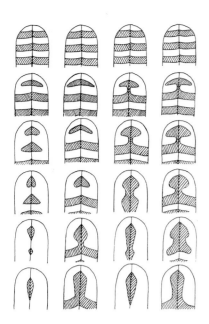

Feather patterns from the breast of immature hawks. Most patterns derive from simple transverse barring. Once started, the process appears to spread and run its course, gradually changing the whole. When a change in pigment distribution produces a new pattern on the exposed tips of overlapping feathers, the hidden part retains the earlier pattern.

Five stages in the pattern changes by which simple barring develops into the complex sphere-shaped patterns on the feathers of the Great Argus Pheasant.

Top left *In the Argus Pheasant (Argusianus argus) the long and subtle-colored feathers of wings and tail are erected in display in a great screen with rows of striking patterns like metal spheres, seen here along a displaced secondary wing feather. Plumage is frequently arranged so that there is maximum contrast to increase the effect of the displaying bird.*

Left *Lawes's Six-wired Parotia (Parotia lawesii) has iridescent plumage confined to the breast, but in display waltzes around a ground area with black plumage spread like a skirt and the fine head plumes raised and spread.*

Following pages *The male Peacock (Pavo cristatus) has the most resplendent plumage of all the birds. The "eye" patterns are not made up of different colored feathers but of bands of color along individual barbs. As in many species with elaborate male displays, peahens are comparatively drab.*

and all preserved museum specimens, even if shut away from the light, soon turn completely blue.

Another factor that can produce apparent changes of color without molt is the effect of wear. Most feathers are used for about one year, during which the natural abrasion to which they are subjected tends to wear away and fray the edges. The presence of melanin, particularly black pigment, within the feather structure strengthens it. This seems to be the reason why many feathers have dark bands at or near their tip or rim. Such feathers are often present on the larger flight feathers and most obvious in the dark wing tips of birds such as gulls.

Feather wear is used by some species to produce a seasonal change to breeding plumage. It may be relatively inconspicuous in some waders, such as Curlew and Whimbrel where most body and wing feathers have an irregular brown center and white edges. The white edges give the winter plumage a paler appearance that may have cryptic value on mudflats. In late winter and spring the white edges wear away, giving the spring plumage a warmer brown appearance.

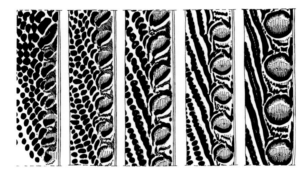

A more striking type of change is clearly shown in the plumage of another northern migrant, the Brambling. After its late summer molt, this finch has a winter plumage in which the feathers of the head and back have a buff edge and the inner part of the feather is black. These parts of the plumage then appear uniformly buff and inconspicuous. Because the black melanin parts of the feather are stronger than the edges, there is a point of weakness on each barb where black changes to buff. In late winter and spring, wear and tear causes the buff fringes to break away along this line of weakness, leaving a sleek black head and neck for spring display.

Finer feathers

The main function of feathers is utilitarian, the contour and down feathers forming an insulating layer over the body and the longer flight feathers of wings and tail controlling movement in the air. However, the possession of feathers may confer another useful advantage.

Sight is of primary importance to birds that tend to signal their feelings and intentions by postures, and visual information based on shape and pattern becomes important. Feathers are

ideal for this purpose because not only can they be used to change shapes or produce striking signals but they can also be folded away or concealed when not needed. Obvious examples of this can be seen in the enlarged and sometimes brightly colored crests, ear tufts or ruffs that ornament the heads and necks of underwater swimmers, such as grebes and some auks and penguins, erected in display but folded back for streamlining when hunting.

Taking advantage of the potential of feather use in display, birds have evolved oddly-shaped or unusual feathers that can play a part in attracting attention or signaling threat. These may occur on any parts: head, nape, breast, flanks, lower back, wings or tail.

Exceptional elongation of feathers is not uncommon, and such feathers may be slender and tapering. They occur most frequently on the head, in the form of crests, and in the tail feathers. In some species, tails may be several times the length of the bird's body and in the small Paradise Whydah, one of the male's tail feathers may be laterally twisted and as large as the bird's head and body.

Another frequent feather form presents elongations of both rachis and barbs, the latter often not interlocking and with the barbules sometimes reduced or lost. This produces a fine, loose and filmy structure. Erectable tufts of such feathers may occur on the bodies and heads of breeding egrets and in the cascades of feathers on the flanks of some birds-of-paradise. On the Lyrebird, the outer tail feathers show partial reduction of barbules on parts of the vane to produce a pattern of translucent or transparent zones.

Parts of feather vanes may be reduced as though cut away to change the shape of feathers and the appearance of wings and tails. This may have a practical use, as in the reduction of width at the ends of primary wing feathers to produce the splayed-finger effect that aids birds in fast maneuvering or riding turbulent air. In contrast, oddities like the expanded tips of the Hawfinch's primaries appear purely decorative.

A recurring adaptation takes the form of a larger feather, usually in the tail, having an extended bare rachial shaft with a flat vane at the end of it, separated from the rest of the plumage. South American motmots have an odd version in which the central barbs of long tail feathers are fragile, soon breaking away during preening to leave a length of rachis supporting a terminal section of the vane, which the bird swings like a pendulum when perched. The more typical examples can be seen in the racquet tails of a hummingbird and some drongos. In the drongos, shafts of the outer pair of tail feathers are as long as the bird and carry an elongated large vane.

Birds-of-paradise show extreme variations. The parotias have tiny vanes at the ends of wire-like head plumes. The little King Bird-of-paradise has the outer tail feathers as two long wires, each with a narrow, rolled-up vane at its tip. In a few the vanes are absent and the tail feathers tend to become bare, curled, wire-like structures.

The male Standard-winged Nightjar has racquet feathers on the wings. Their thin shafts are half as long again as the bird itself and extend back from midwing, slightly raised, and carry a vane about half head and body size. In flight in the dusk, it is said to look like a bird closely followed by two smaller ones flying in formation.

A few structures are unlike typical feathers. At the tip of the secondary wing feathers of waxwings there is a small elongated scarlet lump that reminds people of the sealing wax that used to be used for closing letters, and this gives the birds their name.

The King of Saxony Bird-of-paradise is a small dark bird with two movable plumes extending from the back of the head. These are twice the bird's length and consist of a thin shaft along the outer side of which is a series of small projecting rectangular flanges of solid material, the whole colored light blue. It is a decoration without parallel — but looks a little like cheap plastic!

Wattles, casques and shields

Although mostly covered with feathers, birds may have conspicuous areas of bare skin, usually on the head and neck. Possibly originally evolved to facilitate heat loss, such areas may be brightly colored and form a part of the display pattern. In cassowaries the gaudy face and neck skin varies in color and pattern with species and with age.

The skin of the throat and neck can be temporarily and variably inflated in display. It produces bright swellings like paired poached eggs on the necks of Prairie Chickens and Sage Grouse, and the great scarlet balloon of the male Frigatebird.

In other birds, bare skin may be thickened to form ridges and large wrinkles, and produce wattles that become swollen with blood, to

make prominent adornments that are brightly colored or tinted by the presence of blood. The comb and wattles of domestic fowl and the head and neck of turkeys are typical examples.

Other gamebirds show extremes. Bulwer's Pheasant has forward- and backward-projecting wattles on the head, swelling to produce a pale blue, very elongated and slender hammerhead with an eye in the middle of each side. The tragopans can shake down a wrinkled throat wattle temporarily to produce a large hanging apron over the breast, patterned in vivid colors

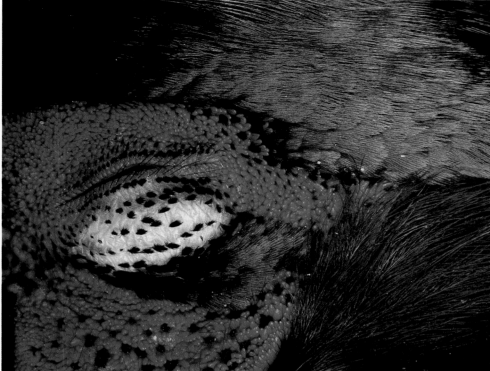

with a pair of thin horns rising from the head.

In addition to plumage and bare skin, the heads of birds may show other conspicuous structures. The Coot has a projecting shield extending up from the bill onto the forehead. Many hornbills have a solid or hollow casque, sometimes large, surmounting the bill. Some guineafowl, and one of the megapodes, the Maleo, have a rounded bony bump on the back of the head. Although functions are tentatively assigned to some of these features, they may be mainly ornamental.

Bare skin is also used in display. Here the closed eye of a male Ring-necked Pheasant (Phasianus colchicus) shows unswollen red wattles above and below the eye and the few tiny feathers on the outside of the closed eyelid, which in birds closes upwards. Rows of bristles are also clearly seen.

Below *The Wild Turkey (Meleagris gallopavo) is usually a slender skulker, like the bird on the left, but in display fans its tail and makes the wattles of head and neck enlarge and redden.*

Camouflage

In contrast to use for display, color and pattern may be important in making a bird inconspicuous. Such colors and patterns are often described as cryptic. Many birds, especially females and young, have plain brown or olive tints for this purpose, others use pattern. To match a background pattern, elements must be of suitable size; as a result feathers of larger birds may have a distinct pattern whereas on small birds each feather only bears a tiny part of the whole.

Many gamebirds, and shorebirds such as woodcock or snipe, have feathers with light and dark transverse barring and a bright yellow streak down the center. Hidden among dead grasses, this produces a three-dimensional effect like the grass blades. The striped neck of bitterns hides them while standing upright in reed beds. All the patterning on the down of young precocial birds helps conceal them against the right background.

Plumage for concealment does not have to be dull: strong sunlight through foliage can hide birds with a mixture of green, blue, yellow and black. The bright colors of parrots and fruit pigeons help to hide them as they feed.

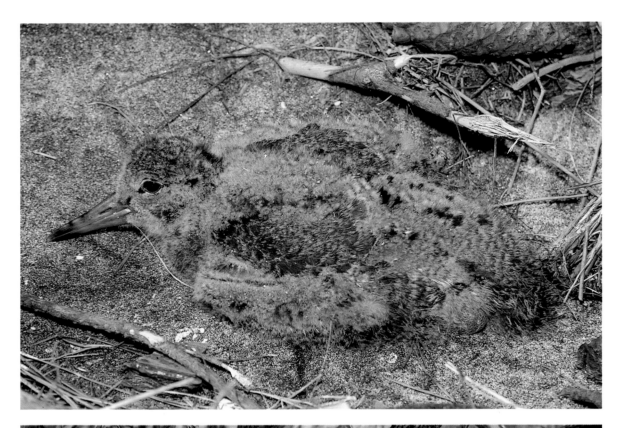

Against the right background the downy chick of the Variable Oystercatcher (Haematopus unicolor) shows the possible value of plumage as camouflage.

A pair of Tawny Frogmouths (Podargus strigoides) resting by day with plumage sleeked, uptilted bill and closed eyes try to look like dead branches.

Right *Flying against a lake full of flamingos, Crowned-Cranes (Balearica regulorum) show the movement of the flying wing: the first beginning to raise the wings from the downstroke, the second lifting them further, the last partway through the body lift imparted by the downstroke.*

FLIGHT

From early times, people dreamed of flying and tried to work out how birds did it. In Greek legend, Daedalus made wings out of feathers and there have been many other human attempts to imitate a bird, none of them successful; indeed scientists still do not understand all the mechanisms involved in avian flight. When humans first managed to travel through the air, it was in balloons, carried upwards by heated air that became lighter than that around it or by gases that were lighter.

Lift and drag

We talk of things being "light as a feather" but though a feather may be carried by a current of air it will not stay airborne. It is heavier, and although a bird's anatomy avoids carrying unnecessary weight it is certainly not lighter than air. Propulsion, whether by flapping wings, propeller blades or jet stream, is produced by pushing against the air but flight, in birds and airplanes, depends upon the "lift" provided by a difference in the pressure in the air that creates a lifting force. Neither birds nor aircraft have simple flat wings. The upper surface is

A bird's wing is shaped to generate lift when it moves forward through the air. Its convex upper surface causes the airstream to travel further and faster over the wing, which creates pressure above it. Below the wing, pressure increases to push the bird up. If the angle of attack is too large, the wing stalls, as the airflow becomes turbulent.

Lift
Low pressure
Leading edge
Trailing edge
High pressure
Bird's wing in normal flight
Angle of attack

Airflow becomes turbulent
Bird's wing when stalling occurs

Below right *American Cliff Swallows* (Hirundo pyrrhonota) *exploit the thermals and upward currents rising against a cliff. Their nests of mud pellets with downward-facing entrance tubes are stuck under rock overhangs.*

An Egyptian Vulture (Neophron percnopterus) *hovers, about to join its mate on a Pyrenean mountainside. The splayed wing tips help it to control its movements in the air currents.*

slightly rounded, giving a longer distance for the air to travel so that it moves faster than air passing beneath. This creates a greater pressure below the wing, which pushes it upwards — gives it "lift." Lift is greater as wing size, air speed and angle of the wing to the air current increase. However, if the angle, known as the "angle of attack" becomes greater than about 15 degrees, turbulence is created above and behind the wing and this cancels out the lift, causing stalling. To counteract the effect, airplanes have "flaps," sections at the front of the wing that open to allow air to pass through. Birds achieve the same effect with the alula, a group of feathers attached to their "thumb" which normally lie flush with the front edge of the

wing but open up to create a slot when the angle increases (as when a bird slows down to land), smoothing the air flow over the upper surface.

As well as creating lift the force of air against the wing opposes lift and forward motion, an opposition known as "drag," which also increases with the angle of attack, requiring more effort in propulsion.

Powering flight

The bird propels itself by pushing against the air with its wings. It may look as though they are just flapping up and down but — as some of the early would-be aviators discovered — that alone does not produce a forward motion. The inner part of the wing, the "arm," provides the plane to give lift, the outer part, the "hand," flaps from the wrist, producing power on the downbeat when the wing twists slightly so that it pushes not only against the air below but the air behind as well. On the upstroke, the primary feathers separate so that instead of forming a solid paddle, which would push the bird downwards, they allow air to pass through them, and at the same time the front of the wing fans backwards and propels the bird forward. These basic movements are varied considerably according to the structure and needs of different species and to generate changes of speed and direction.

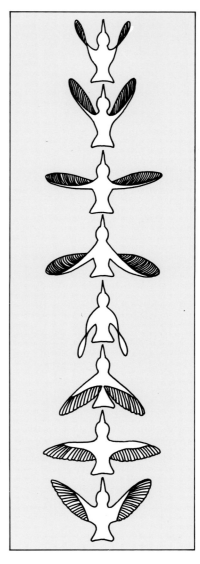

Soaring and gliding

As well as producing its own lift, a bird can take advantage of rising currents of air to carry it higher. These may occur where a cliff face, building or other obstacle — even a ship at sea — deflects a breeze upwards. Even a gently sloping hill will produce an upward current, and when a strong wind is blowing will create turbulence on the far side with further upward waves on which a bird can soar. Upward currents can also be produced over level ground when this has been warmed by the sun, by thermal activity or by heat produced by man. Rising warm air currents are known as thermals.

Many birds, including some of the larger-bodied migrants such as storks and eagles, follow hill ridges to use rising air currents, or soar up in tight circles in a thermal and then glide off at a height in search of the next one. Such birds will watch other soaring birds, or even glider planes, for indications of where thermals are present.

The oceans heat and cool more slowly than the land, so do not produce thermals, but seabirds can make use of the upward currents produced by the height of the waves in a swell, and exploit the difference between air speeds above the water, where it is slowed by friction with the surface, and that at higher levels.

Birds such as albatrosses and shearwaters, which traverse oceans in gliding flight, alternate gains of height from rising air currents

The hummingbird's rather rigid wings beat forward and backward, not up and down as they do in most birds, and pivot at the shoulder so that they can flip over at the end of the forward stroke and provide lift on the back stroke as well, describing a figure-eight pattern.

Above left *The wings of the hovering Costa's Hummingbird (Calypte costae) move forward in a figure-eight stroke as it hangs in front of a flower to feed.*

Left *A Skylark (Alauda arvensis) rising from its nest. The big broad wings impart the lift that allows it to soar and hang high in the air, facing into any wind while it sings aloft.*

Winds blowing against hills, cliffs or buildings produce strong upward currents of air that birds can exploit.

An offshore wind blowing over a cliff creates an eddy that also gives an updraft, important in getting cliff-living birds to nesting holes and ledges.

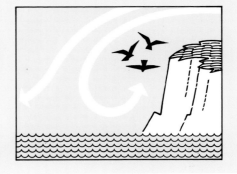

from waves, or from head winds, with long gradual downward glides.

Upward currents of air are also created as part of weather systems when cold air moves under a warmer mass pushing it upwards to great heights. On cold fronts, the mixing of the air often produces storms and birds can use the rising air to soar above them. Similar conditions occur on a smaller scale when on- and off-shore breezes meet the different air masses above the land — one reason why birds are almost certain to be seen soaring on air currents in coastal areas.

Wing forms

As birds have evolved, a wide variety of wing and tail shapes and forms have developed that suit the flying techniques that are most appropriate to particular environments and ways of life.

Large seabirds, such as this Giant Petrel (Macronectes giganteus) *exploit rising air from the edges of waves, or sea winds. Having gained lift to take them higher, they then move downwind in a long glide without wing flapping.*

Right *Different kinds of ground and ground covering (including buildings) do not absorb heat equally and where there are "hot spots" the air above them rises. Even if cold air streaming down the sides of the rising column undercuts it, a bubble continues to rise until it cools or becomes too unstable. Birds use such warm columns to soar in a rising spiral.*

Far right *Approaching its nest, the Spotted Flycatcher* (Muscicapa striata) *spreads wings and tail and uses them as brakes.*

Below *Albatrosses and other large seabirds turn into the wind with wings held stiffly to gain maximum lift and so soar upwards. Turning, they then glide down diagonally across the air current gaining speed before turning into the wind and rising again, carried forward as well as upward by their momentum.*

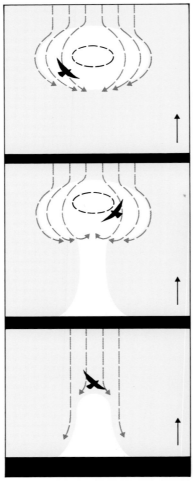

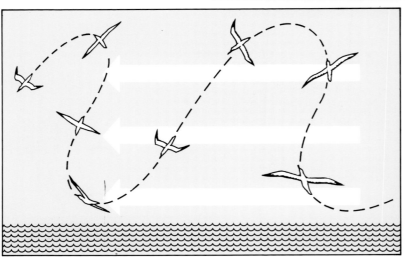

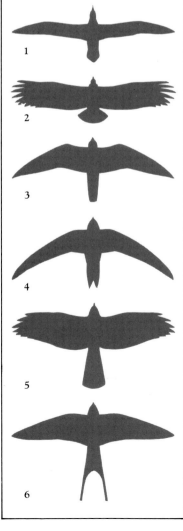

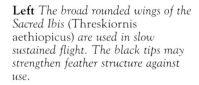

Left *The broad rounded wings of the Sacred Ibis (*Threskiornis aethiopicus*) are used in slow sustained flight. The black tips may strengthen feather structure against use.*

*As it leaves the nest, the Great Spotted Woodpecker (*Dendrocopus major*) raises the legs and the wings begin the backward and downward stroke that will lift it and propel it forward.*

Below left *The White-fronted Tern (*Sterna striata*) shows the tapering wings and strongly forked tail used for agility and rapid reaction in flight.*

Left *The form of a bird's wing is closely matched to its flying techniques.*
1. *The albatross has a lengthened narrow wing for almost effortless gliding.*
2. *Old World vultures also have wide spans but these are not long in proportion to their depth and give greater maneuverability in limited space. Splayed feathers at the wing ends help to give stability in turbulent air.*
3. *Falcons and* **4** *swifts have tapered wings for fast flight but the deeper wing of the falcon and the forked tail of the swift provide special abilities unique to each bird.*
5. *The sparrowhawk has large and powerful wings for its size. The splayed primaries help with maneuverability in varied air currents and tight turns, the long tail makes rapid movements easier among branches and vegetation.*
6. *Swallows have a strongly forked tail and a relatively narrow wing, which helps them to hover and to dart to snatch an insect.*

1

2

3

1. *Penguins enter water cautiously, then with a rush. These Adelie Penguins (Pygoscelis adeliae) launching themselves into the sea show the vestigial winglike use of the flippers.*

2. *In underwater movement a Magellanic Penguin (Spheniscus magellanicus) shows how the flippers are used for propulsion.*

3. *If forced to jump from the nest through fear of a predator, the Hoatzin (Opisthocomus hoazin) chick can swim in the water underneath, then use its wing claws to scramble back up to it again.*

Water wings

As wings advance a bird by pushing against air, so they can also be used to propel it through water. The large wing area that provides the power needed for efficient flapping flight in air, however, finds too much resistance in the denser medium of water, and birds for whom swimming is of great importance tend to have proportionally smaller wings with stronger feathering. This specialization may be at the expense of more efficient flight. Many such birds, particularly the auks and diving ducks, have very rapid wing beats and direct flight with poor maneuverability. Underwater flight is fast enough to catch fish and may take birds to considerable depths. Penguins do not fly at all and their wings are adapted for efficient swimming under water.

Flightless birds

Among the auks, the Great Auk, or Garefowl (*Pinguinus impennis*), completely lost its power of flight, becoming a northern counterpart of the penguins, and this made it especially vulnerable. Hunting and egg collection led to its extinction. A food source on some north Atlantic islands up to the seventeenth century, the last authentically recorded specimens were killed on the island of Eldrey, off Iceland, in 1844.

Some nonswimmers have also given up the use of their wings for flight. Ground-feeding inhabitants of islands that are free of predators or of Australasia which separated from the rest of the world's landmasses before the evolution of the mammals that provide most predators of birds, found no need to fly as a way of escape and gradually lost the means of doing so. Most famous was the Dodo, a relative of the pigeon, which lived on the island of Mauritius in the Indian Ocean. It grew to considerable size and weighed about 50 pounds (22.5 kg). Sailors found it easy prey and a good food source, and introduced monkeys and pigs that killed eggs and young in its ground nest. It too had been wiped out by the end of the seventeenth century.

An even larger bird, the half-ton (500-kg) Elephant-bird of Madagascar, extinct from about A.D. 1000, laid the largest eggs recorded. They are still sometimes found intact after nearly a thousand years, their volume more than 80 times that of the average farmyard chicken's egg.

In New Zealand there were flightless Moas up to 10 feet (3 m) tall. They were browsers, taking the place of plant-eating mammals and evolving species of similar appearance but with a wide range of sizes.

Such birds are at tremendous risk when predators arrive in their territory, whether they are human hunters or introduced animals like dogs and rats, but some flightless species still exist today: the rheas of South America, emus and cassowaries of Australia, kiwis of New Zealand and the Ostrich of Africa. Unlike the island birds, the Ostrich has always lived among predators but its size, watchfulness aided by its height, speed on its long legs and the powerful blows it can inflict with them have helped ensure its survival.

John Tenniel's illustration of the Dodo for Lewis Carroll's Alice's Adventures in Wonderland, probably much like the bird's actual appearance.

Right *A New Zealand Weka (Gallirallus australis) feeding its downy chick. This bird is a rail that, in the absence of predators, has lost the power of flight. Although flightless birds are particularly vulnerable to introduced predators, this chicken-sized bird is itself a predator on introduced rats and mice and other small creatures.*

SENSES

Birds need their senses not only to obtain food for themselves and their young, to find a mate, to warn them of predators and other dangers, to orientate themselves and for the other things common to all living animals, but they must be able to do these things from the air and to provide all the information necessary for interpreting air conditions and controlling flight.

Birds, like humans, rely mainly upon sight and hearing to provide information about the rest of the world, and both these senses are highly developed. Taste and smell seem to be relatively unimportant to them, although some birds do find their food by scent and others rely mainly on touch. Touch sensations are probably also important in interpreting air conditions and the state of their plumage.

Although we normally think of there being only five senses, there are others, including a response to magnetic fields, which we may also have and that are certainly used by birds.

Birds' brains are comparable in plan and relative size to those of mammals much less highly evolved than our own. The cerebrum has a large area devoted to instinctive activity and a comparatively small outer cortex, the area concerned with learned action. The cerebellum, which coordinates movement, and the optic lobe are large, as might be expected. Information from the sensory organs is carried to the brain along chains of nerve cells, known as sensory neurons, and instructions for action needed in response is sent out to the muscles via similar chains of motor neurons.

While the neurons carry messages between specific parts of the body there is another communication network, the endocrine system, that floods out signals throughout the body in the form of hormones, which then produce reactions in those organs where it is appropriate. They control cyclic events such as molt and sexual development. There is some difference in the relative size of the various parts of the brain in species with widely differing ways of life, with varying demands for elaboration of movement, sight or hearing.

The bird brain has developed to be an efficient controller of bird life. It is tempting to link brain size with intelligence and to declare that birds are not really very bright. Certainly some never seem to learn things that seem obvious to us. Eurasian Blackbirds, for instance, will year after year nest in the same garden in a location easily accessible to domestic cats that regularly take their young. But while you, taking all the observations you have made into account, decide that that is a foolish place to build a nest, the birds see exactly the mixture of cover and accessibility in proximity to convenient food sources, which they find ideal for rearing young. Only ringing could prove that the same birds came back once the predator risk was known; it could be a different pair each year choosing the same location for its positive advantages. At the opposite end of the scale, think of the bird who not only has the

Opposite *Birds of prey have acute sight. The keen eyes of this Peregrine Falcon* (Falco peregrinus) *on a Manhattan skyscraper can watch the pigeons in the streets below for a possible meal.*

Fields of view:

The pigeon has a narrow arc of binocular vision but a wide overall field so that it can see predators in all but a narrow sector.

The owl has much wider binocular vision to enable it to judge distance when hunting but must turn its head to see behind it.

The woodcock has narrow binocular vision focused at its bill tip and the same behind, but sees through all 360 degrees of arc and, because its eyes are set high on the head, can see well above itself as well.

physical ability to fly enormous distances but can precisely navigate, without maps, radar, radio or air-traffic control across two hemispheres. Think, too, of the variety and virtuosity that some songbirds can attain and the skills in mimicry that other birds display. Can it really be pure chance that they always seem to repeat the perfect phrase in exactly your tone of voice at precisely the wrong moment?

Such apparent stupidity and wisdom might be inherent ability — just elaborate programming. The most intelligent birds, in the way that we define intelligence, are probably the more generalized species that can adapt to new experiences. That is why we see crows as intelligent but not highly evolved in terms of specialization.

Sight

Compared to their body size, birds have eyes very much larger than our own. Hawks' and owls' eyes, for instance, are about the same actual size as human eyes and those of the Ostrich are considerably larger. They take up a considerable amount of space in the skull and the occiputs leave little space between them, but most are rather flattened, which does reduce some of the depth they occupy. The flattening is achieved through a ring of fine horny plates that surrounds the iris, which is linked with small muscles that can modify the cornea shape and allow some focal adjustment.

Raptors, which need to see particularly well to spot their prey, have more globe-shaped or even tubular eyes, which gives a greater distance between lens and retina.

The life-styles of the different bird groups demand a number of other variant adaptations in the eye. The most obvious difference is the placing of the eyes. In most birds they are on the side of the head. This enables them to see through a very wide arc — in some birds, such as the woodcock, this is effectively all-around vision — and in the woodcock's case it is possible that it may even be able to see right over the top of its head as well! The skull shape and placing of the eyes in other birds gives a variety of lesser vision angles but the raptors are the only group with forward-facing eyes like those of humans, and only the owls have the linking up of nerves from each eye to both sides of the brain, which provides full stereoscopic vision. The area covered by both eyes in the owl is as much as 60–70 degrees (compared to human 180 degrees) but in most birds the area of where vision of both eyes overlaps is comparatively small, though in the woodcock's case it is at both front and rear.

It might be expected that for the judging of distance in flight — particularly when coming in to land — stereoscopic vision would be essential but, although this certainly is of advantage to the owls, the comparatively small amount of noncrossover binocular vision birds have is generally sufficient for their purposes. In many birds that hunt flying insects, a system of binocular vision within each individual eye has

developed, which involves two foveas, two areas at which vision is concentrated and sharper than over the rest of the eye. Most birds have a single fovea, an indentation at the center of the retina where there is a concentration of cone cells (which give a sharp image and record color). The rest of the retina is a mixture of cone and rod cells (which are more light sensitive, giving vision in poor light, but provide a less clear image).

Another way in which birds judge distance is by cocking their heads to one side, comparing the difference between two viewpoints, which binocular vision does at the same time. Even owls improve their vision by bobbing the head about. Humans and other mammals focus their eyes with the muscles around the lens. These provide much less alteration in birds and there may be some degree of lens control by changing the pressure in the aqueous humor behind it. One suggestion is that this is effected by erecting the pecten, a folded membrane that projects from the back of the eye and which is not known in mammals, though this organ is not properly understood and may have other functions. It is filled with blood vessels and probably helps to nourish the retina.

Birds can also change the curvature of the cornea and most species have about twice the focusing power of human eyes. They have both the distant vision they need in flight and the ability to focus on food at very close range. Birds have the advantage that a much greater part of their field of vision is in sharp focus than with human eyes — about 20 degrees compared with our 2.5 degrees; we have to continually move focus to view the same scene. However, birds can swivel their eyes much less than us (2 degrees compared with our 100 degrees) and to change their view must move the head. This is helped by having long and flexible necks; owls can turn theirs through at least 180 degrees. Humans tend to scan a scene fairly slowly as they take in each small segment; birds, viewing much more at a time, can probably pick out details more quickly and consequently change their angle much more noticeably.

There are many other modifications among the birds to match particular ways of life. Herons, for instance, though their eyes are not frontally placed, have them set well forward to give good binocular vision when stabbing the bill forward for a fish. Birds of various species that, like starlings, do open-bill probing, forcing the bill into soil or a crevice and opening it to lever an opening, need to peer down the bill and have close-set eyes.

When birds swim under water, it has a reflective index very close to that of the corneal tissue of the eye and this has the effect of reducing focusing ability and making them long-sighted. To compensate, many diving birds close the nictitating membrane (the third eyelid that helps to protect the eye from dirt and wind in flight and to spread fluids across it). In penguins, who spend so much time diving, the cornea is very flat, so it does not much affect vision and the lens is particularly

powerful. Other species, such as cormorants and diving ducks, have specially soft adaptable eye lenses to increase vision accommodation under water.

Birds see in color much as we do, but birds, like the reptiles from which they developed, have tiny drops of colored oil in the cone cells of the retina that are believed to filter out some wavelengths of light. The oil is mainly of the red-orange-yellow part of the spectrum, removing colors from the other blue end with short wavelengths and letting past those with long ones, thus emphasizing sensitivity in the red-yellow-green range. Photographers use red and yellow filters to cut through haze and this probably helps seabirds, especially, to see more clearly. However such filters make the sky look darker and would also produce poor visibility in the blue-green world beneath the waves. Diving birds and those that catch flying insects have much less colored oil in their cones, as do night hunters, for whom the drops would reduce the amount of already dim light recorded. However, the droplets would emphasize foliage, both when green and in autumn color, and the many yellow and red fruits and berries. It is

Silver-eyes feed partly by probing with bill forced open, peering along it for possible food. As this nesting Silver-eye (Zosterops lateralis) shows, there is a break in the white eye rim at the point where the bird looks down the beak.

Birds recognize ripe berries by their color. This migrant Fieldfare (Turdus pilaris) feeds on pyracantha berries in a winter suburban garden.

probably also relevant that the great majority of the flowers that attract birds for their pollination are red.

However, these droplets do not cut off the extreme end of the blue range. Birds have a sensitivity to ultraviolet light, which humans lack. It is possible that objects that look dull and black to us reflect brightly to them, and ultraviolet light may help birds to orient by the sun even when the sky is overcast. It is known that insects are guided to nectar (and hence to the position where they best effect pollination) by ultraviolet markings on flowers and it is probable that birds can also see these "nectar-guides."

Birds also appear to be able to detect polarized light. The sky pattern of light polarization differs through the day with the sun's position and a perception of this may help in navigation when the position of the sun seems to be used as a compass.

For animals without strong binocular vision the surroundings seem to shift back as they move forward. Birds overcome this in steady movements such as walking by keeping the head position fixed, then shifting it rapidly and briefly to a new forward position. This produces the head-nodding walk of birds such as pigeons and the head thrust of stalking herons. A hovering kestrel keeps the head fixed no matter what body, wings and tail are doing.

Hearing

Because our ears, and those of other mammals, stick out from the sides of the head, it is easy to imagine that birds have no ears at all, but the ear you see is only the pinna or outer ear; beneath their feathers birds have a complete hearing system located at the side of the head. It does not differ greatly from our own but has only one slender bone (the columella) across the cavity of the middle ear, which transmits and amplifies vibrations striking the eardrum (tympanum), whereas three bones do this job in the human ear. There is also a connecting passage through the skull that links the two eardrums and makes it possible very precisely to register the difference in pitch and timing of sounds from the same source as they are received by each ear, despite the relatively short distance between them. This is extremely important in locating a sound source.

The bird's ear opening is usually covered with special feathers, ear coverts or auriculars, that lack barbules and so give protection without seriously interfering with the sound waves. The birds' hearing range differs considerably from species to species both in range and sensitivity, but research so far covers only a limited number of species. Their sensitivity peaks at about the same levels as humans, between 1.5 and 4 kilohertz. It is this similarity in hearing that allows us to recognize and interpret vocalizations of birds. However, the hearing ranges of some species extend to some sounds of very high or very low pitch beyond the human range. Capercaillies are known to produce low frequency sounds that are too low for humans to hear, but there is no evidence that they can hear them themselves either!

Some of the swift family, including the Oilbird of Venezuela, can use an echolocation system like that of the bats. They produce a series of clicks — at a much lower frequency than those of bats, so it is possible for humans to hear them — and the bird's inbuilt radar system compares the time each takes to come back to identify the distance of objects. This is especially useful for cave dwellers such as the Oilbirds and the cave swiftlets, which must find their nests and roosting places in darkness.

Owls do not have this ability but they are able to locate prey in total darkness with an accuracy of 1 degree by the acuity of their hearing. The use of infrared photography to record their hunting has revealed that they move their heads from side to side to enable them to build up an accurate three-dimensional audio image much as they and many other birds use head movements to judge visual distances by parallax. The owls also have their ears placed asymmetrically — the left placed higher and tilted slightly downwards. They have a ruff of feathers around the eyes on each side of the beak that channel soundwaves back to the ears, which are, in their case, hidden beneath a flap of skin.

Whereas some birds use sound for hunting, or locating prey, all use their hearing to give

The Great Gray Owl (Strix nebulosa) has the big facial disks that help owls gather sound for the ears, which are placed low down behind them on either side.

warning of the approach of predators. Even more important is the use of sound for communication. Birds have developed a sophisticated system of calls and songs that are used to announce their occupation of territory, advertise for mates, keep contact with others of a flock and give warning when danger threatens.

Taste and smell

The areas of the brain that handle smell are not very well developed in most birds, so it is reasonable to assume that scents play only a minor role in most avian life. However, there are species in which these olfactory lobes are considerably bigger and where smell is known to be used for specific purposes. The African honeyguides, for instance, probably locate bees' nests partly by the scent of their beeswax, for it was long ago observed that they would fly into churches when beeswax candles were burning. The North American Turkey Vulture also hunts by smell as well as sight. It is possible that this evolved because these smaller vultures were mainly forest birds, living where dead animals are difficult to see. Related New World vultures do not have this ability and watch the Turkey Vulture to find out where carrion may be. The Old World Vultures and other carrion eaters are not able to hunt by smell either and must rely on sight. North American oil

engineers have made use of the Turkey Vulture's sense of smell to help them identify leaks in underground fuel pipes, for these birds tend to congregate in the area of a fracture. Why the smell of petroleum attracts them is still a mystery.

Kiwis certainly hunt by smell. They explore below the surface of the ground with the tips of their long bills (where their nostrils are located) sniffing for earthworms.

Shearwaters, storm petrels and other tube-nosed birds have large scent lobes and probably locate food partly by smell. They will come to fish-oil slicks on the sea surface and the tube-nose may aid their ability to detect scent. It is probable that those living in colonies may use scent to guide them to their nest burrows, which they visit at night.

It is possible that scent plays a part in general navigation; experiments with homing pigeons seem to suggest this. Pigeons kept for a time in a loft where special baffles distorted the directions from which scents came, set out at angles to their home routes equivalent to those of the distortion of the apparent direction smells had come from, whereas birds housed without the baffles flew more directly home.

Taste is closely linked to smell. The cells that carry information on the scent particles, or pheromones, which are carried through the air, are received on the surface of the folded membranes in the nasal cavity at the base of

A Brown Kiwi (Apteryx australis) *has its nostrils right at the bill tip and smells the worms that it is hunting. The small ear hole can be seen behind the eye.*

Left *Wood-storks and ibises, such as this White Ibis (Eudocimus albus) feeding at the tide's edge in Florida, probe in water and appear to find food by touch rather than sight.*

These touch cells, known as Herbst's corpuscles, provide information on the positioning of each feather and may be the way in which birds gain information about atmospheric pressure. Those in the legs are particularly sensitive to vibrations — especially useful as a warning of ground predators — and may respond to airborne signals beyond the range their ears will register. There are also bristle-like vibrissae, comparable to a mammal's whiskers but set throughout the plumage and evolving as a modified form of feather. They are sensitive to any deflection and probably provide information concerning the flow of air over the body, giving the bird a greater awareness of the currents in which it is moving.

Navigation

For creatures of enormous potential mobility, birds are often surprisingly sedentary. It has sometimes been suggested that birds had powers of flight in order to stay where they were, or at least to get back there if blown away.

If you have the power to travel long distances then you will need to know how to go where you wish and how to get back again. Birds are no different and, in order to survive, they need the ability to navigate. Since they lack the power of reasoning, this must be through one or more inherited sensing abilities.

It is probable that hearing is of negligible importance in this respect, although most species have recognizable call notes that they use in order to keep together, and in both night-flying and day-flying migrants these tend to be used continually.

In the past it was assumed that the sense of smell played no part in bird movements but there is increasing suggestion that it may be of importance. As already mentioned, experiments suggest that pigeons can recognize the location of their loft by scent. Polynesian seamen used to claim the ability to recognize their whereabouts by the smell of the sea and most people would recognize a familiar neighborhood with strong industrial or farmyard odors, or know a part of their garden from the scent of flowers and herbs, though scent does not normally have an important role in human orientation. If, as it now appears, the tubenosed seabirds have a fine sense of smell, then perhaps some

the bill. The taste buds, which in humans and other mammals are carried on the tongue and on the inside of the mouth and lips, are placed mainly on the back of the tongue and in the throat around the pharynx and epiglottis; the tongues of most birds are covered with a horny surface. Although they have the same sensations of bitter, sweet, salt and sour, this placing of the buds means that most birds get no taste sensation until food has almost been swallowed. It is claimed that they also have many fewer taste buds: rabbits have 15,500, humans 9,000, but parrots only 400, most passerines 30–70 and the Allen's Hummingbird only one! Certainly birds appear to appreciate the taste of some items when they are touched or held with the tip of the bill, but the small number of buds and the probable lack of much supplementary scent information, which forms part of our appreciation of flavor, would suggest that taste is not of primary importance to most of the birds.

Touch

Touch is not simply a matter of contact, it involves a response to air pressures and vibrations. There are touch receptors on the soles of the feet, on the tongue and in some birds at the tip of the bill (although not over most of its horny surface). Woodpeckers have particularly sensitive tongue tips, which they use to find insects in the holes they make in tree trunks with their bills. Shore- and waterbirds that sift through mud or sand and take animals living below the surface or sweep their bills through water, all have sensitive bills to detect foodstuff that makes contact. There are other minute and very fine sense organs on the legs and areas of bare skin and in a circle around the base of every feather.

Migrating birds that fly by night are likely to use the star pattern for navigation. The abnormal bright light from a lighthouse throws them off course and birds fly toward the light and flutter around the lighthouse.

seabirds, and landbirds also, may have scent-maps of some extensive and regularly used areas.

Sight is obviously of importance. Birds recognize the localities that they live in and that they regularly pass through. Returning migrants, once they have reached a known area, can find their way back to a previously used nest site. On longer migratory flights, the lower-flying day migrants tend to follow the visual cues of hill ranges and shorelines.

More specific ability to recognize direction is difficult to test and establish. We know that birds can recognize the directional polarized light of the sun's rays, and use the changing polarized light pattern during the day to establish direction of flight. In one instance, ducks with an habitual seasonal migration in one direction were kept in a dark room where their daily light regime was gradually modified. They were released at midday, having been physiologically persuaded that it was sunrise, and using polarized light they set off at right angles to their proper course.

Experiments using the artificial sky of a planetarium have shown that night migrants can identify their desired direction by the pattern of the stars. This pattern alters in position through the night just as the polarized light pattern alters during the day. The birds must therefore possess some way of judging the passage of time relative to what they can see. They can use this ability even when only a few stars in a small part of the night sky are visible among clouds. If the sky is completely overcast and the wind changes after the birds have begun their night movement, then large numbers of migrants may be blown off course and appear next morning in unexpected places. Subsequently they appear to be able to reorientate themselves and to get back on course again with the necessary adjustments.

Birds tend not to migrate in unfavorable weather, but it has been noticed that when weather improves they may already be moving and must have started off before the changes were apparent. This suggests that they must be sensitive to changes in barometric pressure. This has recently been confirmed experimentally and domestic pigeons have been found to perceive such changes.

It has also been found that birds can detect the earth's magnetic field and might therefore use this to aid migration. Study of this is difficult and it is still uncertain how it is done. It has been claimed that magnetite crystals occur within the head and neck of birds and that magnetism may act on these, but there is some doubt about this hypothesis. An alternative possibility is that the magnetic field can be detected by special sensitivity or structures in other more normal sensory organs of birds such as eyes and ears, or even by the pineal gland of the brain.

With these various sensory possibilities it seems likely that the navigational abilities of birds result from the use of an interacting group of faculties, rather than relying wholly upon the presence of a single specialized factor.

An Australian Gannet (Morus bassana serrator) soars high above the ocean. When not breeding, it disperses widely at sea, but, even after an absence of four years while growing up, it will return unerringly to breed at the same small colony where it was hatched.

THE LIFE OF THE BIRD

THE DAILY ROUND

As with all creatures, a bird's priorities are survival and reproduction. It must find food, avoid danger, seek shelter from extremes of weather and keep itself healthy. Some species achieve this by dividing their year between different territories, perhaps thousands of miles apart, others spend all their lives in the same locality. Each has developed a particular way of life to fit a particular niche in the ecosystem. Even within the same species, there may be wide differences in the way in which birds have adapted to fit different geographies and the many changes wrought by human beings. Some activities in a bird's life — mating and migration for instance — will be dependent upon season or the annual cycle, but most are a day-by-day matter of survival.

Like humans, birds may rest in midday heat as well as at night. A party of Little Corellas (Cacatua sanguinea) rest from digging in a gum tree.

Scarlet Ibises (Eudocimus ruber) *are sociable birds, feeding, roosting and breeding in flocks. Here they assemble to rest on mangrove roots as rising tides force them off the mud where they feed in the Orinoco delta.*

Because birds use up their energy so rapidly and need frequent replenishment, they tend to have a daily, or nightly, routine — perhaps not unlike that of some people. Soon after waking, the most important activity is taking in food and drink for fueling the activities of the day. As the need for these eases, other things can be fitted in, such as plumage care. There tends to be a lull in activity around midday, then a second and more leisurely period of activity with feeding in readiness for the coming night. The routine is shattered and rearranged during the breeding season. The bird must reassert its presence through territorial advertisement, involving song and possibly display, at the beginning of the day and perhaps at intervals later. Further into the breeding period comes the nestlings' constant demand for food.

Nocturnal birds have a similar routine, beginning at dusk instead of dawn. The longer days nearer the Earth's poles may impose some overlapping in routines of day and night birds. In temperate zones, Barn Owls and a North American nightjar, the Nighthawk, often hunt in the late afternoon, whereas in the Arctic, the Snowy Owl and other species must cope with up to 24 hours of summer daylight. At such times birds tend to have short naps at intervals rather than a long period of sleep. Another group with broken routines is the shorebirds. These species include some that must feed with tidal exposure of food, whether by day or night. In every case, however, the primary and overriding need is for a constant supply of food.

Feeding

Food is necessary to fuel the energy used up in all the body functions and in powering flight and other activity, to generate heat to keep the body at a comfortable temperature and to supply materials for the growth and replacement of all body tissues. How much food obviously varies according to the size of the bird but the difference in need is not of the same proportion as the difference in size.

In small birds the ratio of surface area to body volume is much higher than in larger ones. They lose heat much more rapidly than large birds when the air temperature is colder than the air. Very small birds, such as some tropical hummingbirds, lose so much heat at night that they slow down all their metabolic processes and become torpid, so reducing the energy demand and maintaining minimal temperature. Birds living in colder climates could not survive if they were too small; they would use up energy faster than they could find food to replace it. Birds, especially small ones, burn up so much of their reserves that there is a noticeable weight loss from evening to morning. For many it is essential that they begin to feed as soon as they wake and they must find enough food during the rest of the day to build up sufficient reserves to see them through the next night.

Building up sufficient reserves for mating, laying eggs and feeding and rearing young is only possible at those times when food gathering

becomes easier. Molting and replacing feathers makes further energy, and hence food, demands, and birds that migrate to exploit resources in two areas must also find food to accumulate sufficient reserves to fuel the exhausting migration flight. The need to get food influences almost all aspects of a bird's life and sometimes may leave time only for essential grooming and for sleep when it becomes too dark to hunt for food or too cold to leave the roost.

In some species the possession of an assured food supply may be the primary reason for having a territory, and birds that feed in an extensive but defined area such as a shoreline may defend temporary feeding territories when not breeding. This can be seen for example in the European Gray Heron and Ringed Plover. Highly aggressive birds may tolerate other species on their territories but this usually indicates that they are not competing for the same food source or, if they do show similar tastes, have different feeding methods or take different items from the range of food available.

Diets vary widely. Some species, such as crows, are omnivorous, others are oddly specialized feeders — as for instance the Everglade Kite, which eats only large freshwater snails. Most birds are not wholly reliant on one food source but, as far as their general feeding is concerned, they can be divided into two groups: the animal eaters and the plant eaters. The second group tends to be more specialized and perhaps evolved later. In the first group are the insect eaters, the larger hunters for flesh

and fish and the scavengers of carcasses; in the second the feeders on seeds, fruits, nectar and other plant parts. Bill forms often give a clue to a bird's diet, but it is simpler to observe birds foraging to discover what they eat.

For short periods adult birds of some species may be able to get by on a restricted diet, provided it generates enough energy to keep them going, relying on their body's store of calcium, certain vitamins and other nutrients. Overall, however, the diet must provide a complete balance of the proteins, vitamins and minerals necessary to build and replace bone, tissue and feathers. The demand for different components will vary according to age, sex, and the annual cycle. Chicks and young birds, for instance, need plenty of calcium to help build their bones, and hens have a special need for it for creating eggshells during the breeding season. The growing young will sometimes be given food that differs from the adult diet — fruit, nectar and seed eaters, for instance, collect insects for their chicks to provide the additional protein that the growing young require.

To meet these varying needs and any alteration in the availability of particular foods with the seasons or the bird's migration, some species even undergo changes within their digestive systems to enable them to cope with a different diet. Dunnocks and Bearded Reedlings are species that switch from an insect diet in summer to a seed diet in winter: during the winter their gizzards develop a thicker muscular wall to cope with the change.

A Morepork (Ninox novaeseelandiae) *with a Huhu beetle. Spiders and insects are taken by many birds. They are a rich supply of protein, especially for feeding growing chicks.*

Above left *The Goldcrest* (Regulus regulus) *must feed most of the day to maintain itself and build up reserves to last through the night. It and the Firecrest* (R. ignicapillus) *are the smallest European birds, weighing only ⅕ ounce (6g).*

Eaters of insects and other small invertebrates

Many birds rely on other small creatures as their food. For birds that are not specialized to take other prey, insects provide the obvious source. They are abundant in most regions of the world and not too difficult to catch. Many birds take other similar small invertebrates — spiders in particular, but also centipedes, small crustaceans such as woodlice, and tiny shrimps and crabs in wet situations. Worms and snails are sufficiently abundant to have their own bird specialists as well as feeding the less fussy foragers.

Birds that normally have a different diet may turn to insects when a good supply of protein is needed, for themselves as well as to nourish growing young. Some are insect specialists, particularly the swifts, swallows, wood-swallows

Rainbow Birds (Merops ornatus) *are bee-eaters but take other insects such as this fly, hawking them on the wing and snatching them in flight.*

and nightjars that hunt on the wing, swooping through the air to catch them in flight. The watch-and-wait birds — shrikes, jacamars, puffbirds, rollers and others — that dart out from perches to take unwary insects, and the beeeaters, like most that take large insects, will carry them back to their perch to eat. The seemingly upward-looking todies snatch insects from the undersides of forest leaves and the gleaners, such as warblers and tits, systematically search leaves, twigs and buds for resting insects. Treecreepers and woodcreepers peer and probe in bark crevices and moss on trees for hidden invertebrates. Thrashers and thrushes, such as the Eurasian Blackbird, rake and toss aside dead leaves on the ground, and scimitarbabblers and the longer-billed lark species probe soft soil. The Hoopoe probes with its long curved bill into cricket burrows and other hiding places. Wagtails and pipits chase insects across bare open ground.

"Search image"

Birds generally sample food at random but experiments show that they will quickly learn to reject insects with colors and patterns that they associate with unpleasant experiences. But how do they react to edible insects? In an experiment with birds feeding on short grass, such as thrushes and Eurasian Blackbirds, food was scattered around in varied mixtures and densities. Because an ideal spread of different insects is hard to find, edible models of colored pastry were used as well.

When a bird ate something it liked, it appeared to hold a mental image of it and to look around for more of the same thing. If it found them it would concentrate on this search, seeming to ignore items it might at other times have investigated. If what it was hunting became scarce it would try other things, and if they occurred with the right frequency would switch its search to this new food. This "search image," looking past other items, is something you use yourself when looking for a particular object. It helps the bird to feed more quickly by concentrating on the food most readily available.

A researcher called De Ruiter tested Eurasian Jays and Chaffinches. When shown a twig-mimicking caterpillar or other highly camouflaged insect, a bird would eat it and then begin to discover others it had overlooked before — and to do this more rapidly than might be expected. There appears to be an element of learning and memory involved to enable the bird to concentrate on a new-found object and successfully exploit a food resource.

Insects have evolved a host of elaborate camouflages and ways of hiding themselves from such predators. Sometimes they are disturbed or flushed accidentally and one hunting bird may make prey available for another. Fantail flycatchers, which spread the tail erect over their heads and tilt it from side to side and move through the foliage using this action to flush out insects, may well find other birds taking some of them. There are advantages in birds with slightly different techniques hunting together. In northern forests, after the breeding season, mixed flocks of tits, warblers and treecreepers may move about together, each foraging in their own fashion. Such mixed flocks are much more common in tropical forests where numbers of species that feed at particular levels, but by different techniques, regularly hunt together.

The insect flushers may not be other birds. Grazing mammals disturb insects and wagtails and Cattle Egrets may run around the hooves of grazing cattle while European Robins follow digging wild boars and gardeners.

The bodies of cattle and other animals also attract insects and ticks, providing a kind of moving feast to birds who feed on them. An extreme example of this are the oxpeckers. These two species, related to the starlings, move over the big grazing animals of Africa — antelopes, giraffes and rhinos — like woodpeckers on trees, removing insects, ticks and mites, and taking blood and tissue from the edges of wounds.

Left *The ornate Asiatic Paradise Flycatcher* (Terpsiphone paradisi) *is a monarch flycatcher with the typical strong, broad-based flycatcher bill.*

The Yellow-billed Oxpecker (Buphagus africanus) *travels with the cattle, rhinos and giraffes of Africa feeding on their ticks and sometimes taking blood from wounds.*

Insects themselves may be inadvertent providers. In tropical forests some birds occasionally, or habitually, follow columns of predatory ants. They keep out of harm's way themselves by hanging onto low perches, swooping and snapping up the insects and small animals that the ants flush out of cover. The antbirds of South America are named for this habit, although only some of these species practice it.

Adaptations for insect eating

Simple insect eating does not require much specialization but in a few groups adaptations have been extreme. Keen sight is an obvious advantage and the aerial feeders and flycatchers usually have wide bills with bristles fringing the gape, whereas those that probe have long slender bills for searching crevices and holes. The thrush-like dippers of fast-flowing streams walk into and under water, or swim using their wings, to feed on aquatic insects among the stones of the streambed. The small grebe species will also hunt aquatic insects.

Woodpeckers are insect hunters. The small, songbird-like piculets glean insects from branches and foliage but typical woodpeckers use their stout chisel-like bills to hack into dead and living wood in pursuit of wood-boring insect larvae. They can hammer hard and constantly with their bills because their skulls are especially strong, with cushioning for the brain so that their staccato pounding blows do no harm. Their tongues are very long and can be thrust out for a considerable distance. They are often equipped with barbs at the tip and can be extended far down the tunnels of boring insects and withdrawn with the insect impaled.

Some species have become principally feeders on ants. They tend to feed on the ground, digging into ants' nests or probing in the ground for them. They have even longer tongues, sticky ones to which the ants adhere. The tongue of the ant-eating Wryneck is two thirds the total length of the bird. Ant-eating woodpeckers mainly feed on the ground, like the flickers in North America, the Green Woodpecker in Eurasia and the Ground Woodpecker in Africa.

Even if ants are vulnerable to woodpeckers, despite their formic acid, social insects with stings, such as bees and wasps might be expected to deter birds — but bee-eaters feed mainly on bees and wasps taken in flight away from the insects' colonies. They are held by the tip of the abdomen and rubbed on a perch to discharge their venom before they are swallowed. Other birds also learn to remove the sting. The Honey-buzzard goes straight to the source. It digs out bees' and wasps' nests and eats the larvae. It does not appear to suffer, but it is hard to believe that its dense feathering completely protects it from stings. Honeyguides are more cunning. Several species are known to lead susceptible mammals, such as men, baboons and ratels, to a bees' nest, displaying excitable behavior to attract attention and encourage

them to follow. After the mammal has broken open the colony, the bird feeds on both the bee larvae and the wax of which the honeycombs are made. It appears to have bacteria or an enzyme in the gut that can digest the wax.

Bees and wasps warn off casual predators by their color and pattern. Bright combinations of red, orange or yellow with black usually indicate an inedible or poisonous animal. This marking occurs in a variety of insects and in other creatures. The colors of fire-bellied toads and some salamanders give the same warning. There seems to be a basic rule that, among smaller creatures, if they hide or are camouflaged they are probably edible; if bright and conspicuous they are probably not good to eat. Birds learn by seizing and trying to eat a distasteful insect when young, finding it an unpleasant experience and subsequently recognizing the warning color and pattern. Some young birds may learn from warnings given by their parents. Some edible insects have also gained protection by adopting similar warning colors.

Right A New Zealand Robin (Petroica australis) *with a worm that it has pecked along the body to incapacitate it.*

Below right A Song Thrush (Turdus philomelos) *whacks a snail against a stone to break its shell. The old shell debris shows that this is an "anvil" that is regularly used.*

Honey-buzzards (Pernis apivorus) *feed on bee and wasp grubs, digging open their nests. This parent has brought a comb of grub cells back for its chicks.*

Eating worms and mollusks

Worms and mollusks form a significant source of food for some birds. Earthworms exist in enormous numbers in moist places. They come to the surface to seize and pull leaves into their burrows, to copulate and to excrete their casts. In the first two activities, which normally occur on damp nights, they lie vulnerable on the surface. They are easy prey for owls and form a large part of the diet of some of these birds. It is only the early birds among the songbirds that find the worms before they return to their burrows during the early morning, although a few will be present later in the day. They are also hunted by the smaller gulls and inland shorebirds such as plovers.

A thrush or Eurasian Blackbird, hopping or searching over grass, will suddenly seize a worm and pull. The portion of the worm still in the tunnel will help it resist and a strong persistent tug may be needed. Once out, the worm is pecked at intervals along the body to break the muscles and incapacitate it before swallowing. Such birds may stand with head cocked to one side, as though listening. This is, in fact, the action of a bird with eyes set towards the sides of the head, watching for some small movement or indication of the presence of a worm.

Worms may come to the surface in the daytime in response to subterranean disturbance like a burrowing mole. Drumming rain also seems to bring them up. Some birds, such as plovers, may drum on the ground with one slightly raised foot and it has been suggested that this might bring up worms. Shorebirds feeding on tidal sands and mud may also show the same habit, which has then been interpreted as possibly deluding the buried mollusks into believing the tide is coming in and consequently coming to the surface. Some gulls have a more heavy-footed technique, standing in shallow water and steadily trampling with

both webbed feet, occasionally looking down hopefully.

For underground worms, a bird must probe more deeply. Starlings use open-billed probing, jabbing and then prying the soil apart with the opening bill. Rooks may feed similarly, hunting cranefly larvae in grass roots but also finding worms. Shorebirds can go more deeply but need soft wet soil, mud or sand into which to probe. Snipe and woodcock have long strong bills and probe deeply into small muddy patches in marsh ground, feeling for worms with sensitive bill tips and drawing them into the bill. Pride of place for worm-probing probably goes to the kiwis, whose flexible bill tip bears their nostrils to detect the food.

The muds and sands of estuaries and shorelines are full of worms and small mollusks and prove a rich feeding ground when uncovered by falling tides. Shorebirds exploit these areas, particularly when not breeding, and may assemble in good areas in huge numbers. The bills of the various species cover the whole range of lengths, allowing probing at all depths and, in general, birds do not appear to look for signs of moving food but simply probe likely areas with rapid jabbing as they move forward, often feeding in large and fairly close flocks.

Mollusks are an alternative to worms and probably more nourishing, but often encased in a hard shell. Slugs do not offer the shell problem but are usually confined to moist terrestrial situations. Although they may hide in the soil or among dead leaves, they become active by night and may be poorly hidden by day. Birds find them by searching likely places. When seized, a slug tries to defend itself by exuding slime and birds like thrushes that regularly feed on them, will wipe them vigorously on the ground before swallowing them.

Snails have shells that must be broken. Small snails with less tough shells may be treated like seeds and crushed by seed eaters, such as cardinals and bullfinches, and swallowed by pigeons. Stout-billed trogons eat tree snails. Some thrushes and the pittas have a technique for opening larger snails. The shell is seized by the lip or rim and carried to a stone or similar hard surface where it is vigorously hammered against the stone until the shell shatters and

Little Stint — Dunlin — Knot — Bar-tailed Godwit — Oystercatcher — Curlew — Turnstone

Different length bills enable different species to exploit food sources at various depths in the mud and sand of estuaries and shores. Curlews probe worm burrows and may go deepest. Oystercatchers only use probing part of the time. Turnstones flip over stones and seaweed at the surface and small plovers are mainly surface feeders.

An American Black Oystercatcher (Haematopus bachmani) finds an incautious limpet that has loosened its grip and pries it from the rock.

the snail inside can be eaten. Crows can hammer open land snails with ease but, when hunting the shoreline for marine snails, they have trouble with the thick tough whelk shells. They pick up whelks, tending to choose the larger ones, fly to some rocks and drop them from heights of 7–26 feet (2–7 m) to break them open. They use a similar technique for feeding on bivalve shellfish such as large mussels. The large water snails of shallow marsh waters in countries around the Caribbean region are predated by two species of snail kites. These raptors have slender curved bills that can be inserted into the shell to cut the muscle that holds the snail in place, and it is then extracted from the unbroken shell.

Many of the bivalve mollusks of coastal waters and seabeds are eaten by birds. Tiny ones in sand and mud are eaten by shorebirds and gulls. Some of the heavy-billed seaducks, such as scoters, eiders and steamerducks, feed on these shellfish, diving to reach the types

such as mussels that occur in exposed masses. They are swallowed, crushed partly by the bird's bill and partly in its gizzard. Oystercatchers feed on mussels and cockles. Their long heavy bills have a laterally flattened chisel tip. They can open the shell by cutting the hinge muscle, or simply smash in the side. They also chip limpets off rocks with a quick lateral hack of the bill and eat them out of the shell. They are adaptable birds and their feeding also ranges to catching small fish in tide pools and digging for earthworms in riverside meadows.

Crustacean food

Of the crustaceans, creatures such as woodlice and freshwater shrimps tend to pass unnoticed among the small invertebrates eaten by birds. Brine shrimps are an important food source in regions that are arid for long periods: they survive as eggs when saline lakes temporarily dry

up, hatching and breeding in abundance when water returns. The great breeding flocks of Banded Stilts on Australia's inland lakes rely on them and Avocets and ducks also take them. The rich but hidden swarms of sand-hoppers on beaches support shorebirds, starlings and rock pipits. The abundance of coastal crabs and shrimps of varying size are taken by many birds, including herons, seagulls, sea-ducks, shorebirds and crows. Where mangroves occur on tropical coasts there are swarms of tiny crabs, taken, in addition to already mentioned birds, by rails and some of the larger insect-eating songbirds and minor raptors such as butcherbirds.

The Crab Plover of the Indian Ocean is a crab specialist. Like a large pied plover, with big heavy bill, it feeds on crabs on coasts and for a shorebird is peculiar in nesting in a burrow and bringing food to its chick.

Possibly one of the most important crustaceans is the shrimp-like krill, the main food in cold polar waters. It is a primary food source for penguins, some auks and many of the petrels and shearwaters of colder seas.

Flesh eaters

There is no clear dividing line between the birds that feed on insects and similar prey and the more raptorial flesh eaters, other than the matter of size. Larger insect eaters will take small amphibians and reptiles. The Eurasian Blackbird, bathing or drinking at a pool, will take a tiny frog or a newt, or even a small fish. Among the birds of prey, the pygmy falcons feed largely on insects, as do the small owls, and the long-legged Burrowing Owl will chase insects on foot. The huge European Eagle-Owl is an unfussy feeder with a range of prey from geese and hares to beetles. Others too may be unpredictable: an elegant Pavonine Quetzal has been seen inelegantly swallowing a large frog and a Peacock casually snapping up mice.

Eating larger nourishing prey gives an advantage in that meals may be more widely spaced with less need for activity between them, but capturing prey may be hard work. The two principal raptor groups are the day-hunting birds of prey — hawks, eagles, falcons — and the mainly nocturnal owls. These birds differ from minor predators in their hunting habits. Birds such as shrikes, Australian Butcherbirds, and even New World vultures, can make little use of their feet and rely on their bills for catching and killing. The typical raptors use their large strong feet with long sharp claws to seize and strike prey before bringing the bill into use for the final killing. Prey is carried in the feet to where it will be eaten. They use slightly different hunting techniques, with the diurnal birds of prey usually moving fast and striking hard, the owls approaching more slowly and silently to seize their prey. Owls usually swallow prey whole, or dismember it in large pieces. Other birds of prey strip off flesh to remove and eat as small portions, sometimes leaving a major part of the skeleton. Notable

Owl pellets

The owls' feeding methods involve the ingestion of a considerable amount of unwanted bone, fur and feathers. This could impose a burden on the digestive system and instead of passing this material through the bird it is cast up from the stomach as a pellet. This consists of bones and other hard material encased in a padding of the softer remains of fur and feathers. Such pellets can be large and one or two may be cast nightly.

Similar pellets are produced by diurnal birds. These are usually smaller and, since digestion is more efficient, bones may be partly or wholly eroded and dissolved. Even in cases where bones would be cast up, the young of both diurnal and nocturnal birds of prey tend to digest bones more completely in order to obtain the minerals that they need in growth.

exceptions are the snake-eating serpent eagles that tend to swallow their prey whole and headfirst.

Eagles, hawks and buzzards mainly watch for their prey from a high perch, using their incredibly keen sight. Flying towards their quarry they swoop on it with an accelerating, slanting stoop. Some species hunt by gliding and soaring over the ground and then swooping down in similar fashion. In the final descent

The typical shrikes have a habit of impaling some of the prey they catch, from insects to small mice or fledgling birds, on thorns or spikes in their territories. Exactly how they use these "larders" is not clear. Here a Loggerhead Shrike (Lanius ludovicianus) has impaled a beetle grub on barbed wire.

they rely on speed rather than surprise and this also provides a greater impact when their clawed feet strike the prey. The smaller sparrowhawks that hunt in this way tend to rely on surprising the birds they feed on, catching them with a final agile dash, their long-toed feet grasping them in midair.

The long-winged harriers glide low over the ground in hunting, to surprise and drop onto smaller and weaker prey. Kites and buzzards may spend long periods soaring and searching the ground below, but these rely partly on carrion food.

Food may be eaten on the spot or carried to a perch or ledge where they hold it firmly to tear it apart. Large prey may be only partly eaten and, if scavengers have not got there first, the raptor may return for further meals. Such birds eat fast and food is accumulated in the crop for later digestion.

Falcons have a more compact build with tapering wings. They rely on speed in hunting. They are bird-eaters, pursuing their prey in the air by flying above it and then rapidly down onto it, often closing the wings and rocketing down at speed. It is claimed that Peregrine Falcons reach 188 mph (300 kph) during such a swoop, although 80 mph (130 kph) is about the fastest measured speed. The falcon strikes with the feet and the impact, and in particular the penetration or tearing with the large claw of the hind toe, is usually fatal. The prey may fall and is caught or followed to the ground. This type of high-speed killing is effective in the air but could be risky for the falcon near ground level — ground impact at that speed would cause serious injury. For this reason prey that refuses to fly is usually ignored.

Eagles and hawks may kill large prey, although they prefer those about half their own weight and size, which they can carry away. Falcons tend to have a narrow prey-size preference. The large Gyrfalcon takes duck and ptarmigan, the Peregrine is best adapted for Rock Doves (or domestic pigeons), the small agile Hobby can catch swallows in flight (but will also use its expertise on dragonflies), and the Bat Hawk takes bats emerging at evening from their roost. The large Brown Falcon of Australasia is a sluggish hunter of small prey, and kestrels hover and slowly descend to drop on mice and voles, with an occasional sparrow or even a grasshopper.

Most of these birds of prey are solitary hunters, but pairs sometimes hunt together and, intentionally or accidentally, may help each other. Harris's Hawk, a buzzard-like hawk of Central America, lives in social family groups and these deliberately cooperate in hunting, to the mutual benefit of the group. Their hunting methods appear to include both synchronized raiding from all directions and using one bird to flush out prey for the others to attack. These birds are popular with falconers because they are more cooperative in falconry. Raptors have less need than most birds to use other species to aid their hunting, but the all-white phase of the Australian Gray (or White) Goshawk appears to move around with flocks of white cockatoos in order to surprise its prey.

Most owls, whether day or night hunters, usually watch and wait from a perch, or a series of perches as the bird moves through its territory. The exceptions are the aerial hunters of more open country such as the Short-eared Owl, Snowy Owl and sometimes the Barn Owl. Owls have very keen vision. As well as hunting mainly by night they may be active in the half-light of dusk and dawn; their large eyes can be effective even in poor light.

The owls have a special advantage in that they hunt in silence. Their feathers have fine downy fringes and the feather surface has a very fine raised downy structure; these deaden any sound of flight. As far as prey is concerned, the owl appears and strikes in silence. It is significant that this adaptation is absent in owls that catch fish.

For hunting in the dark, owls make considerable use of hearing. A woodland owl such as the Tawny Owl will listen from its perch for the rustling made by small animals on the ground.

Rain can be a serious handicap in such circumstances, for the widespread sounds of its falling make it difficult to distinguish the sounds of prey.

An owl can hunt by sound in total darkness. Using its ears to locate the sound, the bird flies with its head low and its legs and feet swinging backwards and forwards in readiness to grasp its quarry. When it is very close and its ears have given a positive fix, it brings its feet forward to replace the head position and close down on the prey. With hunting methods such as these, owls are generally uncritical feeders on whatever happens to be moving at the time, from birds and mammals to earthworms.

Other nocturnal hunters are the nightjar's relatives, the frogmouths, owlet-nightjars and potoos. These have small feet, camouflaged plumage and large eyes that are shut by day when they pretend to be dead branches in trees. At night they are alert. Their bills seem relatively small but, like the nightjar's, their great gape seems to split the head open. They watch from a perch, then swoop down to seize and engulf moving prey on the ground, whether mouse, reptile, amphibian or large insect.

The larger long-legged birds are also casual predators of vertebrates. Herons, storks, cranes and bustards will snap up mice, small birds, lizards and amphibians. The Marabou Stork, although often a scavenger, will snatch up any small animals in its heavy bill and has been seen to kill and eat adult flamingos. The Secretary-bird, although a bird of prey, comes into this long-legged walking and random-hunting category. In addition it is an expert snake killer, although rodents are its main prey. It strikes and stamps with its long slender legs, helped by the open wings that also distract and mislead the snake, then finally kills it by biting behind the head. If snakes prove difficult it will fly up with them and drop them from a height.

Birds provide opportunity for another kind of predation. Seabirds, and most waterbirds, breed in large open colonies and, if parents cease vigilance for even a short period, they may lose eggs or young to other predatory birds. Night Herons will raid the nests of other species in the heronry. The big skuas of the Antarctic rely on breeding colonies of penguins, albatrosses, other seabirds and seals for their food when nesting. Gulls of various species are the main exploiters. On lakes, marshes and coasts, wherever birds breed colonially, they are likely to be on watch to snatch a meal. They may also breed in such colonies and even rob each other. Attack from predators appears to be the reason why the smaller petrels and shearwaters wait until nightfall to come to their nest burrows, because being relatively helpless on land, by day they run much greater risk of being killed.

Fish hunters

Except for specifically studied diets it is almost impossible to separate fish-eating from taking occasional crustaceans such as shrimps, whereas polar birds may feed largely on shrimp-like krill and many seabirds also rely extensively on the abundance of squid. What unites the birds considered here is the need to take their prey from water, whether it be fish, crustaceans or cephalopods.

Although they are seabirds, Frigatebirds try to avoid getting their plumage wet. They fly back to land to roost. They ride the air currents and are experts at skimming along the water at speed, their long necks and heads bent down so that the sharply hooked bill can snatch fish or squid just below the surface, or catch flying fish when these break surface and fly over the waves.

The fish-eagles, sea-eagles and Brahminy Kite are aerial fishers that usually watch from a perch, though sometimes soaring, and swoop down to fly near the water and snatch a fish at the surface with a rapid downward and backward grab of their clawed feet. The Osprey uses a similar technique, but not infrequently has to become a plunge diver. It is equipped with bare legs, large feet with long thin curved claws and a spiky-surfaced sole to the foot for extra grip. It soars over the water watching for a fish at or near the surface, plunging down to get it and often hitting the water with a great splash and being temporarily submerged before coming up with its prey. While flying with its catch to a perch it will shake off water like a dog. Large fish may be carried head foremost in both feet.

Other birds cautious of water are those that merely wade in shallows. Ibises and woodstorks hunt in muddy water and appear to find fish as much by touch as by sight, wading slowly and deliberately up to belly-deep in water. There is a trigger-like kink in the neck vertebrae of the heron and from its Z-shaped stalking posture it can be suddenly flipped straight, the head darting forwards to seize the fish.

Some small egrets fish by running into the water, disturbing and snapping up small fish, but the most striking technique is that of the Black Heron, which spreads its wings around in front of it with ends touching and the lower edge at the water's surface. This tent of shadow attracts fish looking for shelter and makes it easier for the bird to see into the water when it puts its own head below its wings. The Green-backed Heron floats a feather or small object on the water and snaps up the little fish that stop to investigate it.

A number of birds fish from the water's surface. Most pelicans swim along and then suddenly duck and reach down with neck and bill, filling the inflated pouch with fish and water and raising it. The pouch contracts and the water is squeezed out, leaving the fish to be swallowed with the typical upward tilt of the head that allows gravity to lend a hand.

There are surface feeders among the tube-nosed seabirds. The small storm-petrels (named after St. Peter for their apparent attempt to walk on the water) flutter over the surface, sometimes with legs dangling and feet pattering over the water, snatching small prey and plankton. This snatching at the surface while on the wing is a typical feeding method for many larger petrels and for many terns, gulls and the smaller skuas. Large species, such as albatrosses, take food on or just below the surface while paddling on the sea, and many also make shallow dives. They may feed at night on squid near the surface, made visible by their phosphorescence. Large shearwaters and petrels also feed in this way, often making shallow dives with half-opened wings.

Many birds will swim under water to fish. Some start from the water's surface; they usually look for prey by dipping the bill and eyes below the surface, diving and pursuing anything they sight. Divers (loons), grebes and the fish-eating sawbill ducks, such as Goosander and Mergansers, may swallow small prey under water, but bring larger ones to the surface to eat. Each species tends to have a preferred size of prey, usually the largest that they can swallow without difficulty.

When swimming under water, such species have to overcome the buoyancy given by air trapped in the plumage, which can be seen as a silvery sheen beneath the surface. They can overcome this to some extent by sleeking down

Right Wilson's Storm-Petrels (Oceanites oceanicus) "walking on water" as they feed in the Antarctic.

Far right A Black Skimmer (Rynchops niger) in action, the longer lower mandible cutting the water and the bill closing if anything is touched.

An Osprey (Pandion haliaetus) returns to its nesting mate carrying a large fish in both feet. The rough surface of the foot helps its grip.

Right A Black Heron (Egretta ardesiaca) and a Gray Heron (Ardea cinerea) feeding in shallows. The Black Heron has spread its wings into a tent to make it easier to see into the water and to attract fish into the shadow.

Below right A Pied Cormorant (Phalacrocorax varius) swimming with the body partly submerged — they are quite capable of traveling with just their necks above the water — has caught an eel which it will swallow whole, headfirst.

Left *A Little Pied Cormorant (*Phalacrocorax melanoleucos*) dries its feathers in the sun after fishing. Opening up the feathers to enable them to become waterlogged helps shags, cormorants and anhingas to swim under water but necessitates careful drying and preening after feeding.*

Right *A Gannet (*Morus bassanus*) plummets down from a considerable height targeted on a fish below and easing its wings back as it nears the water.*

Below far left *A Sacred Kingfisher (*Todirhamphus sanctus*) dives for a fish, folding back its wings as it enters the water.*

Below left *A Common Kingfisher (*Alcedo atthis*) seizes a fish at the end of its dive, the wings ready for use in swimming back to the surface.*

the plumage to force out surplus air. Cormorants and anhingas (or darters) have feathers with a greater gap between the barbs than in most species and, by raising their feathers, they can allow water to seep between them and displace the air. This enables them to submerge more easily, and to swim with only head and neck above the surface. The disadvantages are loss of warmth when the insulating air is lacking, and the need to dry out the wet plumage afterwards.

Cormorants have a hooked bill tip and often seize large fish that are difficult to handle. They are brought to the surface, juggled until they are headfirst down the throat and then swallowed in the expandable gullet.

Anhingas prefer fresh water. They are cormorant-like, but with slender neck and head more like a heron, and with a similar neck kink. They literally stab a fish in the water, transfixing it in the side with partly opened dagger bill. They must then come to the surface to remove the bill and manipulate the fish into the right position for headfirst swallowing, often using a quick upward flip and catch. Headfirst swallowing, common to all fish hunters, ensures that projecting spines or fins do not hinder the fish's passage towards the stomach.

The wing-propelled auks and penguins are most efficient underwater fish chasers. Both can move fast under water and travel extensively and deeply. Since many of the penguins are krill eaters, their abilities may be more closely linked with travel (since they cannot fly) and with predator evasion than with hunting. Survival, however, makes some demands on them and Antarctic-wintering Emperor Penguins must be able at times to hunt in darkness under the ice. Penguins spend most of their lives in water, their dense short fur-like feathering and a thick layer of fat helping to keep them warm. They breed and molt on land but appear not to know how to feed out of the water. Captive birds have to be force-fed for several weeks before they learn to pick up fish thrown to them.

Some of the best-known fish-hunting birds are the plunge divers. These birds focus on their prey while in the air and then plummet down headfirst. As they reach the water the feet point backwards and the wings are extended back so that the bird hits and enters the water like a great arrowhead. The prey is usually at no great depth and the bird must level out quickly, relying on buoyancy to help it to the surface. The birds that practice this kind of fishing range from the 4-inch (10-cm) kingfisher to the 5-foot (150-cm) pelican.

Only the alcedinid and cerylid kingfishers are divers, the others feed on land on insects and larger creatures. Kingfishers watch from perches, or fly and hover before plunging. They carry fish back to a perch, against which they often hammer it to stun it before swallowing it headfirst. A kingfisher seen with a tailfirst fish held in its bill is about to feed a mate or young.

Terns and tropicbirds fly into the wind and hover before plunging, often raising small plumes of spray. The Brown Pelican and its Chilean counterpart, of coastal waters, make spectacular plunge dives with wings held in a W and head drawn back, extending the neck forwards and wings backwards as they hit the water.

Gannets and boobies are expert plunge divers. The Northern Gannet, streamlined and with a layer of air sacs in the skin to cushion the impact with the water, may hurtle down from up to 100 feet (30 m) aiming at a fish or a small shoal only a few meters below the surface: herring and mackerel are its typical food. The heaviest of the boobies, the Masked Booby, which is of similar size, has been recorded plunging from 330 feet (100 m) up!

Most of the fish-eating birds are seabirds. The seas are not uniformly rich in food and, as on land, there are zones and areas of greater productivity. In the oceans, the lines where the major currents converge produce upswellings, sinkings and mixing of waters and in these places food is far more abundant. Such zones are also affected, and sometimes enhanced, by the presence of sandbanks and islands, whereas the main coastlines themselves, where sea and land interact, may be richer than the adjoining seas. Birds tend to concentrate in these areas and the distribution of birds at sea is very uneven, depending on richer feeding grounds or zones that may be very narrow, and on migration routes.

Where food is present, a variety of species will be attracted and sometimes interact. Most seabirds have plumage that is white on the underside and this has been shown to make them less visible to fish. However, the conspicuous white or pied plumages of gulls, terns, boobies, tropicbirds and some other species may function as signals so that a feeding bird can quickly be seen as an indicator of the possible temporary presence of rich feeding, both for its conspecifics and for other birds.

There is some cooperation in feeding on water. Swimming pelicans frequently move abreast in a line or arc driving fish into shallow water and then ducking their heads almost simultaneously to feed. Flocks of some cormorants follow similar maneuvers, concentrating fish together before feeding on them. It is possible that a rain of plummeting gannets hurtling into a shoal of fish may result in a better catch. The small Blue-footed Boobies also fish in parties, a group plunge diving simultaneously in response to a whistled signal.

Birds can also profit from the activities of other animals. Large shoals of predatory fish, such as tuna, may force numbers of the small fish on which they feed up to the surface where they even leap out of the water in an attempt to avoid being caught; then hunting seabirds quickly move in to help themselves. Fish-eating whales also scare large numbers of small fish to the surface, and fishermen have long watched for feeding seabirds to indicate good fishing grounds.

The unwanted fish and fish-gutting waste from fishing boats provides another source of food. Many birds, including gulls, shearwaters and gannets, learned to associate such boats with food and sometimes followed them. It has been suggested that the spread of the Northern Fulmar in the past few centuries was linked with human fishing activities.

Scavengers

Creatures that die in places out of reach of terrestrial predators, and the remains of carcasses left by people and animals, could be a source of pollution and disease if left to decay. Scavengers that take them as food are valuable in disposing of such material.

A number of bird species are partial scavengers. Crows and magpies will clean up small carcasses and take what they can from larger ones. Human garbage dumps attract crows, gulls in abundance, kites and, in places, other species. Unlikely additions may include Hoopoes, after rubbish-eating crickets, and nightjars after nocturnal insects. Carcasses of sheep or deer outside vultures' ranges may attract ravens, crows, magpies, kites, the larger gulls and such unexpected species as Golden Eagles. In the Arctic most seabirds go south to unfrozen waters but Ivory Gulls remain, surviving by scavenging on the seal kills of polar bears. In Australia, which lacks vultures, the Wedge-tailed Eagle is an efficient hunter that also takes advantage of carcasses of kangaroos, sheep and rabbits.

Fish-eagles and sea-eagles, including the American Bald Eagle and the Brahminy Kite, are habitual scavengers of dead fish, bodies along the shoreline and the holocaust of dead salmon after spawning; usually with gulls in

Below right
Herring Gulls (Larus argentatus) and Lesser Black-backed Gulls (Larus fuscus) scavenging offal at sea.

Bottom *A line of Australian Pelicans (Pelecanus conspicillatus) joined by a Little Black Cormorant (Phalacrocorax sulcirostris) swim in line abreast, driving fish into shallow water where they can catch them.*

Like all frigatebirds, unwilling to enter water, Lesser Frigatebirds (Fregata ariel) snatch up fish frightened to the surface by dolphins in the Sunda Straits.

attendance. They will also snatch floating debris. The real sea-eagles and ravens that the sagas describe attending the battles of the Norsemen were more interested in the carrion than cheering on the warriors.

Buzzards and kites that systematically quarter the land below them are as keen to discover carrion as to hunt live prey. Kites were always recognized as skillful scavengers that would take food from your hands or the plate in front of you: army recruits posted to the Middle and Far East were warned to keep plates covered when they emerged from the cookhouse. The Red Kites that received official protection in sixteenth-century London for clearing up decaying rubbish were also notorious for snatching the food from children's hands and for stealing clothes from washing lines as nest material.

Marabou Storks are frequently scavengers around lakes and villages. They have moved to garbage dumps where they compete with vultures and other species such as Tawny Eagles. They also eat garbage dump rats. With assured food sources they have greatly increased in some places and, like gulls, have become a nuisance.

In Central and South America the falcons produced the caracaras, weaker-footed and longer-legged running birds that are generalized scavengers. In the south they attend the

breeding colonies of seabirds and seals for what they can find. In such colonies the larger skuas are also partial scavengers and carrion-eaters. The colonies of the Antarctic have a pair of scavenger species derived from shorebirds: the sheathbills. The more highly-evolved scavengers have bare heads to avoid the problem of fouled feathers. The sheathbills show an early stage. Looking like heavily-built pigeons, they have a short, stout bill with a heavy sheath at the base. They feed on carcasses, offal, feces and afterbirth at penguin and seal colonies.

A Pied Crow (Corvus albus) *feeding on a dead sandgrouse chick. Crows are both scavengers and predators of sick or helpless small animals.*

Hood Island Mockingbirds (Nesomimus trifasciatus) *on the Galapagos Islands must exploit any possible food source. If the eggs of Waved Albatrosses* (Diomedea irrorata) *are broken, or if they can break them, the contents are a useful source of food.*

White-backed Vultures (Gyps africanus) and a few larger Rueppell's Griffon Vultures (G. rueppellii) squabble at a carcass in Swaziland.

Gulls are opportunist feeders and these Common Gulls (Larus canus) have discovered that a plowing tractor uncovers worms and insects as it turns the soil. They probably have a breeding colony nearby.

The principal scavengers are the New World and Old World vultures. American vultures have weaker bills than those of the Old World and meat must be partly rotted before they can tear it. They can often be seen patrolling highways of the southern states of the United States on the lookout for animals that have been run over.

The seven species of New World vultures have bare heads, varying in color and ornamented with wattles in the King Vulture. The smaller Black and Turkey Vultures are common where rubbish is found. The King Vulture is a forest species, not very numerous. The mountain ranges of the Andes and Rockies produce the great soaring condors. These once ranged far over mountain areas in search of carcasses, although the California Condor now nears extinction. If food is found a vulture must take its fill while it can, and Andean Condors used to be caught after eating because it was known that they would fill the crop so full that they would have difficulty in taking off until they had disgorged some food.

The Old World vultures are also bare-headed or downy. They often share ranges. They wait until the day has warmed and they can conserve energy by using rising thermals, and then soar slowly, watching the ground and each other. If a carcass is sighted there is a rush of birds to the place. Some kind of hierarchy occurs, depending on the species present. The larger, heavy-billed Lappet-faced or Cinerous Vulture may be needed to tear open a tough carcass. In the scrum that follows, the Griffon Vultures and White-headed Vulture (which alone among the vultures will occasionally kill other birds or small antelope itself) get the main feast, with smaller species such as the White-backed, Egyptian or Hooded Vultures coming last. The Lammergeier or Bearded Vulture is the final visitor, breaking the bones and using its scoop-shaped tongue to extract the marrow but also swallowing and digesting pieces of bone. To break large bones it will fly high and drop them on rocks to smash them; it will do the same to break a tortoise or turtle shell. The advantages of such eating strategies may seem questionable but meat eaters can assimilate up to 90 percent of what they ingest and decaying carrion can be digested more rapidly than fresh meat.

Thieves and pirates

Finding food is hard work. If a nearby bird has found some already it is easier to snatch that than to look for one's own, provided that the other bird is not bigger than you are. Such behavior has been dignified by the name of

kleptoparasitism. At its simplest level it is just bullying by individuals, not always successfully. If hierarchies exist in a species, as in the social grouping of Junglefowl or domestic hens, an individual lower down the line may lose an item to a higher-ranking individual if it does not swallow fast enough. In gull and tern colonies, food may be taken from adults and young of other pairs.

Outside such colonies theft is between species. In a London suburban garden, for instance, a Eurasian Blackbird snatches a worm from under the bill of a slightly smaller and weaker Song Thrush; a House Sparrow tries to carry off a piece of bread too big to eat at once, and loses it to a Starling, which in turn is robbed of it by either a Carrion Crow or Black-headed Gull, both waiting on the rooftops rather than venturing into the more enclosed area of the garden. In the meadows, wintering Black-headed Gulls rob Lapwings as the latter dig up earthworms, but may lose their prize to a slightly larger Common Gull. At a garbage dump a Carrion Crow loses food to a Red Kite. Larger raptors of various species snatch prey from other birds of prey of smaller and weaker species. As an overloaded pelican empties some of the water from its bill, gulls swoop to snatch at fish that are exposed. A Bald Eagle may rob an Osprey of its fish.

It is difficult to draw a clear line between systematic piracy and the more casual occurrences of this kind. Most of the more highly evolved examples appear to involve coastal and nesting seabirds. Arctic Skuas habitually parasitize other seabirds, forcing them to disgorge their collected food. In one study some were found to gain 90 percent of their food in this way when breeding. The skuas are active and agile and can outfly species such as terns that are their main victims. Harried Puffins in some colonies appear to have learned that, when returning to the nest fish-laden, flying among nonbreeding birds gives them cover. Puffins are also robbed when they reach the nest burrow by gulls or even Jackdaws.

Great Skuas harry Gannets, not chasing but surprising them by swooping down, often seizing them in midair by wings or tail to try to force them to disgorge or crash land. Frigatebirds may harry almost any birds but behave towards boobies as do the Great Skuas towards Gannets. The attacks may be more violent since the frigatebird would prefer to be able to catch the disgorged food before it hits the water. Although such actions often appear highly successful, statistically in 12 to 66 percent of incidents, it can only benefit a small proportion of individuals in the population of predatory species present.

Eating plants

Plant eaters have some advantages over those that eat animals. Their food source does not move and it may be deliberately designed and colored to attract birds and be eaten by them, and it is often a plentiful resource. Most plant food has the disadvantage of being bulky, digested more slowly and requiring the use of crop and gizzard. This makes it less suitable for nestlings and young birds who need high-protein food that can be assimilated rapidly. Most birds that rely on vegetable food when adult, turn to some animal source when feeding their young.

In addition to strict plant eaters, there are omnivorous species that take plant or animal food as the opportunity arises. Large birds, such as ratites, cranes and bustards, tend to be of this type, as are some of the crow group. A surprisingly large number of insect eaters will take berries at times and many birds that are mainly fruit eaters will take occasional insects. Among vegetarian feeders, the diet may be mainly of one type but it is likely to include small but significant amounts of other types of food. As with animal-eating birds there is a tendency to label birds according to the principal component of a diet, which, if studied in detail, shows a broad spectrum with very few species wholly specialized for food of one type.

Seed eaters

Seeds are the part of a plant a bird is most likely to eat because they are a stored food source and provide the greatest nourishment for the smallest bulk. There may be competition for temporary resources and a few birds have special strategies for obtaining them. The small finches, such as Redpolls and Siskins, and the tits have short strong legs and sharp bills and can hang acrobatically on small twigs to extract the seeds from catkins and cones of trees. Goldfinches have a clinging ability and bill design to remove seeds from the drying heads of thistles

Acorn Woodpeckers (Melanerpes formicivorus), *often working in social groups, drill rows of holes in tree bark, storing an acorn in each as their winter food supply.*

and teazle. Weavers and grassfinches can cling to vertical stems of grasses and similar plants to strip the seedheads. Jays and wood pigeons take acorns from the twigs; crows and rooks remove ripening walnuts. Most birds, however, seem content to pick up seeds that have ripened and fallen to the ground.

Typical pickers-up of seeds are the gamebirds, buttonquails, pigeons and sandgrouse. These birds swallow seeds whole, relying on digestion to do the rest. However, seeds tend to have a hard outer husk that is not a necessary part of the bird's diet. Small birds such as finches, buntings, grassfinches and weavers have a specially adapted bill to deal with this. Parrots have a similar ability: in their case the seed is held at the tip of the bill, the lower jaw providing pressure, the sharp tip of the upper bill cutting the husk and the tongue helping to hold and to revolve the seed. In all these birds the whole process is remarkably rapid.

Seeds are an important food in colder regions with short winter days. A crop full of seeds can help ensure the survival of a bird at roost. On the arid cold uplands of South America the shorebirds have evolved the four species of seedsnipe. These birds have come to resemble partridges or sandgrouse in build and have short stubby bills. They live on seeds and the leaves of plants. Larks are another group of birds that mix a seed diet with other parts of plants.

Seeds form some part of the diet in a wide range of birds from ratites, ducks and jacanas to woodpeckers, babblers and dunnocks. In the ducks the dabbling and diving ducks eat seeds of marsh and water plants; the Mandarin feeds mainly on acorns in autumn, together with chestnuts and beechnuts, and the little pygmy geese of the marshes and lagoons of Africa, the Oriental region and Australia are to some extent feeders on water lily seeds.

Most seeds are only available for a season. Birds must switch from one source to another or turn to some other food. If seeds can be stored this will enable birds to continue to exploit the same source for longer, and seed stored in autumn that will keep through the winter can enable a bird to survive without having to migrate. This usually involves the larger seeds and nuts and the birds that have the skill or strength to split them or hammer them open.

Tits and nuthatches will cache or store food. Tits can cope with surprisingly large items: Willow Tits have been seen to split small stones of wild cherry and remove the kernel for concealing; Coal Tits will hide beechnuts that look far too big for them to feed on. Nuthatches take seeds and nuts up to the size of hazelnuts. They will wedge them into a crevice in the bark and then, by swinging the body and head like a pickax pivoted at the legs, they will hammer away until they crack them. These birds use dispersed storage or "scatter hoarding." Objects appear to be hidden at random, among foliage or in crevices or holes, and the hidden item may be there for only a short period. In fact, each bird has a series of hiding places. They

know where they have hidden the food and it is the sites, rather than the individual items, to which they return and which they may reuse. Although some hiding may be short term, this behavior is used more systematically in autumn in colder regions.

Birds of the crow family will also show scatter hoarding and it is highly developed in the Siberian and Gray Jays of the northern conifer forests. These birds hide a much wider variety of food objects that they coat with saliva and hide among conifer foliage and twigs. These tend to stick to the twigs and will be available even in conditions of deep snow.

Some other corvids show more systematic storage or "larder hoarding." The Eurasian Jay is closely linked for much of its distribution with oak trees. It will hide food objects after the fashion of Siberian Jays, but when acorns ripen it spends most of its time filling throat and bill with ripe acorns from the twigs and carrying them for a distance, usually to an open grassy

A Crimson Rosella (Platycercus elegans) *presses a nut fragment against the hard inner plate of the upper jaw with the blunter edge of the lower jaw.*

The Eurasian Spotted Nutcracker (Nucifraga caryocatactes), which buries enough hazelnuts to feed it through the winter, can remember where it did so and then retrieve them, even if covered by a layer of snow.

Top *A Steller's Jay (Cyanocitta stelleri) at a bird table fills its throat pouch and bill with food before carrying it away to cache it.*

conifer seeds and it has been observed that they only retrieve those they bury themselves. Between them these birds must play a significant part in maintaining the continued existence of forest.

It is not only the birds that "plant" stores of seeds that help to spread them around. Fruit pips and stones swallowed with their fruit and other undigested seeds are deposited with droppings and seeds are carried in mud stuck to birds' feet or lodged in their feathers. The fruit pigeon of New Zealand was probably responsible for introducing the variety of fuchsia whose fruit forms its specialized diet, early arrivals bringing the plants on which later arrivals were able to live.

Fruit eaters

Fleshy fruits are an important food, used to some extent by a high proportion of landbirds. As an habitual diet, fruit is often less nutritious for its bulk than animal food or seed, so usually a greater quantity has to be eaten. It is rich in sugars and may be used by migrants preparing for long flights and by birds fattening against a coming winter. It tends to be less rich in protein and if it is used to feed young birds these generally show a longer and slower period of growth before maturity.

In tropical regions there is often an abundance of fruits and they may be available for most of the year. Fruit is often not as brightly colored as in those regions where fruit is seasonal, may be more nutritious and is utilized on a long-term basis by birds more closely associated with the trees and shrubs that produce it. Because less time and energy are used in obtaining food, birds may have more time for other activities. Within these regions are groups of birds that have evolved elaborate display rituals and often elaborate plumages, which may be linked to their mainly fruit diet.

In other regions, where fruit crops tend to be seasonal, fruit is often brightly colored and appears designed to attract the attention of passing birds who may be wandering in search of food. When the berry crop that determines the movement of waxwings is insufficient for their needs the birds will irrupt well beyond their normal range in search of winter supplies.

Color both attracts attention and indicates when fruit is ripe, and the ability of birds, monkeys and humans to discriminate color may be related to the need to recognize this food and its condition.

Birds may be forced to share any temporary abundance of fruit, but, in the late fall, the Mistle Thrush will look for trees with a good crop of mistletoe, or a holly heavy with berries. It will defend this against all comers in an attempt to ensure a winter supply. In severe winter conditions the normally more sociable Fieldfare will behave in a similar way with

area. Here they are usually buried in the turf, one at a time, the hole carefully covered. Enormous numbers must be buried; they represent a winter's supply. The bird does not need visual clues but can find them readily months later and even under a cover of snow. It will probably not retrieve all and some will be left to grow into seedlings, since burying keeps them moist: when a bird dies it leaves as a memorial a potential small plantation.

Similar behavior is shown by the American Blue Jay, which hides nuts in the same manner, allegedly shaking them to ensure that they are ripe and sound. The Spotted Eurasian Nutcracker behaves similarly. The thick-billed northern race buries hazelnuts; the slender-billed race of southern European mountains buries the seeds of the Arolla Pine. The latter have been estimated to bury 32,000 seeds each, thought to be about three times what they need to ensure survival. Clark's Nutcracker of the Rocky Mountains does the same with

a food supply such as windfall apples in a neglected garden.

Birds take fruit in a variety of ways. It may be snatched while swooping or hovering on the wing by trogons, some of the cotingas from Calfbirds to Swallow-tailed Cotinga, and some of the little New Guinea berrypeckers. The nocturnal Oilbird of South America, inhabiting dark caves by day, flies out at night to snatch oil-rich fruits while on the wing and it is suggested it may use its sense of smell to locate food in the dark. Although it may help seed dispersal, most of the large seeds it swallows are regurgitated in the caves, covering the floor.

Most species pluck fruit directly from trees or shrubs. Typical fruit eaters include turacos, parrots (especially lories and lorikeets), orioles, bulbuls, leafbirds and starlings. The mousebirds differ in hanging onto fruit, digging into it and hollowing it. Other groups feed at ground level, often on ripe fallen fruit, and these include some of the big ratites, curassows and some other forest gamebirds and pigeons. The pigeons are a family that has produced a number of arboreal fruit-eating birds, some as brightly colored as the fruit they seek. They tend to be more squat and short-legged and adapted for climbing on twigs to reach fruit.

Bill size, or perhaps throat size, will determine the upper limit of fruit that can be eaten. In fruit-rich areas it can create a range of feeding niches within the same area. The Pied Imperial Pigeon is exceptional in that it can eat

nutmeg fruits bigger than its own head by stretching the elastic articulations of its jaws wide enough to ingest items up to 2 inches (5 cm) across.

It has been suggested that among the birds with oversized bills the long swollen bills of toucans and the long bills and bony casques of some hornbills have evolved partly from a need to force the bill through a barrier of twigs and foliage to withdraw a fruit. The fruit eaters are not readily identified by their appearance: the slender curved bills of the Madagascan False Sunbirds look as though designed for nectar-feeding, those of the broadbills for insect snatching and the tiny pointed white-eye bill is another insect catching structure, although very efficient at puncturing small soft fruits and sucking the juices, whereas the tanagers look like seed eaters with mainly short stout bills. Perhaps most unexpected is the Palmnut Vulture. This large semi-scavenger type of raptor can vary its diet but prefers to live mainly on oily palmnuts, which limits its distribution.

The flowerpeckers are small birds with short sharp bills. Some live mainly on berries, especially the tropical mistletoes. Both they and the Euphonia Tanagers have evolved special short guts and rapid digestion to expedite the processing of berries with a low food content. The excreted seeds stick to the bird's perch, where they germinate. Some cotingas also eat mistletoe berries and the small White-cheeked Cotinga appears to wholly rely upon them. Its feeding behavior differs in that, after five to ten minutes, it regurgitates the seeds of the berries, wiping them off its bill against twigs, where they stick.

Nectar feeders

Nectar, like fruit, is a food high in sugar for energy but low in protein for growth or tissue replacement. Most nectar-feeding birds overcome this by also feeding on insects, and some take fruit as well. In the parrot family the nectar-feeding lories have broad tongues with an irregular surface. They take nectar from blossoming trees, such as eucalypts, in which the flowers occur in unspecialized massed heads. Their tongues appear to be used for gathering pollen as well as nectar and, since pollen is protein rich, this might help to balance their diet.

Abundant nectar can be sipped from open flowers but most nectar feeders probe deeply into flowers that are often long and tubular with nectar not readily available. To do this the tongue must be modified so that the nectar can be drawn out. It is often long and extensible, folded around at the edges and in its most highly developed form becomes a long double tube up which nectar can be drawn by capillary action. In a simpler form the end of the tongue becomes split into a number of fine divisions to form a brush-like structure that can be used to lap up nectar.

Brush-tipped tongues occur in the Old World honey eaters, leafbirds, lories, lorikeets and white-eyes. The sunbirds, Sugarbird and flowerpeckers have a tubular tongue of which the final third is split, and tubular tongues occur in New World Hawaiian Honeycreepers and honeycreeper tanagers, reaching the highest development in the tiny Hummingbirds.

The amount of nectar available from flowers varies considerably, some flowers producing nectar for a relatively short flowering period. This may be of limited use for highly adapted feeders wanting a year-round supply, but can be briefly exploited by nonspecialists such as babblers or warblers. Smaller nectar-feeding species tend to cling to stems or flowerheads.

Plants have become adapted to attract nectar-feeding birds in order to ensure pollination. Some have inflorescences with perching places apparently evolved to ensure the bird is in the right position to carry pollen or pollinate the flowers. Hummingbirds do not use these, but hover while feeding. Flowers that provide nectar and need to attract birds for pollination are usually tubular in structure and advertise themselves by red or orange color.

The nectar feeders tend to be aggressive and to defend feeding territories around flowers or flowering shrubs and trees. Hummingbirds may have territories containing a number of nectar sources, some of which they may share with different species. Some flowers, such as bromeliads, that depend on hummingbirds for pollination have inflorescences that produce one or two nectar-rich flowers at a time over a long period. The birds can exist by regularly visiting

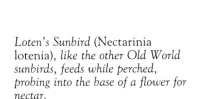

Opposite above A Waxwing (Bombycilla garrulus), *part of a flock irrupting from the northern conifer forests in search of berries in fall and winter, feeds on rosehips in a garden.*

Opposite below Small birds like this Silver-eye (Zosterops lateralis) and the African Mousebirds (Colius species) will burrow into large juicy fruits as they eat them.

A Tui (Prosthemadera novaeseelandiae) *drinking from a leaf with the brush-tipped tongue with which it also laps up nectar.*

Loten's Sunbird (Nectarinia lotenia), *like the other Old World sunbirds, feeds while perched, probing into the base of a flower for nectar.*

a series of them. It has been found that the nectar-feeding Hawaiian Honeycreeper can remember which flowers it has visited.

There has been some coevolution of birds and flowers. Hummingbirds have varied bill shapes and some are closely adapted for feeding on flowers of particular form. The hummingbird hovers with the humming figure-of-eight wingbeat that enables it to hang in the air, advancing and retreating as it probes the flower. The very long straight bill of the Sword-billed Hummingbird may be the only one that can reach into the hanging trumpets of *Datura* shrubs and the curved bills of the sicklebills fit into flowers with an outward-curving corolla tube.

The mountain Buff-tailed Sicklebird does not always hover and has been seen scrambling over inflorescences to probe the flowers. Hummingbirds cheat in other ways. Some have very short sharp bills with which they pierce the base of a flower and reach the nectar by a short cut. A flower may then be visited by other species that take advantage of the piercing. Among the honeycreeper tanagers there is a small genus of flowerpiercers, small birds whose bills are uptilted with a sharp projecting tip to pierce the base of flowers for nectar.

Although they must rely on flowers for nectar, birds use another source of liquid sugar. This is found in the sap of some trees, particularly in the rising spring sap carrying food to growing stems. Such sweet sap is best known to most people as maple syrup. Some woodpeckers have the habit of drilling a row of holes in the bark of a tree and returning later to drink the oozing sap. The American woodpeckers known as sapsuckers use this extensively as a part of their diet. Various small birds, including hummingbirds, may also visit these holes to drink.

Eating leaves and flowers

Other parts of plants are a useful source of food as well as seeds, fruit and nectar, though their nutritional value is generally low relative to their bulk. Buds carry the embryonic structure of flowers and growing shoots and are a potential food source. Some birds are addicted to eating buds. They tend to have stout seed-eating bills but these are usually very short, deep and rounded at the tip. Buds form an important part of the diet of bullfinches. Presumably because of the small amount of food in each, they eat many and the Common Bullfinch is notorious for stripping fruit trees and bushes of flowerbuds in late winter and early spring. The House Sparrow is well known for ripping apart and eating various parts of spring flowers, including petals, and will also eat fruit-tree buds.

Buds and leaves of herbaceous plants are important as primary foods or supplements in the diet of arid country and desert birds. Sandgrouse, larks and seedsnipe eat them. Larger birds can cope more easily with a leaf diet and

they form part of the food of ratites, trumpeters, curassows, guans, chachalacas and screamers. Wood pigeons are notorious for eating green plants in gardens and fields; birds shot when flying to roost in winter may have crops packed with the green leaves of clover or similar plants. The softer, sappier aquatic plants are eaten by diving ducks and coots that seize them under water.

For most of these birds the food value is limited to the juices and soft material that can be extracted directly from the plants, with fiber and cellulose being excreted. An aberrant cuckoo, the Hoatzin of South American waterways, feeds on the leaves of arums and eats large quantities. These are stored in a very large crop that is muscular and capable of squeezing out the sap and juices from the leaves. It tends to unbalance the bird, which is heavily built and sluggish and has a callus on the breast that it rests on its perch to help take the weight when in repose. The related Anis cuckoos also include leaves in their diet at some seasons of the year.

Birds of the grouse family feed on buds and young shoots, including those of heather and conifers. They have caeca — blind-ended extensions to the gut — in which the plant material can be held while bacteria act upon it, breaking it down to produce nutritious material. Capercaillie feed extensively on conifer shoots and were traditionally regarded as inedible because of the resinous flavor of their flesh. Caeca for bacterial digestion are also present in swans, geese and ducks such as Maned Ducks and Wigeon, which graze on grassy areas, and the Brent Goose, which relies mainly on the *Zostera* grass of marine mudflats.

In some herbaceous plants, such as grasses, food materials may be stored in the fleshy swollen bases of stems. The big flightless swamp-hen, the Takahe of New Zealand, uses its deep stout bill to shear away grass tufts to reach the bases. Arid-country birds also make use of this, possibly for liquid as well as for food. The stout bill of the Trumpeter Finch is used to shred such material and the heavy bills of some desert larks may be adapted for this purpose.

Roots are another part of the plant where food may be stored. In addition to eating grass and green plants, geese and the Magpie Goose make use of their stout, hard-tipped bills to reach and break up stout shallow roots and bulbs for food. Geese will feed in carrot and turnip fields in winter. Ground-frequenting cockatoos, such as the Sulphur-crested Cockatoo and corellas, use their bills to dig grooves and trenches in the soil to find shallow storage roots and rhizomes of plants.

Some birds feed on what might be regarded as marginal plant material. Pygmy Parrots of New Guinea forests feed on tree fungus. The arctic/alpine zone Ptarmigans feed on lichens. Lesser Flamingos strain out blue green algae from saline lakes. Dabbling ducks, rapidly dabbling a thin layer of water through their broad flat bills, may also be extracting microscopic plant material.

Diet supplements

Birds need calcium, and females need extra quantities annually in order to produce eggshells. Raptors may get it in the bones of their prey. If lime-rich stones are used as grit these may gradually contribute some material. In addition, snail shells, old eggshells, small bones and similar sources are used. In some species calcium is stored in the hollow limb bones and can be seen as a distinct layer when bones are broken.

Left *Slender trumpet flowers offer nectar to the Rufous Hummingbird* (Selasphorus rufus) *in return for pollination. Hummingbird bills vary in form to suit the shape of flowers on which they feed and the flower's stamens are placed so that the bird will receive pollen on its forehead as its bill reaches the nectar at the flower's base.*

The Takahe (Porphyrio mantelli) *feeds on the seed heads and tender bases of grasses.*

Following pages *A Blood Pheasant* (Ithaginis cruentus) *scratching in the snow in Nepal. Seed eaters must find grit for the gizzard, which they rely upon to grind up the seeds ready for digestion.*

Small quantities of other minerals are needed by birds and may account for the apparently unusual foods that they eat at times. Birds may take soil and salt licks like mammals, and the macaws of the South American rainforests are known for their habit of visiting exposed soil and rock faces to eat minerals.

Drinking

Birds are very economical in their utilization of water. They do not sweat and little is lost through the skin. Most water is reabsorbed through the gut well before excretion, further reducing loss, which is mainly through breathing. Although they need to replace water, they get most of what they want from their own food if they are eating nectar, insects, fruit, meat or green plants. The one diet certainly deficient in water is seed eating. A bird that depends on a dry seed diet in an arid environment might experience the greatest loss and would need to replace about one tenth of its weight in water each day, or even more under hot conditions.

Birds do not appear very fussy about water, but do show a preference for drinking from a dripping source or running water rather than still water. Fresh water is preferred, and flamingos on saline lakes and shorebirds and gulls on a seashore will visit a place where fresh water runs in if possible. In areas where water is scarce birds may sip up drops of dew or condensation, or eat snow. They are often able to find and remember small water sources and forest birds may use little rain-retaining hollows high in trees.

Most drinking in birds is gravity aided. The bird sips a small amount of water in its lowered bill, then raises the head to allow the water to run down the throat, the tongue helping to aid swallowing. Some birds, particularly those of drier areas, need to take in larger quantities. Sandgrouse suck up water until the mouth is full before raising the head to let it run back. Continuous sucking with the bill remaining in the water is used by pigeons, some arid-country grassfinches (Australia) such as the Zebra Finch, and mousebirds and shorebirds.

Birds like swallows and swifts that spend most of their time in flight also drink in flight, skimming low over the water and scooping some up with the open bill as it touches the surface. Birds that take nectar with specialized tongues also use these in drinking.

Birds in arid areas have problems in finding water, and many species have ranges limited to a particular waterhole or similar source. Some may fly long distances to reach it. Australian Pratincoles usually stay within about 1.25 miles (2 km) of water, but desert sandgrouse will make a daily round trip of up to 100 miles (160 km) to drink. They overcome the problem of supplying water to their nestlings by carrying it in belly feathers adapted to soak up and hold water, but this limits them to about a third of their normal distance.

Raptors may get fluid from the blood of their prey, and plant-eating birds get some from plant tissues. For others there is evidence of adaptation. Arid-country birds with dry seed diets — some grassfinches, parrots like the Budgerigar, and desert larks — may survive for long periods without drinking or losing weight, but only at mild temperatures. Hot dry weather will rapidly reduce their chances.

Possibly to avoid heat and water loss, or to avoid predators that gather at a place to which they know they must come, desert birds may visit water holes at or just after dusk and at dawn. Bourke's Parakeet, an Australian grass-parrot of dry areas with large eyes, habitually comes to drink after dark. Small birds on dry diets may need to visit water several times a day.

Not all birds can avoid drinking salt water. Oceanic seabirds must drink it and any harmful effects of salt accumulating in their bodies are overcome by its excretion through a pair of glands, the salt glands. These are usually situated in small hollows that accommodate them in the bone structure, either within the eye-socket or on the skull just over the orbit. Here the salt is removed and concentrated, and the resultant fluid passes forward into the nasal cavity, from which it passes to the bill, seemingly through the roof of the mouth, along inside the upper jaw and is periodically flicked away as droplets from the bill tip.

Comfort behavior

A bird must keep its plumage undamaged and in good order if it is to maintain body temperature and move from place to place. Most routine daily care behavior is to ensure that the plumage is properly groomed and functional.

Bathing

Where conditions allow, a bird will wet and wash its plumage prior to preening, but with plumage wholly wet it can be vulnerable, so a number of strategies are adopted. In typical bathing the bird cautiously ventures into shallow water, fluffs its plumage, wets the belly feathers and dips its face into the water. Then it ducks the head in and throws water over its back, squats and tilts first to one side and then the other while fluttering or beating the wings to throw a shower of water and wet parts of the plumage that are normally dry and hidden while also depressing and raising the tail in the water. Some landbirds may stand at the water's edge and splash themselves, or make short forays into the water and out again, as though scared to stay there too long, a method often used by babblers.

Kingfishers, flycatchers, some reed warblers and tyrants, plunge from a perch into water, then fly back. Aerial birds that normally avoid getting wet may swoop down and splash into water but stay on the wing, a method used by swallows, swifts, orioles and seabirds such as frigates and the less waterproofed terns. Seabirds as a whole bathe while swimming. They may dip the head or rear end, splashing and threshing the wings and rolling from side to side, or dive with part-open wings and ruffled plumage. Geese and boobies may roll over on the surface with legs kicking in the air.

Although most bathing involves getting into water, some species deliberately rain bathe during rain. Pigeons squat and tilt over on one side, raising a wing to wet the underwing and flanks. Parrots perch with wings open, twisting body and head with feathers ruffled or hang

A bathing Blue Tit (Parus caeruleus) *soaks itself with water but typically does not go far into it, retaining a hold on land.*

A bathing Mallard (Anas platyrhynchos) *splashes water over itself with its wings.*

Opposite above *Preparing to preen its plumage, a Southern Black-backed Gull (Larus dominicanus) parts the feathers of the lower back and takes oil from its preen gland with its bill.*

Opposite center *A preening Ground Hornbill (Buceros leadbeateri) runs each flight feather through its bill while its companion nibbles the small contour feathers.*

Opposite below *Birds of the heron family, like this Intermediate Egret (Egretta intermedia), remove fish-slime from their plumage by applying powder down and then scratching it away with a serrated-edged toe.*

A dust-bathing Golden Pheasant (Chrysolophus pictus) *shakes the dust into its fluffed feathers.*

upside-down with wings spread to soak themselves. After rain, small woodland birds may rain bathe by lying on the surfaces of large leaves; bigger birds flutter among wet leaves. Hummingbirds will deliberately fly into fine spray from waterfalls or fountains.

All such bathing may be accompanied by other plumage-cleaning movements and usually precedes more deliberate preening. Afterwards, birds dry themselves with feather ruffling, by whirring of the wings and tail in small birds, and plumage shaking, rearing and wing-flapping in waterfowl.

Dust bathing

Many birds, like bobwhite quails, ruffed grouse, wild turkeys, larks, wrens, wren-tits, and certain other hawks and owls, indulge in dust bathing; most are ground birds or live in dry open places where water is scarce. Birds usually begin by scraping and wallowing in soft soil until they form a hollow, then throw dust onto the plumage with the bill and rub the head in the dust, then ruffle and shake the plumage vigorously. This does not appear to be a substitute for proper bathing but seems to help clean off surplus preen oil. Larks dust bathing, especially on harder surfaces where only a thin layer of dust is present, may push themselves along with lowered head, breast on the ground and feet kicking out behind.

Preening

Most birds have an oil gland just above the base of the tail that is revealed when feathers are raised. The bird reaches back and squeezes oil onto the bill, rubbing chin and head on the gland too, if it can reach. Songbirds can transfer oil from the bill to their feet and to the head by scratching. Bill and head are then rubbed on plumage generally, feathers being rubbed by or run through the bill until all are oiled.

At one time it was thought that the oil made plumage waterproof, but its function appears to be maintaining condition and pliability of the keratin of which feathers are composed. Waterproofing is achieved by the overlapping meshes of barbs and barbules, through which water droplets held in shape by the water's surface tension are too large to pass. Household detergent and other pollutant chemicals can change the surface tension of the water and destroy a duck's waterproofing.

Pigeons, some of which lack a preen gland, have fine powder down patches where disintegrating down produces a powder used to treat plumage in place of preen oil. Herons have both and apply powder down to plumage fouled by fish slime, scratching it away with a comb-like claw before applying oil. Pratincoles and nightjars also have a serrated-edged claw on each foot, but for less obvious purposes.

Once plumage has been oiled the bird begins more systematic preening, working over its feathers with nibbling and smoothing bill

movements that close divisions in the feather vanes and knit barbs and barbules together again. Long and large display feathers in some species may necessitate extreme posturing as all are run through the bill. Feathers are smoothed back into place.

Bill and feet are also cleaned, the bill often stropped against a perch or hard surface. Head feathers cannot be cleaned with the bill so birds rely on scratching and foot movements, with two types of scratching, consistent for the groups in which they are found. Most birds scratch indirectly by lowering one wing slightly and raising the foot over it to scratch the head; some others raise the foot directly to the head in front. A very few use both movements for different ends.

Sometimes birds of pairs or social groups may preen one another, usually on the head or neck, in some instances two preening each other simultaneously. This is called allopreening, behavior that occurs in a wide range of birds from gannets to white-eyes. In some highly social groups, such as some *Turdoides* babblers, a number of birds may huddle together and several be involved in simultaneous allopreening. The parts preened are those a bird cannot reach itself, but such behavior does not occur very often and close study suggests it is practiced by birds that must remain in close proximity for temporary nesting or for long-term social bonding, serving to redirect and reduce aggression between them.

Stretching and shaking

Birds often show typical comfort movements while resting or walking. In one, a leg is stretched almost horizontally sideways and at the same time the wing on that side fully extended over it. In perching birds, the tail is often spread simultaneously. In another, perching birds raise both wings, half open above the back, followed by an upward straightening of both legs.

A typical shorebird movement is to spread both wings vertically above the back accompanied by a lowering and forward stretch of neck and head. There may be lateral head shaking and, in some species, an upward tilting or rotating of the head. Waterfowl tend to stand or swim upright and give a vigorous double wing flap, and may also wag the tail. There may also be jaw stretching, which looks like yawning, but does not appear to involve any exhalation of air.

Keeping cool or warm

Although plumage helps birds regulate their body temperature, they may have difficulties in extremes of heat or cold. They may hold heat in air trapped between the feathers and in hot conditions birds sleek down plumage close to the skin to reduce air spaces. In cold they fluff up their feathers, producing the rounded outline that people often assume indicates well-being but is the bird's attempt to increase insulation and retain body heat.

In areas exposed to hot sun birds may avoid full heat, confining activity to early morning and evening and resting during the day in patches of shade, however small, or even in rock crevices and holes. Parent birds, instead of brooding eggs or young, may stand over them, and some birds spread their wings to shade the nest. Ground birds on nests in open places gradually move around to keep facing the sun and reduce exposure. Standing birds shade their own legs and feet and turn away from the sun. Wings are drooped and, although plumage is usually sleeked, mantle feathers may be raised to help the body lose heat.

Heat is also lost through the open mouth and in hot times in tropical climates most birds may go about their activities panting with open bills. A number of nonpasserine species, from cormorants to nightjars, are capable of gular flutter in which the floor of the throat is rapidly fluttered up and down to increase the rate of heat loss.

To take advantage of cooler moving air, birds may keep off the ground; larks and similar species perch on bushes. Birds may stand with legs stretched, as though on tiptoe, and raise the wings away from the body as though waiting for takeoff, and hold this posture. Flying birds may let the legs hang down.

Evaporation helps in cooling. Birds squat in wet areas at the water's edge. Gulls and terns fly out from the colony to splash legs and belly in the water, cooling themselves and returning to cool the nest. Storks and the New World vultures urinate on their legs so that the evaporation will cool them.

To warm themselves birds may "sun bask," which differs from the more extreme sunning behavior described below. They tilt towards the sun and fluff up parts of plumage, often while in a spot sheltered from the wind. Herons and storks may face the sun and spread out wings, tilting the flight feathers forward so that the underwing is exposed. Birds that are

Contour feathers hold air and conserve heat. This European Robin (Erithacus rubecula) fluffs out its feathers to keep warm.

1

2

3

4

tolerant of each other may huddle together in pairs or rows on a perch. Wood-swallows, bee-eaters and some grassfinches such as munias show this behavior. When a number of munias are huddled on a perch the outermost birds may hop onto the others, run along the row and force themselves into the middle, pushing others to the outside.

Some birds appear to deliberately "smoke bathe" on chimneys or similar places. It has been suggested that this provides a sensation similar to sunning or anting (page 96), but may merely be enjoyment of rising heat.

In colder conditions loss of heat due to wind can be critical. Birds that cannot find shelter in vegetation rest and feed in sheltered hollows, crouching low close to the ground. The habit of Willow Grouse and Ptarmigan of burrowing in snowdrifts may help them to avoid chilly winds.

Sunning

This is behavior in which birds adopt a variety of postures, sometimes very atypical, that allow the sun to penetrate the plumage and reach the skin. The head may be exaggeratedly twisted, with feathers raised and bill open; birds may flop with wings and tail spread and body feathers raised. Small gamebirds sometimes appear dead, lying sprawled on one side, head extended and bill open, with both legs raised off the ground. Wings may be raised and tilted by many birds, with all postures highly exaggerated.

These birds are deliberately seeking extreme exposure to the sun, behavior that may be related to sunbathing in other groups of animals, including humans, and connected with Vitamin D synthesis, but with the possible addition of a beneficial effect on the bird's plumage.

1. *Eggs and nestlings can become too warm. This Phainopepla (Phainopepla nitens) shades its nest with its body and wings to cool it.*

2. *A White-necked Cormorant (Phalacrocorax carbo lucidus) pants to reduce its temperature, fluttering its throat to increase heat loss.*

3. *An Openbill Stork (Anastomus oscitans) on a temple in Thailand tilts its spread wings in sunbathing to expose the undersides.*

4. *Perfectly camouflaged, White-tailed Ptarmigans (Lagopus leucurus) dig cavities and burrows in the snow to conserve their heat and avoid loss through cold winds.*

Anting

Superficially resembling sunning, this behavior may involve more manic activity. In a typical example a starling feeding among grasses will suddenly appear to go into a frenzy, squatting with partly spread wings and tail and using its bill to smear ants on the underside of its flight feathers. Alternatively it may sprawl on an ants' nest with wings and tail spread and feathers raised like a sunning bird, allowing ants to run over its plumage. Individual birds respond to stimulants of many different kinds, from mothballs to cigar butts, soapsuds to walnut juice. The reason for, and function of, this behavior are still being debated.

Roosting

Birds normally must rest and sleep during either the night or day according to their period of activity. They need shelter that will prevent undue heat and energy loss and provide safety from predators. Most birds are solitary roosters and even when pairs are nesting they prefer to have individual and separate roost sites.

Birds seek cover among foliage, twigs and branches, in sheltered sites where wind and rain cannot do great harm. Hole nesters often use holes or crevices for roosting and birds that build domes or enclosed nests may also use such structures. Some woodpeckers may excavate holes purely for roosting and some manakins and Australian babblers may build special domed nests for use as communal roosts. Ground birds usually seek ground shelter but forest birds, such as forest game-birds, may roost up on branches to avoid predators. Others may roost in open spaces, huddled in groups with individuals watching in different directions, whereas small birds like Skylarks or Woodlarks create small single hollows in grass in which to spend the night.

Roosting habits differ with circumstances. In warmer climates Turtle-Doves or Diamond Doves roost high on open twigs and will fly off in the dark at the least disturbance. In cooler areas small doves, such as Scaled Doves, huddle together on low perches in thickets and are reluctant to move. Roost sites may be regularly used until disturbance occurs, after which a new one is chosen. For safety's sake, seabirds and waterbirds may sleep on the water or by the water's edge and islands are popular roosts for many different birds.

Some birds use communal roosts. In the case of shorebirds and seabirds this may simply be a matter of limited choice of sites. Communal roosts appear to have some advantages to offset the distance traveled and conspicuousness. They may indicate a safe site, spread the potential threat of predation and reduce individual risk, enable birds to meet conspecifics and, by accompanying them subsequently, to discover good food sources, and increase the shelter effect by sheer numbers. Some roosts can be huge. Those of starlings or the mixed

Right *Some species rest and roost huddled together to conserve body warmth, as do these Silver-eyes (Zosterops lateralis).*

Above left *Although Helmeted Guineafowl (Numida meleagris) are ground-living birds, like some other gamebirds, they roost in trees for greater safety.*

Center left *Roosting Yellow-billed (Intermediate) Egrets (Egretta intermedia) show the individual distance maintained by most roosting birds.*

Below left *Common Starlings (Sturnus vulgaris) roost in enormous numbers. They often circle and maneuver in a large flock before pouring down into the crowded roost.*

A hybrid of the New Zealand Black Stilt (Himantopus novaezelandiae) and the typical Pied Stilts (H. leucocephalus) (behind) in the typical resting posture, balancing on one leg. Birds do this perched, standing on land or standing in water.

roosts of American troupial species can run into hundreds of thousands. In such cases birds may assemble in subsidiary gatherings before they fly to roost and there may be elaborate mass maneuvering over the roost before a flock settles.

Some roosts can only be used seasonally and may be reused from year to year, but damage caused by huge numbers of roosting birds may necessitate an occasional shift of site. Within roost species many still maintain an individual distance, with a small gap between roosting birds. Other species conserve heat by huddling together in both large and small roosts. Such individuals may conserve up to 50 percent of their energy reserve. Species such as the Long-tailed Tits or Fairywrens huddled together in a sheltered spot look like a single mass of feathers with a number of tails. Wood-swallows may roost clinging to the sides of hollow trees or on

rough surfaces; other birds huddle closely around the first to settle.

Northern Wrens are highly aggressive and solitary individuals but, in cold winters, will use communal roost holes, the birds entering and leaving singly but spending the night in a closely packed mass.

Although much is known about large communal roosts the roosting habits of the more solitary species are still poorly studied.

Resting and sleeping

Birds have the same basic problem when resting and roosting as in standing and moving: they need positions that will offer limited wear and damage to plumage. Although an overriding need for warmth and shelter in periods of cold or in bad weather may force them into a confined space, they will normally rest on a surface using legs and feet, and spacing themselves at a little distance from each other to avoid actual contact.

In general the postures for resting and sleeping are similar, but some of the larger long-legged birds, from Emus to Stone-curlews, may rest by squatting on their leg joints with the lower part of the legs and the feet resting above ground level in front of them. They do not sleep in this position.

The majority of birds rest and sleep standing on one leg, on a perch, on the ground or standing in shallow water. Gamebirds and pigeons squat, on the ground or across a level perch, resting on both the lower legs and presumably the keel of the breastbone, and nightjars rest on the ground or along the top of perches. The more aquatic ducks and oceanic seabirds rest and sleep floating on the water.

Northern treecreepers, and probably other climbers, rest and sleep clinging to upright surfaces.

Standing on one leg might be expected to put a strain on the bird, but there are specializations of leg structure. There is a locking device in the foot where the ridged surfaces of tendon and tendon sheath interlock as the bird's foot presses down. The tendons pass over the back of the leg joints higher up the leg and their pressure will keep the leg straight while the tension on the tendons will also tighten the bird's foot grip, helping it to stay in place on its perch. The other foot is drawn up into the plumage.

During resting and sleeping, plumage is usually fluffed up to keep the bird warm. In squatting birds the head rests on the shoulders and the bill is tucked down into the fluffed breast feathers. In the resting nightjars and their relatives the head is tilted back on the shoulders.

In birds that rest on one leg, or float, or cling, the head is turned and rests on the back. The bill and nostrils are tucked down and concealed in the mantle feathers or behind the longer tertials or inner secondaries of the closed wing. Only nestlings appear to lie down and rest the head on the surface in front of them.

In sleeping birds the closed eyes remain visible and, although there may be continuous periods of deep sleep, for most of their normal sleeping period birds will open one or both eyes for a second or two at intervals of a few minutes or even more frequently. This appears to be part of sleep behavior but, if disturbance or danger is visible, the bird wakes. It would seem that the eyes of birds perform the constant monitoring during sleep that hearing supplies in sleeping mammals.

It is usually thought that most Common Swifts sleep on the wing at high altitudes. This has recently been questioned, although without other evidence. A bird sleeping while gliding and presumably circling in constant flight is difficult to envisage, but if a bird typically opens its eyes at very frequent intervals while sleeping, it should in theory be able to monitor its airborne progress in an environment without obstructions.

Some birds lapse into torpor at times, a state like deep sleep but in which all body processes slow down and energy is conserved. Hummingbirds burn energy at a high rate when active and appear to become torpid when sleeping, especially in places where night temperatures fall. It is also a safety device for birds in abnormally cold or deprived situations.

Nestlings of swiftlets and some shearwater-type seabirds, where adults may be absent for unpredictable periods, are capable of torpor. Adult swifts, and the nightjars and their relatives appear capable of resting in torpor in unexpected cold weather. There is evidence of a North American Poorwill apparently hibernating in a rock crevice during winters in the desert and hibernation is also claimed for the Green-backed Firecrown Hummingbird of the mountains of the extreme south of South America.

BIRD TERRITORIES

A bird's territory is the area surrounding it that it will defend against other birds. It may range in size from not much more than a body length in a colony, or a linear streamside strip for a kingfisher or dipper, to several square miles for eagles and other raptors. Territories are not necessarily for breeding. There may be a feeding territory providing a temporarily reserved food supply, a defended area around the family as in migrant geese with young, or a territory temporarily established in a wintering area by a northern warbler or European Robin. They may be required for only a few hours or for a lifetime. They may be needed to provide a secure nesting place, to offer sufficient sustenance of plant material or prey to hunt, either for the individual or for rearing young, or possession of a territory may be necessary for courtship to be initiated. Often a bird requires a territory for all these reasons. In some, occupation is for a brief time only. In the case of some of the grouse, the ruffs and birds-of-paradise it is only a small patch of ground required for short and intermittent periods as a stage on which to display to attract a succession of females, who go off to nest and produce eggs and chicks with no male help.

A territory must provide the facilities a particular bird needs, not just a place to nest or food supplies but features such as an elevated position or "song post" for some species, or a hillock or mound from which Ptarmigans and other heath birds can oversee surrounding country. A Woodlark requires an area with very short or sparse vegetation where it can easily run around and find food, a few scattered trees or shrubs from which it may watch and sing, and small areas of coarser grass or heather, approachable on foot, in which it can conceal its ground nest cup. If not too heavily disturbed by humans, golf courses often offer the combination of facilities it requires.

Extent is not determined by the ground area but by what it contains — a group of berry-bearing trees will take up less than a dispersed supply — and the defended area may change to reflect both a transition from one major food source to another and the greater demands of raising young. Once the young have fledged territorial boundaries tend to break down, if only through sheer weight of numbers. The tendency in some species for adults to divide the fledged brood between them and go off with certain young ones will also break down the territorial pattern.

Not all birds manage to establish a clear territory, though it is usually a requirement for successful breeding. If they cannot find space for a territory of their own, nonbreeding individuals must operate on or between the limits of the territories already established, taking the opportunity to rush in and claim one if the "owner" dies or fails to return after migration, or expanding the area they occupy by gradual encroachment until it becomes a viable territory. A small territory will be actively defended, but birds with a large territory cannot be everywhere at once and some birds that initially defend a large territory may confine themselves to a smaller area around the nest when actually breeding. In some species other birds that keep a low profile may be tolerated and allowed to nest and breed within a territory provided they do not feed in the same places at the same time as the "owner." Perhaps the resident bird is too busy raising a family to have time to bother — most birds are less active in defense in the breeding season, which usually coincides with a time of food abundance — or he may not even notice that they have moved in but assume that they are simply transients, for such intruders do not confront the resident or attempt to announce any claim.

It is usually only birds of the same species that are excluded, except for cases where other species are competing for a limited source of exactly the same food, or feed in the same places in the same manner.

Opposite *Territory is usually advertised by song, and since the western population of the European Robin* (Erithacus rubecula) *defends a territory for most of the year, it may still be singing there at Christmas.*

A hunting territory and a ledge nest site do not need to be in open country. A male European Kestrel (Falco tinnunculus) *at its nest on a high-rise apartment block may not have access to the small mice and voles that have made highway embankments a favorite hunting ground but probably finds easy prey among urban sparrows.*

Left *Two male Green Jays* (Cyanocorax yncas) *display aggressively when disputing territory.*

Male Oystercatchers (Haematopus ostralegus) *come together at the territory edge and display, running side by side or standing, the neck arched, bill open and down-pointed, and uttering a constant loud piping that can accelerate into a trill.*

Two closely-related warblers, the Willow Warbler and the Chiffchaff, have different habitat preferences, the first in low scrub, the second preferring trees. In areas of mixed vegetation both may occur but produce a mosaic of territories, mixed together without overlap, neither tolerating the other.

Most of these territories are highly vegetated, but birds in more open bare habitats, steppe, moorland, grassland or grassy swamp, must make themselves conspicuous in song and often in plumage. Pipits flutter up and then spiral down in song. The Australian Brown Songlark behaves similarly but in addition the male is large and blackish in color. *Cisticola* warblers and larks circle over territories in song, with the aerial boundaries rather imprecise. Bishops float over their territories as fluffed scarlet and black balls with buzzing songs. Extravagantly long-tailed widowbirds show off plumage in flight. Overflying territory appears to be all that is necessary in birds of prey.

Some shorebirds, such as the trilling Curlew or the Lapwing, with extravagant flight and wild calls, also show aerial displays. The black bellies of breeding Golden and Gray Plovers and Dunlin seem designed for this purpose, but in these birds the critical feeding areas and nest sites may be small plots in the areas that they overfly and the display may be for sexual rather than territorial reasons.

Birds can fight with beak and claw if they must, but confrontations over territory are rare. It is usually enough for the occupant to advertise his presence. The European Robin is an example of a small bird that is often very pugnacious. Many are migratory but western European populations tend to be resident. In Britain, after summer molt, males and females (including the new young adults) stake out individual territories using song and threat displays and defend them through the winter. There are two typical displays: a lateral pivoting with head raised and throat puffed, indicating a territory edge where an intruder should not proceed further, and a frontal approach with head raised and the whole red breast displayed,

meaning that the intruder has gone too far and attack is imminent. In spring males and females become cautiously more tolerant of each other, and there is a revision and some amalgamation of territories by pairing birds. Some females will have migrated and returned after having held feeding territories in winter quarters. The breeding territories are retained until the molt, then it is every bird for itself again.

Display and song enable birds to assess their neighbors. Boundary disputes are usually threats that are not taken to the point of violence and merely test the zone in which some interactive response is likely. The whole point of displays and songs is that birds need to parcel up the available areas between them but have a vested interest in avoiding actual conflict that might harm them as well as the challenger.

When close-knit social groups breed, the defense of territory is in the interest of the group as a whole. In some it may rest largely on the dominant male. In some species of Fairy-wren, such as the White-winged Wren, the dominant male appears to achieve the full gaudy breeding plumage but the other males do not, even though their testes may have enlarged. In other species all the males may be involved in defense, usually communally, and in some all individuals, including females. Even in pairs, females may help in defense and, if two pairs of coots disagree, all four birds join in the fight that follows.

In polygynous species, where males have several mates, whether Northern Wrens, Reed Warblers, Scarlet Bishops or Eurasian Bitterns, the maintenance of the territory and its defense are the male concern. The female merely nests within the defended space. In a number of instances, both in species regarded as polygynous and in others usually monogamous, the situation may vary, apparently as a result of the ability of territory to support one or more nestings, thus determining the number of females present since their behavior depends on territory suitability rather than male behavior.

In Corn Buntings the polygynous male sits watching and singing a constant jingling song from a perch while his females — the number depends upon the territory — nest and rear the young in low herbage, the male seeming to do nothing other than chase off possible rivals.

Some species have limited territorial areas in the immediate vicinity of nests, which are not necessarily close together, and share feeding grounds further removed. Common Starlings, and possibly House Sparrows, seem to be examples, as too may be the Rock Dove and Domestic Pigeon. Nests are usually in cavities that are jealously guarded, holes always being in short supply. Intruders may be chased away. A sparrow pair may take over an occupied nest and throw out eggs and live young. Away from the nests, birds of these species feed and meet on apparently friendly terms in open spaces where food is available or at bathing and resting places. It is not clear whether colonies of these birds are formed by choice or are merely chance aggregations of suitable nesting sites.

Bird colonies

True colonies are those in which birds choose to nest close together and do so even if unused space is available nearby. They are often in clumps of trees, or in raised areas of marshland, groups of holes or crevices in rocks or buildings, or on coasts and islands as masses of burrows or crevices, nests covering open ground that may be high or low, or crowded assemblies on rock faces. The size and continuity of such colonies appears primarily to be determined by the availability of a suitable quantity of food within reasonable reach.

The birds that nest in colonies assemble by choice. Even if not in pairs throughout the year, birds are likely to return to the same nest site and may either breed together over a period of years or have an immediate chance to find another mate if necessary. There is competition for the sites towards the center of the colony, which may be occupied by the same experienced pairs. Young birds and newcomers often have to nest at the edge of the colony where they are more vulnerable, and will move towards the center if the opportunity arises.

The territory may be a nest burrow, a small area with a nest site on it, as with some gulls and terns that use level grassy areas, or it may be only the nest and its immediate surroundings that can be guarded against encroaching pairs by the sitting bird.

The patterns of territoriality so far discussed are based on the assumption of a single annual breeding period, but in some tropical areas, where the food supply is more assured, the pattern of territory use will differ. On one island in the Galapagos two populations of Madeiran Storm-Petrel breed at different periods of the year, using the same sites again, whereas on another island the same occurs with the Madeiran and the Galapagos Storm-Petrels. There is also evidence of use of a site by successive species during the year among birds nesting on islands in freshwater lakes in Africa.

A colonial nest site tends to increase the intensity of breeding behavior and to enhance breeding success, ensuring encounters with the same species. Food is more likely to be found by watching other individuals, parties or flocks dispersing outwards. It offers a sure nesting and roosting site. Predators are likely to be deterred or to have plenty of alternative victims. This may be a critical factor: where the smaller gull species nest on freshwater marshes, other species such as ducks, grebes and terns may nest on the colony's edge, apparently to take advantage of protection against predators, even though eggs or small chicks may be at risk from the gulls.

The disadvantages are the need for one bird always to be on guard at the nest, the inability of easily protecting the female from other males' approaches, theft of nest material or eggs, loss of young or injury to them, injury to the pair in fights arising from limited space and competition for food.

Large colonies may contain a number of different species. On coastal and cliff sites this may be the result of birds exploiting different

Gannets nest colonially, building nests two bill-stabs apart on all the level ground or flat ledges available. This colony of Australian Gannets (Morus serrator) covers a cliff top on Cape Kidnappers in the North Island of New Zealand.

sites when choices are few. Mixed colonies often occur where waterbirds — herons, cormorants, ibises, spoonbills and storks — nest in trees or on islands. Here sites do not always seem to be a limiting factor and it is possible that an inherent tendency to choose colonial nesting is involved.

Interaction between individuals

Some animals allow physical contact between individuals and others keep a distance from each other. Birds are usually individual-distance species and the relatively few contact species may represent secondary adaptations.

Each bird maintains a short distance between itself and the next. This can be seen in a feeding flock and in resting birds, in spaced swallows on a wire or starlings at a roost. Individual distance may be advisable for greater freedom of movement, but birds do not ignore each other and when the same or different species meet interaction is likely. The normal reaction is likely to be suspicion and aggression and, if it is desirable for individuals to approach each other, a code of signals is needed that will indicate intention.

Many of the postures, movements, calls and displays of birds are information signals of this kind. Individual-distance birds must temporarily modify their social behavior in order to function as a pair, but aggression may not be far below the surface and may break out at times.

Basic signal postures usually have simple components but will have differences of detail and elaboration in different species. An aggressive bird will often extend the head and neck towards the other and sleek the plumage. The other bird may react by withdrawing but, if it wishes to stay, it may signal a fleeing or submissive tendency by lowering or turning away its head and adopting a hunched position with fluffed plumage.

Maintaining a critical distance between individuals entails fairly simple posturing.

During the breeding season, however, individuals of a pair may experience conflicting impulses of approach and withdrawal or of aggression and submission. It is likely to have been inner conflict of this kind, with alternating impulses, that has given rise to the often strange and unexpected postures and movements that often characterize mating displays, especially in species where the birds do not have a long-standing pair bond and pairing involves strangers.

Birds can behave sociably without losing their individual-distance tendencies. Birds in flocks usually retain them and occasional aggressive interactions can be seen in small squabbles between individuals or in supplanting attacks where a bird is forced to move as another takes its place.

In closer social groupings, where individuals have longer periods of acquaintance, hierarchies often develop. One individual will dominate and lead the group and the rest may form a descending succession of individuals with fewer and fewer of the group that they can dominate. This tends to be flexible and less precise in the wild than in some laboratory studies, where individual scope for evasion is limited, but it can be useful in enabling a group to function and interact while reducing the likelihood of conflict, since each bird knows where it stands in relation to the others.

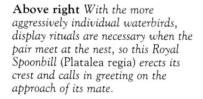

Above right *With the more aggressively individual waterbirds, display rituals are necessary when the pair meet at the nest, so this Royal Spoonbill* (Platalea regia) *erects its crest and calls in greeting on the approach of its mate.*

Two Ring-necked Pheasants (Phasanius colchicus) *show how threat display is used to determine the boundaries of territories.*

BIRDSONG

Birds can be recognized as much by their songs as by their feathers. The sounds they use vary enormously but, in general, song is loud and clear because birds must constantly use it to announce their presence to each other. Songs have only been studied in detail in a few species but it seems that seabirds, for instance, may have only about ten different calls, whereas songbirds have about twice as many.

Calls are often short and it is usually possible to recognize contact calls between individuals, flock calls of small birds on the move or of flying geese, and the alarm calls that our presence may elicit. Other calls are concerned with threat or courtship, and there are begging calls of young and those used by adults to chicks or nestlings. Vocabularies may be more complex. The Azure-winged Magpie, a bird that lives in groups, has different calls to warn of furry predators, fast-flying hawk-like birds and slow-soaring eagle-like birds.

We can differentiate the bird species and the meaning of the call it uses but our ears obviously miss subtleties. When a penguin or a tern returns to a colony crèche of hungry young, parents and young recognize each other's voices among the clamor, although to us all adults, and all young, are using the same calls.

The structures of various birds' vocal apparatus can produce an extraordinary range of sounds, from the low hoot of owls and churrs of nightjars to the warblings of the Nightingale, cackling wails of Great Northern Divers or the tiny shrill songs of Goldcrests and hummingbirds, only just within the human range. Neotropical bellbirds produce far-carrying notes like large metal bells being struck, the Calfbird bellows, Sickle-billed Birds-of-paradise make a deafening metallic clang, the Pied Butcherbird's notes are as pure as a flute and the low-pitched thrumming of the displaying Blue Bird-of-paradise sounds almost machine-like.

Typical songs are elaborate, personally variable sounds used by birds to advertise their presence within an area or to attract a mate. As a result such songs are usually sung by males only, although when a female European Robin holds her own territory, she too will sing. They are usually uttered by a single bird, but Australian Magpies live in social groups and males will perch near each other to produce a chorus of loud musical notes for territorial advertisement. In some resident species with long pair bonds, ranging from tinamous and Magpie-larks to bush-shrikes, duetting may occur. The mated pair produce a song phrase that may sound as though it comes from a single bird, though both birds have contributed to it; the second contribution may be in the middle of a phrase. These songs appear to be used as territorial advertisement directed at another pair. Shorter rhythmical antiphonal duets can be heard from pairs of Toucan Barbets, and can be detected from the dominant pair in the confused chorus of a social group of

Many birds obtained popular local names from attempts to render their calls into words; the cuckoo is named for its call wherever it is heard. Musical transcriptions may be more accurate. Top here in Athanasius Kircher's record, published in 1650, of the Nightingale's song. Below, with attempts at Latin vocalization are: A Cock crowing, B and C Hen laying and calling chicks, D Quail, E Cuckoo and a Parrot, for whose harsh croak he has resorted to Greek.

Left *Bitterns live in reed beds and advertise their territories by sound. The American Bittern (Botaurus lentiginosus) seen here makes a repeated deep note described as "thunder pumping" while the Eurasian species (B. stellaris) makes a soft deep and far-carrying booming noise.*

White-crested Laughingthrushes and probably from similar birds.

In typical instances a bird sings its song when moving into a territory, singing from various perches within it. Birds in open places without perches sing on the wing on short or long advertisement flights. Any replies establish that other birds are present. The vigor, complexity and rapidity of response may give some indication of the age, experience and aggressiveness of the other bird. Song combined with aggressive displays will be used to determine the mutual boundaries of territories.

Song is also used to attract females, which recognize and respond to it. The nocturnal songs of Nightingales may be aimed at night-migrating females. Females may also gain information about the singer from the song, and male warblers with the longer and more complex songs have been found to be more successful in attracting females. In some species song becomes less elaborate and less frequent after pairing has occurred.

In some species, such as Great Tits and Chaffinches, the songs have a familiar basic pattern with small and subtle variations that are of importance to the birds. In other species songs may be lengthy, complex and variable. A male can be recognized by his song, but this is not a fixed repertoire. Experiments have shown that young birds reared in isolation without hearing the complete song of a male would only produce a short incomplete version, even if this were a phrase of a short and fairly stereotyped kind. As soon as they heard the complete song from a male they would learn to imitate it. Singing birds appear to constantly add to the pattern of their songs and, like young birds, often borrow song phrases of other males.

As a result, within an area, singing males may have individually distinct song repertoires but also include phrases that are common to district males. This may have a function since each male will recognize and share the songs of its neighbors. The shared component may act as a reassurance that the rivals and their distribution remain unchanged. The presence of a male lacking the shared song phrases would indicate that a stranger had moved in, with a potential threat to territorial boundaries. This sharing of song phrases may be the origin of more marked local song dialects. The pattern of songs used by a particular species, even normally stereotyped songs like those of Chaffinches or Yellowhammers, have distinct differences in distinct geographical regions.

This tendency to imitate and add phrases to the song repertoire may be why mimicry is fairly widespread in birds. We are inclined to notice only those species that imitate the human voice, such as parrots and Hill Mynahs, whereas the Cockatiel and in the past the Eurasian Bullfinch were taught to whistle tunes. Studies reveal that many birds imitate sounds both natural and mechanical and these may become part of the regular song. The suburban Common Starling offers an example, imitating calls of other birds and the ringing of telephones, and one bird, singing in spring, took less than a

week to perfect an imitation of a Siamese cat recently arrived in the neighborhood.

It is sometimes suggested that the Superb Lyrebird has the biggest repertoire of imitations, including most local birds and mammals, and a few extras such as axes and saws, whereas the Marsh Warbler is credited with borrowing sounds from one hundred different species of European birds, but the human ear is sometimes deceived in such matters when attempting to match sounds. For a bird, song is the advertisement noises that it makes in the kind of contexts described and includes the yodeling of a large gull, the caw of a crow, the reiterated single note of a Wonga Pigeon or the almost inaudible whines, clicks and hisses of the Gouldian Finch, sung vigorously but sounding as though the bird has been nearly strangled.

Some of the sounds used by birds to advertise themselves are mechanically produced noises in place of song. Woodpeckers hammer rapidly on resonant branches or metal poles to produce far-carrying drumming sounds. Pheasants and displaying Black Grouse whirr their wings and Ruffed Grouse produce a loud rumbling drumming by rapidly beating their wings across the breast. Common Snipe fly up, then dive with outer tail feathers spread to produce a whinnying sound, and American Woodcocks use outer primaries to produce a musical whistle in the air. Wood pigeons and nightjars clap their wings in flight and Common Swifts produce a loud wing flutter. Flappet Larks make an odd burring sound with their beating wings in place of songs and some manakins and birds-of-paradise produce sounds with wings or tail during displays.

Opposite page The Nightingale (Luscinia megarhynchos) *usually sings a series of separate phrases, often sudden warbling notes, sometimes a soft start with a strong crescendo. The song is loud and far carrying but its fame is partly because it is also sung at night when most birds are silent. It is not only advertising its territory but hoping to attract a female, since these arrive at night.*

Above left *The male Ruffed Grouse* (Bonasa umbellus) *advertises its presence by standing upright and beating its open wings against its breast at about 20 times per second to produce a loud drumming sound.*

Center left *Birdsong-recording pioneer Ludwig Koch sets up his equipment in the 1930s. Advanced recording techniques and computer analysis have made birdsong study more precise.*

The Dunnock (Prunella modularis) *also sings to advertise territory but although a good territory may attract several females, a female may use territories of several males if they offer poor facilities.*

THE BREEDING CYCLE

The age at which birds reach sexual maturity differs from species to species, as it does with all animals. In general small birds start breeding earlier and have shorter lives, but produce a greater number of offspring during that time. Size may be a factor but relates to groups rather than species and produces exceptions.

The majority of birds, including the small songbirds and many up to the size of ducks, owls or penguins, tend to breed at one to two years old, and the Gray Heron also breeds at two years. Terns, gulls and birds of prey breed at three to five years, as do pelicans and White Storks. Larger species of eagles and seabirds may wait a few years more. The big albatrosses and Great Frigatebird are later still at 10–11 years old, while the smaller Fulmar, which may live for 40 years, breeds at 7–11 years old.

Breeding may not occur under adverse conditions, as in polar regions if the snow lies too long, or in arid regions in time of drought. Competition for territory may prevent breeding and in some species individuals may spend some years waiting as helpers to breeding pairs. Sexual imbalance may also mean that birds do not find a mate.

The breeding season

The breeding season, when a bird produces eggs and young and when it is most likely to succeed in rearing them will vary from species to species but in any particular region it is likely that major groups of species will breed at certain periods. It appears mainly linked to food supply.

The two most critical factors are that prior to nesting a female must be physically capable of producing a clutch of eggs, which will depend on food, and a good supply of food for the young when they hatch. The availability of food in turn depends upon plant and prey animal cycles, or plankton and marine life at sea, and these in turn are linked with climate.

In the cooler regions of the world, from the subtropics to the poles, this results in a single breeding period in spring and summer, although in warmer regions birds may rear a succession of broods within that time. The precise conditions that each requires will determine the timing for individual species. Northern crossbills using conifer seeds to feed females and young are independent of the factors controlling other finches and begin about two months earlier, in February; in the Mediterranean and around Arabia the Eleanora's Falcon and Sooty Falcon breed late, relying on the abundant autumn migrants moving south on which to feed their young.

In theory, birds in tropical regions should not have this problem, and in tropical forests the tendency is for birds to produce well-spaced nestings with small broods. Only a few species seem to have a pattern of nesting at any time,

with each individual having its own period of rest and molt, though a few landbirds and seabirds such as Masked Boobies and tropicbirds are known to have a breeding pattern. One effect of tropical nonseasonality is that seabirds are freed from the need for an annual cycle. Some species breed in different months on different islands and some breed at less than twelve-month intervals. Bridled Terns may breed every seven to eight months, Sooty Terns every nine months and Swallow-tailed Gulls at nine- to ten-month intervals. These may be synchronized breeding in some instances, or spread over a year in others.

Intervals of longer than a year may be influenced by the need to build up reserves for laying or the time taken feeding slow-growing young, mostly involving the large birds. Although the Emperor Penguin, with the male sitting out the winter on Antarctic Ice, can breed annually, the similar King Penguin only rears two young every three years. The larger albatrosses and frigatebirds breed once every two years, as do big raptors such as the California Condor and Harpy Eagle.

Opposite page Although precocial, young Coots (Fulica atra) are in no hurry to leave the nest, which is also used as a brooding site. Adults feed them to some extent until they are well grown.

King Penguins (Aptenodytes patagonicus) have no nest. The egg is incubated resting on the adult's feet, covered by a flap of belly skin. Here it is exposed as the adults prepare to change shifts, rolling it from one set of feet to the other.

Below *Emperor Penguins (Aptenodytes forsteri) also incubate the egg on the feet, under the bulging flap of belly skin. After four months of nonstop incubation on the Arctic ice by the male alone, the egg hatches. The chick (center) also being brooded on the feet.*

For most of the tropical regions there is in fact a seasonality linked to the rainy seasons. These are not necessarily annual, there may be two rainy seasons and two peaks of breeding activity within a year. Some seabirds also show a double season, with semiannual breeding by the same population. They include the Silver Gull in Australia, Sooty Tern on some Pacific islands and Cassin's Auklet of the western North American seaboard.

Rain is also a critical factor in arid areas, where although rainfall may be unpredictable in occurrence, it tends to have a seasonal pattern. After even brief rainfall, birds may need to breed quickly within the short period that follows of plant growth and the accompanying availability of insects. An unseasonal rainstorm in inland Australia, activating the overriding impulse to breed, may temporarily halt or inhibit other cycles such as molt. The need for rain and the plants and seeds that follow accounts for the almost continuous breeding in captivity of birds such as Budgerigars and Zebra Finches, for which an urban house is a desert with an assured supply of water.

Breeding seasons are therefore to some degree adapted to the locality and to the needs of the species involved.

The physiological background

Breeding totally changes a bird's activity pattern with a series of hereditary impulses or drives that need to be satisfied. The sexes have different roles to play, some independent of each other but some that must be synchronized if mating is to succeed.

Factors such as availability of food affect breeding behavior but the trigger that sets the cycle in motion must occur much earlier, for aspects such as defense of territories or nest sites may be evident in the fall. It appears to be the gradual change in day length, apparent to some degree almost everywhere except the equatorial zone. This activates various hormones within the body that control the stages that follow.

Birds perceive daylight change. It has been suggested that this is directly through the skull rather than the eyes, and it causes a reaction on the hypothalamic region of the brain resulting in the release of a hormone that stimulates the pituitary gland, lying just under the brain. This gland produces hormones that stimulate the gonads — the testes and ovary — which in their turn produce various steroid hormones.

The steroids initially active produce breeding plumages and changes in such things as bill color and also induce aggressive behavior. In the female they stimulate the production of ova and later of eggs.

In the fall these effects are limited, though initiating the beginnings of territorial and aggressive behavior in some species, and in some favorable years small numbers of individuals may show unseasonable breeding behavior. There is some slowing down and inhibition of activity during the winter and the principal rise in breeding behavior accompanied by increase in hormone activity is in the lengthening days of spring.

Later, under the influence of longer days and as a reaction by the bird to the presence of eggs, the pituitary gland also produces the hormone prolactin, which stimulates parental behavior, makes birds broody and causes the development of brood patches and the production of secretions such as pigeon's milk.

Birds in tropical regions with minimal daylength change appear to show a continuous level of stimulation, making potentially continuous breeding possible, but with some evidence of a cycle that allows a seasonal change and resting stage.

The thyroid gland, also stimulated by the pituitary gland, produces hormones some of which are involved in the later inhibition of

Penguin parenting

Breeding success in the Emperor Penguins depends upon a strong pair bond and precise timing between a pair who may be hundreds of miles apart.

These penguins leave the sea for the shore-ice in late March, returning to the location where they were born and bred in previous years. Here courtship takes place and some seven or eight weeks later the female lays a single egg and goes off leaving its incubation to the male. By now the ice has spread far out to sea and she may have a long journey before she reaches open water and can feed.

The male now spends another 64 days without food carrying the egg upon his feet to keep it from contact with the ice and tucked under a belly flap. He lives off reserves of fat, losing about one third of his weight. The males huddle in large groups for protection from temperatures that fall to -40°C (-40°F) and 100 mph (160 kph) winds, milling about so that each spends some time in the warm center. At hatching the male exudes food still in his crop to feed the chick for a day or two. The female then returns — if she is late the chick will die — fattened up and able to take over feeding while the male, who has gone 16 weeks without eating, now heads for the sea. The male spends a few weeks away and then returns to share rearing with his partner from about the end of August. At four months old the chick is grown sufficiently to begin fending for itself.

King Penguin males also incubate the egg, though conditions for them are not quite so extreme.

gonadal stimulus, bringing an end to the breeding season and the onset of molt.

Bird pairings

Bird pairing and breeding is 90 percent monogamous, most typically with male and female remaining together for the period of nesting. The male may defend a territory, a more limited nest area or be a member of a breeding colony and in some species his contribution to nesting is small, a situation most likely to occur in territorial situations. In some the male only feeds the young, possibly feeding the female also during earlier stages of nesting; in other species he may participate in incubation and brooding as well.

Unless conditions are adverse, individuals of many species that move away or migrate when not breeding return annually to breed at the same site, with the likelihood that the same individuals will encounter each other in subsequent years. In some species, particularly short-lived small passerines, pairings may change each year, seemingly at random. In others, although separated for part of the year, the same two will pair again and show a long-term breeding bond. This has been studied more closely in colonies of nesting seabirds such as gulls. There is evidence of what might be called an experience factor. Birds that meet and pair again each year try to use the same site again, and tend to pair early and retain the better sites. They have a stronger bond, defend the site more effectively and are more efficient in the various stages of nesting, producing young to fledgling stage more regularly. Such pairings may break down, possibly through failures at some stage or an inadequacy of one partner, but not always for obvious reasons.

Long-term pair bonds certainly exist in birds as diverse as babblers, Jackdaws, geese and cranes. In the last two groups some species are migrant, pairs migrating together accompanied by young of the year. More usually long-term bonding is more likely to be evident in resident and sedentary species.

Choice of partner

Be cautious of over-generalizations concerning bird pairings. Individual choice may be difficult to prove in the wild, although obvious at times in captive birds. In Derek Goodwin's study of Blue-breasted Waxbills he took two males and two females at random from imported consignments. They were liberated in a bird room in order to study breeding in two pairs. A male and female paired almost immediately and began to show nesting behavior. The second male displayed to the other female but she ignored him and made a determined effort to break up the first pair and to mate with the first male. For years the situation persisted with the first male paired with his choice, the second female trying to oust her, and the second male trying to persuade the second female to pair with him.

Similar problems were experienced with two of each sex of Lanceolated Jays in which both females wanted one of the males. This indicates a strong degree of personal preference, even in small birds, that could affect interpretations of behavior and of which students of birds in the wild should be aware.

A female Satin Bowerbird (Ptilonorhynchus violaceus) (left) inspects the avenue of twigs the male has built and the blue objects he has collected to decorate it. Bowerbird species each have different color preferences — this one is obsessed with blue and green. To make the bower more enticing he paints it with berry juice, sometimes applied with a twig. Visiting females are greeted by plumage fluffing, a wheezing ecstatic display song and the holding of some objects in the bill. After mating takes place in the bower, the female goes off to nest alone.

From field studies of birds and from DNA fingerprinting methods, by which body fluid or tissue can be used to establish individual relationships, it becomes increasingly apparent that in many instances, often involving theoretically monogamous birds, extra-pair copulation occurs. This may be controlled to some extent by patterns of behavior such as the guarding of females by their mates. However, evidence suggests that, if the opportunity occurs, individual birds of both sexes are likely to copulate at times with birds other than their mates on a random basis. The likelihood that this will lead to fertilization of the eggs varies and depends upon the stage in nesting at which it occurs. Much appears to depend upon who copulates last before laying. That individual may fertilize about four fifths of the eggs in a clutch.

Pairing behavior may vary even within a species, as in the Dunnock, and shows several other patterns.

Momentary pairing

In this pattern, pairing usually follows a display by the male on a display ground. After copulation the female goes to nest and raise young alone, usually in a different place. It involves solitary males, as in bowerbirds and some birds-of-paradise, and most birds that have communal lek displays, such as Sage Grouse, Ruffs, cocks-of-the-rock and manakins.

In ducks, pairing tends to take place in flocks and association may be brief, and sometimes promiscuous, or may continue, the male guarding the female until gradually deserting her during incubation. In Eider Ducks the male conscientiously, if reluctantly, helps her search for a nest site on land, flopping down at intervals and needing encouragement from her. When, possibly after several visits, she settles on one he leaves her for good, joining other males on the shore.

Polygyny

Polygyny (one male mated to several females) appears in a number of forms. Males in colonies of open-country nesting weaverbirds will build a new nest for a succession of mates. In some birds a male defends a territory in which he mates with a number of females, sometimes his involvement in nesting being minimal but in other species playing a part in each.

In the Northern Wren, the male builds a series of basic nests, constructing the outer part from dead leaves and other coarse material, which he presents to a potential mate who will line the one she chooses. The male may offer the others to the next female he attracts, or build more. He will attempt to help feed a series of broods of young.

Some Pied Flycatcher males establish a territory and settle a mate in a nest hole in it. While she lays and incubates he establishes a new territory and tries to install another mate there. Later he returns to the original female and helps her rear her brood, leaving the second female to cope on her own.

Polyandry

In polyandry the female has more than one mate, enabling her to devote herself to egg production. It usually occurs where the female is bigger and brighter than the male and takes the dominant role in pairing. It is seen in various groups but gamebirds and shorebirds show a gradation in nesting behavior that may explain its origin. In the simplest form, as with the Gambel's and Bobwhite Quails, the female may lay a second brood while the male tends the first. In the Red-legged Partridge she may lay two broods, one of which the male incubates, the young of both being reared together. The female Temminck's Stint lays a clutch tended by the male closely followed by another for which she cares; the Spotted Sandpiper lays clutches for several different males but may help the last with nesting. Ultimately, in species such as the Dotterel a female pairs with more than one male and leaves them to do all the nesting and rearing. Banding (ringing) revealed one Dotterel who in the same season mated in Norway, left the male with a clutch of eggs then flew across the North Sea to leave another clutch with a male in Scotland. This sort of behavior is called sequential polygamy.

In the Greater Painted Snipe the female has a territory in which several males incubate clutches of her eggs. Northern Jacana females have a large territory in which they lay eggs for three or four males, each defending a small territory on floating water plants. Female Galapagos Hawks copulate with several males, all of whom cooperate in rearing the brood.

Communal breeding

About 150 bird species nest in social groups, not isolated pairs. The way such groups are

Opposite above *In the African Golden Weaver* (Ploceus subaureus) *and related species, the male builds a nest and displays by hanging onto it, flapping his wings and singing a harsh wheezy song to attract a female. Females will only consider fresh green nests, which they then line. If a nest goes brown before he finds a mate he must build a new one.*

Left *A Pied Flycatcher* (Ficedula hypoleuca) *brings food back to its young. Males sometimes have two mates but only help with rearing one brood.*

Opposite below *A young male Royal Albatross* (Diomedea epomophora) *displays before two young females. Young unmated males display on open ground at the colony, waving wings, exaggeratedly waving the head and producing braying calls, watched by young females. This may be repeated for several seasons before pairing occurs.*

organized varies considerably but only a few have peculiarities in the pattern of actual pairings. In some, several pairs simply share and defend a single territory. A large number involve a dominant pair aided by helpers, who are often the young of earlier broods and years, though sometimes strangers may be involved.

Some are more exceptional. Australian Magpies live in groups in which a dominant male mates with up to three females and females rely on male help in feeding young. Additional males may help and try furtively to mate with the females. In the Ostrich, a dominant pair nest but additional females copulate with the male and are allowed to add eggs to the nest. The dominant pair incubate and tend the young. There are more eggs than can be brooded and the dominant female is said to recognize and favor her own eggs.

In the Tasmanian Native Hen, nesting groups are formed by two, or rarely three, related males mating with one female. In the swamphens, the brood is cared for by a group of adults that usually consists of a pair with additional subordinate males that also copulate with the female. Occasionally a second female joins the group. Something similar in terms of relationships seems to occur in the Acorn Woodpeckers.

The most confused pairings are found in the colony-nesting Noisy Miner, an Australian honeyeater. Males appear to have small overlapping territories but defend the area in larger groups, with some birds possibly dominant. Females have their own small territories in which nesting females copulate freely and frequently with any males, and in return rely on these males to feed the young.

Courtship behavior

To attract a mate, a bird (and in most cases the male, for females mainly do the choosing) must advertise his presence by songs and displays that are usually the same as those which declare his ownership of a territory. He must first of all be recognizable as a mature male of the right species. Mature plumage often differs from that of the juvenile bird and sometimes there are other seasonal changes that indicate mating potential, such as the development of wattles, the bill adornments of auks and the color changes of bill and facial skin in herons. He usually must have established claim to a territory, though sometimes a territory will be established after pairing. Sometimes the male may have to show special skills such as nest making.

If they are to pair, mate and breed the two individuals must, at least briefly, overcome their aversion to immediate proximity and many will need to spend some time in each other's company without disagreement. To do this they must signal their intentions to each other. Some of the displays used to attract and reassure a potential mate may differ little from that used to repel a rival but their message must be read quite differently. The initiative is usually

Great Crested Grebes (Podiceps
cristatus) *have a repertoire of
striking courtship displays, performed
with most intensity when a mated
pair reunites. Here both birds have
dived to gather waterweed of the type
used for nest building, swum toward
each other and rear up treading
water. Other displays include a head
shaking ceremony, face to face with
their crests raised, and a sequence in
which one bird is stationary with
wings out sideways while the other
dives and emerges with its back to it
and then comes close, or alternatively
may rise out of the water instead of
diving.*

taken by the male and, to some extent, his
exceptional reactions can be interpreted as a
conflict between the more normal aggressive
behavior and more appeasing tendencies. The
end result of this confusion is abnormal
behavior, some of which may become stylized
as a part of the typical behavior repertoire of
that species.

Our interpretation of this can be complex
and difficult. It is possible that simple behavior
components are involved. One example might
be in the positioning of the bill. Thrusting the
bill towards another individual is aggressive;
whereas withdrawing it or turning it away
removes the aggressive threat. In breeding pairs
of Black-headed Gulls standing close together,
a bird will deliberately turn the head and bill
away from the other bird, the movement now
ritualized and enhanced by the brown hood on
the head.

Lowering the bill in head bowing might be
equally significant. Bowing occurs in a number
of species and has become a ritualized display in
pigeons, where it is enhanced by color markings
and patterns on the top of the head and nape
of the neck.

The large category of birds that must pair
annually, birds found especially in cooler
climates where many species migrate, use courtship displays to persuade the female to allow
the male to mate with her, and to reconcile
each to the other's proximity and so aid them
in nest building, incubation and rearing of
young. These displays are likely to include
movements such as spreading of wings and tails
and tilting of the body, together with fluffing of
some feather tracts, all intended to enhance
color and pattern, and to display it to best
advantage. They are usually accompanied by
movements and types of songs and calls that
are not typically used in other contexts.

The often-domesticated Mallard duck seems
an unexceptional bird, but the breeding male,

trying to attract a female, suddenly changes his
usual staid habits. Even the bottle green head
will be shown off with the feathers fluffed to
make it appear black with two green stripes. A
whole group of drakes will suddenly lower their
heads, dip their bills in the water, rear the foreparts while flicking water to one side with the
bill, then lower the foreparts and at the same
time elevate the rear to show off the black and
white of curly tail and tail coverts. As they do
so they utter a musical whistle-and-grunt call
quite unlike their usual notes. The whole
appears as a solemn quadrille dance to attract
the attention of an unimpressed female.

A constant and varied series of displays
reconciles a pair to each other's presence and
the female gradually gains the confidence and
dominance that, in songbirds at least, she
appears to need before mating can be successfully achieved. The danger of the absence of
such display and recognition has been shown
when captive birds have been put together in
an aviary in spring. In enforced proximity,
without the gradual ritual of territorial advertisement and mating displays, the aggressive
male may kill the female with which he might
otherwise have paired.

The most striking displays are those given by
species where one bird (usually, but not always,
the female) nests and rears the young and the
other has only brief moments in which to
startle the partner into sexual awareness before
the short period in which copulation occurs.
The displaying bird must invest the whole
season's energy into a few brief and eccentric
moments. In such species the males, usually
with time on their hands, tend to have elaborate
display plumage and may meet with other
males to show this off competitively in display
areas called leks.

Many grouse species use such displays. In the
Black Grouse the glossy blue black males puff
scarlet eye wattles and spread the lyre-shaped
tail in an arch, exposing fluffy white undertail
coverts. Gathering on open turf at dawn they
frantically leap, flutter, fizz and coo, with
swollen necks, to persuade a visiting female to
pause long enough for mating.

Among the shorebirds the male Ruffs grow
great neck fans and crests over the eyes, individually colored and patterned. These are spread
and shown off on the display lek where frenzied
outbursts of activity alternate with silent, static
and rigid posturing.

Some birds-of-paradise display communally
in trees with loud ringing calls, sometimes
perching side by side to show off masses of
shimmering plumes and even swinging to hang
upside down to appear to better advantage to
a female perched above.

The Brown Sicklebill shows what startle-
effect can achieve. It is an exceptional-looking
brown bird-of-paradise, long-tailed, with a
scrawny neck and slender curved bill. In display it draws itself up and suddenly erects a
couple of "false wings" arching on either side
above its head like those of a symbolic angel in
a church carving. As an upright oblong object
with a long tail it opens the bill, the gape

showing as a vivid lime green lozenge, and emits a series of ear-splitting clanging notes, like a huge metal sheet struck with a hammer. Equally suddenly it reverts to its normal appearance. The effect on a human observer is considerable, when directed at a female of its own size the experience must be overwhelming.

Birds that have long pair bonds typically show mutual and more subdued courtship behavior with the least extraordinary display by the male prior to nesting. The pair will have been together for a long period and recognize each other as individuals. Display behavior shown prior to copulation tends to be subtle rather than outrageous. It may involve a slightly unusual posture with parts of the plumage accentuated, head feathers ruffled, a swaggering or unusual gait or flight, and atypical calls.

However, a more conspicuous feature of the behavior of such species is the mutual displays that help to reinforce the pair bond. Antiphonal singing, in which the notes uttered by the two birds fit together to sound like a single phrase, occurs in diverse species. There are more vigorous mutual displays, as in the neck waving and calling "triumph displays" of geese and shelducks, and the mutual trumpeting and crazy dancing of cranes.

Nesting

Birds usually build a nest after pairing has taken place, although for many, including some seabirds, colony-nesting waterbirds and various hole nesters, the displays and pair-

Black Grouse (Tetrao tetrix) *gather on an open display ground or lek, each defending a small display territory where mating occurs. This male shows the spread tail, fluffed undertail coverts and swollen head wattles that enhance its cooing and hissing displays. Grouse display is effective from every direction.*

Above left *Mandarin Ducks* (Aix galericulata) *have a simple head-dipping display, enhanced by raising the head feathers to produce bold eyebrows and crest while lowering the bill to fluff out the spiky cheek feathers. This is accompanied by sneeze-whistle calls. The movement also throws into prominence the erect, sail-like inner secondary feather on each wing and the male then tucks his bill behind one of these feathers to ensure the female notices it.*

Left *A male Great Frigatebird* (Fregata minor) *displays to a seemingly uninterested female, inflating his normally crumpled-looking throat wattle like a balloon. At the peak of the display he will flap his wings and rattle his bill against the inflated pouch.*

bonding begin on the site, the possession of which may be critical in attracting a mate. The males of a few birds, such as weavers and polygynous wrens, build at least the outer nest structure first and offer this as an incentive to the female.

Most nests seem primarily designed to help keep the eggs warm when they are laid, though they may have other functions and sometimes, as in the Australian babblers and some arid-country munia, similar but quite separate sleeping nests are built, whereas woodpeckers may make holes in which to roost.

A nest may be just a layer under eggs to insulate them from cold or wet ground, or a cup that fits around the sitting bird, retaining the heat it generates and hiding the eggs from view, or it may enclose bird and eggs entirely, insulating and concealing them. Holes in the ground and in rocks or trees may serve a similar purpose to the enclosed nests. Nests raised above the ground help to conceal eggs and sitting bird from passing predators and make it possible to nest in areas that are unsuitable at ground level.

Nest structures range from the simple to the very complex but that should not be taken to indicate that one kind developed from another. There is no ideal nest; each has evolved to suit the life cycle of the species that makes it.

Nest evolution must have been very varied, occurring in different ways in different places, though often resulting in superficially similar structures. The similarities are due, in part, to the limited facilities birds have to help their nest building: a bill that can seize, hold and thrust and, in some species, feet that may be used to hold material. In general only a few basic movements are used to create the variety of nest forms.

A very few species appear to make no nest, and lay their eggs on bare, open sites. Most such species, however, appear to have originated from ancestral groups that do make nests and, even when no nesting material is apparent, the bird may make movements suggesting the nest-building repertoire of its evolutionary past. For instance, a sitting Ostrich on its bare scrape may pick up a pinch of sand and place it carefully to one side or the other with a sweep of its head, whereas a guillemot, brooding its single egg on a bare rock ledge, may carefully sift or place one or two tiny rock fragments.

Making the nest

On a bare site, where no real nest is visible, a bird will usually make a "scrape." The standing bird lowers its breast to the ground and by pushing a little with its feet and rotating its body it makes a small hollow. If nothing else is added the hollow will ensure that eggs do not roll away, but a scrape is often the first stage of a more substantial structure on the ground.

A nest is usually a fixed spot but nightjars, which mostly nest on dead litter under trees, make no formal nest and rely on camouflaging plumage for concealment. They usually have only one or two eggs and, if necessary, can shuffle brooded eggs or young for a short distance.

Small sketchy nests, like those of shorebirds, often on open sites, are assembled by two simple movements in "sideways building." The birds walk away from their chosen site picking up small items — stems, stones or shell fragments — and throw these behind them with a sideways movement of the head. Thus a mass of small items gradually moves back towards the nest hollow. A bird sitting on the nest site picks up objects within reach and places them to one side or the other around itself so that this pulled-in material gradually forms a small pad or platform, sometimes with a raised edge. Such nests will vary according to what is available nearby. Plovers and terns nesting on a bare beach may have a scrape that is empty or with just a few stones or shells or, if plants grow nearby, they may create a sizeable shallow nest cup. The groups and species that may use such methods include most shearwaters, gamebirds and waterfowl. Waterfowl also pluck the downy layer of their underside, to form their brood patch and line the nest hollow with down, which makes a warm insulating layer for the eggs.

Birds that, unlike those already described, carry nest material, can build a more substantial nest on any site. The selection and transport of material provides the potential for the evolution of complex nest structures, though the nest will vary considerably according to what material is available or chosen. Waterbirds may snatch up floating debris and often limp weed, resulting in the shapeless mound with a hollow top that is the typical nest of birds such as noddy terns, gannets and cormorants. Grebes' nests are similar but may be floating in shallow water or loosely anchored in growing plants.

The collection of firmer material offers better opportunities for construction. Stems, twigs or sticks form the basis of nests for a great many bird species. Not just any twig will do: it should not be rotten or too brittle. Birds seem to select a stick or stem that offers some resistance when pulled from a growing plant, bush or tree. Those on the ground are mostly ignored and twigs that fall may not be retrieved. Where vines or climbing stems are used, those selected are again the ones that need some tugging before they yield.

Stems and twigs are not just piled onto nest sites. Another widespread building movement now comes into play. The lateral movement of the head is used, together with a rapid quivering or shaking movement of the bill, as the bird tries to push a twig end into the material already present. This helps entangle and incorporate the new twig. The sitting bird will seize any projecting ends and try to tuck them into the nest, gradually consolidating and strengthening the structure.

Some twig nests, such as those made by pigeons, herons and ibises, are barely more than raised platforms with little specialized structure. More solid nests are built by birds of prey and storks who also add a scanty lining of

1. *An Australian Gannet (Morus serrator) carries back material found floating to add to the nest mound. Many birds collect material and carry it to the nest site.*

2. *Fairy Terns (Gygis alba) use tiny raised sites for their single egg, sometimes balancing it on a rock pinnacle or tree branch. The small site these two are investigating will probably be used for such a nest.*

3. *A Variable Oystercatcher (Haematopus unicolor) nest illustrates how shorebirds will use a scrape with no nest material. The footprints are made by birds walking away from the nest. As they do so they will pick up a fragment of nest material and flick it back towards the scrape, gradually assembling enough for a lining.*

4. *With the "throw-back" method of nest building any local objects are used and this New Zealand Dotterel (Charadrius obscurus) has assembled a mass of seashell fragments.*

5. *Nest building can be a cooperative affair and this Common Coot (Fulica atra) brings a stick to be incorporated by its sitting mate.*

finer softer material, changing the texture of what they collect as the nest nears completion. Birds of prey may also bring leafy twigs to add to the lining during the nesting period. Larger songbirds, such as crows, still use a large twiggy base but make more typical cup-shaped nests.

Large nests represent a considerable investment of time and energy and, since they may be solid and weather-resistant, may be reused in later years. They may need a new lining, but both storks and such birds as eagles, buzzards and Ospreys go on adding to the structure year by year to produce great twiggy masses. Small songbirds — weavers, sparrows and starlings, for instance — sometimes see the sides of these large nests as convenient sites into which they build their own nests. They are usually tolerated by the larger birds, whom they nevertheless may try to attack as though they were a threat. Falcons and owls, species that do not build nests, may also take advantage of a large well-constructed nest if an old one becomes available, seeing it as a ready-made alternative to the cavity or sheltered ledge they usually use.

Nest building

Nest building is too important to be left to learning. This behavior is inherited. The bird instinctively recognizes what material to use and how to collect it, rejecting material that does not pass tests to ensure that it not only looks right but will fulfill its purpose.

Twigs on the ground may be rotten, so crows tear twigs off trees. If one falls it may become a "twig on the ground" and be left there. The ground under rookeries is sometimes carpeted with dropped twigs.

A pigeon builds a platform of stiff twigs. This is tested each time a bird brings a fresh twig for incorporation, for it lands on the back of its sitting mate, ensuring the structure will bear the weight of at least two adults. Pigeons collect twigs from the ground, but

selectively: grasped near the middle, tested for thickness, each twig is raised above the head. If rigid enough to be lifted and light enough to carry it is taken to the nest.

A pair of Laughingthrushes, nest building in an aviary, needed strong thin stems that could be wrapped around supports and fine rootlets for nest lining. Dead stems of bindweed were offered, but were only accepted when hung so that one or two strong pulls were needed to detach them. Having passed this test they were used to build a cup bound to upright supporting twigs. Rootlets are thin, wiry, probably white and attached at one end. For a substitute coarse string was offered, cut in short lengths, unraveled and tied so that a pull was needed to free each piece. The birds accepted this as suitable, added an inner lining and laid eggs in the nest.

Cup nests

The cup nest is always regarded as most typical. It may have a rigid twig base but the important part is an inner cup of more pliant material, shaped around the body of the sitting bird. Material carried to the nest is tucked into place but the important work is done by the bird squatting in the nest, turning as it works tucking ends in and compressing the material to mold a cup around itself. As it shapes and builds it brings in finer material and some cup nests may use plant fibers, hair, feathers and plant down, the coarsest items on the outside, the finest to the center. The nest rim is formed by pressure from the bird's chin and downward-flexed tail. In theory, nests made like this would be a tight fit for bird and eggs but the bird's movements usually involve a forward pressure of the breast and backward thrusting of the legs similar to those used in making a scrape. This enlarges the inner cup sufficiently to accommodate the eggs or young under the sitting bird.

Where nests are built in growing vegetation or among branches they do not need to rest upon supports but can be supported at the sides. Where this occurs a bird can take a strip of nest material, push it around or over the support, seize the end and tuck it back into the nest structure. For cup nests, outer strands or stems can be wrapped around upright stems or twigs to hold the nest. The Reed Warbler's cup nest is bound between upright reed stems and rises as the reeds grow.

Thick insulated cups are valuable for birds nesting in temperate or cold climates, but for tropical species they are often much more sketchy structures, through which daylight may be seen. Materials vary with the size and weight of the building birds. Some small birds of tropical rainforests use fine black, fiber-like hyphae of fungi. Spiders' webs are useful too; they are strong, elastic and adhesive. In temperate climates webs are mostly small and used mainly to bind fragments of moss and lichen to form nests by Chaffinches, Goldcrests, Firecrests, Long-tailed Tits and some parulid warblers and small tyrants of America. In tropical areas webs tend to be stronger and used more extensively, often to form tight cups

Above *A European Spoonbill* (Platalea leucorodia) *returning with a stick, finds it difficult to incorporate it into the nest. For larger birds nesting together on a restricted site, the return of a mate with a gift of nest material is an important and ritualized event.*

A small colony of Bank Cormorants (Phalacrocorax neglectus) *nest on a rock, utilizing the seaweed available. At least one bird must attend each nest to ward off marauding gulls.*

1

3

2

4

1. *Hair and similar fine fibers are valued by birds for nest linings. Usually they are collected from bushes or fences, but this Jungle Crow* (Corvus macrorhynchos) *tugs a tuft from the base of a horse's mane.*

2. *Temminck's Horned Lark* (Eremophila bilopha), *like most larks, excavates a small hollow in the shelter of a plant tuft or stone and then adds a normal nest lining.*

3. *The tiny cup of the nest of an Emerald Hummingbird* (Amazilia *species) of Colombia, only about 1.2 inches (3 cm) across, is bound to the supporting twig with spiders' webs and made of soft fibers bound with spiders' webs with fine flakes of bark stuck to the outside.*

4. *A Yellowhammer* (Emberiza citrinella) *nest, tucked down in the herbage, presents the more solid cup built by temperate climate songbirds.*

Above right *House-Martins* (Delichon urbica) *from a small colony collect mouthfuls of mud mixed with a few bits of plants for fiber and use these to gradually build up the walls of a nest stuck to a wall under an overhang.*

Below right *A North American Dipper* (Cinclus mexicanus) *clings to the rock just below its nest entrance. Dippers build domed nests with downward-tilted entrances on supports or ledges overhanging water so that the bird can enter or leave over the water but predators will be deterred.*

and to bind them to supports, as with the nests of monarchs and fantailed flycatchers and larger birds such as cuckoo-shrikes. These webs may be spread or smeared over the outside of the nest. Flakes of lichen or moss, like those on nearby twigs, can be stuck on to aid camouflage. The Australian Sittella's cup nest, fitted into a fork, may be so finely coated with bark flakes that it appears a continuation of the branch.

A coarser nest material, which birds as diverse as White Storks and crows may incorporate to strengthen a nest, is mud. Some European thrushes use a layer of mud in the thickness of the nest and the Song Thrush uses it to line the cup. Mud will stick to a rough surface and can be used to form a cup on rocks where an overhang will keep out rain that might destroy it, the structure being built up with plant fibers mixed in as strengthening. Some swallows and martins will stick cup nests on house walls sheltered by eaves. Similar, but bigger, cups are used by Rockfowl in West African forests and by cocks-of-the-rock in South America. Where the breeding season is reliably dry, mud may be used in open sites. In Australia the Magpielark, Apostlebird and White-winged Chough all build fine bowl-shaped mud nests on horizontal branches.

Domed nests

The simple type of domed nest, resting upon a twig or other support, is an extension of the cup nest. The bird builds up and over itself, the size of the cavity relating to the size of the bird, though it must use longer strands of material to form an outer shell enclosing a finer cup. Most domed nests hide the sitting bird, but the Common Magpie builds a large dome of open, loose sticks to deter predators. Some species extend the entrance as a short horizontal tube, among them the American Cactus Wrens and some Australian greenfinches. The thrush-sized ovenbirds of South America build domed nests of clay that bakes hard in the sun. They are exposed on open, raised sites but with an entrance passage that curves around the nest.

Most domed nests are built by the smaller songbirds but the African Hamerkop, which is like a small stork, also builds one, usually in a big tree. It is about 5 feet (1.5 m) across with an upward-sloping entrance passage.

Suspended nests

Nests can hang from vertical or horizontal supports. Cup nests are most frequently slung like hammocks between horizontal twigs, bound to them with plant fibers, bark strips, wool and similar materials. The Old World orioles and many small species suspend nests in this way.

More obviously hanging are nests suspended from a single support such as a twig tip. They are difficult for predators to reach but demand ingenuity in their construction. They are usually begun by making a hanging loop, big enough

for the bird to perch in, from which the nest is extended, often with the initial ring as entrance.

Among the troupials, the American orioles include species that build bag-like nests with several points of attachment, whereas others are elongated into pear-shaped bags up to 2 feet (60 cm) long. Within the same group the bigger caciques and oropendolas build very long, sleeve-like bag nests with a small loop entrance at the top. They may be suspended up to 5 feet (1.5 m) hanging in colonies from the higher branches of trees.

This Masked Weaver (Ploceus velatus) *has built two nests for different females. He is working on the earliest stage of a third, making a hanging ring of material within which he clings, building a nest chamber out of one side of it and the entrance on the other.*

Right *The hanging nests of the Lesser Masked Weaver (Ploceus intermedius) are built like those of the Masked Weaver. The long pendent attachment to a slender reed and the longer entrance tube on a nest that overhangs water give greater defense against predation.*

The haystack-like mess of a group of Sociable Weaver (Philetairus socius) nests, their entrances on the underside. The pairs build domed nests, one against the other, then thatch the whole lot over as a great solid mass.

Tiny, bag-like hanging nests are also made by sunbirds and other small songbirds but, in the Old World, the primary builders of pendent nests are the weavers, most of whom nest in colonies. They build out from the ring using fine strips of grasses or fibers that are intricately knotted and woven to produce a tautly-constructed nest that is strong and springy. Some simply have a rounded nest chamber built out on one side with the entrance at the loop but others also build on the other side to form a downward-pointing entrance tube that varies between species: in the Asian Baya Weaver it may be nearly 39 inches (1 m) long.

Penduline tits and kapokbirds build similar hanging nests with a round nest chamber and downward-pointing entrance tube, but made of plant down and fluffy seeds amazingly felted together by rapid bill movements into a solid material.

Cavity nesting

Using a natural cavity seems an easy way of gaining an enclosed nest, but tree cavities are in short supply. Barbets and woodpeckers solve the problem by hacking their own holes, which may subsequently be used by a range of other species from starlings and bluebirds to owls, parrots and ducks. Songbirds apart, many of these hole-nesting species make no nest and add no lining.

Various species enlarge holes to a suitable size, parrots and even some trogons biting wood away. Only the nest liners reduce cavity size but nuthatches may also plaster mud to reduce the entrance to suit their size. The female hornbill, sometimes helped by the male, uses droppings and debris to reduce the entrance to a slit through which the male can pass food while she settles down to incubate and rear young while shut in.

Birds also make use of holes in the ground or in banks or cliffs. Ready-made cavities may be found where there are rocks and stones but ground hole nesters must make their own burrows, although the small American Burrowing Owls will take over holes of other animals. Where to burrow will depend on habitat: most kingfishers burrow into banks but they also use termite mounds, and forest species may burrow into tree-termite nests.

Non-nesting birds

Some birds dispense with nests. The White Tern precariously balances a single egg on the tiny support of a twig, ledge or rock pinnacle and the first need of the little hatchling is to cling on tightly to the site. The Emperor and King Penguins balance the single egg on the feet protected by a feathered flap of the lower belly and protect small young in the same way.

The megapodes dispense with personal incubation completely. They provide the warmth needed by burying the eggs in warm sand or rotting vegetation. The male Brush Turkey scratches up a huge mound of decaying leaves in which the female buries her eggs. The Mallee Fowl gathers rotting vegetation in an earth mound that the male tends all the time, testing temperature and modifying the mound structure accordingly. With these birds the eggs hatch underground, unattended, and the young must dig themselves out and fend for themselves.

The specialized swifts

Swifts, who are unable to use their legs for more than clinging and short shuffles, make some very specialized nests that employ a copious glue-like saliva. Common Swifts seize feathers and fragments blowing in the air and use their saliva to glue them to the floor of the nest hole or ledge. Palm Swifts glue a scanty nest — and two eggs — to a hanging palm leaf. Cave Swiftlets produce strands of saliva that quickly harden and use them with moss to make shallow cups stuck to rock, whereas the Edible-nest Swiftlet makes cups of pure coagulated and solidified saliva strands.

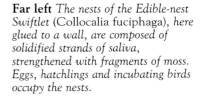

Above *Suitable vertical surfaces for tunneling are always in short supply. By nesting colonially Sand-Martins* (Riparia riparia) *have taken advantage of a weak layer in a quarry to make a row of nest burrows.*

Left *The Gila Woodpecker* (Melanerpes uropygialis) *treats a Saguaro cactus as a tree, pecking out a nest hole in the sappy interior. This must then dry out and scar tissue form before the hole can be used.*

Far left *The nests of the Edible-nest Swiftlet* (Collocalia fuciphaga), *here glued to a wall, are composed of solidified strands of saliva, strengthened with fragments of moss. Eggs, hatchlings and incubating birds occupy the nests.*

A pair of Malleefowl (Leipoa ocellata) *cooperate in closing up the mound in which they bury their eggs to incubate. The male builds up the large mound by burying plant material and then opens it out or closes it up according to its inner temperature, which it tests with the mouth.*

Following pages *Ceylon Green Bee-eater* (Merops orientalis) *pairs dig a tunnel by loosening material with the bill and kicking it behind them. Up to 10 feet (3 m) long, it ends in a nest chamber. These well-grown young have moved up the tunnel to meet a food-bearing parent. Such burrows can be foul with insect remains and droppings: perhaps it is to keep them clean that chicks' feathers stay sheathed until the bird is almost ready to leave.*

Courtship feeding

When the hen bird is involved in nest building as well as in egg production she not only reduces her feeding time but needs more energy. Feeding by the male then fulfills not just a ritual role and indication that the male will be able to feed her on the nest but is a practical help at this stage of the cycle.

A female, seeing a male with food, may crouch, shiver her wings, open her bill and make calls similar to those of a hungry young bird. The male responds by feeding her.

Before egg laying, a Blue Tit may receive 40 percent of her food from her mate. In birds of prey, the female may cease hunting and rely on the male for food both prior to egg laying and throughout the nesting period until she begins to help hunt food for the young.

A male Kokako (Callaeas cinerea) brings food to his mate as part of his courtship.

Great Crested Grebes (Podiceps cristatus) copulating on a partly-built nest site. The nest is usually a pile of water plants, partly or wholly floating in shallow water among emergent vegetation.

The mating

Copulation is a more awkward activity for birds than it is for humans and other mammals because most birds lack a penis. Some bird groups do have a penislike projection: the ducks, geese, swans, coracid gamebirds and Ostriches, but these are species that mate while in the water or on the ground.

The birds that lack a penis must bring their cloaca into direct contact. In both birds the feathers around the cloaca are turned back to expose it and its lips everted so that the opening of the male's *vas deferentia*, the tubes that carry his sperm from the testes, is placed directly against the mouth of the oviduct of the female.

To achieve this contact and transfer his semen, the male must mount his mate and, while balancing on her back, bend the rear end of his body over and around until the cloaca come together. The female must keep very steady if this is to be possible and both birds twist their tails sideways to keep them out of the way. This is a little easier if copulation takes place when the female is on the ground, though it still looks precarious. On a tree branch it is even more tricky to accomplish, though the female may lie with her breast against the branch to increase stability. Swifts manage to copulate in the air.

Copulation between a pair usually takes place many times, most frequently in the day or two before the first egg of a clutch is laid, to ensure that it has been successful.

The spermatozoa, once in the female, must move up the oviduct, because fertilization of the germinal cell on the surface of the developed ovaries must occur before the egg develops further. As females may produce fertile eggs after being apart from a male for some days, there must be some retention of the sperm.

Birds lay their eggs one at a time, usually at daily intervals, although in the larger species the intervals may be longer; in the Golden Eagle two eggs are laid three to four days apart. Most small species lay in the morning. This allows the latter stages in the egg's development, when it will be most heavy, to take place overnight and the hen does not have to carry a nearly fully formed egg around with her during the day. By the time that one egg is laid the next is fertilized and begins its development.

The egg

The egg is an effective way of overcoming the problem of what to do with an embryo or off-spring to ensure it does not interfere with flight mobility. It is left in relative safety in the nest while the female is on the move and does not have the extra weight to carry. However, she is still encumbered by having to carry a single egg just before laying, and also the possible additional weight of the enlarging yolks of eggs that will later be added to a clutch. The advantage is so obvious that it would seem to have been an ideal adaptation, but the bird did not have to evolve it; the reptiles from which the birds developed already laid eggs.

The eggs of aquatic or partly-aquatic animals such as fish and amphibians are mostly simple structures: a cell-like mass with a jelly-like cover but, for land-living reptiles, a more elaborate structure was needed. Their eggs include a food mass, the yolk, to nourish the growing embryo and the whole is protected by an outer coating, sometimes leathery, but with hard eggshells coming into being quite early on in reptile evolution.

There is no very early fossil evidence regarding eggs, but it is possible that birds inherited their capacity for shelled-egg production directly from reptiles and retained it because it fitted their evolving life types.

There is evidence of some degree of parental care in various reptile species. It is not known how early such behavior occurred but it is suspected that dinosaurs tended nests of eggs and brought food to their young. In such circum-

Making the egg

The yolk with its germinal cell, held in a fine vitelline membrane, passes from the ovary into a large funnel at the end of the oviduct, most of which is a thin-walled tube that enlarges for the breeding period but must still stretch to twice its diameter to accommodate the yolk. In the first 20 minutes the egg passes through 10 percent of the oviduct length but nothing significant occurs. In the next 60 percent, over a period of about three hours, the albumen (white of the egg) is added in several layers. First is a thin fibrous layer which forms strands that extend to each end of the developing egg as twisted bands, the chazalae, helping the yolk to maintain a position in the middle of the egg. Then come a layer of liquid albumen in which the yolk floats, a more extensive tougher layer that cushions it if it is displaced and another more liquid outer layer.

The egg slows down in the next, narrower 15 percent of the oviduct, remaining in it for about 70 minutes. Here two fine shell membranes are deposited around it, one tight and one loose. The egg spends about 19 hours in the next 15 percent where it first absorbs a watery solution and swells to the limits of the membranes, creating a firm outer surface on which the shell is gradually built up before passing into the last short section for laying.

The simple-looking thin layer of eggshell is actually complex, differing in some aspects from one group of birds to another but composed of a crystalline calcite structure incorporating a network of protein fibers. The main crystals are arranged radially, like the stones in an arch and, like them, imparting enormous strength against pressure from outside but vulnerable to damage from inside, which helps the relatively weak young to escape at hatching.

The shell is penetrated by a mass of tiny pores through which gases pass enabling the embryo to obtain oxygen from outside and to rid itself of carbon dioxide. After the egg is laid the contents cool and shrink a little, pulling the two shell membranes apart at the larger end of the egg. Since the outer shell is rigid, an air pocket forms inside the shell, allowing the young bird, when fully developed, to breathe air before it finally breaks free.

The egg is pushed through by muscular contractions of the oviduct and the pressure on the soft egg gives the front end a more pointed shape. Once the shell is added this shape is fixed. A weakness of the wall near the end of the oviduct causes the egg to catch and allows it to turn to pass out at laying with the larger blunt end foremost.

The egg is a complete structure, containing all that is necessary to produce the baby bird, which to function needs one thing only — a constant supply of warmth to trigger off the division and growth of the germinal cell. In most birds this is provided by the body of the parent bird during a prolonged period of incubation, although this conflicts with the day-to-day function of the plumage of preventing undue loss of heat.

1. Germinal cell
2. Vitelline membrane
3. Yolk (in concentric yellow and white layers)
4. Shell
5. Chalaza
6. Inner shell membrane
7. Outer shell membrane
8. Air-space
9. Liquid or fluid albumen
10. Dense albumen

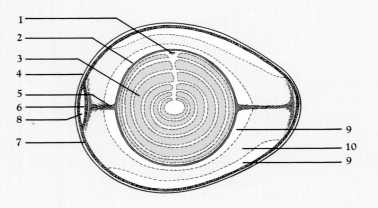

stances it is possible that birds may have inherited not only the ability to produce eggs but also a tendency to evolve patterns of parental care.

Whereas insects, amphibians and some reptiles lay many eggs, birds show an evolutionary trend to expend less energy in egg production and to invest more in brooding and rearing young. Some species, usually small birds such as the wrens and Long-tailed Tit, lay large clutches, and some populations of Gray Partridge have about 19 eggs, whereas those with smaller clutches may have several during a single season. Others produce only a single egg: the Emperor and Adelie Penguins and the albatrosses, for instance, who then devote many months to incubation and raising their single chick. This development reaches its ultimate in modern birds in the Wandering Albatross, which lays one egg every two years. This species, which lays the largest egg in this group, devotes 11 weeks to hatching it and the chick spends a further ten months in the nest before it flies.

The egg of a bird consists of a minute fertilized germinal cell that will grow to form the young bird, the food source that will nourish it and the protection around these vital parts. It must be built up within the breeding bird, layer upon layer, mainly as the egg passes down the oviduct. After laying, its development continues, requiring constant warmth. This is usually provided by the body of the parent bird brooding the eggs. A few species are exceptions, such as the megapodes, the Australasian group of gamebirds that bury their eggs in warm sand or rotting vegetable material to provide the necessary heat.

Egg form and color

The typical shape of eggs, a little larger towards one end, appears to be the result of accidental shaping and compression as it passes down the oviduct during formation. In some species the eggs are almost spherical. Rounded eggs tend to be laid by hole nesters, such as rollers, kingfishers or owls, where it could be argued that there is no danger of rolling, or by the ground-nesting Ostrich, but they are also found in the arboreal twig cups of turacos. The size of the oviduct may limit the girth of the egg, tending to make larger eggs longer. Although the Ostrich egg is the largest in dimensions, relative to the size of the bird itself it is small compared with a Goldcrest's or white-eye's egg. Eggs with more contents may need to be longer and thicker with round blunt ends. Such eggs are laid by megapodes who must provide for a fully-formed and well-developed chick, but also by swifts and hummingbirds.

More pear-shaped tapering eggs are found in shorebirds. It has been suggested that such eggs may be larger in order to lose heat more slowly if uncovered and that the shape allows up to four to fit together and be just covered by the brooding bird. The large tapering egg of the Guillemot is usually instanced, somewhat

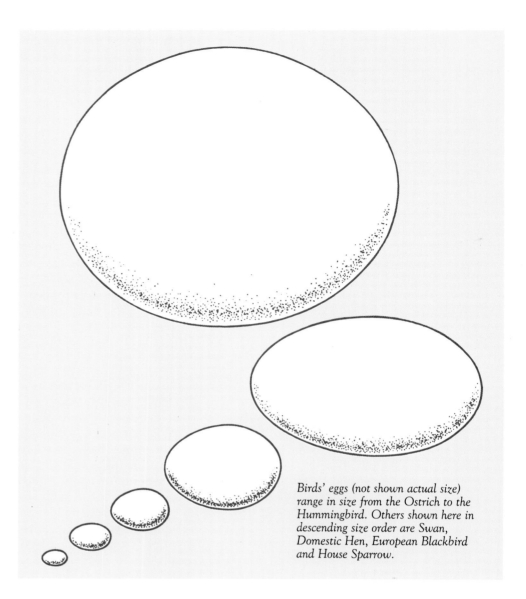

Birds' eggs (not shown actual size) range in size from the Ostrich to the Hummingbird. Others shown here in descending size order are Swan, Domestic Hen, European Blackbird and House Sparrow.

doubtfully, as a design that will spin rather than roll on a narrow ledge. It is also a large egg laid by a narrow-bodied bird and may be the ideal shape for incubation in a semi-upright posture without a nest.

The color of eggs is linked with where they normally occur. Eggs are usually a basic white or blue in color, coated and/or patterned with reddish or brownish pigments that turn them

Below An Xray shows the body space occupied by a fully-formed egg of the Brown Kiwi (Apteryx australis). Only a sedentary flightless bird could accommodate and produce an egg of this size, up to a quarter of the female's body weight. Two of these huge eggs may be laid in the type of tunnel kiwis excavate for roosting as well as nesting.

pinkish, buff or olive, with the markings reddish, brown or black. Only a few eggs have a yellow pigment that turns them really green.

Eggs incubated in cavities or those of larger birds that cover them most of the time are usually white. Birds that have evolved from nesters in more open sites to nest in holes have eggs pale blue or buff, or white with fine speckling, suggesting that stronger patterns and colors are being lost. Whiteness is thought to help a bird to see its eggs in a dark cavity. A dark egg might be overlooked, and this may explain the dark olive eggs of some small glossy cuckoos that lay an egg into a domed nest with whitish eggs.

The frequency of plain or spotted blue eggs in the cup nests of tree-nesting birds seems to suggest that such colors are less visible to other birds than they are to us. Because it is known that occasional individuals produce abnormally colored or patterned eggs, and that these are more conspicuous and tend to be lost to predators, resulting in a perpetuation of the more standard type, it may be assumed that the color and pattern of the typical egg aid its survival. The pattern and color of many eggs appear designed for camouflage. Pattern may be spots of dark color, or these may be elongated into streaks and scrawls. In the spotted eggs of plovers, terns and gulls it is possible to see how the color and pattern are likely to make the egg difficult to see against the right background.

In some this is less obvious. Most jacanas' eggs are highly polished and bronze-colored with heavy black scribbling all over them, not immediately suggesting camouflage. The plain buffs and browns of some gamebird eggs appear linked with nesting in grass and similar vegetation. It is difficult to explain the surprisingly glossy eggs of tinamous that nest in similar situations. These may be pink, buff, purple, gunmetal gray or vivid green according to species. They do not seem to be cryptic and it can only be assumed that the dull-colored parent birds keep them covered. Although the *Turdoides* babblers lay the plain blue type of egg in their cup nest, in one area of Africa the eggs are pale strawberry pink or purple and still appear to survive. In fact the local *Clamator* cuckoos lay eggs that mimic them.

One egg variation that can be more easily explained is the large range of individual differences in color and patterning in some species. In birds with open nest sites such as Guillemots and Crested Terns it appears to be a means of allowing the bird to identify its own eggs. The highly varied egg clutches of some weavers with closed nests, where camouflage is not needed, appears to help baffle the small cuckoos that parasitize them. These can only produce one version each and may find their eggs rejected in the nests where they do not match the rest.

Incubation

To be warmed, the eggs must be brought close against the body. A bird can do this, to some extent, by fluffing out its feathers, but in most species the females, and in some the males too, have areas of the underside on which feathers are lost during the breeding season leaving bare patches. Known as brood patches, they have more blood vessels near the surface that

Jacanas walk and nest on water plants. This Lotusbird (Irediparra gallinacea) broods its typical scribbled eggs in a sketchy nest on floating leaves.

increases the heat available. The way in which birds settle on the eggs so that these brood patches warm them can best be seen in shorebirds and others that make little or no nest. The crouching bird fluffs the belly feathers and with a characteristic shuffle and wriggle eases the eggs into position against the brood patch, settling so that there is a draft-excluding wall of feathers all around the eggs. Some species have two or three brood patches to match the number of eggs in a clutch. Gannets and cormorants lack any. They settle with their webbed feet spread against their eggs; the feet of waterbirds usually lose little warmth but, in this case, it would seem that they help with incubation.

The body temperature of a bird is usually much higher than our own, about 105–108.5°F (40.5–42.5°C). In a nest where incubation is in progress egg temperature may be around 95°F (35°C) or a little higher, cooling if brooding stops; and the egg may experience temperature variation of 39–40°F (4–4.5°C). The embryo is in danger if temperatures are too high or too low and development may temporarily cease if they fall below about 81.5°F (27.5°C). In the early part of the incubation period eggs can withstand cooling but, as the embryo develops, periods of chilling are increasingly likely to kill it.

Development within the egg

Given warmth, the embryo develops rapidly on the upper yolk surface from a rapidly dividing and developing germinal cell mass on the first day to a minute tadpole-like embryo on the third day with a tiny heart surrounded by a network of blood vessels bringing food material.

The embryo needs protection and space to grow. It must absorb food and be able to get rid of wastes. This is achieved by three membranous sacs that fill the spaces left in the egg as food material is absorbed. One, the amnion, surrounds the embryo and is filled with fluid in which the body floats. A second, the chorion, surrounds the empty spaces, lining the inner wall of the shell and gradually surrounding the yolk sac. It has a layer of blood vessels that absorb the yolk and pass it by a narrow canal, the yolk stalk, through the amnion and into the intestine of the embryo. Waste passes from the embryo's hind gut into another sac, the allantois, which spreads around the chorion, just inside the shell, as the waste increases.

During the first part of incubation, water from the albumen is absorbed into the yolk. The shrinking remaining albumen, increasingly pushed to one side by the spreading sacs, gradually passes through a small channel, the sero-amniotic connection, into the fluid surrounding the now rapidly-forming bird within the amnion, is taken in by the embryo and digested.

Some of the calcium on the inside of the shell is also absorbed via the sac membranes and blood vessels and is passed to the growing chick to help form the skeleton. This makes the shell thinner and more liable to yield at hatching.

During incubation, brooding birds occasionally "turn" the eggs, though more accurately described as "stirring" them. In the early stages of incubation this may cause the eggs to rotate and, since the yolk floats with the germinal cell uppermost it will stay, tightening the twisted bands of fibers and ensuring that it remains at the center of the egg. Later, as the embryo develops, the weight will become one-sided and the egg will come to rest with the heaviest part at the bottom, the correct position for the hatchling young to rest.

When it has reached the hatching stage, the young bird will occupy most of the space within the shell, usually lying on its back with the head forward and turned under the right wing. The remnants of the yolk sac, resting on the belly, are the last relic of development and are drawn into the body for absorption. In most of its initial movements the baby bird can only stir slightly, with only the head and bill able to shift significantly. The bill breaks through the membrane to the air space and the bird begins to breathe air.

Hatching

The development within the egg is related to how soon the young will leave the nest, but in all types some days before hatching it may be complete and the chick begin to breathe. At this stage the bird is vocally and aurally in touch with the outer world. It may call while in the egg and can hear and respond to the calls of the parents, who may in turn react to the sound of the young bird in the egg. In some birds — gamebirds for example — chicks within eggs seem to communicate with other unhatched eggs at this stage. The sounds appear to help to synchronize the hatching and shorten the period during which a clutch of eggs produces chicks. This can be useful for species that have downy young that are led away from the nest within hours of hatching.

Curled up in the egg, the bird's main movement is confined to shifting the head and lifting the bill in its restricted position between the folded right leg and right wing. This lifting movement brings the bill tip up against the inside of the shell with sufficient force to raise a tiny bump on the outside. At this time many hatchlings have a small blunt prominence on the tip of the bill. Called an egg tooth, this little horny lump increases the efficiency of the bill tip in piercing the shell. It drops off soon after the hatching.

With repeated bill-raising, the tip breaks through the shell and, as the hatchling struggles to bring its head to a more natural position, it creates a break extending from right to left of

the bird and towards the larger end of the egg. The convulsive movements of the young bird as it tries to straighten its posture finally results in the egg breaking open. Hatching of this type can be seen in shorebirds.

In some other groups of birds the head-raising, combined with other attempts at movement, cause the hatchling to gradually turn inside the egg, shifting towards the bird's right-hand side. The resulting row of tiny breaks caused by the lifting bill move around the egg and sometimes virtually cut the shell in two, facilitating rapid emergence.

Effort is not continuous. The young bird may rest at intervals and the total time taken to emerge may vary from possibly a matter of minutes in small songbirds to several days in some species.

A Black Swan (Cygnus atratus) turns the eggs in the nest. By doing this incubating birds prevent their contents sticking to the sides in the early stages and later it ensures that the young are in the right position for hatching.

A Lesser Black-backed Gull (Larus fuscus) chick is breaking out of the egg by shifting slightly and raising the bill. The "egg tooth" on the top of the bill helps it to break out.

THE NESTLING

With the final breaking of the shell, the baby bird emerges. The eggshell has served its purpose. The adults may break it and eat fragments, replacing minerals lost in egg laying in the case of the female, and perhaps preparing for a later brood. Broken shell is conspicuous and might be noticed by a predator, and adults will lift it and carry it a short way before dropping it. Only birds like gamebirds or waders, ready to desert the site as soon as the down on the young is dry, are likely to ignore it.

The young birds are of two main types, different in appearance. One, familiar from the songbirds, is helpless, mainly naked and blind and wholly reliant on the adult — the altricial or nidicolous nestling. The other is downy, with its eyes open, able to stand, if a little unsteadily, and ready for almost instant activity after a short interval to rest from breaking out of the shell and to allow the down to fluff out.

This is the precocial or nidifugous (=nest-fleeing) nestling. These are convenient descriptions but perhaps a little too broad: there are really four basic categories of young, with subdivisions.

Altricial birds are hatched with eyes closed, a little down and confined to the nest. They embrace a wide range of birds including songbirds. **Semialtricial** birds are down covered but remain in the nest. Some, owls for instance, have eyes closed at first. Others have eyes open and include tubenose seabirds, herons, storks, ibises and birds of prey.

Semiprecocial birds have eyes open and are down covered and, although able to walk, stay near the nest. They include flamingos, gulls, terns, auks and nightjars. **Precocial** birds have eyes open and are down covered and leave the nest almost immediately, or within a few days, and with a very few exceptions normally follow the parents, sometimes until fledging. They include divers (loons), grebes, cranes, rails, bustards and some shorebirds. The majority

As one chick hatches and another begins breaking the eggshell, an Avocet (Recurvirostra avosetta) prepares to remove the first eggshell to avoid making the nest more conspicuous.

In the nest of a Ring-necked Pheasant (Phasianus colchicus) the first-hatching nestlings of its large clutch, some still damp, are ready to run when disturbed, although others are still hatching. No effort is made to remove eggshells from a nest that will soon be deserted.

find their own food, including most of the waterfowl and shorebirds. Others rely on parents to show them food and include game-birds and some plovers.

Altricial young

These helpless young birds, with small legs and wings and a big belly, cannot control their temperature and huddle together, relying on brooding by parents and the construction of the nest to keep them warm. Songbird young may have little or no down, or some on back and head — the parts exposed — or with larks in more open nests a denser growth of down seems to cover the brood. Swifts may be bare or downy. Pigeons have a coarse hairy down. The larger hole nesters such as rollers, king-fishers and woodpeckers have naked young, and those in holes in trees often have a callus pad on the leg joint on which to rest. Pelicans' and cormorants' young are hatched blind and

Left Kingfisher nests become foul with droppings, regurgitated fish bones and insect parts. Although the young Sacred Kingfisher (Todirhamphus sanctus) comes to the burrow entrance for food now that it is well grown, the evidence of drainage and droppings shows the state of the nest.

Chicks of the Australian Pelican (Pelecanus conspicillatus) in their shallow rough nest, hatch blind and naked, only later growing a coat of down. At first, a parent is always present to guard and feed them.

Right *During the nesting season most adult birds have an instinctive urge to feed young and those without their own young for some reason, and on occasion those with, will sometimes put food into the gaping mouths of young that are not their own. Here a male Northern Cardinal (Cardinalis cardinalis) reacts to the open red gape of a goldfish expecting to be fed and gaping at the water's edge. The bird returned again and again to this backyard pond in North Carolina, bringing food to satisfy a number of demanding goldfish.*

naked and need care at first; later they grow a coat of woolly down.

At first the nestlings recognize the adults from the vibrations of the nest and learn their calls, raising their heads and gaping in response. The adults put food into the mouths of the young, and it is swallowed. At intervals the parents will peck at the cloaca of a nestling, which raises it and excretes a dropping encased in a jelly-like coat, which the adult can carry off and discard, although these contain undigested food and are sometimes swallowed. Woodpeckers have sensitive swollen gape edges at the back of the jaws and these are stimulated by feeding adults to make them gape. Small pelicans and cormorants are brooded continuously at first and fed on regurgitated food.

Although such young are less well developed at first, their digestive system is large and efficient, processing large quantities of food to provide rapid growth. Many will be fully grown

and fully developed in a fortnight, eyes will open in about a week and feathers begin to sprout rapidly. Feeding becomes a full-time job. The young clamor for food, each reaching up and opening its bill wide in the hope of being fed first. Legs, growing more rapidly than wings, may help it to compete. The open mouth displays color, and sometimes pattern, characteristic to each species and encouraging the adult to feed. Food may be shared around at first; later for insect eaters one visit will only fill one mouth.

Tits and similar small species may have to make a thousand journeys a day. Insects are carried back in the bill, large ones singly, and killed first, small ones packed together. Finches feeding seeds regurgitate from the crop into each bill. Swifts travel the air and pack insects into a bulging throat pouch, glued together with saliva, 300–500 at a time and possibly 20,000 a day. Pigeons grab the sensitive bill-base of the young and, holding the bill crosswise, pump up liquid crop milk for it to swallow. Young pelicans and cormorants thrust head and neck down into the parents' gullet in pursuit of food, looking as though they are fighting and trying to choke them. Droppings are still carried away from songbirds' nests but others defecate over the nest edge.

During this period birds become very fierce in defense of the nest and against possible dangers to the young, although they may cease their attack once the predator has actually reached the nest.

Birds that remove droppings try to keep nests clean, picking at the lining and removing objects. Nests accumulate a number of parasites — fleas, lice, fly larvae and mites — which can be discarded with the nests, but reused nests, particularly holes with linings, are likely to carry parasites from previous years. It is thought that the leaves and parts of plants that birds that use such nests often add to their linings may deter or destroy some parasites. Some grassfinches and sparrows will carry in burnt wood or charcoal fragments to add to the nest lining, possibly for similar purposes.

Once feathered and able to warm themselves, nestlings turn their back on each other. With some ground-nesting altricial birds such as larks, the young may leave the nest before they are fully fledged and hide in surrounding cover where they are less vulnerable, returning when parents bring food.

A male Greenfinch (Carduelis chloris) regurgitates seeds for the begging young. Because the young are well grown their parents are not carrying away the droppings, a tendency frequent in cardueline finches, and these accumulate on the rim of the nest.

Right *The scarlet gapes of the young of a Magpie-lark (Grallina cyanoleuca) reach up to be fed in response to the female's presence. Any broad level support is suitable for the neat mud basin this species makes as a nest, even a telegraph pole.*

One of two well-grown and nearly-feathered young begs for food from the feeding Gray Fantail (Rhipidura fuliginosa). The nest, tightly bound and smoothed on the outside with spiders' webs, shows the tapering base characteristic for these birds.

Below left Coucals are nonparasitic semiterrestrial cuckoos that build a domed nest at ground level. Nestling Pheasant Coucals (Centropus phasianinus) show typical hair-like down and the scarlet gape of the young bird. The gaping mouth of chicks demanding food seems to provoke an instinctive urge to feed in adult birds.

A pair of Curve-billed Thrashers (Toxostoma curvirostre) attack a red racer snake attempting to rob their nest, built in a cactus in Arizona.

A brood of young Great Horned Owls (Bubo virginianus) watch from a nest site in a palm tree in the Mojave Desert. Like all young owls they will be dependent upon their parents for several months after fledging.

The herons feed their young by regurgitation and this Australian Bittern (Botaurus poiciloptilus) brings up food for small downy young in a nest on the ground among reeds.

Semialtricial young

These young, with open eyes and a warmer down covering, are mostly larger birds of more open nests. Owls begin as helpless nestlings. The female stays with them at first and the male brings food from which she takes small fragments to feed them. If the food supply has been good she will have laid a large clutch and started incubating with the first egg, so that the young hatch at intervals and there is a big difference in size between the first and last. If the food supply dwindles, the smaller young will starve and die. If it is good, a large brood is reared.

Tubenosed seabirds, usually in nests in burrows or on ledges or islands, grow a heavy coat of down that may be necessary to survive, for adults may travel huge distances for food and leave them for several days. The food is partly digested and is fed as an oily fluid regurgitated into the young bird's bill. Growth is slow, often 50–70 days in the nest for smaller species, but the young may be heavier and look larger than the adults before they start growing feathers. In the last stages they are deserted by the adults, starve and grow plumage and then leave on their own.

The downy young of herons, ibises, spoonbills and storks, with eyes open, and with bills of ibises and spoonbills small and straight compared with adults, are at first closely guarded by at least one parent. Young grab at the parent's bill, persuading it to regurgitate food into the throat, then taking it from the bill. Later larger food may be disgorged onto the nest and picked up. Adults also bring water in hot weather, regurgitating it into the bills of the young or over them. The young become active and in later stages, although unable to fly, will leave the nest, climbing on branches or in reed beds nearby.

Birds of prey tend the downy young closely. Leafy twigs are brought and added to the nest, possibly to keep it cleaner. At first the female stays brooding and guarding the young while the male brings prey for them; and she feeds them carefully on small pieces of food. Later both parents hunt for the growing brood and the young learn to dismember prey for themselves. The larger eagles usually have two young, hatching at an interval of a few days. As they grow, the older fights and kills the younger, so getting the parents' undivided attention. The young have two successive coats of down as they grow. Helpless at first, they become more and more active, snatching at twigs, clapping the wings and sometimes climbing into nearby branches and returning before the first flight.

The New World vultures, like the storks to which they are related, regurgitate food that the young take from the adult's throat. They are more active than typical birds of prey and will move around more, but grow more slowly.

Semiprecocial young

These young are apparently active when they hatch but remain reliant on parents for food and stay at or near the nest site. Their down is spotted and blotched for camouflage in some species, and more uniformly dark or pale down in auks that may hide them against rocky backgrounds. Possibly the young sandgrouse, with their beautiful down patterns, should go into this group for, although the chicks pick up their own food, their movements are constrained by the fact that the male must bring back water for them from some distance. The other birds with semiprecocial young are the gull group of shorebirds (skuas, gulls, terns and auks) and the nightjars.

Adults fly out in search of food for semi-precocial young. Terns and auks bring fish that, like those of kingfishers, must be offered headfirst. There may be less ceremony for the puffin's mouthful of sand eels, crammed cross-wise in the bill. Nightjars are fed on insects put into the big open mouth, but gulls and skuas regurgitate food. In most species of gull, the chick triggers off regurgitation by pecking at the red spot on the tip of the adult's bill. Food is taken from the bill at first, later regurgitated on the ground.

Conditions for the young vary. At first they may be brooded but, except for auks, may be later left to hide while parents hunt. Auks may be in holes, burrows or crevices, with Kittlitz's Murrelet on a bare mountain top scree and the Marbled Murrelet on a platform of lodged twigs and moss in the top of a high conifer up to 5 miles (8 km) inland. Others of this group are in nests, usually on the ground or a rock ledge, within a small territory. Gradually the young can move around and perhaps hide in low vegetation but, except for nightjars, run the risk of being attacked, injured and perhaps killed if they stray into another territory.

Most species nest in colonies and adult gulls, terns and skuas combine to attack predators, and the last two at least will strike them, however large. The young learn that, at a parent's alarm call, they must crouch motionless, hoping to be overlooked. Even the feathered young of large gulls will do so and allow themselves to be picked up, if the adults keep up their warning.

Young penguins belong in this group, beginning life often on a small heap of stones, in a burrow or balanced on their parents' feet. They grow fast, fed at first on regurgitated food and then on more solid fish. In more open colonies with nests on the surface, young penguins, and the larger young of some terns and those of pelicans in the altricial category, tend to gather together in crêches, waiting near the water's edge for returning parents. The arrival of one with food creates a rush, but adults and young recognize each other's calls and only their own young get fed.

Like tubenose seabirds, young penguins have a thick coat of down and when fully grown appear larger than the adults, but lose this in a starvation period as they grow their feathers and wait to go to sea.

Flamingo chicks are fed on a pigeon-like secretion from the parent's crop, dribbled into the bill at first, and continue to be fed for about two weeks, although taking about six weeks to grow an adult-type bill. Young ones leave the nest after a few days and wander through the colony in large groups.

Precocial young

In many species, precocial young are active as soon as their down dries after hatching, and able to run, stagger or swim after the parents. Most maintain contact with small high-pitched calls, returned by low call notes from the adults. Even so, in the early stages losses,

particularly to predators, may be high in large broods, such as those of ground-living game-birds and ducks. At an alarm call young will scatter, hide and remain motionless. The adult may explode into noisy flight, or run or swim around conspicuously.

A number of ground birds appear to feign injury on such occasions. Some will run trailing a wing, or stagger with spread wings or tail. Others will just lower the head, close the tail

Above *A well-camouflaged European Nightjar* (Caprimulgus europaeus) *feeds its young by regurgitating the insects collected in flight. The young spread their wings and the farther bird already shows a great gape like that of the adult. No actual nest is made at the site.*

Left *A New Zealand Dotterel* (Charadrius obscurus) *moving and flapping in injury-feigning distraction display near the nest.*

Top *A Silver Gull* (Larus novaehollandiae) *regurgitates food for its young, who seize it from the parent's mouth, competing for possession. The spotted down is an ineffective camouflage against the background of this shell beach.*

and run around looking more like a small rodent. It is not certain that the bird does so purposefully, and it may be a kind of temporary paralysis arising from fear. On occasion it draws attention to hidden nests or young but in general has a diversionary effect.

A duty of the attendant parent is calling together and brooding young that are tired and cold. Small young birds hide under a crouching parent. With larger young the parent stands and one may see an apparently multilegged plover or sandpiper. Where the young are on water this is more difficult. For ducks or rails any slightly raised support above the water level will serve as a brood site. Divers (loons), grebes and swans supplement this by allowing small young to climb on their backs and support them between slightly raised wings. Young rails tend to stay closer to the nest than most: moorhens and coots, being almost semiprecocial, need nests as resting islands and adults may make extra nests to brood them on.

Alarmed woodcocks have been observed apparently transporting a chick, but this may be a misinterpretation of the result of sudden feather sleeking and movement by a bird brooding young. In jacanas such transport appears more deliberate. They walk over floating water plants and movement may be difficult for young. In moments of alarm the male that broods them, usually crouching with one or two under each wing, closes the wings and walks with the young held between wing and body, long legs protruding.

Feeding methods vary. Many young find their own food, accompanying parents who lead them where food is plentiful. Gamebirds scratching and pecking food will call the young with a special note and indicate the food by pecking at it. Young Stone-curlew are fed for the first week by parents, then shown food in a similar manner, as are young cranes. Some long-billed probers such as oystercatchers and snipe, whose young hatch with short bills, bring food to them at first. Divers (loons) and grebes are fed for much of the time on fish brought by adults, and young grebes are fed a few feathers to help them form pellets of hard fish bones and throw them up. Young rails are fed by adults for the first few days, and partially fed for longer. Moorhen young of earlier broods may help feed those of later broods, remaining around the nest site.

Cooperative rearing

There are varied and complex relationships among the birds that breed communally, working together to ensure the success of a single nesting, with the young bird cared for by an extended family. Many such groups consist of a pair with additional young of earlier broods and years that remain with the adults, in a subordinate status, helping with later matings. Possible origins of this cooperation can be seen in species like the Moorhen, when young of earlier broods may help with the feeding of later ones.

Other groups may involve several adults, which implies more tolerance. The possible forerunners of these are apparent in species that normally nest in pairs but where an additional adult may occasionally help in feeding a brood, as in the Swallow or Long-tailed Tit. Eider ducks nest in dispersed groups and, after taking their broods to the sea, tend to flock. The young form crèches, gradually deserted by adults that leave a few individuals on watch. Some females that have failed to nest, or lost their eggs early, attach themselves to another brooding female, the males having left when incubation began. When the nest these so-called "aunts" are watching hatches the extra female joins in and helps to tend the brood and guard it on its journey down to the sea. She is more likely than the mother to stay with the young and become an adult watching over a crèche of ducklings, and may perform a useful role in rearing.

With tendencies for young and adults to help care for young, communal breeding can evolve. The question of relationship is irrelevant to the young awaiting food, although a little extra always helps. Communal breeding can become very important in species nesting in areas where food is hard to find or in arid places where only a short time may be available after rain within which nesting must occur. The presence of extra birds bringing food to the young is likely to make a critical difference between success and failure.

Such efforts are not always more successful. There may be some confusion in unorganized communal efforts. A researcher who studied the communal nesting of some desert babblers in a marginal situation worked on the hypothesis that the young helpers were, in fact, trying to ensure that the brood did not survive in order to reduce potential competition. However, this was an exception.

Brood parasites

Some bird species avoid all the effort of incubating and rearing by laying their eggs in the nests of other birds and leaving them to take on the responsibility. The best-known example is the cuckoo, but many other species use this method; it is very easy to leave an egg in the nest of another bird. Some birds may occasionally lay an egg in the nest of an individual of the same species. Ducks frequently lay in each other's nests, and this is fairly common in cavity-nesting species where there is a shortage of holes. The young only need a little brooding at first and have a fair chance of survival. It has been discovered recently that some Common Starlings also lay their eggs in neighboring nests. Birds may also lay in nests of other species where the nest is of similar appearance to their own and in the same type of habitat, and the habit may be more widespread than has been suspected.

In other species, parasitism is part of the regular life cycle. The Black-headed Duck of South America dumps its eggs on other ducks,

or even on waterbirds such as coots, rails and herons, although not always with success. Where the chick requires more sustained rearing special adaptations will frequently occur. The parasitic wydahs and indigo-finches, for instance, lay their eggs in nests of particular African waxbills and firefinches, in which the young of each species has a different mouth pattern that shows when they beg for food. The young wydahs not only resemble the young of the particular host but have similar mouth patterns and imitate the call notes of the birds they are with and they are reared alongside their nest mates.

Some birds are less selective. The Common Cowbird, one of the parasitic group among the American troupials, typically lays a single egg in the nest of small insect-eating birds but may use a wide range of nests, some of quite unsuitable hosts. The young of smaller species may not be able to compete for food, attention and nest space with the vigorous interloper and may not survive.

Some species strengthen their chance of success by measures against the chicks of the host species. Among the honeyguides, for instance, of those species in which nesting habits are known and all parasitic, laying in the cavity nests of barbets, woodpeckers, rollers, starlings and similar birds, the newly hatched honeyguide is equipped with temporary needle-like hooks on its jaw tips. With them it chews and kills the host's own young, removing competition.

Not all cuckoos are brood parasites, in fact only about half of the 127 species in the family. In some, such as the Koel, which mainly parasitizes crows, and the *Clamator* species whose hosts range from crows to babblers and bulbuls, young of both cuckoo and host are reared together, especially if more than one cuckoo lays in the same nest. The sociable *Turdoides* babblers' young have a better chance of survival with the parasite chicks, for additional adults assist the nesting pair.

The Common Cuckoo and others of the genera *Cuculus*, *Chrysococcyx* and *Cacomantis* are highly adapted to their own chicks' advantage. The nestling has a hollowed, sensitive back and in the nest it squirms under the host bird's eggs and young until they touch its back and rest there. It then rears up against the side of the nest and heaves them out. Since the host parents have no behavioral adaptation for retrieving them, the tiny, naked, blind nestlings die. The young cuckoo then gets all the pair's attention.

The Cuckoo-finch, a weaver that parasitizes small African warblers, usually ends up with the nest to itself, unless it has to share it with a second nestling of its own species.

Success as a brood parasite seems to depend on the ability to fool the host and more rapid development, achieved by rapid egg laying, a shorter incubation than in the host species and making more vigorous, noisy and conspicuous demands for food. In some cuckoo species, males appear to accompany the females when they lay, distracting the host pair while the nest is visited. Earlier hatching may be helped by the cuckoo's eggs being retained in the body for a day before they are laid, for it is suspected that embryo development is then already begun.

A young Common Cuckoo (Cuculus canorus) *seems too large for both the nest and the Reed-Warbler* (Acrocephalus scirpaceus) *that is feeding it.*

FLEDGING AND MATURING

The young birds' wing and tail feathers begin to grow before the rest. These are the largest, still not completely grown in songbirds when they leave the nest; the contour feathers of the body and head grow while these are still lengthening.

Young birds grow fast in the latter stages of the nestling period, some may temporarily overtake adults in weight. Their main energies are directed towards growing their final plumage. In most altricial birds this means the growth of flight feathers that, although wing and tail feathers begin to grow before the rest, will probably not be complete until after the birds have left the nest. However, they will be large enough to carry them in their first fluttering efforts at flight.

Maturation of the nestling is usually measured by the point of fledging, when it leaves the nest, but this can be misleading. Fully precocial birds are quickly active so are assumed to be growing faster than helpless nestlings and, because they may grow wing feathers and be able to flutter some distance while still downy, this is seen as rapid development. Yet they may take half as long again as the altricial birds in acquiring their first full set of feathers. The stage that small songbirds reach in 12–14 days smaller gamebirds probably reach in about three weeks.

If flying ability is the criterion for "fledging" then the megapodes are instant fledgers; their downy chicks struggle out of a mound unaided and are able not only to run but also to flutter for some distance on their first day. Whereas precocial young gamebirds are beginning to fly at 10–14 days old, small songbirds are leaving the nest at 12–14 days. Sea Terns take four to

A Brush-turkey (Alectura lathami) *egg is incubated in a mound, like that of the Mallee, for about eight or nine weeks. This hatchling has dug its way out unaided and with wings already feathered, is able to fly immediately and lead an independent life.*

At a colony of Australasian Gannets (Morus serrator), *dark-plumaged young birds on a nest site, almost ready to fledge, stretch and beat their wings.*

five weeks, although Wideawake Terns, whose parents must forage further, take about eight and a half, cranes and swans about 10–15, whereas the Wandering Albatross needs 40 weeks and Ostriches, with no need to fly, take about a year to reach full size.

Achieving independence

The nestling's final break with the nest site and gaining the ability to look after itself is achieved in different ways and at different speeds. For many birds, becoming able to fly is the important thing. Gamebirds, shorebirds, ibises and gulls may quickly learn to move around with adults and may have begun to emulate them before fledging. Others take more time. Seabirds are difficult to observe but certainly young terns, and possibly others such as gannets, follow adults. They beg and may be fed when they are flying and well out to sea. Raptors, both day-flying birds of prey and owls, have to learn the difficult art of hunting, and may rely on adults for food for months after they have flown.

Leaving the nest is a simple act for an altricial bird, although learning to land successfully in the right place may take longer.

For the parents, the sudden dispersal of a brood of young still needing to be fed is a period of stress. Unsophisticated birds must learn from alarm calls how to recognize predators. In their early stages they will become motionless when the warning sounds. Parents must watch and try to remember where young ones last landed. Some species, from thrushes to grebes, make their task easier by dividing the brood, each parent being responsible for certain young and ignoring the others. This enables them to exploit a larger area for food gathering with less effort.

Leaving the nest site may be dangerous. Tree-nesting ducks may seem to have problems for the duck calls from the ground and the ducklings scramble from the hole and just fall, as do the young of cliff-nesting Barnacle Geese. However, at that stage there is a lot of elastic cartilage in the skeleton instead of bone and the young appear to hit the ground, and even bounce, without damage. Cliff-nesting Guillemots and Razorbills may call their incompletely fledged young down off the ledges at night and accompany them out to sea where they will live and feed, hoping to avoid marauding gulls. Young shearwaters and petrels, deserted in their burrows, must also hope to find a takeoff site and fly to sea under cover of darkness. For others it is more difficult: a Marbled Murrelet, raised in a nest high in a conifer, must in one flight travel alone up to 5 miles (8 km) over forest to reach the safety of coastal waters. If it falls, it will not find its way out.

Precocial and semiprecocial birds, although less directly reliant on adults, tend to remain with or near them in social groupings from which they may gain some help in survival by learning the daily life patterns. Nonprecocial

First flight

Birds look as though they learn to fly. Nestlings of birds of prey, especially, when development is well advanced, will jump up and down in the nest, vigorously flapping their wings. From such incidents and because birds are found not long out of the nest and unable to fly well it was once assumed that birds needed practice before they could fly.

In the 1870s, Douglas Spalding showed that young Barn Swallows, if prevented from spreading their wings while in the nest could still fly without difficulty if released at normal fledging time. More recent experiments holding young pigeons' wings in paper tubes proved that at the right time birds flew instinctively, whereas in the megapode chick there is a bird that can run and fly almost immediately after it digs itself out of the incubation mound.

Though for some first flight must be well executed, for others success comes more gradually and, even for those that start off well, take-off, and more particularly landing, appear to need some practice. Songbirds leave the nest with a fluttering flight that may carry them no further than the first convenient perch, with rests needed between flights. The nest is a potentially dangerous place to which they do not return. Gradual improvement is not a learning process but, since survival requires fledging as soon as possible, birds leave the nest when flight feathers are still in the last stages of growth; complete plumage brings better flight.

If a nestful of young approaching fledging are disturbed by a predator they will leave the nest even earlier, scattering into whatever cover is available, even though unable to fly. This desperate reaction may allow some to survive. Anyone studying birds in nests or banding (ringing) birds must be aware of this problem. This, and the earliest stages of flight when fledging will usually explain why seemingly helpless young birds are sometimes found. The begging calls of the young help parents to locate a scattered brood to feed them. If a young bird is disturbed and flies to a new spot, parents will sometimes accompany it for part of the way and note where it settles so that they can find it again.

birds are reliant on adults for longer. They will continue to beg for food until the parents become reluctant to feed them. Experiments suggest that the longer the adults continue to feed them, the slower the young are to learn to feed themselves.

The period differs according to the birds involved, since parental support must last long enough to allow the young bird to learn the skills it needs. This is especially true for birds of prey and fish hunters, which have the longest periods of reliance. Independence can range from beginning at eight weeks in a Pygmy Owl to 20–24 weeks in a big European Eagle-Owl; and in the White-tailed Sea-Eagle 15–16 weeks. The true point of independence is difficult to discover since by then both adults and young may be on the move and away from the nest.

Instinct and learning

The way in which a bird fits into its world is governed mainly by instinct: inherited patterns of behavior appear at the right place and time to ensure survival. This was the general view on all animals until recent times; only humans used learning and intelligence, but the picture is not so clear-cut in either direction. Like birds, we are conscious of the world mainly through sight and hearing, making bird behavior more easy to observe than that of

other animals and we are also increasingly aware of human instinctive behavior.

A precocial chick, which must follow its parents from the first, would be expected to recognize them, but it was long ago discovered that very small precocial young of many species could be persuaded to follow people and behave as though they were the bird's parents — a considerable aid in the domestication of geese, ducks and fowl. More careful twentieth-century study, when this was given the name "imprinting," gave some clarification.

A feathered and fledged young Eurasian Jay (Garrulus glandarius) begs food from an adult that has already begun to collect acorns for winter and has both throat and mouth full.

Blue Tits (Parus caeruleus) help themselves from milk bottles.

Learning and instinct in starting to feed

Precocial birds may have to start searching for food as soon as they begin to run around. In one of his 1870s experiments, Douglas Spalding hooded domestic fowl chicks from the moment of hatching for three days and then offered them live and dead flies. They pecked at them, preferring the live flies, easily locating them.

While hooded these chicks recognized the hen's calls. A female gamebird will make a special call to which young respond and lead them to where food is available, pecking at a food object. The chick, following her example, will pick it up and eat it. If she is not actually teaching, she *is* facilitating discovery of where food is found and providing objects to search for.

Some learning is probably involved. Gilbert White, a century before Spalding, observed

"take a chicken of four or five days old, and hold it up to a window where there are flies and it will immediately seize its prey, with little twitterings of complacency; but if you tender it a wasp or bee, at once its note becomes harsh, and expressive of disapprobation and a sense of danger."

Some precocial shorebird families have species that feed the downy young at first. Stone-curlews do and, when young were raised artificially because aviary adults tend to eat each other's eggs, there was a need to feed them. After feeding for six days with food given in the fingers or in forceps held between them (which they accepted as substitutes for the parental bill), food was offered held near the ground. The chick had to peck down at it and, at intervals, the fingers merely pointed closely at an object, which the young bird seized. It was now picking up objects and soon finding them for itself. Is this learning or only helping to trigger off an instinctive change in behavior that was increasingly present?

Altricial birds that have left the nest to follow parents, begging for food, are led to places where food is found, watch parents finding it and know what it looks like. When parental indifference and hunger drive them to peck around for themselves, the knowledge of place and the food images will already be there.

There is evidence that both precocial and altricial young will show some preference for objects of the color of what will be their usual food, whether insect, seed or plant, but may also peck experimentally at other things.

During a brief period after hatching, sometimes only hours, a gosling will identify the first thing that it sees moving as a parent goose, even though that be a person, a part of a person such as hand, leg or foot, or an object. Young ducklings showed similar behavior, but for them it was important that, as well as moving, the object make a constant sound, such as quacking. It seems incredible that something so important should be triggered off so easily but under normal conditions instantaneous recognition is necessary.

People who take and rear a newly-hatched or nestling altricial bird discover that it will come to regard them as parent but, since this can occur with partly-grown nestlings, there appears to be some learning needed to recognize what it is that offers food and should therefore be the parent.

More problems arise if a young bird is reared in human hands without seeing others of its kind. On maturing it will try to socialize with and to pair with human beings. This is often called "human fixation." It is the bane of aviculturalists who, even if they do not themselves hand-rear the bird, may buy one raised in this way. People often find that they have a wonderfully tame parrot or some similar bird that shows not the slightest interest in others of its kind and cannot be used for breeding.

Similar problems arise with fostering, resulting in a young bird of one species behaving as though it belonged to another. In nature this probably occurs with any regularity only with brood parasites, such as cuckoos, where it might be advantageous for the young cuckoo to become fixated on the host species so that both male and female cuckoos return to where they can find that species and its nests. This would make successful rearing of young more likely and help gradual selection for eggs resembling those of the host. If a shortage of such nests forces experimental laying in nests of different species, the young would be fixed on that host, establishing a new line.

A hand-reared and isolated young European Robin that developed "human fixation" behavior, when adult, saw all humans as robin-like invaders of its territory and promptly displayed aggressively and attacked them. However, two other Robin nestlings reared together looked to the human feeder for food but, with the right companion to provide the image, behaved as normal birds when adult. A bird reared in isolation learns the wrong identity and sees humans as other birds of the same kind as itself; reared with another bird it does not have the same problem, although a human is a parent substitute in both cases.

Much bird behavior seems to be a mixture of instinctive behavior and learning; there is no definite evidence of new intelligence or insight. Tool using, when some implement is an indirect means of obtaining a desired object, is often regarded as evidence of intelligence. The few examples shown by birds need consideration.

The undisputed example is shown by the Woodpecker Finch of the Galapagos Islands. Without competition, the short-billed Gala-

The Huli Wigmen of the highlands of Papua New Guinea hunt the Cassowary (Casuarius bennetti). A chick taken when a hen is killed becomes imprinted on the hunter who tends it, attacking other humans it regards as sexual rivals. Eventually it is ritually killed and its feathers used for decorating ceremonial headdresses and weapons.

A Galapagos Woodpecker Finch (Camarhynchus pallidus) uses a twig to force insects from a crevice.

One of the Galapagos Island finches, the Sharp-beaked Ground-Finch (Geospiza difficilis) has been called the Vampire Finch because it has discovered that by pecking at the quills of growing feathers on molting seabirds, such as the Masked Booby (Sula dactylatra), it can draw blood and use this as a source of nutrition.

pagos finches have tried to use all the sparse food sources available. There are no woodpeckers, and insects in deep crevices or burrows in wood are out of reach of other birds. This finch holds a short twig or cactus spine in its bill and probes with it into holes and crevices, forcing out insects that it can seize and eat.

This behavior has no parallels elsewhere, although the Egyptian Vulture is also credited with tool use. Among other food it eats eggs, taking them in its bill and dashing them on the ground to break them. Confronted with enormous Ostrich eggs it shows behavior that might be interpreted as frustration. It seizes egg-sized stones near by and throws them down instead. When done at an Ostrich's nest with a large spread of eggs, this sooner or later results in an egg being broken. Are the movements purposeful and expected to result in broken eggs?

The oddest "tool use" is that of the little Green-backed Heron of North America. It has been seen floating small feathers or fragments of bread on water and catching the small fish that come to investigate.

More obvious learning used in feeding is seen in the Sharp-beaked Ground Finch. These finches on some Galapagos Islands explore nesting seabird colonies where broken eggs may provide free food. They have discovered that they can approach resting Masked Boobies and, by pecking at the growing quills where feathers have been molted, make them bleed. The finches drink the blood. This behavior appears to have been discovered by some individuals, learned by others and presumably remembered for periods.

Another learned behavior is that of raiding milk bottles left on doorsteps, breaching through the cap and drinking some of the cream or milk; the principal culprit being the Blue Tit. This was first observed at the end of the 1920s, when cardboard caps were used, and has occurred intermittently into recent times when metal foil caps have been pierced. The habit appears to be learned at times by individuals, then learned from them by others and may spread through an area. The relatively short life span and periodicity of the behavior may result in the need for it to be relearned.

"Milk stealing" is not limited to Blue Tits. In Queensland, Australia, the loss of larger quantities of milk proved due to Greater Bowerbirds, and the latest discoverer of this potential food source is the Common Magpie. The crow tribe, like the tits, will explore and examine promising food. With their recent increasing tameness as persecution is relaxed, and with their curiosity and relative intelligence, Magpies are possibly more exploitive than the Blue Tits but also more cautious. There has been some alarm following claims that they have introduced harmful bacteria into milk bottles. In places where this is a problem it is probably easier to change the way in which milk is made available than to eliminate all potentially exploratory birds.

Recent experiments have been made to see to what extent such birds could learn to obtain food from increasingly complex devices. Individuals of tit species, varying in ability, in some instances learned to withdraw a series of pegs or sticks to release a nut, and a town pigeon to peck in sequence on three buttons and wait while each activated machinery finally releasing food. These show some evidence of learning indirect sequences that ultimately result in obtaining food. It would seem that for those species that normally exhibit some inquisitiveness a definite if limited ability to learn is combined with the instinctive responses that they already possess.

Integration

Once independent in moving and feeding, young birds must integrate themselves into the world of adult birds. For most the opportunity will depend upon losses among older birds, providing territories and nest sites where younger birds can establish themselves. Mortality will have been highest among the growing birds, with from one in five to one in twenty of eggs laid developing to adulthood. The chances of young surviving are shown by annual mortality rates, which average 30–60 percent among most birds, only some large raptor and seabird species losing as few as 5–10 percent per year.

A tendency to wander and to disperse into areas where adults may not normally occur or breed is a feature of immature young, once they are independent of parents. In species that take longer to mature and do not breed for several years, such vagrancy may be apparent over most of this period. At the end of it, the young are likely to return to their own area of origin, but if changes in those parts result in population pressure to accommodate new individuals, or if they make areas unsuitable, there is a possibility that this dispersive habit will facilitate spread or changes of range.

For migratory songbirds and similar species, maturation involves, from the first, joining in migration, which in most birds appears to be an inherited character. A bird will migrate in particular directions for a particular period. This is a time that contributes heavily to bird mortality in general. Having survived migration and wintering, the returning bird finds itself competing with other returning migrants. Although it will tend to return to the place where it was reared, it lacks experience of establishing territory or of nesting and knowledge of the area from an adult viewpoint.

Cranes, geese and similar birds grow fairly slowly and remain with the adults. They migrate with them to traditional wintering areas and stay there with them, possibly traveling and associating with other family units to form flocks. Young return with adults to the breeding ground and then will gradually separate from them as nesting occurs. Pairing of the young with others may happen on the wintering areas or at the time when nesting is occurring. It has been suggested that, since many of these species have relatively circumscribed areas for breeding and wintering and tend to used fixed routes between them, having young travel with the adults may enable them to learn the traditional routes and sites in a way that might not be necessary for species with more dispersive migratory movements.

In species that tend to flock, the young birds may integrate themselves more easily by simply becoming part of these associations. A flock will move to areas providing facilities for feeding and roosting, and so help ensure the survival of the new generation. The competition that occurs in flocks may create a problem, young losing out to more experienced and aggressive adults who may take the best food or sites by supplanting attacks that force a bird to give way to another. Lack of expertise may also mean a young bird feeds more slowly and fails to take as much as others if a flock is on the move.

Birds nesting in large colonies may move away and wander outside the breeding season but, during that period, they are likely to return, having reached maturity. They will attempt to establish themselves at the borders of colonies and are likely to be less successful breeders in their earlier seasons. In such situations females may have a better chance than males to establish themselves, since they do not have to cope with the need to gain a site or territory.

In birds that have communal or lek-type displays, it is likely a young male will gradually join the displaying groups of males. He may be chased away but in some birds-of-paradise, such as the *Paradisaea* species, where males display in small groups, young birds may begin to emulate dominant displaying males before they have fully acquired display plumes and may mate in immature female-like plumage. In these species, young females would appear to have similar opportunities to older ones.

For nonmigratory birds of warmer regions, the young would only appear to need to integrate themselves slowly into their surroundings in the appropriate habitat. For territorial species, the problem would be that of finding a vacant space. It is mostly among birds of this type that communal nesters occur. The broods are usually small, perhaps one to three young, of which not all will survive. The young bird continues to stay within the parental territory, assisting the parents or becoming part of a slightly larger social unit. It may gain experience of helping with nesting but, since most species appear to manage without previous experience, this may not be important. What is more relevant is that the individual can continue to live in these surroundings without provoking aggression and, if and when the opportunity arises, may establish itself in a vacant territory, assume a dominant role on the death of a parent, or pair into another group.

Migratory birds gather where there is ample food. On a stretch of Australian coast a local Caspian Tern (Sterna caspia) is surrounded by a flock of northern Siberian shorebirds in winter plumage, including Eastern Curlew (Numenius madagascariensis), Bartailed Godwits (Limosa lapponica) and Lesser Knots (Calidris canutus).

MOLT

The end of the breeding season usually sees the beginning of molt. Most birds have one flight-feather molt each year, with body feathers being molted at the same time. Some have a second molt of body feathers only, usually just before breeding. Albatrosses have a single slow body-plumage molt that takes two years and pigeons and parrots with a single year molt also tend to do this slowly and patchily. The large eagles and vultures take three years of annual partial molts to complete their feather change. Because it affects their way of life, molt shows many variations in timing and extent not only between different groups of birds but between related species.

Molt makes extra food demands, and reduced mobility while replacing feathers may make feeding and escape from predation more difficult. Molting birds tend to be subdued in behavior and reluctant to show themselves conspicuously. The waterbirds that lose all their flight feathers rapidly, such as shearwaters, divers (loons), grebes and waterfowl can take to the water to evade predators. More terrestrial birds such as geese have more of a problem and usually resort to large lakes and swamps. Their flightlessness usually coincides with that of their growing young that accompany them. Some fly long distances to secure locations, deserting the young.

To molt in safety from mammal predators a large part of the European Shelduck population — about 1,000,000 birds — gathers from August through October on the Grosser Knetchsand, a sandbank island off the German coast in the Wadden Sea. While most birds from Britain and Ireland congregate there, some 3,000–4,000 congregate in the Bristol Channel; others in the Wash, Humber estuary and Firth of Forth. They leave the growing young, cared for at first by a few late adults.

Flightlessness may also affect arctic-breeding songbirds that compress a rapid all-over molt into a brief period between breeding and migrating, even beginning in the latter stages of nesting. The female Hornbill finds safety by molting all her flight feathers after walling herself up in the nest.

Molts may be interrupted. Some arctic-breeding shorebirds and the Turtle-Dove begin flight-feather molt, then wait to complete it in winter quarters. Delaying the whole molt until after migration occurs in some songbirds and the Common Swift. Birds nesting in arid country where nesting is triggered by rain, appear to temporarily suspend molt at any stage if this occurs, the rapid attempt at breeding having priority.

Seasonal plumages

In many species plumage may show conspicuous differences according to age or sex, difference often achieved by molt. The first plumage that a young bird grows when leaving the nest usually differs from that of adults. In species where the female has a plumage that is duller and less boldly patterned than the male the

Young birds may have different plumage from adults. A blackish young Gannet (Morus bassanus) in its second year will take another year — and a total of three molts — to resemble the white adult flying with it; each molt will decrease the number of dark feathers.

juvenile plumage may resemble that of the female, but if both adults have conspicuous plumage it is likely to differ from both. In general juvenile plumages tend to be drab and more cryptic in color and appearance. They may be more streaked, barred or spotted than the adults', usually to aid concealment within the habitat.

Some juvenile plumages may relate to adult aggressiveness. Adult European Robins have red breasts, but juveniles are brown with pale buff spots; adult hawks may have fairly uniform and finely-barred breast patterns, but young are white-breasted with heavy streaking, spotting or barring. In both, the difference may ensure the rapid recognition that the possible intruder is a nonthreatening juvenile.

Many juvenile plumages are similar in both sexes but some show dimorphism. Young Green Woodpeckers are more speckled than adults and lack the black face mask, but males already show the distinctive scarlet mustache mark from the first.

The juvenile plumage is short-lived. In late summer to early fall there is a postjuvenile molt, sometimes involving only body feathers, in which the young lose their first body plumage and those that will breed in their first adult year acquire the adult type.

In some birds that do not become breeding adults for several years, this period is covered by a sequence of molts like those of adults in which some may gradually acquire adult plumage. This can be seen most clearly in seabirds, where the Gannet takes several yearly molts to change gradually from a blackish to a white plumage, and gulls, according to their

species, may take two to four years in which the mottled brown juvenile plumage is gradually changed at successive molts into the gray, black and white of the adult.

In birds with a single annual molt after breeding, the new plumage will be the breeding plumage of the next year. Often this will be brightly colored in the male. If the species passes through a nonbreeding winter period it may be preferable for the male to be less conspicuous. In some species of colder climates such as finches and buntings the male's noticeable new plumage may be concealed by overlapping dull tips to the feathers that wear away during the months after molt so that the breeding plumage is visible by spring.

In other species, from shorebirds to wagtails, both sexes gain a dull plumage in the postbreeding period. Before breeding they molt again, partly or wholly, to get a new breeding plumage. This is particularly relevant in birds like widowbirds that have ornamental plumage such as long tails that might be a hindrance at other times.

Ducks tend to pair up early and the males to desert their mates soon after mating begins. They gain their bright breeding plumage in the late summer molt. During the breeding season the male molts the body plumage and has a short "eclipse" period in which the plumage is dull and more like that of the female.

Breeding birds of some species also grow temporary ornaments such as the bright-colored plates on the bills of some auks or lumps on the upper bill of some pelicans. Like feathers, these are shed after breeding, and grown again just before the next breeding period.

Waterfowl molt all flight feathers at once, relying on water for protection against predators. These part-molted Pink-footed Geese (Anser brachyrhynchus), on Spitzbergen, cannot yet fly properly.

DISPERSAL AND MIGRATION

Migration can be described as a seasonal movement backwards and forwards between two locations. There is no doubt about what birds achieve from it: a winter passed in a more comfortable climate and with supplies of the food to which they are habituated when those things are not available in their breeding grounds. But why do they do it? How did it start? We have maps to show us what lies beyond the lands we know, travel books and tourist promotions to tempt us to exotic climes. Birds do not have any way of knowing about other lands beyond their own and their inherited experience. Why would they embark on long, exhausting and risky flights into the unknown? The answers are still not certain but there are a number of possibilities that probably all played some part.

The origins of migration

The simplest form that migration takes is a bird's progression up and down a mountain side as the snow and ice advances and recedes, winters being spent in the warmer and more sheltered valleys, whereas in summers the bird exploits the heights. This does not involve long journeys in short time spans but a gradual movement through the different altitudes and, for all except the ground-living birds, over terrain that it is already possible to know through their daily experience.

If the territorial claims of others do not hinder them, birds might also move around following food availability, perhaps returning to areas where it has proved abundant at a particular season in an annual pattern — a behavior known as nomadism, and which is also a form of migration. Where occupied territories prevent a bird foraging through adjoining areas, and especially when a bird needs to establish its own territory, it will have to overfly those that are occupied and go further afield. Some young adults squeeze within the fringes of territories that belong to others, hoping later to take one over, but at times that favor population growth they will be forced to find unoccupied ground that offers the habitat and food supplies they need. Thus they extend the overall distribution of their

An Arctic Tern (Sterna paradisaea) feeds its mate, resting on Arctic ice. This species breeds around the Arctic and annually journeys south halfway around the world to spend its winter in the Antarctic summer season. Its seasonal haunts may be as much as 10,860 miles (17,500 km) apart.

The spread of the Common Starling

The Common Starling, along with the House Sparrow, has been introduced by man to every corner of the globe except the polar regions. There were a dozen or more attempts to introduce Starlings to the United States and Canada in the nineteenth century but only one proved successful: a flock of 60 released in New York's Central Park in 1890, followed by 40 more the following year. These birds bred successfully at once; the first nest was found, most appropriately, under the eaves of the American Museum of Natural History in the summer of 1890.

For the first few years the Starlings stayed within the New York area but with increasing numbers they moved further afield, especially in fall (autumn) and winter. Even where conditions proved good, many often returned to where they had been reared at breeding time but some stayed in the new territory. When these areas became occupied, new generations moved on further.

By the end of the century there were Starlings from New Haven, Connecticut, to Bayonne, New Jersey. In another ten years they had spread through most of New England and the Middle Atlantic states. In the 1930s, they were spreading through the Middle West, into southern Canada and south into Florida and they were first seen in California in the 1940s; they had crossed the Rockies. From those 100 birds in Central Park are descended all the millions of Starlings that are now spread through the whole of North America.

Starlings have also been introduced in Australia, New Zealand, South Africa and Hawaii with similar startling population explosion and dispersal.

---

species. This can happen quite rapidly as is evidenced by the Common Starling in North America.

It is not only birds that have not established a territory that have to seek new places to live. Changes in conditions, as when a natural cataclysm or some human activity destroys or ruins a habitat, or due to the slower alteration of the global climate, make long-established territories no longer viable and birds must move elsewhere.

Like the Starling in North America, the Serin provides a very recent European example of a migratory pattern developing. Only a hundred years or so ago this species was known only in the Mediterranean region. In the past century it has gradually spread northwards and is now found in southern Sweden and has occasionally bred in Britain, though it is not yet established there. The Mediterranean birds are sedentary but, as Serins moved further and further north, they found food supplies in winter insufficient and so they migrated back to the original range.

The Starlings of North America returned to their breeding areas but this is not necessarily how the original migratory patterns developed; the Serins returned to winter. It is a measure of the dominance of Northern Hemisphere cultures that they have identified birds as "theirs," wintering elsewhere. But try looking at things the other way around. Consider migration not so much as a means of replacing a dwindling food supply but providing an enriched one that makes it easier to breed and to raise young. Food competition is greatest at this time, both within and between species; it is worth finding somewhere where it is easily available and competition less.

After an Ice Age, as the retreat of the glaciers and the ice caps made new terrain available, birds moved gradually further north, following the melt. At first, plenty of territories were available without having to compete for them, plenty of food and, since summer day length increases as one moves closer to the poles, more daylight hours to hunt or forage. Again as territories fill, growing populations must move further north, but this provides no problem as the ice caps continue to shrink. There is one disadvantage. When winter comes conditions are worse than in the original breeding grounds so birds are forced to return and, since their original reason for moving north was that populations were already too dense, they find even heavier competition and so fly onward to new territories further south. The process is slow and the distances involved increase gradually but what may have started as a relatively short journey for the first migrants becomes longer and longer.

The Rock-Thrush (Monticola saxatilis) *of open rocky places and ruins in mountains, is a summer migrant to southern Eurasia, wintering mainly in northeast Africa.*

It is always difficult to think of the evolutionary time scale involved. The geologically recent periodic fluctuations of climatic conditions, which we think of as ice ages but that affected the whole earth, began about two million years ago in the Pliocene period. The 1.7 million years of the subsequent Pleistocene ice ages is now known to include about 17 pairs of cold and warm periods. Our Holocene period, a mere 10,000 years, may just be the current warm interglacial phase. From fossil bird bones there is evidence of combinations of species at various places that suggest that migration, of the kind that we recognize, has been going on for nearly two million years. Through this period the movements of species would have had to adjust to the slow changes of glacial and interglacial, or arid and pluvial, phases. We merely see the latest version of this. The number of species that are migratory in part of the range, resident in others, indicates its potential plasticity.

The pattern in which some species spread can today be seen in the routes along which they now migrate. The Wheatear, for example, "winters" in Africa but migrates north not only to Europe and Siberia but across to Greenland and Baffin Land and Nova Scotia. The American and Eastern Asian birds would have much shorter distances to travel if they "wintered" in South America or Southeast Asia but they have never explored these territories; they still follow the route back to Europe or across the Middle East along which they originally moved northwards. Similarly, those Willow Warblers that have spread to Alaska return to South Africa and Alaskan Arctic Warblers to Southeast Asia, as do Arctic Warblers that have flown west to Scandinavia.

Migration routes

However a migration route developed, and the suggestions above are hypotheses rather than proven methods, a bird must sustain itself on the journey, or have developed the endurance to go without rest for long distances. It may be unaware of unexplored territories but the original journeys must have proved viable for sufficient numbers to survive, maintain the species and establish the pattern. The routes of migrants through the Americas show a broad division into birds who travel down the west of the continent and those who keep to the east. Eastwards of the 100° meridian tends to be settled, wooded country and in springtime great waves of small songbirds can be seen migrating north. To the west are open grasslands and mountains where there are plenty of small mammals for migrating birds of prey. Along the Pacific coast travel vast numbers of waterfowl, beside which the passerines taking that route seem insignificant.

In some instances a different route is taken for each direction, exploiting either wind patterns or seasonal availability of food. Some species, both shorebirds and songbirds, fly south to Africa via Spain and Portugal in autumn but return in spring through Tunisia and Italy to take advantage of more favorable winds. The Golden Plover flies north from the Argentinian pampas to the Arctic tundra following a route through Central America, but traveling south in the fall exploits rich crops of berries on the Atlantic coast of North America and then takes a route across the Caribbean.

Where migrants fly for long distances over terrain that offers no chance to feed, or even to rest, the routes emphasize the apparently random way in which they must have become established. One generation made it and came back and others followed, but how many of each generation failed to make it? And how many birds have tried a different route and failed? Does the repetition of the journey from generation to generation strengthen the genetic coding that guides the birds? It would seem so and that experimentation with new routes is comparatively rare.

It is difficult to know whether to speak of migration routes or migration direction. Once

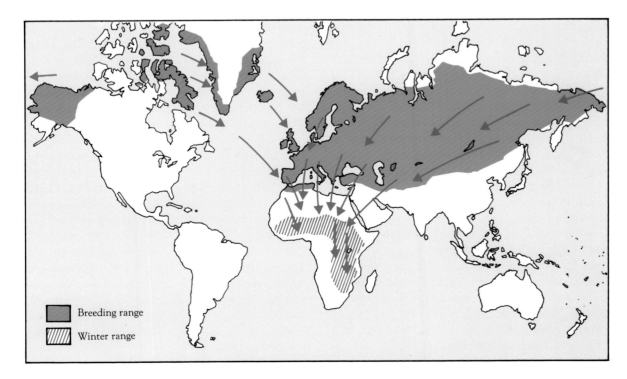

The Northern Wheatear (Oenanthe oenanthe) is a species that after the glacial periods has spread back into Eurasia and invaded North America from both directions. In spite of this, in winter it migrates back to ancestral wintering areas in Africa.

Breeding range

Winter range

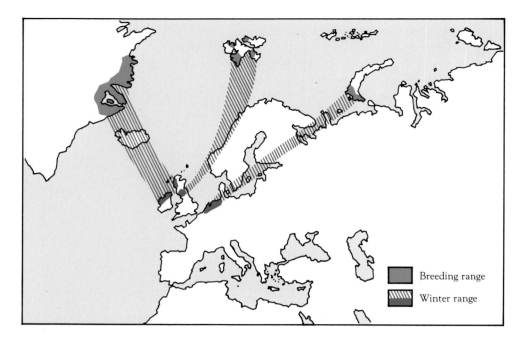

Some migrant species, particularly some waterfowl, follow fairly well-defined routes. In the Barnacle Goose (Branta leucopsis) the three populations have separate wintering areas and follow clear routes to them. Such species may also have traditional stopping places along these routes.

Breeding range

Winter range

across to North Africa, preferring a shorter route overall, or make use of the Greek islands, Crete and Cyprus as staging points.

The demands of migration

The demands imposed by migration differ. Some seabirds fly prodigious distances — the Arctic Tern down to the Antarctic and back — but many conserve energy by gliding on prevailing winds, if necessary they are able to rest on the water and can feed along their way, pacing the journey to take advantage of areas where food is plentiful. So, huge though such distances may be, their challenge is not so great as that to landbirds that have to traverse great stretches of water where they have to keep on flying, or desert and other terrains that provide no chance to feed. It is met twice every year by such birds as the Bristle-thighed Curlew, which flies from its breeding territories in Alaska south to the Polynesian islands, including a nonstop stretch without landfall of over 1,800 miles (3,000 km). The Greenland race of the Northern Wheatear crosses the North Atlantic from Greenland to Africa, some going by Iceland and Britain but others flying nonstop for 1,800 miles (3,000 km) until they reach the Spanish coast. Most migrants from Europe cross both the Mediterranean Sea and the Sahara Desert in one hop, probably flying very high, whereas Siberian migrants cross from the northern edge of the Caspian Desert to Africa, over both Iran and Arabia. In the Americas the Blackpoll Warbler covers more than 2,480 miles (4,000 km) nonstop south from New England across the Caribbean, unless bad weather forces it to stop in the Antilles, whereas the tiny Ruby-throated Hummingbird makes a 500-mile (800-km) flight across the Gulf of Mexico.

These long flights expend an enormous amount of energy and when no rest is possible must impose a tremendous strain. Birds must be in good flying condition and new feathers grown or molt delayed until migration is complete. Fuel reserves must be built up to power the flight, and when it is a long haul with no intermediate feeding opportunities these must be considerable. They consist of fat, which produces more energy than the same weight of protein or carbohydrates and has the advantage that as this is burned up it generates water, a life-saving bonus for a bird that may have no opportunity to drink as it crosses sea or desert. Part of the fat stored is a subcutaneous layer spread around the body just below the skin, but a large amount is stored within the body cavity where, although adding weight, it will not interfere with the bird's flying ability.

There is a limit to the extra fat that each bird can carry, for extra weight requires much greater effort to lift it into the air. Large birds add on proportionally much less than the small species, but some of these double their weight, as do the Blackpoll Warblers of North America, which gather on the eastern seaboard to feed for two to three weeks, the small warblers, such

migration began to be observed it was noticeable that the birds that could be seen migrating often followed what at times appeared to be quite narrow tracks across land. When evidence of migration was searched for, it tended to be found along coasts and at coastal headlands. On this basis, migration routes could be traced as lines across maps.

With the advent of radar and similar aids it was discovered that other migration was occurring, usually most marked at night but also by day, and this was taking place at much higher altitudes, with birds widely dispersed and seemingly not reacting to physical features such as hill ridges and coasts. This broad-front migration, as it was called, appeared to involve by far the greatest number of birds and was regarded as the more important type.

It is now apparent that broad-front migration is used by the majority of migrants, flying at altitudes of 3,300–6,600 feet (1,000–2,000 m) and occasionally much higher. Altitude is varied to take advantage of following winds or avoiding adverse ones. However, this type of flight is directional, and direction may change during the course of migration. It can therefore be said that such migrants have a kind of route, since they start from a certain general area and fly in a certain direction.

Day-flying migrants also fly high when possible, but in less favorable conditions such as adverse winds they fly lower and take advantage of ground topography. Storks, pelicans, birds of prey and other large soaring birds that normally depend heavily on thermals tend at most times to fly lower, along more precise routes and to use higher ground and thermals to aid their passage.

The ways in which birds fly often determine the routes they take. The soaring birds avoid large stretches of sea where thermals are not available. Those that migrate between Africa and Europe, for instance, do not cross the Mediterranean Sea but cross at the Straits of Gibraltar or take a route around its western shores. Some other birds take these routes too, though they may mean longer journeys, but others fly the length of Italy and head straight

as the Sedge Warbler in western Europe, and small arctic shorebirds.

It has been calculated that Blackpolls have the potential for about 115 hours flying time. Their journey to South America takes about 85 hours in favorable conditions but, even so, unexpected and adverse winds could prove disastrous.

The presence of suitable feeding grounds where fattening up can take place probably has a major influence on migratory routes and types of journey. Sedge Warblers, which fatten up in southern Britain, for instance, generally fly over Europe without stopping, but the English Reed Warblers fly first to Spain and fatten up there for the journey onwards. The Marsh Warbler makes a much more leisurely journey from Europe to South Africa with several long feeding stops, but it has to leave earlier and stays for a much shorter period in the south.

Birds fattened ready for migration provide hunters with a bonus. In the north the Eskimo Curlew, once so numerous that it was known as the Prairie Pigeon after the Passenger Pigeon, used to fatten up on snails and crowberries in Newfoundland and Nova Scotia so that its breast developed a thick layer of fat looking like dough and it became known as the Doughbird. Hunting reduced its numbers and it is now brought near to extinction; but the greatest blow came from habitat loss at the end of the last century when, following the failure of Russian harvests, the pampas grasslands of

Argentina were converted to agriculture to meet the demand for grain, followed by the disappearance of its habitat across the Great Plains and the prairie provinces of Canada.

What triggers migration

While the reasons for migration lie in the need to find food when conditions make it hard to come by or there are too many birds in competition, birds do not migrate in response to the increasing shortage of food. They leave well in advance of winter conditions developing, for they need a time of plenty to build up their resources. A major signal is probably the reduction in daylight hours as the summer moves into fall, which encourages them to eat in preparation as well as finally to set off. However, this is probably only a "fine-tuning" control for the bird's built-in "body clock," an annual hormonal cycle that will operate even without environmental factors.

For the bird's survival it is essential that this biological clock can be overruled, for it would be fatal for the bird to make its flight in bad conditions. There is plenty of evidence that birds will wait for bad weather to pass or for a wind to change to their advantage before beginning or at part stages of their migration, often responding to barometric pressure. Delay cannot be indefinite, however, and to stay beyond the period when food is plentiful could risk depleting the reserves needed for the flight,

Horseshoe Crabs, which evolved long before these Laughing Gulls (Larus atricilla) feeding upon them, have for centuries come to the beaches of Cape Cod and Delaware Bay to breed. Stranded crabs, eggs laid in the sand and, two weeks later, newly hatched crabs, provide a feast for shorebirds, including many migrants such as turnstones, sanderlings, dunlins and knots on their way north.

Following pages *White-fronted Terns (Ternus striata) over a breeding colony on the New Zealand coast. After breeding they move westwards to winter on the coasts of southeastern Australia.*

or no longer match with the best times for making later stages of the journey. Yet some birds do stay right through the winter when others of their kind make the journey to distant lands.

Who stays, who goes?

Over 60 percent of bird families have migrant members and more than half of all birds migrate. Even in the tropics a large proportion are not resident all year-round. In Mexico, for instance, out of some 950 species, 750 (79 percent) are resident and the other 200 (21 percent) either winter visitors or birds of passage migrating further. The proportion of migrants tends to rise as latitude becomes higher. In Britain about 50 percent of the 240 species regularly recorded are visitors, about two thirds of these southern birds moving north to breed and one third northern breeders flying south to winter. In addition a large number of the resident birds migrate for shorter distances within the British Isles. Moving up into the Arctic there are fewer species overall and more of them migrate; in Greenland at least 36 of the 64 known species leave and most of the remaining birds move south within the island. In Greenland probably only the Ptarmigan, Black Guillemot, Snowy Owl, Fieldfare and Raven spend the whole year in the same area as they breed.

Of long-distance migrants between the hemispheres, most breed in the north. The great stretches of tundra and subarctic swamp, scrub and forest stretching across Siberia and North America have huge populations of birds such as nesting shorebirds that are strong on the wing and must get out in winter; they pour south. Arctic-nesting Dunlins reach the southern tip of Africa; Godwits, Greenshanks and Curlew Sandpipers from Siberia reach Australia and New Zealand, as do Wandering Tattlers from Alaska. The Alaskan Bristle-thighed Curlew freely crosses the Pacific to islands from Hawaii almost to New Zealand and the Whimbrel and Hudsonian Godwit of arctic North America reach Tierra del Fuego.

Among coastal seabirds the Arctic Tern moves from a breeding range bordering north polar regions south to Antarctic seas and back during winter migration, a round trip of about 22,000 miles (35,000 km) each year. Since some birds live 10–12 years, it is estimated that their total travel would be as far as from the earth to the moon. This is an incredible distance but one wonders how it would compare with a swift flying nonstop for most of its life.

Seabirds such as tubenoses, riding the winds, perform great figure-eight tracks north and south across the oceans. The Manx Shearwaters of western Europe move southwest, down the South American coast to the Antarctic, presumably fly nearer to Africa on the return and then cross to the western side of the North Atlantic for the final part of their journey. Their track depends upon the prevailing ocean winds. Southern birds follow similar tracks. The Great and Sooty Shearwaters that breed on islands in the South Atlantic and Antarctic seas move on a northward track through the Atlantic similar to that of the Manx Shearwater, but in reverse. Other Sooty Shearwaters encircle the Pacific Ocean, whereas the Short-tailed Shearwater of southeastern Australia circles through the northern end of the Pacific on a clockwise track before returning to breed.

Not all such seabirds seem to follow predictable routes. Many of the seabirds breeding in southern and Antarctic seas, from albatrosses downwards, may move in seminomadic fashion around these southern oceans.

There are Southern Hemisphere landbirds that travel great distances too. For instance, after breeding, some of New Zealand's Banded Dotterels migrate across to Australia, and the Shining and Long-tailed Cuckoos, which lay their eggs in the nests of other New Zealand

The Arctic Tern (Sterna paradisaea) makes possibly the longest migrations, breeding in the Arctic and wintering in Antarctic seas. It is a coastal migrant, with routes mainly near coasts or across islands.

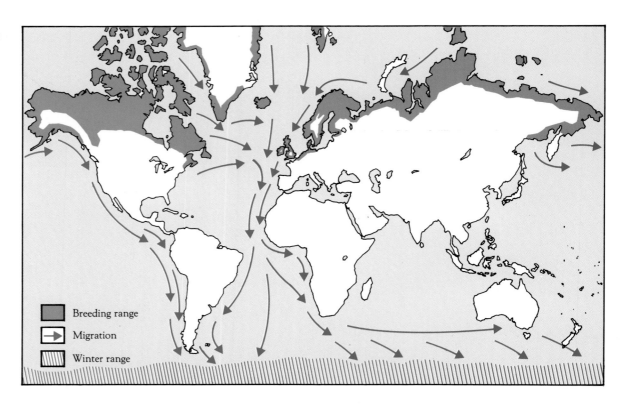

Breeding range

→ Migration

Winter range

birds, winter in Polynesia. However, none of the southern land birds migrate across the equator. Except for the extreme south of Chile and Argentina there is little land in the south, other than the Antarctic continent, where the landbirds are the flightless penguins. Without the temperate conditions with cold winters and seasonal food shortages that occur in the Northern Hemisphere there has been no reason for a cross-hemisphere migration pattern to develop.

It is not always obvious that birds will be migrants. Although the rails and the gamebirds are mostly sedentary, Corncrakes and Common Quail will migrate to Africa from Europe. Nor is it possible to make a hard and fast division of all species into migrants and nonmigrants. Among the migratory bird species there are many in which only some of the birds migrate. Climate and local conditions are obviously important in deciding whether an individual migrates or not — and some will make mistakes.

A few individuals, already near the colder margin of their winter range after migration, may remain instead of moving on — warblers such as Blackcaps and Chiffchaffs in Britain and the western European seaboard for example, where with luck conditions may be a little milder. They may sometimes survive more successfully than if they had migrated. With a mild winter or if extra food sources are available — bird-table feeding, for instance — it is possible that a bird may stand a better chance by staying. It may then gain the advantage of already having an established territory when the others arrive in spring.

Migration can take a heavy toll of birds not strong enough to complete the journey or who get blown off course. Of the estimated more than 5,000,000,000 birds that move south into Africa each autumn it is thought that only about half will survive to be back on their breeding grounds the next year.

Improvement in climatic conditions or the availability of new food sources may encourage

The Manx Shearwater (Puffinus puffinus), like other small tubenosed seabirds, returns to its burrow in a breeding colony at night to escape the attention of the larger gulls that would kill it while it is relatively helpless on land. The young, abandoned by their parents one to two weeks before fledging, make the long migration to South America unaided.

Left An Eastern Bar-tailed Godwit (Limosa lapponica baueri) probing the mud for crustaceans and marine worms. These long-distance migrants breed in the Arctic tundra but may travel south as far as Indonesia and Australasia.

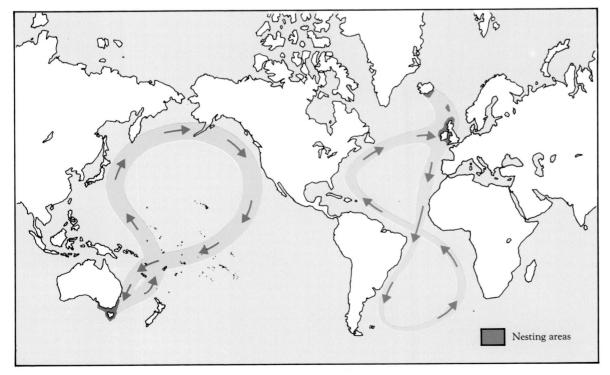

Nesting areas

Seabirds which economize on energy by gliding most of the time, travel at an angle to the prevailing winds. As a result, on long journeys their main course is around the ocean basins, clockwise in the Northern Hemispheres, anticlockwise in the Southern. For migrating species this produces a figure-eight track, shown here for the northern-breeding Manx Shearwater (Puffinus puffinus), wintering in the South Atlantic, and the southern-breeding Short-tailed Shearwater (P. tenuirostris) moving north in the southern winter in the Pacific Ocean.

a former migrant to become a resident species. Auxiliary feeding by bird lovers has some effect and the unintentional food provision in the increased amount that can be scavenged from garbage dumps seems to be responsible for a change in at least one species: the Hooded Crow, which early in the twentieth century was a migrant in western Europe, is now almost entirely sedentary.

Though climate is usually the reason a species is resident in one area and migrant in another, age and sex can produce differences within a local population. There is no broad rule by which this operates. The Juncos, which breed in the forests of western North America, migrate southwards but adult males winter further south than juveniles of either sex and adult females go further still. Among Chaffinches, juveniles are more likely to migrate than adults and, towards their northern limits, it is the females among adults that move furthest. Linnaeus, in Sweden, observed the deserted males and gave them the scientific name of *Fringilla coelebs* or "bachelor finch." They stay probably because in competing for food the dominant males benefit most from keeping an established territory, whereas females and juveniles, who may not yet have begun to breed, gain more advantage by migrating to a better food supply. Similarly, in Britain, although most are resident, some female Robins move south in winter.

The Ovenbird Warbler (Seiurus aurocapillus), a North American Wood Warbler named for its domed nest and not one of the Ovenbird family, is an insect eater which migrates down to the tropical areas of Central and South America for the northern winter.

warmed by the North Atlantic Drift. This can sometimes result in a huge influx of a particular species, known as an irruption, usually caused by the failure or at least a considerable reduction in the crop of seeds or berries on which they feed, or a cyclic reduction in prey species. In 1983, a failure in the acorn crop in Europe saw flocks of Jays, normally relatively solitary birds, arrive in Britain, and similar smaller movements are shown more frequently in the thick-billed race of the Nutcracker that relies on hazelnuts.

Migration patterns

There are many more bird movements than seasonal north-south, south-north patterns. Altitude migration has already been mentioned and Alpine Water Pipits moving to low altitudes may end up in lowlands of northwest Europe. European Lapwings move westwards after breeding towards the milder regions of the Atlantic coast and Woodcock show a south-westerly shift.

Many sedentary birds move short distances to take advantage of a more protected winter habitat or a winter food source, sometimes adopting a radical change of diet, but this is not usually classed as migration, any more than the daily journey that many birds make from roost to feeding grounds is described as such. These movements may not be for the whole season but reflect more restricted weather changes, such as the cold snap that ices up a pond, freezes ground so that it can no longer be probed for worms or coats berries in frozen snow. The Capercaillie, a member of the Grouse family that lives in European highlands feeding on leaves and seeds on the forest floor in summer, eats pine needles when snows make its summer food inaccessible. They often winter in higher altitudes to gain access to conifers and, though few travel far, some reverse the normal pattern and go north instead of south.

When a winter is unusually severe or other conditions create food shortages, birds on the European continent may move west to Britain,

The magnificent Royal Albatross (Diomedea epomophora) breeds around New Zealand but in winter disperses through the southern ocean across to the east coast of South America and possibly beyond.

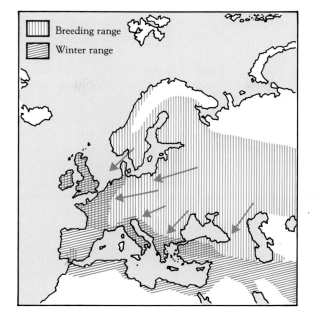

Not all migration is north-south. The Lapwing (Vanellus vanellus) breeds in Europe on moist meadows and requires similar unfrozen ground in winter. The bulk of the European population moves west or southwest toward the milder Atlantic coastal region as soon as nesting is over. Other inland shorebirds needing soft and muddy ground, such as Woodcock and Common Snipe show similar westward winter movement.

Breeding range

Winter range

Arctic birds feeding on lemming frequently irrupt elsewhere when the lemming population falls, Snowy Owls, for instance, sometimes appearing in California and other northern areas south of their normal range, as do Rough-legged Buzzards.

In other animals affected by food shortages there is a balancing cycle. Starvation reduces populations so that the following year fewer seeds or prey will be eaten, giving those species a chance to recover — as in the balancing of population of the Bobcat and Snowshoe Rabbit in North America — but birds can escape to feed elsewhere. Those that stay may die and the dangers of moving from home ground will take others but, in the long term, occasional years of extreme plenty that lead to an increase in population are balanced by bad winters that cull all except the strongest and most resourceful birds.

Nomads

Not all bird movement is as regulated as that of the migrants. In desert areas where rainfall is spasmodic and plants and animals must respond quickly to it with a short-lived burgeoning, birds may wander from place to place to exploit these conditions. A typical example are the Budgerigars of Australia. Even their breeding cycle is triggered by rainfall, for without it they would not have the food available to produce eggs and raise a brood.

Nomadism appears to be an alternative to migration in situations where there is no area of assured food supply to which the birds can move. There may be partial nomads (which could include many seabirds) that wander for much of the year, returning to traditional sites to breed. True nomads wander and settle to breed where and when conditions are suitable.

About a quarter of Australian species are nomadic. They include seed eaters such as parrots, pigeons and grassfinches, insect eaters such as wood-swallows, nectar-feeding honey-eaters, marshland birds such as rails and ibises and, more particularly, waterbirds such as ducks, cormorants and pelicans. All must have a flexible breeding season, possibly breeding at any time, and must respond quickly to improved conditions. Nesting in the Gray Teal will be triggered off by rising water and in wood-swallows a heavy shower may be enough. They must nest simply and be able to do so quickly. If conditions are good they may breed successfully and build up numbers rapidly, but they are cut back by drought and disaster. If a food supply fails, whole breeding colonies with eggs or young in any stage of development will be deserted and die.

The nomadic Black-footed Albatross (Diomedea nigripes) breeds on the Hawaiian Islands, wandering around the North Pacific with a distinct move northward in the winter.

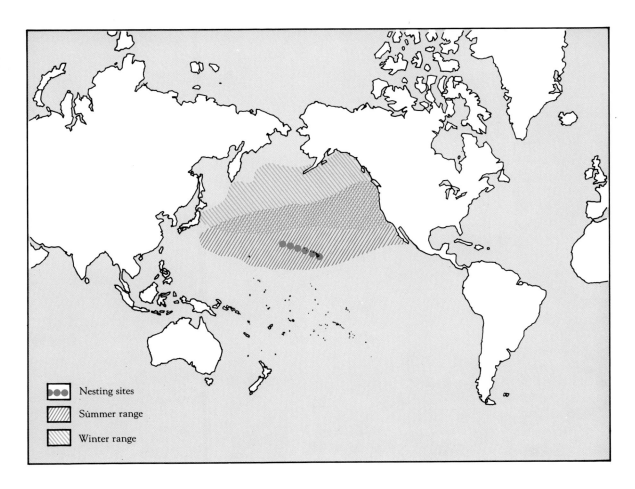

Nesting sites

Summer range

Winter range

Some birds considered rare will appear from the Australian interior in bad times. Flock Pigeons are arid grassland birds that live, feed and nest in flocks on the ground, traveling fast and appearing or disappearing unpredictably. Rarely seen species, such as Bourke's Parakeet or the Splendid Parakeet, may suddenly become widespread in more cultivated areas.

Nomadic species can at times produce very large populations. In areas where food supplies may not be wildly irregular, movement within an area, similar to nomadism, may be used to support very large numbers. The vast natural forests of North America, before European settlers destroyed them, produced great crops of nuts, seeds and fruits. The Passenger Pigeon, which lived on such food, occurred in huge numbers but there appear to have been only a few really vast flocks moving around to crop temporarily on abundance of food. The Redbilled Queleas of Africa show a similar pattern.

Vagrancy

Birds occasionally appear in a place where they do not normally occur, apparently not from choice but as the result of some unexpected event. This can produce odd sightings of unusual birds or in some instances lead to an extension of range. The British Isles are well placed to catch stray birds, off course and trying to avoid the open sea, from both Eurasia and North America. They are also situated along the line of changing weather systems associated with the jet stream. The great numbers of bird-watchers looking out for rarities has ensured the logging of an impressive list of about 450 species seen in Britain, of which about half are vagrants, an indication of the possible magnitude with which vagrancy occurs.

Some of these vagrants in Britain are strays from Europe blown off course, some lost migrants from North America, or carried out of North Africa or the Arctic by unusual weather conditions. There are fairly frequent occurrences of birds from unlikely areas such as southern Siberia, for which one explanation offered is that they are birds that suffer from reverse migration, a kind of navigational defect that results in their traveling in exactly the opposite direction to that which they should. In some cases the birds are immature individuals and some vagrancy may be related to the tendency to random dispersal and wandering shown by the young of some normally more sedentary species.

If a number of birds are displaced, they may try to establish themselves. Small flocks of Lapwings, and more recently Jackdaws, have appeared in eastern North America. A wind-driven movement of Fieldfares accidentally colonized Greenland in 1937. White-eyes reached New Zealand in the mid-nineteenth century and Gray Teal more recently. A few wood-swallows of two species survived and bred there for several years in the 1970s.

Most vagrants appear to be lost birds on their way to disaster. However, in some places, some species turn up intermittently. If they can last out and survive until others arrive they may have a chance of establishing themselves, even though arrivals occur only at long and infrequent intervals. Such changes would seem to be the only basis for colonization and possible later development of endemic species on oceanic islands.

Right *The White-crowned Sparrow* (Zonotrichis leucophrys), *a species which occurs in Europe as a vagrant, is one of the many in the Bunting tribe called sparrows in America.*

A flock of Sulphur-crested Cockatoos (Cacatua galerita) *take flight, some pink Galahs* (Eolophus roseicapillus) *and a Little Corella* (Cacatua sanguinea) *among them. Such flocks search for seeds and roots in open country.*

BIRDS OF THE WORLD

THE CLASSIFICATION OF BIRDS

Evolution is a continuous process of small mutations. When these are advantageous and selection for better-adapted individuals operates as they spread into different environments, an array of isolated and highly adapted non-interbreeding units is gradually produced that are called species. These, in turn, may show further local adaptation to differing pressures and subdivide to produce new species. Each creature must find an ecological niche — a place in the interrelationship of environment, food sources and competitors — where it can thrive. However, conditions can change and whole groups of species that once were best fitted to their life-style may no longer be able to survive or to compete effectively with other species. They become extinct.

The Wood Warbler (Phylloscopus sibilatrix), of the Leaf Warbler family, is a migrant that breeds in forest with a high canopy and little undergrowth, but builds its domed nest hidden among leaves and litter on the ground.

161

Bird evolution can be envisaged as like a tree, constantly growing and spreading in three dimensions, adding new branches and twigs. The birds we see today, some 9,672 species, are the tips of the twigs at the top of the present tree. By studying them we can work out, to some extent, the early pattern of branching by which they were produced. For information on the various "branches" and "twigs" that died off at earlier periods we must rely on the evidence provided by surviving fossils. This study of the relationship between different birds is usually called *systematics*. To list all the kinds involved on paper, a three-dimensional structure is reduced to a continuous flat list, using a hierarchical sequence. This is a *classification* and because of the modifications necessary to produce them, to some degree all classifications are arbitrary.

The Class Aves, to give the complete bird group its scientific name, is subdivided into large groups, known as orders, which in turn are broken down into suborders, families, subfamilies, tribes, genera and species. In an attempt to produce perfect sequences, additional subheadings may also be inserted.

In referring to bird species, either a local language name may be used or a scientific name, which will be internationally understood. This scientific name consists of two words in Latin: the name of the species (the individual form) and the name of the genus, which is a small group of closely-related species with the species as the individual. The name of the genus — the generic name — comes first and with a capital letter, followed by the name of the species, without a capital. For example, in the pigeons the generic name of the typical pigeons is *Columba*. The Rock Dove, from which our domestic pigeons are produced, is the species *livia* and known as *Columba livia* wherever it occurs.

The genera are organized within groups called families, which in turn are set within larger groups called orders. The large division to which pigeons belong is the order Columbiformes and the family within that order is the Columbidae. That order contains another family, that of the now-extinct Dodos, the Raphidae, which form a snapped-off twig on the still-growing tree of evolution.

For ease of use and comparisons, a classification should be as permanent and consistent as possible, but constant additions to the knowledge of bird relationships means that it must also be flexible and capable of accommodating new information. For nearly 60 years a classification has been used that was based on one proposed by Alexander Wetmore, incorporating ideas newly arising from what was then known about fossil birds. Constant additions have required modifications that are at times confusing.

One problem that has arisen constantly is the need to distinguish true relationship from adaptive convergence — the development of resemblances in quite unrelated birds because they evolve similar ways of life and hence similar characteristics. Aerial flycatching is an obvious way for a bird to catch insects, and groups of flycatcher species that are unrelated but resemble each other have evolved independently in South America, Australia and the Oriental region.

In attempting to arrange and classify birds, there is therefore a need to use objective characters that are not affected by this kind of superficial similarity. Attempts have been made using a wide variety of characters.

A classification was recently produced by C. G. Sibley and J. E. Ahlquist based upon the use of the DNA strands in the body cells that carry the characters for inheritance. The double strands in which the DNA occurs were separated, those of pairs of different key species mixed together, and the degree of recombination measured. This appeared to indicate the amount of affinity between species without reference to any external characters.

Only a limited number of species could be treated, and other information was combined with that from DNA that may raise some problems concerning the smaller details of relationships, but a whole new outline of bird evolution has been made available and is followed in this book.

As well as the various divisions described already there is a halfway stage in which large units of birds have been popularly placed in groups such as the finches, thrushes, pigeons, owls and waterfowl. These consist of obviously related species but tend to differ from each other and are readily identified by most people. In past classifications, groups such as these have mostly been listed as families. In the new classification, the elaborate branching sequences of evolution have been followed more closely. Some units that were once regarded as families are now seen to be more closely related and may appear lower down in the sequence of groupings, as subfamilies or tribes. In a few cases groups have been subdivided or upgraded to appear as higher categories.

In this book, to avoid well-known bird groups becoming submerged within scientific families, some family subdivisions into subfamilies and tribes have been discussed as fully as though they were families. As well as common English names for groups (where they exist), scientific names are also given. These provide a guide to the status of the group described in their name endings that tend to remain the same according to the level: "-iformes" for an order, "-dae" for a family, "-nae" for a subfamily and "-ni" for a tribe. The diagram or dendrogram opposite shows the links between the orders; later dendrograms explain the divisions in the two most complex orders — the Ciconiiformes and the Passeriformes.

Unless otherwise specified, the measurements given for each bird family in the following pages refer to the length from bill tip to tail tip.

THE BIRD FAMILIES

RATITES Struthioniformes

1. Elephant-birds (Aepyornithidae) Extinct. Occurred on Madagascar and, mainly on egg-shell evidence, in Africa. Eleven species or more, up to 10 ft (3 m) tall and massively built, probably up to 1,100 lbs (500 kg) in weight. Apparently vegetarian, the last known birds on Madagascar were helped into extinction by man, probably 1,500–1,000 years ago.

2. Ostriches (Struthionidae) 1 genus, 1 species. A huge bird, up to 8 ft (2.5 m), with long legs with two short thick toes, legs and long thin neck bare of feathers, filmy wing and tail feathers. Males are black and white, neck blue or reddish; females gray-brown. Sociable and a fast runner, it has scattered distribution in Africa, living in savanna, thin thorn scrub and semidesert, feeding mostly on seeds and plants and some small creatures. The male has a booming call and wing-waving display. Polygamous, male and chief female incubate a bare nest scrape where several females lay up to 30 creamy-white, rounded eggs, but not many hatch. Striped downy precocial young cared for by both adults. Originally present through Eurasia, possibly not in Africa until the Miocene. In Africa one species with scattered distribution. Small desert subspecies (Arabia and East Sahara) were extinct by the 1940s.

3. Rheas (Rheidae) 2 genera, 2 species. Like smaller ostriches, up to 3 ft (90 cm) tall but short-feathered on head, neck and thighs. Rheas occur in South America, one species widespread on grassland, one mainly in open Andean highlands. Plumage is loose and droopy. No tail. Dull gray brown, white feather tips on one species. Fast moving, it swims well,

RHEAS: A male Greater Rhea (Rhea americana) with partly grown young, which he tends alone. The Lesser Rhea (R. pennata) is a little smaller, lacks the black color on the neck and has most feathers of the body tipped with white.

Below *From a possible origin in the Triassic period, more than 190 million years ago, birds' ancestors produced two branches during the Jurassic (190–136 million years ago): the Archaeornithes (to which Archaeopteryx may belong) and another line, which probably divided to produce three branches during the Cretaceous period (136-65 mya), of which two became extinct but the Neornithes went on to produce the modern birds. All the modern orders were established during the Cretaceous period.*

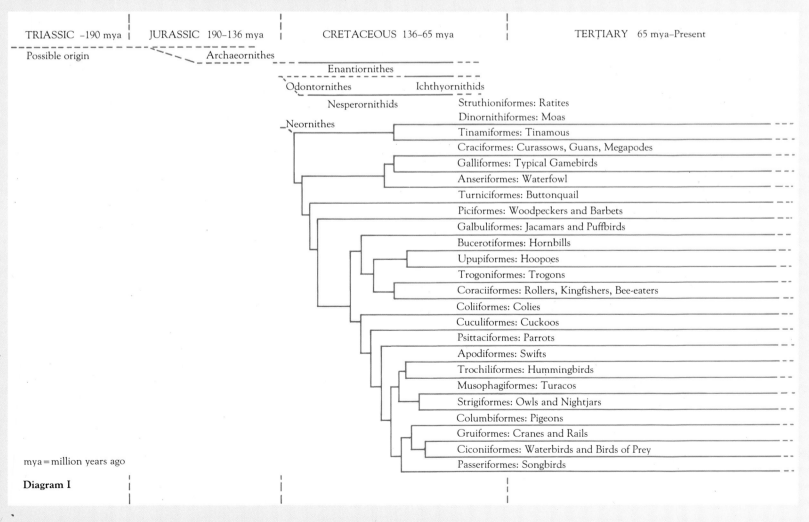

TRIASSIC –190 mya   JURASSIC 190–136 mya   CRETACEOUS 136–65 mya   TERTIARY 65 mya–Present

Possible origin   Archaeornithes

Enantiornithes

Odontornithes   Ichthyornithids

Nesperornithids

Neornithes

Struthioniformes: Ratites
Dinornithiformes: Moas
Tinamiformes: Tinamous
Craciformes: Curassows, Guans, Megapodes
Galliformes: Typical Gamebirds
Anseriformes: Waterfowl
Turniciformes: Buttonquail
Piciformes: Woodpeckers and Barbets
Galbuliformes: Jacamars and Puffbirds
Bucerotiformes: Hornbills
Upupiformes: Hoopoes
Trogoniformes: Trogons
Coraciiformes: Rollers, Kingfishers, Bee-eaters
Coliiformes: Colies
Cuculiformes: Cuckoos
Psittaciformes: Parrots
Apodiformes: Swifts
Trochiliformes: Hummingbirds
Musophagiformes: Turacos
Strigiformes: Owls and Nightjars
Columbiformes: Pigeons
Gruiformes: Cranes and Rails
Ciconiiformes: Waterbirds and Birds of Prey
Passeriformes: Songbirds

mya = million years ago

Diagram I

is sociable and feeds on plants, roots, some small creatures. Polygamous, 6–12 females lay up to 50 yellowish or greenish eggs in a bare nest scrape. The male incubates alone, only covering some eggs, and cares for the striped downy precocial young.

4. Cassowaries and Emus (Casuariidae) Large Australian ratites producing two tribes: Cassowaries (Casuariini) 1 genus, 3 species, up to 6.5 ft (2 m) high; and Emus (Dromaiini) 1 genus, 1 species, up to 6.5 ft (2 m) high.

Heavily built, **Cassowaries** are designed for pushing through thick vegetation of the tropical forest of Queensland, New Guinea and islands to southern Indonesia where they occur. They have an upright bony casque on top of the head and coarse, drooping, hairy-looking, blackish plumage with wing feathers reduced to bare quills and no obvious tail. Legs are stout with sharp claws used to slash in fighting. The bare head and neck, sometimes with wattles, are vividly colored, varying with species and age. Calls are varied rumblings, roars, booms and hisses. The bill is narrow and food mainly fruit, with some plants, seeds and small creatures. Females are larger and at times polyandrous, making several nests; 3–6 finely ridged, bright green eggs are incubated by male, who tends striped downy precocial young. **Emus** occur in arid scrub of open country of inland Australia, from semidesert to open forest. They have coarse, drooping, brown plumage, a blunt tapering tail and bare blue facial skin, vestigial wings and no visible tail. They run fast, can swim and usually live in pairs or small parties, feeding on fruit, berries, seeds, some plants and small creatures. Females are larger and brighter colored. Usually 7–11 dark green, finely ridged eggs, laid in a scrape, are incubated by male. Striped, downy precocial young are tended by male, sometimes for 18 months.

5. Kiwis (Apterygidae) 1 genus, 3 species. 18–24 in (45–84 cm) long, usually with a semi-crouching stance. They are found in moist forest and scrub in New Zealand only. Plumage is hairlike and coarse, brown or grayish. The body is narrow, legs proportionally very large, short and stout, the wings vestigial, tail absent. The neck tapers forwards to a small head with small eyes. Bill long, slender and slightly curved, with nostrils at the tip and long sensitive bristles around the base. Crepuscular and nocturnal, probing with sensitive bill for worms and invertebrates, they also take some berries and seeds. They whistle and snuffle. The male makes a nest burrow for 1–2 huge white eggs (up to 25 percent of the female's weight), which he incubates for up to 85 days, then tends precocial young.

MOAS Dinornithiformes

6. Moas (Dinornithidae 1 genus, ?6 species and Anomalopterygidae ?5genera, ?14 species.) Extinct. A range of species of these two families occurred in New Zealand forest. Ranging from *ca.* 40–156 in (1–4 m) in height, they had long, massive legs, coarse feathering, long necks and small heads with short blunt browsing bills; apparently feeding on vegetation in the absence of browsing mammals. Finally exterminated by hunting and massive environmental destruction by humans in the last 900 years, mainly in the earlier part of that period.

TINAMOUS Tinamiformes

7. Tinamous (Tinamidae) 9 genera, 47 species. Smaller gamebird-like species 6–20 in (15–49 cm). Ground-living birds of Central and South America, where they run and skulk, mostly in forest and scrub, a few in more open grassland. They have a compact body with smallish head, bill narrow and very slightly curved, and legs strong but fairly short. Reluctant fliers with short rounded wings, the plumage usually gray or brown with cryptic patterning, thick body feathering may hide tail. Whistling and piping calls. Solitary, in pairs or gregarious, the females are larger and some species are polyandrous. Nests are poorly lined scrapes with 1–12 eggs that are extremely glossy, bright blue, purplish gray, brown or green. The male incubates and rears the downy precocial young. Occur in Central and South America.

CURASSOWS, GUANS AND MEGAPODES Craciformes

8. Curassows, Guans, Chachalacas (Cracidae) 11 genera, 50 species, 21–40 in (52–100 cm). Moderate to large forest- and tree-adapted gamebirds, found in pairs or groups from southern U.S.A. to northern Argentina, their longish necks, legs and tail giving an impression of slender build. Their large feet, with well-developed hind toe, perch and grasp well. The bill is short and slightly curved. Food includes fruits, seeds, husks, leaves and some small creatures. They are all agile in trees but rather slow and heavy in flight. Nests are small loose twig platforms in a tree, or on the ground in a few species. Eggs, usually 2–3, hatch to downy young with wing feathers; they perch well and fly in 3–4 days.

Curassows spend much time on the ground in forests but roost and take refuge in trees, running easily along branches. They have crests of curled feathers and colored bill knobs or ridges. Chachalacas are small dull colored, more arboreal birds of scrub and woodland. Guans are heavier and almost wholly arboreal, with bright bare throats, wattles or other ornaments.

9. Megapodes (Megapodiidae) 6 genera, 19 species, 10–30 in (25–75 cm). Moderate to large gamebirds, occurring from the Nicobar Islands

Above EMUS: A male Emu (Dromaius novaehollandiae), *a bird of arid open country. The shaggy, drooping feathering makes it less conspicuous when resting. Females have deeper blue skin on face and neck, bordered by darker feathering.*

Left TINAMOUS: The Chilean Tinamou (Nothoprocta perdicaria) *is one of the smaller, skulking tinamou species, of typical appearance. A few of the largest are plain gray. Most are forest birds. The few that live in more open country are browner and more heavily patterned; two have thin, upright crests.*

and Philippines to Central Polynesia and Australia from forest (often coastal) to dry inland scrub in one species. Heads are small with a short stout bill with a slightly curved top; tails sometimes fairly long and laterally flattened as in domestic fowl; wings short and rounded, flight usually short and infrequent, only forest scrubfowl regularly perching in trees. Legs are very large and strong, toes and claws well developed and designed for digging. Head, or head and neck may have bright bare skin, some have wattles and the Maleo has a domed head-casque. Food includes seeds, fruit, plants, roots and some small invertebrates. Nesting is unique. Eggs are large and blunt ended and hatched by the heat of sand, soil or rotting vegetation. Some species lay eggs in hot sand or soil exposed to the sun. Forest-living scrubfowl scratch a soil and leafmould mound shared by several pairs. The male Brush-Turkey builds a huge mound of forest floor debris. The Mallee-fowl has a soil and plant debris mound, tended and temperature checked for most of the year, which is opened for the female to lay. Brush-Turkey and Malleefowl lay up to 35 eggs, separately, and these incubate for *ca.* 50 days. The downy, precocial chick digs its way to the surface after hatching, able to run, feed and fly — wholly independent.

TYPICAL GAMEBIRDS Galliformes

10. Typical gamebirds (Phasianidae) 45 genera, 177 species, 5–44 in (12–110 cm). A large, complex family of small to large gamebirds, including quails, partridges, pheasants, grouse, turkeys and peacocks, that occur in open to forest habitats from the Arctic to the tropics, absent only from Antarctica and South America. They have in common small, stout and slightly curved bills, strong legs and feet for mainly terrestrial existence (spurred in some species) and relatively short rounded wings for sudden powerful flight usually short and low. Food is mainly seeds and parts of plants, various small creatures, and sometimes fruit. Most species are terrestrial but some grouse feed in trees and tragopans nest in trees. The forms include compact, short-tailed quail and partridge types, often similar-sexed with cryptic coloring and patterns. Pheasant types are long tailed, males having vividly colored plumage and wattles and complex display. The most elaborate display plumages occur in Asiatic peacocks and argus pheasants. The grouse occur in cooler climates, having cryptic or elaborate plumage and dense feathering, down to the feet on Ptarmigan. Breeding may be solitary or with males at leks, in pairs, or polygamous or polygynous. The nest is usually a sparsely-lined ground scrape with a large clutch of dull-colored eggs. Incubation and care of the downy, patterned precocial young is usually by the female alone.

11. Guineafowl (Numididae) 4 genera, 6 species, 17–30 in (43–75 cm). Moderate-sized birds of African habitats from semidesert to rainforest, guineafowl have a lumpy body, short tail and rounded wings. The head is small with typical gamebird bill, usually bare, the skin sometimes brightly colored or ornamented with crest, frill of feathers or bony casque on top. Legs and feet are well developed for walking, running and scratching and may bear spurs. Mainly ground-living, they roost in trees but fly little. Food is plants, roots and small creatures. Thick-shelled buff or speckled eggs are incubated by the female in a thinly-lined scrape. The striped, downy precocial young are active after hatching, following the parents, and can

TYPICAL GAMEBIRDS: *A male Reeves's Pheasant (Syrmaticus reevesii),* with its long tail and bright plumage is typical of the pheasants, and the female (left) is more cryptically colored. Other genera, such as Partridges and Quails are smaller and more compact but the family also includes the spectacular Turkey, Argus Pheasant and Peacock.

Top CURASSOWS, GUANS, CHACHALACAS: *A Horned Guan (Oreophasis derbianus),* one of the rarer species of these tree-adapted gamebirds, has an odd bony head ornamentation but is otherwise characteristic of the family.

Left GUINEAFOWL: *Vulturine Guineafowl (Acryllium vulturinum). Other species are very similar, differing in head ornamentation. The blue color, streaked neck and bald head typify this species.*

fly before they are fully grown. When not breeding Guineafowl are highly sociable.

12. New World Quail (Odontophoridae) 9 genera, 31 species, 6.75–12 in (17–30 cm). Small, typically partridgelike gamebirds with short stubby bills and sometimes slender or forward-curved crests. Most have conspicuous facial patterns, more bold on males. Habitats range from tropical forest to arid plain or mountain scrub from U.S.A. to northern Argentina. Ground living in pairs (or nonforest birds in flocks when not breeding), they run well and fly low and fast, but can perch and roost above ground. Food is seeds, plants and insects. They have short, loud calls. The nest is a thinly lined scrape with 7–16 eggs. Boldly patterned, downy, precocial young are tended by both parents, or male alone while female renests.

WATERFOWL Anseriformes

13. Screamers (Anhimidae) 2 genera, 3 species, 32–36 in (80–90 cm). Big, wader-like birds, heavy bodied and small headed, having long thick legs with long toes and often wading though capable of perching, screamers occur by water in South America. Dull colored and crested, with loud antiphonal calls, they fly well and can soar for long periods. Their large wings have two spurs on the leading edge, used in fighting. The bill is oddly short, curved and gamebirdlike. They feed in and around marshes, eating mainly plants and some insects. Both adults build a large nest mound, usually in water. Downy, precocial young remain in or by the nest at first, fed by adults.

14. Magpie Goose (Anseranatidae) 1 genus, 1 species, 28–37 in (71–92 cm). A large, lanky goose, with a knobbed forehead, that occurs in the swamps of northern Australia. Its bill is fairly long and strong, the neck slender, legs long and strong and feet half-webbed. The wings are broad and flight slow and raptorlike. The male's windpipe is lengthened for loud honking. It feeds and breeds in large flocks in seasonal swamps, eating plants and seeds and digging for bulbs of spike-rushes. The nest is a trampled platform. Males sometimes have two females, sharing a nest. The precocial downy young feed on swamp grass seeds, parents show the food and may dribble seed into the young one's open bill, unique in waterfowl.

15. Whistling Ducks (Dendrocygnidae) 2 genera, 9 species, 16–24 in (41–61 cm). Moderate-sized, web-footed ducks with long legs and necks and an upright stance that occur from the Americas to Afrotropical Africa and from Asia to Australia. They have rounded wings and can fly slowly for long distances, neck lowered and legs trailing. They feed in water, dabbling, upending and diving, taking water plants and small creatures, and some graze near water. Highly sociable, often perching, they form long pair bonds, nesting in vegetation near water or in the fork or hollow of a swamp tree, both adults nesting and tending young. The mainly brown, downy, precocial ducklings follow their parents.

16–19. Typical Waterfowl (Anatidae) 43 genera, 148 species. All web-footed, they divide into several subfamilies and tribes.

16. Stiff-tailed Ducks (Oxyurinae) 2 genera, 8 species, 14–29 in (35–72 cm). Smallish, large-headed diving ducks that spend most of their lives in fresh water, occurring through the Americas, southern Eurasia, Africa and Australia. Their stiff tail feathers are rarely obvious

Above NEW WORLD QUAIL: A male California Quail (Callipepla californica), typical of these stoutly-built gamebirds, most with bold but somewhat cryptic plumage patterns.

Right WHISTLING DUCKS: A pair of White-faced Whistling Ducks (Dendrocygna viduata) allopreening, unusual in waterfowl but in this family possibly linked with a habit of perching near each other and long pair bonds. The scientific name means "tree-duck" but several species do not perch in trees.

Below MAGPIE GOOSE: Magpie Goose (Anseranas semipalmata) seems highly adapted for its niche as a semiterrestrial swamp dweller in the seasonally flooded marshes and billabongs. It likes seeding marsh plants and easily transfers to rice as food, becoming unpopular where rice growing has spread within its range.

STIFF-TAILED DUCKS: A male Musk Duck (Biziura lobata) has the typical heavy build, fleshy lobe under the bill and male much larger than the female. Highly aquatic, they seem reluctant to come to land or to fly unless forced to do so.

Below SWANS: Black Swans (Cygnus atratus) are more sociable than most but this attack shows the aggressiveness often present. These swans are typical of six swan species; the seventh, the Coscoroba Swan (Coscoroba coscoroba) looks like an overgrown, long-necked domestic duck.

GEESE: Bar-headed Geese (Anser indicus) feeding on shallowly flooded grassland where roots are more easily pulled up. This species breeds on the high central Asian plateau, migrating over the Himalayas at high altitudes.

Left TYPICAL DUCKS: North American Wood Ducks (Aix sponsa), typical of most ducks in the brighter plumage for the male but one of the forest ducks of inland waters, nesting in trees. The family also includes dabbling and diving ducks and narrow-billed fish eaters.

but bills are often large or swollen, with a big pendent lobe in the Musk Duck. Strong legs are set well back on the body, making walking difficult. They dive deep or feed on the surface on plants and small animals. Flight is strong but takeoff slow. Their nest platform is made in thick waterside vegetation. Downy precocial young are brownish and unpatterned, relying at first on food adults bring to the surface. Species include the Ruddy, Black-headed and White-headed Ducks.

17. Freckled Duck (Stictonettinae) 1 genus, 1 species, 19–24 in (48–59 cm). Longish-necked, dull-colored duck with some swan-like anatomical characters found in southeastern and southwestern Australia. It feeds at night by dabbling, mainly on algae, in freshwater swamps with trees. Nests at water level in bush or debris. Young are plain brownish gray, downy and precocial.

18. Swans (Cygninae) 2 genera, 7 species, 29–61 in (72–152 cm). Large, long-bodied birds, occurring through the Americas, Eurasia and Australia, with short stout legs and feet, long slender necks, small heads and strong bills. Wings long and strong, flight powerful with audible wingbeats in some species. Some have an elongated windpipe with a loop in the breastbone, producing loud trumpeting. Plumage white and/or black with sexes similar. Mainly aquatic, they upend, reaching down for underwater plants; some grazing by the waterside. They form long pair bonds and build a mound-like waterside nest together. Downy gray precocial young are tended by both parents, sometimes carried on the back when swimming. They remain with parents until next spring. Species migrate from coldest areas in winter.

19. Ducks and Geese (Anatinae) Comprises two tribes, the geese and the typical ducks.

The **Geese** (Anserini) 14 genera, 43 species, 12–46 in (30–114 cm), include geese, sheldgeese, shelducks, big perching ducks, diving steamerducks and tiny pigmy-geese. Typical characters are short stout bills for grazing and dipping, long necks and longish legs adapted for easy walking on land. Food is mainly parts of plants, taken from land or water, marine mollusks and crustaceans in some coastal species. Geese are mainly sociable when not breeding. Pairs form lifelong bonds. Young remain with adults for first year but Common Shelducks leave young in crèches and migrate to molt. Nest a down-lined hollow on the ground, or in low rock, stump or higher tree cavities in shelducks and perching ducks. Downy precocial young, plain yellowish or gray, or boldly patterned. Cosmopolitan in distribution, with migration from colder climates.

Ducks (Anatini) 24 genera, 89 species, 14–26 in (35–64 cm). Aquatic birds, cosmopolitan in distribution, found in most habitats where there is water, migrating from cold climates, often for long distances. Usually have short strong legs set well back on a compact body, bill broad and feathered for straining fine material from water, but variously modified and narrow in fish-eating sawbills. Wings narrow, flight strong, swift and direct. Plumage dull or camouflaged in females, usually brightly patterned in breeding males. Species may feed in water at the surface, dive in fresh and sea water or graze on land. Food may be plant material, invertebrates, frogs, mollusks, crustaceans, fish or amphibians. Pairing is often temporary and nesting usually by female, the nest a down-lined hollow on the ground or in a cavity or tree hole. Young are downy, precocial, and boldly patterned or plain and dark.

BUTTONQUAIL Turniciformes

20. Buttonquail (Turnicidae) 2 genera, 17 species, 4–8 in (11–20 cm). These birds, very similar to small quail, occur in Africa and southern Eurasia to Australia. Plump-bodied with rounded wings, small tails and staring, light-irised eyes, but no hind toes, their bill often longer and more slender than in gamebirds and legs well developed for running and scratching for food. They skulk in ground vegetation, preferring to crouch, reluctant to fly, but some species are nomadic or partial migrants. Food is seeds, plants and small creatures. Sexes are fairly similar but females larger, brighter and aggressive. They display and have low-pitched booming or moaning calls. Some are polyandrous, laying several clutches. Eggs are incubated by the male and the downy, striped precocial young are fed at first.

WOODPECKERS AND BARBETS Piciformes

21. Honeyguides (Indicatoridae) 4 genera, 17 species, 4–8 in (10–20 cm). Small perching birds of tree savanna and forest, mainly in Afrotropical Africa, with single species in the Himalayas and southeastern Asia. They look like songbirds with a short, thin or thick bill, short legs, feet with two toes pointing backwards and tapering wings and tail. Food is insects and also wax, especially beeswax, which they can digest. To obtain this at least two of the larger species lead humans, baboons or honey badgers to bees' nests, feeding on wax and larvae when the nest is opened. They are mainly solitary, with weak songs, some having display flights with wings or tail producing loud sounds. Females lay single eggs in other birds' nests, larger species parasitizing barbets, woodpeckers, rollers and similar cavity nesters. Smaller species parasitize swallows, swifts and open nests of some warblers and white-eyes. The young honeyguide has a short incubation period and at hatching uses temporarily inward-pointing bill tips to kill the host's young. The Himalayan Yellow-rumped Honeyguide appears not to be parasitic.

22. Woodpeckers (Picidae) 28 genera, 215 species, 3–22 in (8–55 cm). Tiny to moderate-sized arboreal birds occurring widely, except in Australia, Madagascar and some other islands, in habitats from forest and scrub to grassland. The two Wrynecks are songbird-like with finely camouflaged plumage, tree nesting but feeding on ants. The typical woodpeckers are adapted to feeding upright on vertical surfaces, stiffened tail feathers and turned-back outer toes supporting the body. A strengthened skull and strong, sharp-pointed bill enables hacking and boring into wood. A very long, extendable tongue can extract insects from small, deep holes. Woodpeckers normally feed on tree trunks and branches, hopping upwards, rarely backing downwards, and fly with distinctive swooping flight. Insects are taken mainly, but pine seeds and acorns are eaten, rows of holes drilled for sap by some species and others probe for ants on the ground. Plumage is often brightly colored and patterned. Roost and nest holes are excavated in trees. Nesting is in pairs, with helpers in some species, the nest unlined, eggs white and glossy and nestlings naked. Species include the Sapsuckers, Flickers and Piculets.

23. Asian Barbets (Megalaimidae) 3 genera, 26 species, 6–13 in (15–32 cm). Stockily built birds ranging from forest to cultivated land with trees in the Himalayas, south Tibet, south China to Indonesia and Philippines. Short legged and strong footed, with two toes pointing backwards, they hop clumsily but perch and cling well. Head large, bill stout, tapering and pointed, with long bristles around base. Wings short and rounded and flight rather weak. Usually green plumaged with head brightly patterned. Food is berries, other fruits and insects. They have loud repetitive calls, with antiphonal duetting in some species. Nest is a hole bored into a tree, the white eggs laid on bare wood. Adults share incubation and rearing.

24. African Barbets (Lybiidae) 7 genera, 42 species, 4–9 in (9–23 cm). These resemble Asian Barbets in general appearance but extend to more open habitats of arid scrub and savanna and include some very small species. In larger species bill edges may have projections and notches. Three species are slimmer and longer legged, more terrestrial and more sociable, and feed mainly on insects. These also make nest burrows in banks and may have additional helpers. Other species nest in tree holes.

25. New World Barbets and Toucans (Rhamphastidae) Two subfamilies, New World Barbets (Capitoninae), 3 genera, 14 species, 6–8 in (15–20 cm), and Toucans (Rhamphastinae), 6 genera, 41 species, 11–18 in (27–45 cm) — bill 0.25–0.5 of total length, which appears to be a specialized offshoot.

New World Barbets are arboreal forest barbets resembling African and Asian species of similar habitats. Although usually single or in pairs, they may join mixed-species foraging packs and be active feeders, at times taking small creatures as well as fruit. Toucan Barbets have longer, heavier bills and give loud duetting calls. All are tree hole nesters, occurring in montane and lowland forest and secondary growth from Costa Rica south through South American tropical forests.

Toucans are heavy-bodied birds with longish tails and rounded wings for maneuvering among trees. Legs short and strong with two toes directed backwards. The bill is very large but light-structured, long and deep with curved upper mandible; the cutting edges are serrated in some species. Food is mainly fruit, parts of plants and small creatures. Parts of plumage and bills are often brightly colored. Noisy, with loud unmusical calls, toucans nest in a tree cavity, with white eggs laid in a bare hollow. As in most species of this order, nestlings are naked with thickened heel pads to rest on. Both parents tend the young. Habitat varies from forests to open areas with trees, from Mexico to Argentina.

JACAMARS AND PUFFBIRDS Galbuliformes

26. Jacamars (Galbulidae) 5 genera, 18 species, 6–14 in (15–36 cm) — bill about 0.25 of total length. Slender, perching arboreal birds with long thin straight bills. Tails are long, sometimes tapering, wings short and rounded, legs and feet short and small, with two toes directed backwards. Plumage has bright metallic colors. They occur in southern Mexico to northern Argentina in forest to savanna, usually sitting on low open perches, flying out to catch insects and other small creatures, solitary and sedentary. They have sharp, high-pitched calls. Nest holes are bored into banks or tree-termite nests, with white eggs (3–4) laid in a bare cavity; both sexes incubate, the hen generally at night. Incu-

bation lasts 19–21 days. Nestlings have long white down.

27. Puffbirds (Bucconidae) 10 genera, 33 species, 5–12 in (13–29 cm). Small squat perching birds with large heads and loosely fluffed brown plumage, occurring from southern Mexico to northern Argentina. They have short legs, two toes pointing backwards, short rounded wings, the bill either broad, short and hooked or narrow and decurved. These are sit-and-wait species of lower forest vegetation, watching from an open perch, flying out or swooping down after insects or occasionally small animals such as lizards. Most are rather quiet, solitary or in pairs, but Nunbirds tend to be noisy and sociable, with helpers when nesting. Nests are usually burrows in a bank or the ground, less often in tree-termite nests. Eggs are white, nestlings naked.

HORNBILLS Bucerotiformes

28. Typical Hornbills (Bucerotidae) 8 genera, 54 species, 15–52 in (38–130 cm). Medium to large arboreal birds with long tails, long broad wings and longish necks occurring in Africa and from northern India to southern China south through Indonesia and Philippines to New Guinea in habitats ranging from forest to sparse scrub and tree savanna. Legs are short, giving a heavy hopping gait, flight strong but deliberate — wingbeats may be noisy. The bill is long, fairly deep and slightly downcurved and in larger species may be topped with a long casque. Food is fruit, insects and small creatures. Nest is a tree or rock cavity, bare with white eggs and naked nestlings. The pair seal its entrance with mud and droppings, leaving a slit through which female and young are fed.

29. Ground-Hornbills (Bucorvidae) 1 genus, 2 species, 36–52 in (90–130 cm). Two very large birds that inhabit open woodland, savanna and dry grassland in Afrotropical Africa. They have a bare wattled face and throat and long, slightly curved bill with small low casque, are long tailed and long legged. They hunt as they walk around a territory held by a small social group. Flight is mainly into and out of trees. Food is almost wholly small animals. They have deep booming calls. Nest, with sparse lining, is a large unsealed cavity in a tree. The dominant pair nest, helped by the group, rearing a single young one.

HOOPOES Upupiformes

30. Hoopoes (Upupidae) 1 genus, 2 species, 11 in (28 cm). Slender-built birds with broad tails and large rounded wings, strikingly patterned in black and white with a slender crest that erects into a fan, the neck slender, the bill long and downcurved for probing the ground for insects and other small animals. Flight is deliberate, undulating and flapping. Birds of open areas with some trees, they walk and run easily but also perch and cling. They have a soft, repetitive hooting call. The nest is a tree or rock cavity, bare or sparsely lined. Eggs are drab tinted, incubated by the female fed by the male. Nestlings have white down. They occur in central and southern Eurasia, southeastern Asia and Africa, most Eurasian birds shifting south in winter.

31. Woodhoopoes (Phoeniculidae) 1 genus, 5 species, 10–18 in (27–46 cm). Slender, mainly dark metallic-plumaged birds with long graduated tails, no crest, short wings and short strong legs with long-clawed toes. The bill is long, slender and slightly downcurved. They clamber

TYPICAL HORNBILLS: The Great Indian Hornbill (Buceros bicornis) is the largest hornbill. In some species the casque is reduced to a low ridge and in the much smaller Tockus hornbills of Africa is absent and the bill longer and more slender.

Left WOODHOOPOES: The Green Woodhoopoe (Phoeniculus purpureus) is typical of the family. Scimitar-bills look very similar, but smaller and slighter in build with a more curved bill.

Opposite page above
TROGONS: Narina Trogon (Apaloderma narina). Trogons mainly differ in the presence and pattern of barring on the underside of tail feathers. The five Quetzals (Pharomachrus) of South America have spiky crests, The Resplendent Quetzal (P. mocinno) has a tail twice as long as its body.

Opposite page bottom *TYPICAL ROLLERS: Lilac-breasted Roller (Coracias caudata). The body color may show much sober brown or blue gray in some species but they all reveal vivid blue wings when they fly.*

in agile, jerky fashion on tree trunks and branches, probing crevices for insects. Occasionally they may feed on the ground, hopping along. They also eat some small fruits. They are sociable, usually in small parties, with noisy cackling calls and body-rocking, nodding and tail-flicking displays. The social group help with nesting in a scantily lined tree cavity, with dull bluish eggs. They occur in habitats from forest to sparse arid scrub in Afrotropical Africa.

32. Scimitar-bills (Rhinopomastidae) 1 genus, 3 species, 9–10 in (22–25 cm). Very similar to woodhoopoes, but slightly smaller with longer, more slender and curved bills. These are agile feeders, usually solitary or in pairs, and less

noisy with shrill whistling calls. They nest in pairs, in tree cavities, occurring in woodland and tree savanna in Afrotropical Africa.

TROGONS Trogoniformes

33. Trogons (Trogonidae) 6 genera, 39 species, 9–15 in (23–38 cm). Unobtrusive and sluggish arboreal birds of tropical forests, usually found in the tree canopy, of which two subfamilies are recognized. Plumage is dense and soft, usually metallic green or blue, with red and yellow on underparts. They are plump bodied, long tailed and narrow winged, with large rounded heads. Legs and feet are small with two toes directed backwards but, unlike other zygodactyl birds, it is the inner toe that turns back. The bill is broad based, short and curved at the tip. They hawk insects in rapid twisting and hovering flight and also take them from branches. Nests are in cavities in trees or stumps, partly excavated by the birds, or in tree-termite or wasp nests. Uniform eggs, color varying, are tended by both parents in a bare cavity. Nestlings are naked.

The **African Trogons** (Apaloderminae) 1 genus, 3 species, live in montane forest regions of Afrotropical Africa. The other subfamily divides into the **Asian Trogons** (Harpactini) 1 genus, 11 species, of lowland and montane forest from the Himalayas and southern China to Indonesia and the Philippines, that are mainly rufous on the back and scarlet below, and the **New World Trogons** (Trogonini) 4 genera, 25 species, of forest, woodland and scrub of Central and South America. The latter show greater diversity and include the large quetzals, with brilliant crests and long coverts, forming in the Resplendent Quetzal a glistening green train that adds 30 in (76 cm) to 15 in (38 cm) length. Bill edges may be serrated in New World Trogons and they take more fruit, snatched in hovering flight; larger species also eating small frogs and lizards.

ROLLERS, KINGFISHERS AND BEE-EATERS Coraciiformes

34. Typical Rollers (Coraciidae) 2 genera, 12 species, 10–18 in (25–45 cm). Medium-sized, stoutly built birds with large heads and broad bills, either strong with small hooked tip or very short, stout and curved. Their wings are long and broad and tails of varying length, sometimes forked, legs short and feet small. They hop clumsily. Watching from an open perch, with an agile swooping flight they pounce on small creatures, occasionally also eating fruit. Call notes are loud and harsh. Usually paired and territorially aggressive, they display in a conspicuous twisting and swooping flight and nest in a tree cavity or bank, with sparse lining and glossy white eggs. Both sexes incubate and feed the naked nestlings. They range through forest, scrub and tree savanna in Africa and from southern Eurasia to the Philippines and Australia.

35. Ground-Rollers (Brachypteraciidae) 3 genera, 5 species, 10–18 in (24–45 cm). Medium-sized, more ground-adapted rollers found in Madagascar. Stoutly built with a large stout bill, large head and large eyes. Wings are short and rounded, legs long and the tail usually moderately long — but in the Long-tailed Ground Roller comprising about half the total length. Most live at ground level in thick evergreen forest but the Long-tailed in arid scrub. Usually solitary, they hunt small creatures at dusk. They nest in a tunnel in the ground, the white eggs laid in a bare scrape.

36. Cuckoo Roller (Leptosomidae) 1 genus, 1 species, 17 in (42 cm). A large, slender, arboreal roller, occurring on Madagascar and the Comoro Islands, with smaller and more rounded head than the other rollers, bristling forehead feathers and short-looking bill. The wings are large, flight strong, tail moderately long, legs very short and outer toe reversible. Noisy and fairly sociable, it lives in forest trees, feeding on large, tree-caught insects and lizards, and nesting in a tree cavity where the male feeds the sitting female. Nestlings have white down.

37. Motmots (Momotidae) 6 genera, 9 species, 7–18 in (17–45 cm). Small to medium size arboreal birds, rather stout-bodied and large-headed, their strong, slightly curved bill with serrated cutting edges. Wings are short and rounded, legs short, feet small and the tail long with end parts of feather vanes rubbed away to leave separate rounded tips. The tail is often swung like a pendulum or held to one side. Motmots occur from southern Mexico to northern Argentina, living in forest, often near water, watching from a perch and swooping on small creatures or following army ant swarms for fleeing insects. Fruit is snatched while hovering. They have low hooting or harsh calls. The nest is a long tunnel with unlined cavity. White eggs and naked nestlings are tended by both parents.

38. Todies (Todidae) 1 genus, 5 species, 4–5 in (9–12 cm). Tiny, plump, round-headed arboreal birds with long, tapering, dagger bills. Wings are short and rounded, tail short and legs and feet thin and weak. Found on the larger islands of the Caribbean, usually in pairs, in lower vegetation of forests, often near water. Usually quiet, but constantly alert, they perch with up-tilted bill and fly out to seize insects, spiders or small lizards from under leaves. They have short shrill calls and can whirr wings in flight. Nest is in an unlined cavity in a long burrow, with white eggs. Unsuccessful breeding neighbors may act as helpers.

39. Alcedinid Kingfishers (Alcedinidae) 3 genera, 24 species, 4–19 in (10–23 cm). Medium to tiny, squat perching birds with small legs and feet, short rounded wings and fast direct flight, a largish head with a long sharp dagger bill and plumage mainly of bright blue. Call notes are short and high pitched. These are waterside birds, watching from a perch and plunge diving after small fish or other water creatures, except for the tiny Dwarf Kingfisher, a forest insect eater. Nest is a bare tunnel in a bank, with glossy white eggs. Nestlings are naked and feathers stay in quill until fledging. Both adults incubate and feed young. They occur by water in Africa and from temperate Eurasia south to Australia. Some winter migration from northern Eurasia. Species include the Common and Dwarf Kingfishers.

40. Dacelonid Kingfishers (Dacelonidae) 12 genera, 61 species, 7–19 in (17–47 cm). This family includes the bush kingfishers and kookaburras and occurs in Africa and from southern Asia to Australia, Philippines and Pacific Islands with some migration in Australasia. Small to large birds, similar to Alcedinid Kingfishers but heavier built, with longer tails and stouter, blunt-tipped bills. Some occur by water or on coasts, others in dry forest, scrub or open country. Food is a range of small creatures taken from the ground or from vegetation. Calls are prolonged whistling, rattling or cackling. Nest is a burrow in the ground, or in ground- or tree-termite nests, or a tree cavity. Nesting is similar to other kingfishers. Laughing Kookaburras have help from previous broods. Species also include the Sacred, White-throated, White-collared and Ruddy Kingfishers.

41. Cerylid Kingfishers (Cerylidae) 3 genera, 9 species, 6–18 in (14–45 cm). Small to large kingfishers, often with short shaggy crests, like larger, longer-tailed versions of Alcedinid Kingfishers with longer, stronger wings. They watch from open perches or fly over water, hovering and plunge diving after fish or other small creatures. Calls are mostly harsh rattling. Nest is a burrow in a bank, nesting like other kingfishers. They occur by inland and coastal waters in the Americas, Africa and from northern India and Japan through southeast Asia. Migration from northern North America in winter. Species include the Belted, Pied and Amazon Kingfishers.

42. Bee-eaters (Meropidae) 3 genera, 26 species, 7–14 in (17–35 cm). Slender perching birds with long, slightly curved bills, more curved or heavier in bearded bee-eaters. Wings are long and tapering, tail long and sometimes with elongated feathers. Legs and feet small, with two toes directed backwards. Insects (especially bees and wasps) are hawked from a perch or in agile aerial flight. Some species take small creatures from the ground. Sociable, perched individuals often huddling together when resting

1. MOTMOTS: *Blue-crowned Motmot* (Momotus momota). *The curious tail feathers grow complete but with some weak barbs designed to be soon removed in preening to isolate the racquet tip.*

2. BEE-EATERS: *A European Bee-eater* (Merops apiaster) *approaching its nest burrow. It has the typical bee-eater slender build and long thin bill with tail tips lengthened or forked in some species.*

3. DACELONID KINGFISHERS: *The Kookaburra* (Dacelo novaeguineae) *or Laughing Jackass is the largest of this family at 19 in (47 cm).*

or roosting. Nesting is colonial in many species, the nest a bare chamber of a long tunnel in a bank or the ground. Eggs (2-8) are white, nestlings naked. Both sexes incubate and tend the young, some species having nest helpers. Species occur from open country and scrub to rainforest both in Africa and from southern Eurasia to the Philippines and Australia.

COLIES Coliiformes

43. Colies (Coliidae) 2 genera, 6 species, 12-14 in (30-35 cm). The genera are separated into two subfamilies, Coliinae and Urocoliinae, but are very similar. These are small songbird-like, pot-bellied birds with long graduated tails forming over half their length. The head is rounded, with a small crest, and the hooked bill short, thick and curved. Legs are short and strong with all four toes forwards at times when birds hang on twigs by them, but the outer toe is reversible and they can perch, hop and run fast. The short, rounded wings are used for brief level flights and birds clamber over vegetation feeding on seeds, fruit and parts of plants. Highly sociable at all times, they often huddle together. Nest is a bulky or shallow cup in a bush, sometimes several in a loose group. Eggs are white or with dark markings, young have sparse down. Both sexes incubate and tend young. Colies occur in Afrotropical Africa and Madagascar.

CUCKOOS Cuculiformes

44. Old World Cuckoos (Cuculidae) 17 genera, 79 species, 6-27 in (15-68 cm). Small to large birds occurring from Eurasia south to Africa and Australasia in varied habitats from forest to grassland. Structurally diverse, ranging from small species like glossy songbirds to larger, long-tailed, curved-billed arboreal species and long-legged, long-tailed terrestrial species. The more general form is slender bodied, long tailed, with smallish legs and feet with two toes directed backwards. Wings are long and narrow. The diet is mainly insects but other small creatures are taken and some larger species also eat fruit. Some can feed on hairy caterpillars rejected by other birds. Calls tend to be rather simple, loud and repetitive. Some build shallow cup nests and rear their own young but a number of species are highly adapted to brood parasitism with mimicry of the host's eggs and young.

45. Coucals (Centropodidae) 1 genus, 30 species, 14-32 in (35-80 cm). Medium-sized to large cuckoos that occur in Afrotropical Africa and from southern Asia to the Philippines and Australia in habitats from forest to tall grass and reed beds. They have well-developed legs and feet, short round wings, long broad tails and strong, stout, slightly curved bills. They skulk, walking and running on the ground, clambering in low shrubs, moving with agility through grass and thick cover, but with slow laborious flight. They have bubbling and hooting calls. The nest is a loose, domed structure on the ground or in low vegetation. Sexes are similar but females are larger and may be polyandrous, having several mates with several nests. Eggs are white, young naked but developing spiny quills.

46. American Cuckoos (Coccyzidae) 4 genera, 18 species, 8-16 in (21-40 cm). Medium-sized, slender arboreal cuckoos that in most respects resemble Old World cuckoos, but none are brood parasites. The bill is narrow with a more distinctly downcurved tip. Generally dark colored above, pale below, with long graduated tails, they feed on insects and fruit and take hairy caterpillars. The nest is a shallow loose cup in a bush or tree. Eggs are pale blue or greenish blue and the nestling has sparse down. Incubation and rearing is by both adults. Habitat ranges from forest to savanna and mangrove and they occur from southern Canada to northern Argentina. Northern species migrate.

47. Hoatzin (Opisthocomidae) 1 genus, 1 species, 14 in (64 cm). The family consists of a single clumsy-looking species occurring in the Amazon basin region. It has big rounded wings, a broad tail and short legs. The bill is deep, short and blunt and there is a shaggy crest. Highly sociable and sluggish, Hoatzin occur in small groups in flooded and riverside forest and feed on leaves of marsh plants. Flight is weak and heavy, calls short and harsh. They nest socially, with a group of helpers building a loose twig platform in a tree over water. Eggs are buff with dark spots. The almost naked young become active and can clamber around and swim if necessary before fledging.

48. Anis and Guira Cuckoos (Crotophagidae) Separated into two tribes, they both occur in woodland, open scrub, grassland, swamps or mangroves from southern U.S.A. to northern Argentina. The **Anis** (Crotophagini) 1 genus, 3 species, 13-18 in (33-45 cm), are black, awkward-looking birds with a very stout deep bill with curved upper edge, short wings and a loose-looking tail. The **Guira Cuckoo** (Guirini) 1 genus, 1 species, 15 in (38 cm), is a scruffy-looking, loose-plumaged, slightly crested cuckoo with a moderately deep bill.

All are highly gregarious, usually in small parties, often hunting insects disturbed by cattle or, in tropical forest, by army ants. They huddle in contact when perched, roost together and breed socially with a group of several pairs sharing a large loosely-made cup nest. Earlier young may act as helpers. Eggs are blue with a thin white coating, and blue with a raised white net pattern in the Guira Cuckoo. Nestlings are almost naked.

49. Roadrunners and Ground-Cuckoos (Neomorphidae) 5 genera, 11 species, 10-24 in (25-61 cm). Medium to large, mainly terrestrial cuckoos of slender build with long legs, long tail and sometimes crested, which occur from southwestern U.S.A. to northern Argentina. Smaller species prefer dense undergrowth but typical roadrunners occur in dry open scrub where they pursue prey on foot, but rest above ground. Food is a wide range of small creatures, including reptiles and eggs and nestlings. The smaller Striped Cuckoo, Pheasant Cuckoo and Pavonine Cuckoo are brood parasites of other birds but the rest make cup nests and almost naked young are tended by both parents.

OLD WORLD CUCKOOS: An immature Red-chested Cuckoo (Cuculus solitarius) which will have a red chest when adult. This African species is one of the more typical species in a family that differs widely: from small glossy cuckoos that look like small songbirds to the Great Channel-billed Cuckoo (Scythrops novaehollandiae) that looks rather like a small toucan.

ANIS AND GUIRA CUCKOOS: Guira Cuckoo (Guira guira). These are always scruffy-looking, loose-feathered birds. Like the Anis (Crotophaga) species they are mainly ground feeding.

Following pages *ROAD RUNNERS AND GROUND CUCKOOS: Roadrunner (Geococcyx californianus). Many of the ground cuckoos are forest birds, but the two Roadrunners occur in more open areas where sustained speeds are useful.*

PARROTS Psittaciformes

50. Parrots (Psittacidae) 80 genera, 358 species, 6–27 in (15–67 cm). Mainly arboreal birds, uniform in general structure, but differing considerably in size, tail length and plumage color. Some are crested. They are stout bodied with short, strong legs and powerful feet with two toes directed backwards. Combined feet and bill are used for climbing and feet hold and manipulate food. The short deep bill has a downcurved upper mandible with thin tip and flat inner surface. The short, strong lower mandible fits inside. Bill and tongue can be used for delicate manipulation or exerting strong force. Nectar-feeding species have a brush-tip to the tongue. Wings vary from rounded to long and narrow, flight from leisurely to very fast and direct. Calls are harsh or shrill. Food is fruit, seeds, nectar, various plant parts, exceptionally wood-boring larvae. Sociable with long pair bonds. Nest usually a tree hole, more rarely in a termite mound or burrow; Monk Parrots build colonies of twig nests. Eggs white, incubated by female or both adults. Habitats range from forest to open semidesert. Widespread, except in Antarctica and cold to temperate Northern Hemisphere, except for introductions. Species include Lovebirds, Budgerigar, Lorikeets, Parakeets, Conures, Lories, Macaws and Cockatoos.

SWIFTS Apodiformes

51. Typical Swifts (Apodidae) 18 genera, 99 species, 4–12 in (10–30 cm). Small to medium birds with mainly aerial existence. Body narrow, head broad and rounded with small visible bill but gape as wide as head. Eyes large. Tail short to medium, in some forked or spine-tipped, and wings tapering, narrow and often long. Legs and feet small, usually with all four toes forwards for clinging. Drinking, mating and sleeping may occur in flight, some possibly only settling when nesting. Often sociable and flocking. Insects are caught and eaten in flight. Calls are shrill and some cave nesters echolocate. Nests are windblown debris or small, snapped-off twigs, stuck to a site with saliva. Some cave swiftlet nests are partly or wholly of solidified saliva. They vary from small pads or supports to cups, often stuck to upright supports, or rounded structures. In tiny nests eggs may be stuck in with saliva. Eggs are white and elongated. Both sexes incubate and tend young. They are cosmopolitan, except in polar regions, and some are migrants. Species include Swiftlets.

52. Crested-Swifts (Hemiprocnidae) 1 genus, 4 species, 9–13 in (11–33 cm). Small to medium swifts with long tapering wings and deeply forked tails. The head is ornamented with a crest or mustache tufts. They are more swallow-like than the typical swifts, hawking insects over open forest or clearings, more agile and maneuvering, and frequently perch, normally on high bare twigs. Legs are short and feet small. The nest is a tiny crescent-shaped shallow cup, cemented along the side of a horizontal twig, with a single elongated egg. The incubating adult rests its weight on the twig. Both sexes incubate and feed the downy young one. Crested-Swifts occur from northern India to southern China and south to New Guinea and the Solomon Islands.

HUMMINGBIRDS Trochiliformes

53. Hummingbirds (Trochilidae) Two subfamilies, the **Hermits** (Phaethornithinae) 4 genera, 29 species, and the **Typical Hummingbirds** (Trochilinae) 105 genera, 290 species. Both are similar in structure and general habits, small to tiny, 2–8.8 in (5.2–22 cm) and include the smallest known birds. Most are under 5.2 in (13 cm), the Giant Hummingbird *ca.* 8 in (20 cm), but others longer by virtue of elaborate tails. Their narrow, tapering wings rotate from the shoulder and can be used with a figure-eight beat to hover in one spot. This flight is used mainly to take nectar from flowers, using a long, thin extensible tongue. The bill is narrow, 0.28–4 in (0.7–10 cm) long and may be straight, upcurved or strongly downcurved, the extremes adapted to particular flower forms. Most species also eat small insects and spiders. In the Swordbill the straight bill forms half the total length. Tails are varied in shape, from short to long, sometimes with spatulate tips, and more developed in males. Males also show patches of iridescent color and crests and ruffs, used in display. Song is high pitched and squeaky. Hummingbirds are mostly solitary or in pairs, territorial and aggressive. They are intensely active, feeding frequently and becoming torpid when resting.

Hermits are duller in color, usually inhabiting lower forest vegetation or scrub. Males may form scattered leks of singing birds. Nests are tapering cups bound to tips of hanging leaves with spiders' webs.

Typical Hummingbirds are sexually dimorphic in plumage. The nest is usually a neat thick-walled cup of fine plant material and spiders' webs on top of a level twig. A few cave nesters have pendent cups stuck to vertical surfaces. There are two white elongated eggs. Eggs and sparsely downy young are tended by female alone. Hummingbirds occur from forest and swamp to sparse scrub, through the Americas. Species migrate from north and south extremes of the range.

TURACOS Musophagiformes

54. Turacos (Musophagidae) Two subfamilies, the Turacos (Musophaginae), 2 genera, 17 species, 14–20 in (35–51 cm) and the Plantain-eaters (Criniferinae), 3 genera, 6 species, 14–30 in (35–76 cm). Medium to large birds, they are fairly slenderly built, arboreal birds with short rounded wings and long tails. Legs are moderately long and feet strong with a reversible outer toe. Flight is heavy, but they are agile walkers and leapers among branches. The neck is slender, the head rather small and often crested. The bill is short and deep, often slightly curved. Food is mainly fruit, also parts of plants and some small invertebrates. They are gregarious, often in small parties, with repetitive low-pitched or harsh calls. The nest is a twig platform in a tree with two to three white or bluish rounded eggs. Sexes are similar and both adults incubate and tend young. The downy young, which are fed regurgitated food, are semialtricial and may leave the nest to climb among twigs, aided in some cases by a claw on the bend of the wing. Both subfamilies occur throughout Afro-tropical Africa.

Turacos are green or purple plumaged with bright red on primary feathers. Some have a forehead shield to the bill. They occur in forest or on forest edge. **Plantain-eaters** are duller gray, black and white, but blue in the Great Plantain-eater. They more often occur in open woodland, scrub or tree savanna.

OWLS AND NIGHTJARS Strigiformes

55. Barn and Grass Owls (Tytonidae) 2 genera, 17 species, 9–21 in (23–53 cm), occurring from forest to open grassland, cultivated areas and in towns. Distribution is cosmopolitan except for the polar regions. These are medium-sized owls of rather slender build with large heads. The bill is hooked and fairly long but partly concealed by elongated facial disks around the forwardly directed eyes that form a heart-shaped face in front view. Wings are long and flight is silent. Legs are long and feathered, feet large and strong with large claws, the outer toe reversible. Hunting is mainly crepuscular or nocturnal and prey, detected by watching and listening from a perch or in flight, is pounced on. Any small creatures are taken but mainly small rodents. Nests are unlined cavities in trees, rocks, buildings or on the ground. Eggs are white and the females incubate, males bringing food. Young have white down and broods are large with competition for survival.

56. Typical Owls (Strigidae) 23 genera, 161 species, 4.8–29 in (12–71 cm). Small to large birds, solid looking with large rounded heads. Bills are short, stout and hooked, eyes are large and forwardly directed with the facial disks around them usually rounded. Heads may have ear tufts. Legs are often feathered and feet large and strong with large claws and the outer toe reversible. Wings are long and rounded and the flight silent, except in fish-hunting species. Tails are short to long. Sexes are similar with females usually larger. Most species are nocturnal hunters, but some are diurnal. Hunting is by

TURACOS: *The Purple-crested Turaco* (Musophaga porphyreolopha) *is typical of the family, but whereas most Turacos have glossy green or blue plumage, the similar Plantain-eaters have gray, black or white plumage.*

AUSTRALIAN FROGMOUTHS: *A Tawny Frogmouth* (Podargus strigoides) *feeding its downy chick. By day, motionless, it mimics a broken branch.*

Right TYPICAL OWLS: *A Morepork* (Ninox novaeseelandiae) *with wings and tail spread for braking, about to land at its nest hole. One of the less specialized owls, its appearance is typical.*

Opposite left TYPICAL SWIFTS: *A Common Swift* (Apus apus) *at its nest in the roof space of a building, its throat pouch bulging with insects brought back to its chicks.*

watching or listening from a perch or in flight and prey is seized in the feet. Creatures from small insects up to rabbit and goose in size are included in the family prey range and a few species specialize in fish. Habitats range from forest to grassland and tundra. The nest is an unlined cavity among rocks or in a tree or building, in old nests of other birds or on the ground. Eggs are white, broods sometimes large, with competition for survival between downy young. Incubation is by the female or pair. Distribution is almost cosmopolitan but absent from Antarctica and small remote islands. There is some irruption and migration from colder areas.

57. Owlet-Nightjars or Owlet-Frogmouths (Aegothelidae) 1 genus, 8 species, 8–12 in (20–30 cm). These are small to medium-sized, nocturnal birds like lightly built owls, but with long narrow wings and tail. The head is large and rounded with very large dark eyes and poorly defined facial disks. The visible bill is very small, with long bristles at the base and a head-wide gape. Legs and feet appear slender and weak. The plumage is highly camouflaged. Owlet-Nightjars hide in cavities by day, feeding at night, mainly taking insects from the ground, sometimes in flight. Flight tends to be short and direct. Some species have soft churring calls. Nest is in a tree cavity, bare or sparsely lined, with 3–4 white or spotted eggs. Nestlings have thick white down. These birds occur from tropical forest to open woodland and scrub, from the Moluccas to New Guinea, the Solomon Islands and Australia.

58. Australian Frogmouths (Podargidae) 1 genus, 3 species, 12.8–15.2 in (32–38 cm). These medium to large arboreal birds occur from rainforest to open woodland and lines of trees in Australia, New Guinea and the Solomon Islands. They are stout bodied and large headed with long wings and tail and small legs and feet. The plumage is highly camouflaged against tree bark and sexes are similar. Eyes are very large. The bill is large and boat shaped, with a down-curved tip. It is mostly concealed in feathers, with a tuft of forehead bristles, but opens into a huge gape. These are crepuscular and nocturnal feeders, watching and swooping to take small creatures from the ground or from branches. They roost with bill uptilted, eyes

closed, and plumage and pose very closely resembles a broken-ended branch. The nest is a small, flimsy stick platform in a tree, with 2–3 white eggs, incubated by the female. The young are downy and fed by both parents.

59. Asiatic Frogmouths (Batrachostomidae) 1 genus, 11 species, 9.2–16 in (23–40 cm). Very similar to Australian frogmouths, these birds occur in rainforest to more open secondary growth from the Himalayas to Java and the Philippines. They generally have larger tails, more rounded wings and more boldly variegated plumage. General habits appear to be the same. The known nest is a small felted pad of the bird's own down, camouflaged at the edges with spiders' webs and lichen, set on a horizontal branch. There is a single white egg.

60. Oilbird (Steatornithidae) 1 genus, 1 species, 19 in (48 cm). A nightjar-like bird with long wings and tail and small legs and feet occurring in Trinidad and mountain regions from Guyana to Peru. Its eyes are large and the bill prominent and strongly hooked, with long bristles at the base, the gape wide. It is nocturnal in feeding, resting in colonies by day on ledges of large caves. Flying in caves it uses echolocation clicking but is also very noisy with loud screams and snarls. Flight is strong and it searches at night for oil-rich fruits that it snatches in flight. These are digested by day and the seeds regurgitated. The nest, on a cave ledge, is a bulky cup with a shallow depression, made of regurgitated fruit, seeds and bird droppings. New nest layers are added on a site annually. Both adults incubate the 2–4 white eggs. Sparsely-downed young take 130 days to fledge, becoming large and fat before feathering.

61. Potoos (Nyctibiidae) 1 genus, 7 species, 9–20 in (23–50 cm). These medium to large nocturnal birds are a forest species of tropical Central and South America. Rather similar to frogmouths, but slightly more slender and with a much smaller visible bill. No rictal bristles. The full gape is as wide as the head. The eyes are very large. Wings and tail are fairly long and the plumage well camouflaged. Legs are very short and the feet small. Arboreal and usually solitary nocturnal feeders, they rest along a sloping branch or on a broken branch end in an upright posture. In sleep and in alarm the eyes are closed, plumage sleeked and bill uptilted, the bird very closely resembling an extension of the branch.

They feed by flying out from a perch after flying insects. For nesting they use a natural hollow, usually in the end of a stump or broken branch, or on a branch, and incubate in an upright posture. There is usually a single, spotted egg, incubated by both adults. The semialtricial, downy nestling may move among the branches before it can fly.

62. Eared-Nightjars (Eurostopodidae) 1 genus, 7 species, 10–16.2 in (25–41 cm). These birds occur in forest and scrub from southern India and South China to Australia. They lack bristles around the bill and have inconspicuous, backward-pointing ear tufts. Some species may call when flying. There is usually only one egg. Other habits are like those of the Typical Nightjars (below) and they tend to be larger and darker patterned.

63. Nightjars (Caprimulgidae) There are two subfamilies: the Nighthawks (Chordeilinae) 4 genera, 8 species, 6–11.2 in (15–28 cm), and the Typical Nightjars (Caprimulginae) 10 genera, 68 species, 7.6–20.4 in (19–51 cm).

Typical Nightjars are medium-sized nocturnal birds occurring from forest to scrub and heathland, and in sparse semiarid habitats, being worldwide in regions where aerial insects occur. They have long wings and tails, small short legs, sometimes feathered, and small feet. The neck is short, the head broad and flattened with large eyes. Visible bill is small, short, slightly curved, opening to a head-wide gape fringed with long bristles. The plumage is highly camouflaged against dead leaves and bark, sometimes with white marking concealed when at rest. Birds rest by day on open ground or dead leaves, or lie along branches. They become active at night, hunting insects taken mostly in flight. Usually solitary and silent they become noisy when active with loud repetitive calls, from plaintive phrases to churring or knocking sounds. There is no nest: the 1–2 blotched eggs are laid on the ground, the sitting bird and nestlings relying on camouflage. Both adults incubate and feed the young. The semialtricial nestlings may move from the nest site. Some species migrate.

Nighthawks, which occur through the Americas, are in most respects like Typical Nightjars, but lacking the long bristles around the bill gape. Their wings tend to be long and tapering and the tail often slightly forked. They often fly higher and more strongly and may

hawk insects in daylight or half-light. This is most marked in the Common Nighthawk, which also has a swooping display with loud wing noise. They may call in flight.

PIGEONS Columbiformes

64. Dodos (Raphidae) Extinct, 2 genera, 3 species. Dodos occurred on Mauritius and Reunion and were huge, flightless terrestrial pigeons, large headed and heavy billed with much reduced wings and tail. They appear to have fed largely on fruit, becoming seasonally very fat. They laid a single egg. The Solitaire was a more slenderly built but equally tall flightless species with a bony lump on the wing that was used in fighting. It occurred on Rodrigues. Dodos were exterminated by 1700, the Solitaire by 1760, through the activities of man and mammalian predators.

65. Pigeons (Columbidae) 40 genera, 310 species, 6.8–36 in (17–90 cm). Pigeons and doves, found living in all types of vegetation from forest to open areas and on rocky ground and worldwide except in tundra and polar regions, are small to large, typically plump-bodied birds with thick feathering, the head rather small and rounded, the bill narrow with a blunt tip and a fleshy base around the nostrils. Legs and feet often small, but legs stout and feet strong in arboreal-feeding species, and legs long in terrestrial species. Wings may be tapering, with flight strong and sometimes prolonged, or short and rounded in terrestrial species. Tails may be square or long and tapered. They walk or run with typical head-nodding gait. Food is mainly seeds and parts of plants, taken from the ground, but some species are specialized arboreal feeders, mainly on fruit. Food is stored in the crop and digested later. They typically have low-pitched cooing calls. The nest is a thin twig platform in a tree or bush, or on a rock ledge or the ground. Nesting may be solitary or in colonies. Both sexes incubate the 1–2 white eggs and feed young. Nestlings are fed at first on "pigeon's milk" taken from the adult's bill. They have coarse hairy down. Some species migrate.

CRANES AND RAILS Gruiformes

66. Sunbittern (Eurypygidae) 1 genus, 1 species, 19 in (48 cm). A slenderly-built, narrow-bodied waterside bird with long thin legs, very thin neck, small narrow head and thin dagger bill that occurs on forest rivers of Central America and tropical South America. The spread wings reveal a striking "eye-spot" pattern used in display and threat. Sexes are similar. It walks sedately, feeding along river margins and among rocks and shallows taking small creatures, from fish to insects. Flight is slow and heavy. It perches in trees when alarmed. It has a whistling call. Usually solitary or in pairs its nest is a small mound of mud and plant material on a branch of a tree of bush, with a small hollow on top. Two spotted eggs are incubated by both adults. The downy nestlings are fed in the nest.

67. Bustards (Otididae) 6 genera, 25 species, 16–48 in (40–120 cm). These large terrestrial birds of open country, sparsely vegetated, dry areas from southern Eurasia to Africa and Australia have heavy bodies and stout longish legs with short toes, the hind toe absent. The neck is long, the head relatively small and round and the bill short and blunt ended. The wings are broad and flight heavy but strong, the tail fairly short but broad. Bustards tend to move with a deliberate walk in bare or grassy areas, feeding on seeds, parts of plants and small creatures. They may crouch in alarm rather than fly. They are mostly silent but the often larger males have strikingly odd displays and calls. Males are usually boldly colored or ornamented on head and breast. They are often gregarious. The female nests alone on a bare or sparsely lined scrape laying 1–6 eggs, colored and patterned. Downy precocial young are elaborately patterned and follow her.

68–69. Cranes (Gruidae) have two subfamilies.
68. Crowned-Cranes (Balearicinae) 1 genus, 2 species, 42 in (105 cm). These birds of Afrotropical Africa resemble the typical cranes that follow, a few features excepted. They have a distinctly patterned head with spiky crest, the windpipe is short and straight and they lack the loud trumpeting calls. They can use the foot to scratch for food, feed more on animal food, normally roost and occasionally nest in trees and have larger clutches of eggs.
69. Typical Cranes (Gruinae) 1 genus, 13 species, 36–72 in (90–180 cm). These tall slender birds occur in extensive open habitats, usually near water, and are worldwide except for polar regions. They have long legs, a long neck and a small head (partly bare of feathers in the adult) with a slender, tapering dagger bill. Wings are long and broad and flight deliberate with neck and legs extended. They are terrestrial, feeding on the ground or in shallow water on a wider range of plants and small creatures. Secondary feathers are long and drooping and there are often black and red patterns of feathers and bare skin on the head. Pair displays involve trumpeting and dancing movements. Cranes are gregarious, but nesting in pairs and pairing for life. The nest is a mound of vegetation on the ground or in shallow water. Both parents incubate and tend the downy precocial young who are at first fed by them, often only one nestling surviving from two-egg clutches. Young remain with their parents until spring. Many species are migratory.

70–71. Heliornithidae is a family with two tribes.
70. Limpkins (Aramini) 1 genus, 1 species, 25–35 in (63–88 cm). A large crane-like wading bird that occurs in vegetated lowland marshes from the southern United States to Argentina. It has long legs and neck, a long bill which is slender and slightly downcurved, long wings and a deliberate, crane-like flight with neck and legs extended. It wades and can swim and will

SUNBITTERN: *The Sunbittern (Eurypyga helias) has sober, though finely patterned plumage, but in threat or display its spread wings show two great eye-spot patterns in chestnut and black.*

BUSTARDS: *A male Buff-crested Bustard (Eupodotis gindiana) calling and partly displaying. Bustards are finely patterned for concealment but males are boldly colored on breast neck and head or can erect these parts in display on the ground or rising in the air.*

Below LIMPKINS: *A Limpkin (Aramus guarauna) perches on a rootsnag of a mossy swamp-cypress. Its specialized diet of freshwater mollusks limits it to lowland marshes in the warmer regions of the Americas.*

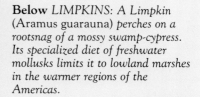

perch in trees. It feeds on large water snails and is mainly active at night. It has loud wailing and screaming calls. The nest is a shallow twig and leaf saucer, on the ground or low in vegetation. Both adults incubate 4–8 patterned eggs and tend the downy, precocial dark-brown young, who still take food after fledging.

71. Sungrebes (Heliornithini) 3 genera, 3 species, 12–24 in (30–60 cm). Medium-sized waterbirds that occur separately as single species in Africa, Southeast Asia and Central and South America. They have an elongated body, longish tapering tail with stiffened feathers, strong short legs and swimming feet with brightly-colored lobed toes. The neck is

TRUMPETERS: White-winged Trumpeter (Psophia leucoptera). The three species vary in the color of wing coverts and tail. Tameness, sociability and keen-eyed watch for predators encouraged settlers to keep them with free-range domestic fowls.

Below KAGU: The almost flightless Kagu (Rhynochetus jubata). Its drooping crest can be raised into a great spiky fan with the front edge vertical above the forehead.

long and thin, the head narrow and the bill strong and tapering. They are birds of fresh waters bordered and overhung by trees and thick vegetation. They swim well, can dive but appear to do so infrequently, run on land with a crouching posture, perch and have a low heavy flight. Food is various small creatures taken on or around water. Mainly solitary, or living in pairs, they are rather silent with low-pitched abrupt calls. The nest is a shallow twig and leaf platform low on a branch over water. Both adults incubate 2–6 eggs and tend altricial young that are first naked then downy.

72. Trumpeters (Psophiidae) 1 genus, 3 species, 17–21 in (43–53 cm). Medium-sized, mainly terrestrial birds of lowland forests in South America, trumpeters have large, rounded and humpbacked bodies, rounded wings and small tails. Legs are long and strong, the neck slender and the head rounded with a stout, short and slightly curved bill. They are highly sociable, living in flocks, feeding on the ground, flying reluctantly and heavily and roosting in trees. Food is small fruits, parts of plants and insects. They have soft booming notes and loud trumpeting calls when alarmed. They nest in a natural tree cavity, the female incubating 6–10 white eggs. The young are downy and precocial.

73. Seriemas (Cariamidae) 2 genera, 2 species, 32–35 in (80–90 cm). These large, but slimly built, birds of open scrub and grassland of lowland South America have elongated bodies, long legs with small feet and long necks. The wings are rounded and the tail long and broad. The head has large eyes and a short, stout and broad-based bill, slightly curved and with a bristly forehead crest above it. They walk deliberately, run fast when alarmed and fly reluctantly but perch and rest above ground. Food is various small creatures, particularly lizards and snakes. They are sociable, often in small flocks, and have loud yelping calls. The nest is a twig platform in a low tree or shrub, with 2 patterned eggs. Incubation and care of the young is by both adults, the downy, uniformly dark young remaining in the nest.

74. Kagu (Rhynochetidae) 1 genus, 1 species, 22 in (55 cm). A heavily built terrestrial bird of forest undergrowth in western New Caledonia, the Kagu has strong legs, a shortish neck and a large head with a long shaggy crest. It has a short tapering bill, the tail short and the wings rounded. Apparently flightless, it can glide downhill. It is sociable, occurring in loose flocks, usually near water. Food is earthworms and other invertebrates dug from the ground. It has harsh calls, and pairs have a loud contact song at early morning. The nest is a thin layer of dead leaves on the ground, with a single blotched egg. The downy young with streaked pattern is semiprecocial but fed for several weeks.

75. Rails (Rallidae) 34 genera, 142 species, 4–14 in (10–60 cm). Small to medium-sized (and rarely, large) rails occur worldwide except in polar regions. They are marshbirds, slenderly built and narrow bodied, usually with a partly crouching posture. Their legs and toes are long, wings rounded, tail soft and short. They fly well, though not readily, some migrating but some island species have also become flightless. Bills vary from short to long, stout to slender, some with a forehead shield. They are mainly terrestrial, adapted for moving through lush vegetation, but also wade and swim well: the more aquatic coots have lobed toes and dive for food. Rail diet includes a wide range of plant

material and small creatures. Most are solitary or in pairs, a few with small groups acting as helpers in nesting, and mainly silent, but with loud unmusical calls. They occur on the water's edge, shores and in damp grassland to forests. Nests are a pile of sticks or vegetation on the ground or in water, usually hidden in vegetation. Either the female or both sexes incubate 1–14 eggs that are usually spotted. Partly precocial downy young, usually black, gradually leave the nest to follow adults on land and in water, and are fed by them. Species include Coots, Moorhens, Swamphens, Gallinules, Flufftails and Corncrake.

76. Mesites (Mesitornithidae) 2 genera, 3 species, 10–11.2 in (25–28 cm). These are medium-sized, mainly terrestrial birds of Madagascar, living in forest cover to dry scrub. Their head is songbirdlike with a small slender bill, straight or downcurved. Legs are of moderate length, wings short and rounded, tail long and broad. They run in pigeonlike fashion, with bobbing head. They fly poorly and only when disturbed, and feed on seed, fruit and insects. Little known, they are thought to be gregarious and may be sociable, with extra helpers, in their nesting. The nest is a thin twig platform, with some lining, in a small tree or shrub, placed to be reached without flying. Both sexes incubate one (rarely 2–3) spotted eggs. The downy young are partly precocial and fed by adults.

WATERBIRDS AND BIRDS OF PREY Ciconiiformes

77. Sandgrouse (Pteroclidae) 2 genera, 16 species, 10.8–19.2 in (27–48 cm). These medium-sized, desert-adapted birds occur in arid, semi-arid or dry steppe areas in southern Eurasia, India and Africa with Madagascar. They are pigeonlike, with compact body, long pointed wings, and thick feathering. Legs are short and feathered in the two *Syrrhaptes* species, toes short and hind toe absent. The head is small, the bill short and bluntly tapering. Wings are long and narrow and flight is fast and powerful, the tail pointed and sometimes elongated. Sandgrouse are ground birds, running swiftly, walking with body held low and feeding mainly on seeds, some plant material and insects. They are gregarious, particularly in daily flights to water at up to 50 miles (80 km) distance. Breeding males soak specially adapted belly feathers and carry water in them daily up to 19 miles (30 km) for nestlings, determining nesting limits. Flocks have noisy clucking and whistling calls. The nest is a bare scrape with three patterned eggs, incubated by both birds. Young are precocial, feeding themselves but shown food by adults.

78. Seedsnipe (Thinocoridae) 2 genera, 4 species, 6–11 in (15–27 cm). These small to medium, partridge- or larklike shorebirds are found on bare mountaintops, high plateaux and arid grasslands of Andean and Patagonian South America. They have a plump body, short neck and rounded head with a short, stubby, slightly curved bill. A thin opercular flap covers the nostrils. Their legs are short but the toes long, the tail narrow and tapering and the wings long and pointed, sandgrouselike, with strong swift flight. Alarmed birds crouch, then rise in a rapid zigzag flight. Seedsnipe are terrestrial, feeding in open, sparsely vegetated or rocky places, eating parts of plants and seeds, apparently not drinking. Their calls are low and snipelike. Sociable birds when not breeding, their nest is a scrape with some plant lining.

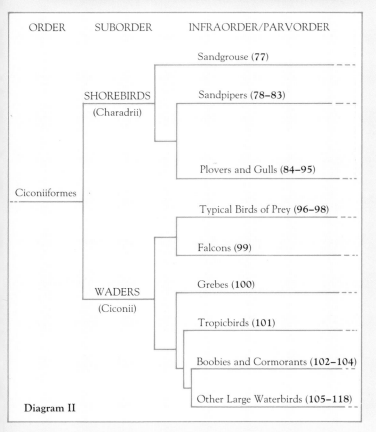

Above SANDPIPERS: *The appearance of the Marsh Sandpiper (Tringa stagnatilis) is typical of these birds which vary considerably in size and in bill: short and stubby in Stints and Turnstones, long and straight in Godwits, curved in Curlews.*

Above left SEEDSNIPE: *Least Seedsnipe (Thinocorus rumicivorus) are shorebirds that have adapted to a seed and plant diet on the open uplands of South America.*

Left WOODCOCK AND SNIPE: *Shorebirds that have adapted to inland life, Eurasian Woodcock (Scolopax rusticola) have large high-set eyes that give all-around vision and feed by blind probing with the bill. Snipe are marshland birds, Woodcock prefer a swampy site in scrub and woodland. The newly hatched downy chicks have short bills and food will be brought to them until they grow longer.*

In this DNA classification the Ciconiiformes differ noticeably from other systems, including a larger group of shorebirds previously assigned to separate orders. The Sandgrouse are birds so highly adapted to arid conditions that their affinities have previously been difficult to assess. The Sandpiper group includes the Plains-wanderer, which, like the Seedsnipe, is seen as an exceptionally adapted offshoot of this group. Flamingos recently thought to have affinities with duck or shorebirds are returned to their place among the larger waders, the Shoebill joins the long-legged Pelicans in a subfamily and the New World Vultures join the storks as two subfamilies of one family. The numbers in brackets indicate the groups in the text belonging to each infraorder.

The female alone incubates the four spotted eggs, the male on guard. The downy young are fully precocial, guarded by the female.

79. Plains-wanderer (Pedionomidae) 1 genus, 1 species, 4–4.8 in (10–12 cm). A small species of the shorebird complex, like an upright button-quail, the Plains-wanderer is found inland in eastern Australia on shortgrass plains. It has a compact body with a short tail and rounded wings and a whirring quail-like flight. The bill is slender. The female is larger, more brightly colored and dominant. It feeds in open short-grass areas of plains, crouching or running when alarmed. Food is a variety of insects, seeds and plant material. The nest is a scantily lined scrape with four patterned pear-shaped eggs. Incubation and care of the precocial, downy young is by the male alone.

80–81. Typical Shorebirds (Scolopacidae) have two subfamilies.

80. Woodcock and Snipe (Scolopacinae) 4 genera, 25 species, 6.8–14 in (17–35 cm). These plump-bodied shorebirds of marsh, moist grass-land and damp woodland occur worldwide, except in polar regions. They have moderate to short legs for wading birds, a short neck and a large head with eyes set high on either side. Their downward-slanting bills are slender and long to very long. They feed by touch, probing deeply in soft soil or mud for worms and similar creatures, detected by and seized in the sensitive, flexible bill tip. They are furtive and semi-nocturnal and plumage is camouflaged. They crouch and fly when forced to do so. Flight is strong and fast. Males have flight displays with calls and noises made by the tail feathers. The nest is a ground scrape in plants or dead leaves with four patterned eggs. The female incubates and the heavily patterned, downy, precocial young have short bills at first and are fed by the adults. Some species migrate.

81. Sandpipers (Tringinae) 17 genera, 63 species, 5.2–26.4 in (13–66 cm). This group, which is found in all manner of open habitats worldwide except for Antarctica and deserts, includes curlews and phalaropes. They are small to medium shorebirds, typically slenderly built with long legs, toes, wings and necks. The head is small and bills vary from short to very long, with some downcurved, a few upcurved, one short and one spatulate. These birds usually occur at margins of all types of inland and coastal waters, taking small creatures by picking and probing at the surface or in various depths of sand and mud. They have slender wings and fast flight. Many are long-distance migrants and a large number breed on Arctic tundra. They

Diagram II

ORDER	SUBORDER	INFRAORDER/PARVORDER
		Sandgrouse (77)
	SHOREBIRDS (Charadrii)	Sandpipers (78–83)
		Plovers and Gulls (84–95)
Ciconiiformes		Typical Birds of Prey (96–98)
		Falcons (99)
	WADERS (Ciconii)	Grebes (100)
		Tropicbirds (101)
		Boobies and Cormorants (102–104)
		Other Large Waterbirds (105–118)

are mostly gregarious when not breeding. Some have aerial displays. The nest is a sparsely lined scrape on the ground in the open or in vegetation, more rarely in old tree nests of other birds. There are usually four patterned eggs, incubated by one or both sexes. Species include Godwits, Curlews, Tattlers, various "shanks" such as Redshanks and Yellowshanks and Willet.

82. Painted-snipe (Rostratulidae) 1 genus, 2 species, 8–10 in (20–25 cm). These snipelike, long-legged shorebirds, found in Africa, from India and South China to Australia and in southern South America, have a slender bill, slightly curved and with a swollen tip. Their plumage is elaborately patterned, brighter in the females, which are larger. Wings are rounded and flight rather weak. Furtive, crepuscular birds of freshwater marshes, swamps and paddy fields, they probe for small creatures and eat some seeds. Females have a display flight. In the Old World species the female is polyandrous, several males caring for clutches. In the New World species both sexes share nesting. The nest is a low hidden mound of vegetation on the ground or floating in a swamp, in which 1–4 patterned eggs are usually laid, hatching as downy striped, fully precocial young.

83. Jacanas (Jacanidae) 6 genera, 8 species, 6–20 in (15–50 cm). Also known as Lily-trotters. Small to medium shorebirds that occur in Africa, from northern India and South China to Australia and in Central and South America, the jacanas have long legs and very long toes and claws for walking on floating water plants. The wings are long and broad, tail short and head and neck slender, the bill short and rail-like. They sometimes have decorative wattles or combs and pale wing patches. They move on water plants in swamps, marshes, lakes and streams, and also in wet grassland, eating various small creatures and some plant material. Where known, females are larger, brighter and polyandrous. Nests are sketchy flat structures on aquatic vegetation. There are usually four eggs, glossy brown, plain or scribbled with black. Males incubate the eggs under their wings and care for the young that are downy, patterned and precocial. They are brooded under the wings of the standing male and may be lifted and carried short distances. The large Pheasant-tailed Jacana is exceptional in being flocking and migratory. The Lotusbird is a Jacana.

84. Sheathbills (Chionididae) 1 genus, 2 species, 13.6–16.4 in (34–41 cm). Medium-sized shorebirds, these are Antarctic scavengers and like heavily built pigeons with short strong legs and an upright stance. The deep stubby bill has a horny sheath. White plumaged, they walk, run and swim, and fly slowly with dangling legs over land, but strongly at sea. They scavenge for eggs and bodies around penguin, cormorant and seal colonies. They are sociable and tame. The nest is a hollow in a rock crevice where 2–4 patterned brown eggs are incubated by both birds who also care for the downy, precocial young.

85. Thick-knees or Stone-curlews (Burhinidae) 1 genus, 9 species, 12.8–22 in (32–55 cm). Medium to large ploverlike birds of dry open places, thick-knees are found in Africa, western Eurasia, from India to Australia, in Central America and in western Peru. Their legs are long and strong with short toes and no hind toe. The head is large and round with big staring eyes. The bill is short, stout and blunt ended; much larger and heavier in some larger

SHEATHBILLS: A Snowy Sheathbill (Chionis alba) searches for eggs or carrion in a colony of Imperial Shags (Phalacrocorax atriceps) and Rockhopper Penguins (Eudyptes chrysocome).

Left THICK-KNEES OR STONE CURLEWS: Another group of shorebirds mostly adapted to inland life, of which this Peruvian Thick-knee (Burhinus superciliaris) is typical. There are also three large and large-billed species, two on rivers, one on the beaches of sea coasts.

Below PLOVERS: A male European Lapwing (Vanellus vanellus) with eggs in an as yet almost bare scrape. The species has adapted well to farmland. Lapwings often show crests and wattles but other plovers are typically round headed.

species. Wings are long and rounded, but birds tend to run and crouch by day, flying reluctantly. They are mainly crepuscular and nocturnal, resting among sparse cover by day and active and noisy at night, with whistling and wailing calls. Often gregarious, they feed on any small creatures. They mainly occur in bare open areas, sometimes near water, with one species coastal. The nest is an almost unlined scrape with two patterned eggs. Both sexes incubate and tend young, which are precocial with short woolly down and fed by the adults for their first six to seven days.

86–88. Plovers (Charadriidae) have two subfamilies, one with two tribes.

86. Oystercatchers (Haematopodini) 1 genus, 11 species, 16.8–20.4 in (42–51 cm). These are medium-sized black or pied shorebirds that occur inland in western Eurasia and coastally around Europe, southern Eurasia, Africa, India, Australia and from the southern United States to the tip of South America. They have strong legs and long tapering wings. The long straight bill with a blunt laterally-compressed tip can open shellfish and chisel them off rocks. These are noisy and sociable birds with loud piping calls. Most occur on shores, but they extend to estuaries and inland rivers. Their food is shellfish, crustaceans, small fish and other shore and water creatures. The nest is a sparsely lined, often stony, ground scrape with 2–4 patterned eggs. Both sexes incubate and tend the young. The downy young are precocial but fed at first by the adults.

87. Avocets and Stilts (Recurvirostrini) 4 genera, 11 species, 14–20 in (35–50 cm). Occurring worldwide on continents, except for polar and tundra regions, these slenderly built shorebirds frequent the shallow waters of marshes and lakes — fresh, brackish or salt in different species. The Ibisbill is like an Oystercatcher with a long tapering downcurved bill and lives on upland stony rivers. Others are long legged, exceptionally so in stilts, with the bill very slender, straight or upcurved. Wings are long and narrow and flight strong with legs extended behind. Their plumage usually has a bold pied pattern. They are gregarious, with short abrupt calls. Stilts wade and pick at small invertebrates, Avocets and Banded Stilts swing upcurved bills through water to find tiny creatures. Nests are scanty, in shallow scrapes or on marsh grass tufts, the eggs patterned and usually four. Both sexes incubate and care for the patterned, downy precocial young.

88. Plovers (Charadriinae) 11 genera, 67 species, 14.8–15.2 in (12–38 cm). Small to medium-sized shorebirds of open places worldwide, except for Antarctica, plovers, lapwings and dotterels have plump, compact bodies with moderately long legs, short tails and long tapering wings for fast flight. A few have broad-tipped wings used in display flight and some have a spur on the angle of the wing. Toes are fairly short and the hind toe may be absent. The neck is short, the head round with large eyes and sometimes ornamented with a pointed crest or colored face wattles. The bill is fairly short, stout and blunt-ended, bent sideways in one species and sometimes with basal wattles. Plovers occur in open places with sparse herbage from short grasslands to sandy shores and semidesert. They feed mainly by short runs, snatching small insects and other invertebrates. Calls are loud and simple. Some species have aerial displays. Nests are a bare or scantily lined scrape, usually with four patterned eggs. Mating may be in pairs, polygyny or polyandry, the females being bigger and brighter birds. Incu-

bation is by the pair or by one sex, who then tend the downy, patterned and precocial young.

89–90. Glareolidae has two subfamilies.
89. Crab Plover (Dromadinae) 1 genus, 1 species, 15.2 in (38 cm). This bird is like a large, long-legged plover with a very heavy bill tapering at the tip and as long as the head. It feeds mainly on crabs and some mollusks. It is often gregarious when resting, dispersing to feed. It has whistling noisy calls. It has long wings but its flight is slow and low. It nests, often in large colonies, in a burrow made in a sandy area. One white egg is laid in an unlined chamber in a sand bank. The young is downy but remains in the burrow, fed by the adults, feeding continuing after it leaves the burrow. Crab Plovers occur around the warmer shores of the Indian Ocean and its islands, from the Arabian Gulf and Bay of Bengal to South Africa and Malaya.
90. Coursers and Pratincoles (Glareolinae) Although closely related, these birds form two distinct groups: the Coursers, 3 genera, 9 species, 7.6–11.6 in (19–29 cm), and the Pratincoles, 2 genera, 8 species, 6.4–10.4 in (16–26 cm).

Coursers are like slenderly built furtive plovers with longer legs, slightly more upright posture, thin neck and a small head with a long, pointed thin bill with downcurved tip. Toes are short, the hind toe absent, and birds run fast, crouching when alarmed. Wings are long and broad and tail short and square. Coursers feed by picking up small insects and seeds, and are

partly crepuscular and nocturnal. They have short low-pitched or whistling calls, occurring in pairs or small parties on more level desert or short grassland. The nest is a bare scrape with 1–3 patterned eggs, incubated by the female or both sexes. In very hot sites, the Three-banded Courser partly buries eggs. The Egyptian Plover, on sand banks, buries eggs and small young at hot times, and cools them with water brought on belly feathers. Young are downy and precocial and can feed themselves, but are also fed for most of the prefledging period. Coursers occur in Africa, through the Middle East and in India.

Pratincoles are shorter legged and longer toed, with short neck, larger head and stumpy curved bill with a wide gape. Their wings are long and pointed and the tail is long and forked. They are mainly aerial feeders on insects, with fast agile flight. They are highly sociable and have high-pitched flight calls. They occur near water with bare open margins. The nest is a bare scrape with 1–4 patterned eggs incubated by both sexes. The downy young leave the nest and hide, fed by parents at first. Pratincoles are mostly migratory or nomadic, occurring in southwestern Eurasia, Africa and from northern India and South China to Australia.

91–95. Laridae has two subfamilies, the Larinae, which consists of the four following tribes, and the Alcinae.
91. Skuas and Jaegers (Stercorariini) 2 genera,

Above COURSERS AND PRATINCOLES: A Collared Pratincole (Glareola pratincola). Pratincoles are another shorebird adaptation, to a bird trying to be a swallow.

SKUAS: A pair of Great Skuas (Catharacta skua) may have a third bird as helper during nesting, here joining them in a territorial display showing white wing patches and calling.

8 species, 20–27.2 in (50–68 cm). Widespread through polar and tundra regions, around southern South America and at sea, Skuas are gull-like, but with a hook-tipped bill, usually stout and strong, but slender in small species. Large species are heavily built with broad wings, smaller species more slender with long narrow wings and elongated mid-tail feathers. Feet are webbed and flight is fast and strong. At sea and on coasts other seabirds are parasitized to disgorge food. Skuas take eggs and young from seabird colonies and scavenge, but will also take fish at or near the surface. Tundra nesters take small rodents and birds, and some insects and berries. They breed mainly on tundra and polar shores, migrating in winter, often across oceans. Nests are sparsely lined scrapes, spaced when inland, in colonies on coasts, usually with two patterned eggs. Both sexes incubate and tend young.

92. Skimmers (Rynchopini) 1 genus, 3 species, 15.2–20 in (38–50 cm). Superficially like large terns, these birds of seashores, estuaries and larger inland waters have single species in the Americas, in Africa and another from India to South China. They have short legs, webbed feet and long slender wings. The bill is deep and laterally compressed, the upper mandible fairly short and straight, the lower bladelike and extending well beyond the upper. They feed by flying low over the water with steady buoyant wingbeats, the bill open with the lower mandible plowing just below the surface, snapping shut as fish are touched. They are gregarious at all times and males are larger than females. The nest is a bare scrape on open ground with 2–7 patterned eggs, incubated almost entirely by the female. Young are downy and precocial, fed by parents, their lower mandible is short at first and only gradually do they learn to skim.

93. Gulls (Larini) 6 genera, 50 species, 15.5–30.4 in (37–76 cm). Medium to large waterbirds, mainly of seacoasts, gulls occur worldwide, mostly in cooler regions. They are mostly white with gray and black wings and backs. The legs are moderately long, the body compact, tail square or, rarely, forked and wings long and fairly narrow — used for strong flight and sustained soaring. The bill is usually stout, rarely slender, blunt tipped and slightly hooked. Gulls walk and swim well, and can make shallow dives. They are mainly scavengers, minor predators and opportunistic feeders, taking fish and small water creatures, insects, eggs, small birds and mammals. Piracy of other gulls, terns and waterbirds also occurs. They are usually sociable in feeding, resting and nesting; and noisy, with shrill or harsh calls. There is usually a long-term pair bond. Nests are usually in colonies, on the ground or on rock ledges, exceptionally in trees. The nest is a sparse to bulky cup of vegetable debris, usually with 2–3 patterned eggs. Both sexes incubate and tend young that are downy with spotted patterns and semiprecocial, fed by adults on regurgitated food on or near the nest.

94. Terns (Sternini) 7 genera, 45 species, 8–22.4 in (20–56 cm). These are medium-sized, gull-like waterbirds but with a more horizontal stance and short small legs and feet. Their wings are long and narrow and the tail forked. In marsh terns the bill is slender and shorter, flight is very buoyant and food such as insects snatched from the surface in dipping swoops. Sea terns have longer, stouter dagger bills and plunge dive for food: fish, squid or crustaceans. Noddies have narrower bills and broader wedge tails and snatch fish at the surface. Terns are gregarious and noisy, with short sharp calls. Nests are in colonies, sometimes very large. Marsh terns build thin nests on floating vegetation. Sea terns have bare or sparsely lined scrapes on the ground near water. Noddies build plant debris platforms on ledges or branches, the White Tern balances a single egg on a small projection of tree or rock and Inca Terns use holes. Both sexes incubate the 1–3 patterned eggs. Downy spotted precocial young are fed at or near the nest. Older sea tern young may form crèches. Most species are migratory and terns are world-wide in occurrence on seas and inland waters.

95. Auks (Alcinae) 12 genera, 23 species, 5.6–14.4 in (14–36 cm). Small to medium-sized, compact-bodied diving seabirds, the auks occur on polar to temperate coasts and seas of the Northern Hemisphere. Their short legs, with webbed feet, are often well back on the body, producing an upright posture on land and walking ability may be poor. Wings are small, strong and tapering, for rapid flight and for swimming under water. Their strong bills vary from tapering and pointed to laterally flattened and blunt and to very short and deep. Food is fish and crustaceans caught in rapid underwater swimming, sometimes deep down. Display plumage ranges from head crests and plumes to brightly colored bill flanges. Voice is low pitched in large species, mostly squeaky in small ones. Nests are usually in colonies on coasts and islands, varying from bare ledges with close-packed birds to crevices or burrows with nest material.

The Murrelets lay inland, Kittlitz's Murrelet nesting on bare mountains, the Marbled Murrelet on branches on debris in tall conifer forest. They lay 1–2 eggs, usually white in cavities, patterned in open sites, which are incubated by both adults who feed the downy semiprecocial young. These must make their first flight from nest to sea. Ledge nesters leave early, fed at sea by parents. Auks include Puffins, Auklets, Razorbills and Guillemots or Murres.

96–97. Accipitridae has two subfamilies.

96. Osprey (Pandioninae) 1 genus, 1 species, 22–23.2 in (55–58 cm). A long-winged but lightly-built, eaglelike raptor, the Osprey occurs on coasts, rivers and larger inland waters and is almost worldwide in distribution, but breeds mainly in the temperate Northern Hemisphere and Australasia. Its head is narrow with shaggy nape and prominent bill with strongly hooked tip. The feet are large with long curved claws and rough sole, outer toe reversible. The tail is fairly short, wings narrow, often held angled and gull-like. It flies over water and plunge dives for fish near the surface, sometimes submerging. It has a whistling call. A big twig cup nest is enlarged annually in a tree, on a rock or on the ground. The blotched eggs — usually 3 — are incubated by both adults and both tend the young, but at first the male brings food for the mate and downy altricial young.

97. Typical Birds of Prey (Accipitrinae) 64 genera, 239 species, 10–46 in (25–115 cm). Medium to large diurnal hunters and scavengers, these birds have compact bodies, legs of variable length, strong, large feet with strong grasping toes and large curved claws. They have large, keen-sighted eyes and powerful hooked bills with a bare cere around the nostrils. Their necks are usually short and their heads and necks sometimes bare in scavengers such as vultures. Tails are short to long and wings long, broad and rounded, their flight powerful, often with prolonged soaring. Food consists of all kinds of creatures, or carrion (mostly dead mammals) and palmnuts in one species. Live food is usually seized in the foot after a rapid

AUKS: The face and bill of the Atlantic Puffin (Fratercula arctica) are decorated in clown-like fashion. The wattle over the eye and some of the colored shields of the bill base fall off after the breeding season.

Left *TERNS: A Caspian Tern (Sterna caspia) gives chicks a fish, probably brought by its partner, offering it headfirst. Some Terns spend most of their time at sea, plunge diving for food, but the three Marsh Terns (Chlidonias species) snatch insects from the surface.*

Left *TYPICAL BIRDS OF PREY: This family varies considerably in size and ability. This Martial Eagle (Polemaetus bellicosus), which has killed a small antelope, is at the upper end of the range.*

Opposite page *GULLS: The Herring Gull (Larus argentatus), noticeable for its loud yodeling calls, is a bird of coast and inland waters, often nesting on ledges.*

swoop on land or water, or after aerial pursuit. Females are often larger than males. They breed mostly in solitary pairs, colonially in some vultures. The nest is a twig cup with finer lining, often bulky, on a tree, shrub, ledge or the ground. Both adults incubate the 1–7 blotched eggs and rear the young, but the female does most incubation and brooding, the male bringing food. Young are downy and semialtricial, active around the nest when older. Found worldwide, except in polar regions, species include Eagles, Kites, Hawks, Buzzards, Harriers and Old World Vultures.

98. Secretary-bird (Sagittariidae) 1 genus, 1 species, 48–60 in (120–150 cm). This is a tall bird of prey of open country with very long slim legs, weaker feet and smaller claws. The wings are long and the tail has long mid-tail feathers. The neck is long and the head small with a spiky crest on the nape, large eyes and bare face with a large hooked bill. It hunts with long deliberate strides, striking prey with its feet and using wings to add movement. Food includes snakes (sometimes dropped from a height), rodents, large insects, eggs and the young of ground birds. It has deep croaking calls and soaring advertisement flights. Usually in pairs, it makes a large shallow nest of plant material on a low tree or bush with 1–3 white eggs. Incubation is usually by the female fed by the male. Young are downy and altricial, fed for about one month after leaving the nest. It occurs as a resident in open grassland, steppe and savanna in Afrotropical Africa.

99. Falcons (Falconidae) 10 genera, 63 species, 6–24.4 in (15–61 cm). Small to large diurnal hunters found worldwide except in Antarctica, in most land habitats, the typical falcons have a compact body with a short neck and largish rounded head. Their eyes are large and sight very acute, the bill strong, short and hooked, often with a notched edge and nostrils in a fleshy cere. The tail is medium to long and wings long and tapering for fast and agile flight. Legs are strong with bare shanks and large grasping feet with big curved claws. Food is birds, small mammals and insects, taken in the feet from the ground or in the air often while in very rapid flight. Females are usually larger. Breeding is usually in solitary pairs, rarely colonial, the nest an unlined hollow on a ledge or the ground, in a hole or old tree nest of other birds, with 2–3 colored or blotched eggs. Incubation and brooding of small young is mostly by the female, fed by the male. Young are downy and semialtricial. Some species are migrants. Caracaras are long-legged, larger, hawklike falcons of the Americas. They are sluggish and mainly terrestrial, able to run fast to hunt weaker prey but feeding extensively on carrion. They build a nest in a tree or among ground vegetation. Falcon species include Kestrel, Merlin and Hobby.

100. Grebes (Podicipedidae) 6 genera, 21 species, 9.2–30.4 in (23–76 cm). These small to medium-sized diving waterbirds are primarily aquatic, occurring worldwide except in polar and desert regions, on open still or slow moving fresh water, some wintering on coastal waters. They have a compact body with thick plumage and a vestigial tail, strong legs with large lobed toes placed well back on the body and small, curved and tapering wings. They fly reluctantly, preferring to dive and swim, and flight is poor or lost in some species. The neck is long and thin, head small and narrow and bill short to moderately long, thin and pointed, or, rarely, short and deep. They swim well, dive abruptly and move rapidly under water, propelled by their feet, to catch fish, crustaceans or insects. In breeding birds the head is ornamented with conspicuous tufts, crests and ruffs. Breeding is in pairs or colonially, the nest an anchored mound of floating plant debris with 2–6 whitish eggs, stained when adults cover them with weed when absent from the nest. Incubation is by

both sexes and care of the downy, striped precocial young is divided between both parents. Small young are carried on adults' backs. The Little Grebe is also called a Dab-chick.

101. Tropicbirds (Phaethontidae) 1 genus, 3 species, 18.4–20 in (46–50 cm), plus the same length in tail streamers. Tropicbirds, which occur on islands and coasts of warm seas, are like heavy-bodied terns, white with black as eye streak and on wings and a tapering tail with two long thin central red or white streamers in adults. The bill is stout and tapering, the legs short with four toes webbed and set towards the rear of the body, so birds cannot stand erect. The wings are long and narrow and in flight strong fluttering wingbeats alternate with soaring glides. Largely oceanic, solitary or in pairs, tropicbirds hover and plunge dive for fish or squid. They are more gregarious at breeding sites, with flying displays and trilling calls. The nest is a scrape in a cavity in a cliff or rocks allowing immediate takeoff. Both parents incubate the single brown egg and feed the downy altricial young.

102. Boobies and Gannets (Sulidae) 3 genera, 9 species, 25.6–40 in (64–100 cm). These large plunge-diving seabirds occur in the tropical to subtropical North Atlantic and Australasian seas. They have torpedo-shaped bodies, wedge-shaped tails and long pointed wings. The legs are short and strong with all four toes webbed. The bill is long, strong and tapering, with a large gape and the eyes close set near its base. Gannets are oceanic seabirds, mainly coming to land to breed, boobies tend to roost onshore. Flight is strong and direct with alternating flapping and gliding. Food, fish and squid, is caught by plunge diving from well above the surface using the wings to swim under water. They are fairly gregarious and breed in colonies on cliff ledges, level or sloping ground, low shrubs or trees. Nests may be sketchy, or heaps of debris or twigs. Chalky white eggs, 1–4 according to species, are incubated by both parents using their webbed feet and both feed the downy altricial young that take food from the parent's gullet.

103. Anhingas (Anhingidae) 1 genus, 4 species, 34–36 in (85–90 cm). Anhingas or Darters are cormorant-like fishing birds found in Africa and

FALCONS: *A Brown Falcon (Falco berigora) usually contents itself with prey that is easily caught but the brown snake it has brought its brood has a potentially lethal bite. Falcons range from fast flyers that strike on the wing to Kestrels and Pygmy Falcons that may pounce on large insects.*

Above left SECRETARY-BIRD: *The Secretary-bird (Sagittarius serpentarius), an efficient snake killer, stamping and kicking with long feet that do not allow the snake a close approach, gets its name from the crest, like quill pens tucked behind the ear of an old-time clerk.*

Above right GREBES: *Great Crested Grebes (Podiceps cristatus) at their floating nest. The young, often carried on a parent's back on the water, have climbed up to rest between the wings.*

Right TROPICBIRDS: *A White-tailed Tropicbird (Phaethon lepturus) with its almost full-grown young. Skillful fliers, but most helpless on land, they must find deep cavities and cliff hollows in which to nest, where they will not be vulnerable.*

Far right BOOBIES AND GANNETS: *Although these birds are awkward on land, a tightly packed Northern Gannet (Morus bassanus) colony leaves little space for clumsiness. Boobies tend to nest in more dispersed colonies.*

through the Americas from the southern United States to Argentina. Their body is long, with short legs set well back for propulsion under water with four toes webbed. Wings and tail are long and the neck very long and slender with a small head tapering to a thin pointed bill with finely serrated edges. They fly and soar strongly with neck extended. They swim well, often with body submerged, and chase fish under water. They stab fish and pick up insects for food. They rest with wings extended for drying. They nest colonially, often with other waterbirds, making a bulgy twig cup in a tree with usually four greenish eggs. Both sexes incubate, using their webbed feet. Downy young are fed by both parents, taking food from the gullet, feeding continuing after fledging.

104. Cormorants (Phalacrocoracidae) 1 genus, 38 species, 18–40.4 in (45–101 cm). Medium to large diving birds, cormorants occur worldwide, except for polar and tundra regions and isolated oceanic islands, on rivers and larger inland waters, islands and coasts. They are long bodied with short strong legs set well back for underwater propulsion with large feet and four toes webbed. Wings are long, flight level, often with intermittent gliding, though one species is flightless, and the tail longish and tapering. The neck is long, head narrow and sometimes crested and the bill strong, cylindrical, hooked at the tip and with a wide gape. The eyes are close set near the base of the bill and the skin of face and throat is often bare. Swimming well, often low in the water, cormorants chase fish under water and also eat crustaceans, squid, amphibians and small water creatures. They spread their wings out to dry when resting. Often gregarious, they nest in colonies, building a bulky drum of debris or twigs on the ground or rock ledges or in a tree. Both adults use their webbed feet to incubate chalky white or bluish eggs, usually 3–4. Altricial young are naked then downy and take food from the gullets of parents.

105. Herons (Ardeidae) 20 genera, 65 species, 12–56 in (30–140 cm). These small to very large wading birds occur by fresh and salt waters of

all kinds and in marshland. They are worldwide except in polar regions. The body is narrow, tail short and wings large and broad. The legs are long to very long, and thin; feet have long thin toes. The neck is long and slender, the head narrow and the bill long and dagger shaped. Flight is slow with legs extended behind. The head rests on the shoulders in flight and when resting. Some forage by open waters, some are secretive in marshes or mangroves. Food is mostly obtained on land or wading in water by slow deliberate stalking and a quick thrust of the head. It is principally fish but any small creatures are taken. They are solitary or gregarious, the calls mostly low and harsh and display plumage is narrow plumes or filamentous feathers on head and back. Breeding often colonially — bitterns may be polygamous — the nest is a shallow cup of twigs or stems on the ground or in a bank or tree. The bluish eggs, usually 2–7, are incubated by both parents, who feed the downy semialtricial young on regurgitated food. Herons include Egrets and Bitterns.

106. Hamerkop (Scopidae) 1 genus, 1 species, 22.4 in (56 cm). This bird of Afrotropical Africa and southwestern Arabia occurs around inland fresh waters with some trees and estuaries. Like a small short stork, it has strong legs and a stout tapering bill with a slightly hooked tip. There is a large shaggy crest on the nape. Wings are large and rounded, tail fairly long and it flies with neck often extended. It feeds by water or wades in shallows, taking amphibians and other small creatures. It is usually in pairs but gathers for social displays with loud croaking or whistling calls. The nest is a huge domed mass of sticks and mud on a tree or rocks with 3–6 chalky white eggs incubated by both parents. Altricial downy young are fed by adults.

107. Flamingos (Phoenicopteridae) 1 genus, 5 species, 32–40 in (80–100 cm). Tall wading birds of saline waters, flamingos occur around the Caribbean Sea, Galapagos Islands, Africa, and from the Mediterranean to steppe lakes of western Asia and the Arabian Gulf to India. Their legs are very long and thin with small webbed feet. The wings are narrow, tail short, neck long and sinuous and the head small. The bill is short, stout and downward angled with a larger troughlike lower jaw and narrow flat upper jaw with filtering ridges inside. They feed with the head and bill inverted and pump water through the bill with the tongue extracting minute animals or algae. Flight is fast with neck and legs extended. Highly gregarious, they live in large flocks and often fly for long distances between salt lakes, lagoons and seashores, feeding in shallows but able to swim. They have gooselike honking calls. They nest colonially by water, making a small rounded mound of mud with the top hollow. A single chalky-white egg is incubated by both adults. The gray downy young, with straight bill at first, is fed on liquid crop secretions of the adults. After about one week young leave the nest and form crèches.

108. Ibises and Spoonbills (Threskiornithidae) The family contains two distinct groups: the Ibises, 12 genera, 28 species, 19.2–40 in (48–100 cm), and the Spoonbills, 2 genera, 6 species, 28–34 in (70–85 cm). Both occur on most continents, though absent from polar, cooler and arid regions.

Ibises are medium to large wading birds with long legs, feet capable of perching, broad rounded wings and short tails. The neck is long, head small and bill long narrow and strongly downcurved. Flight is strong with neck and legs

HAMERKOP: *The Hamerkop or Hammerhead (Scopus umbretta) is like a small stork of fresh waters, its tapering crest looking as though it balances its heavy bill.*

Right SHOEBILL: *Against smooth grass a captive Shoebill (Balaeniceps rex) looks rather out of place. Its great bill is designed to heave large slippery catfish from papyrus swamps.*

Below FLAMINGOS and PELICANS: *Lesser Flamingos (Phoenicopterus minor) and Great White Pelicans (Pelecanus onocrotalus) come to drink where fresh water enters a salt lake. Black-winged Stilts (Himantopus himantopus) swim in the foreground. The special diet of the flamingos has imposed a very patchy distribution on all five species.*

extended. They feed by probing and seizing all kinds of small creatures. Most species feed in shallow water in swamps or wet grassland, a few in drier grass and savanna. They are mostly highly gregarious and have low harsh calls. They breed singly or in colonies, sometimes with other waterbirds. The nest is a shallow twig structure in a tree or shrub, or on the ground, with 2–5 eggs incubated by both adults. Downy semialtricial young are fed by both parents on regurgitated food direct from the adult gullet or from the nest. The bill is short at first.

Spoonbills are similar to ibises but have a long straight bill with a broad spatulate tip. They feed by wading in fresh or salt waters, inland or on estuaries and coasts, swinging the bill from side to side through the water and catching small aquatic animals.

109–110. Pelecanidae has two subfamilies.
109. Shoebill (Balaenicipitinae) 1 genus, 1 species, 60 in (150 cm). This bird of the Upper Nile and central Africa is like a very large stork, but with a big head and huge shoe-shaped bill with a terminal hook, and has a small tuftlike crest. Wings are large and broad, legs long and the feet have long toes. It occurs in large swamps with floating vegetation, standing still and seizing often large fish and may lunge forward onto its breast to do so. Solitary, in pairs, or more rarely in groups, it may remain hidden in tall swamp vegetation. It flies well and may soar high, with head drawn back and legs extended. The nest is a heap of grass on floating vegetation or a small island, with 2–3 chalk-white eggs incubated by both parents. The downy altricial young are fed and brought water by regurgitation by both parents.

110. Pelicans (Pelecaninae) 1 genus, 8 species, 45.6–73.2 in (114–183 cm). Large waterbirds of larger inland waters and coasts of southern Eurasia, Africa, India to southeast Asia, Australia and United States to western South America. Pelicans are heavy bodied with short strong legs and large feet with four toes webbed, short tails and long broad wings. A long neck carries a small head, the bill very long and narrow with a hooked tip and huge elastic throat pouch. They swim well, most species feeding by reaching under water and scooping up fish, sometimes after communal driving of shoals. Two species plunge dive from a height. Flight is strong with intermittent gliding, prolonged soaring at times. Mostly silent, they have low harsh calls. They are highly gregarious, breeding colonially. A tiny platform nest in a tree or a heap of vegetation on the ground or in a marsh usually has 2–3 chalk-white eggs incubated by both parents. Naked, then downy, altricial young are fed by both parents taking

regurgitated food from the gullet. Larger young of ground nesters may form crèches.

111–12. Ciconiidae has two subfamilies.

111. New World Vultures (Cathartinae) 5 genera, 7 species, 24–52 in (60–130 cm). Large to very large scavengers occurring over open and forest country from southern Canada through the Americas, these birds are distantly related to storks. They include Black, Turkey and King Vultures and the Condors. The body is heavy, wings long and broad, tail broad and legs and feet only moderately strong. The small head and the neck are often decorated with wattles. The bill is short, stout and strongly hooked. They feed mainly on carrion, spending much time slowly soaring. The Turkey Vulture can smell decaying flesh and other species may follow it down. Young or helpless animals may be eaten and some fruit and vegetable matter stored in a large crop. Often gregarious, though rather silent, they are solitary breeders. The nest is a bare hollow on a ledge, in a cave or broken tree or on the ground, with 1–2 plain or patterned eggs incubated by both adults. Semi-altricial young are downy with a bare head and fed by both parents on regurgitated food. The Condors have a single egg and nest in alternate years.

112. Storks (Ciconiinae) 6 genera, 19 species, 24–70 in (60–175 cm). Storks are tall, long-legged wading and walking birds of marshland, open areas near water and mixed grassland and woodland from temperate Eurasia to Africa and Australia, and from southern United States to Central and South America. Their legs are long and strong, with toes fairly short, wings long and broad and tail short. The neck is long, head rounded, bill stout, long and tapering, slightly upcurved or downcurved in some species. Some have bare skin on head and neck, or decorative wattles. Most feed by stalking prey near or in water, or on open ground, taking any small creatures, while Marabous feed on carrion. Wood-Storks probe under water with an open bill. Openbill Storks have incomplete closure at mid jaw, using the gap for opening shellfish. Flight is strong and deliberate with much gliding and soaring. They are solitary or gregarious, breeding in isolated pairs or colonies. The nest is a large twig saucer in a tree, on a cliff or building or on marshy ground. Both birds incubate the 3–5 white eggs. Downy altricial young are fed and brought water by regurgitation.

113. Frigatebirds (Fregatidae) 1 genus, 5 species, 28.4–40.4 in (71–101 cm). These aerial, raptorial seabirds that occur on coasts and islands throughout the warmer oceans have a slender body, very long tapering wings and long deeply forked tail, but very short legs and feet with four toes with reduced webs and sharp claws only used for perching. They do not walk or swim, only fly. The neck is slender, head small, and the bill long and slender with a strongly-hooked tip. They fly constantly, soaring with infrequent wingbeats, extremely agile using wings and tail. They hunt coastal seas, swooping low to snatch up fish, squid or offal from the water, small creatures from beaches and eggs and young from bird breeding colonies. They also harry boobies and tropicbirds to disgorge food. They roost perched on trees or rocks. Males are smaller than females, with scarlet balloonlike throat pouches used in display. Often gregarious, they breed in colonies, the nest a stick platform on a low tree, shrub or the ground. A single white egg is incubated by both adults. The downy altricial young is fed by parents for up to a year.

NEW WORLD VULTURES: The Andean Condor (Vultur gryphus) ranges from Venezuela and Colombia to the Strait of Magellan.

Right *STORKS: The bill of the African Openbill Stork (Anastomus lamelligerus) can effectively hold and open freshwater mussels and other shellfish on which it mainly feeds. White-faced Whistling Ducks (Dendrocygna viduata) and Garganey (Anas querquedula) share this waterside.*

114. Penguins (Spheniscidae) 6 genera, 17 species, 16–46 in (40–115 cm). Medium to large flightless seabirds, penguins feed and breed in cold Antarctic seas, extending north in cold currents to South Africa, southern South America and the Galapagos Islands. They are stout bodied with dense, short, furlike feathering, very short legs and short, broad, webbed feet with sharp claws, set far back by the vestigial tail, giving an upright stance. Wings are highly modified to narrow curved flippers for fast underwater propulsion. The bill is short, stout and bluntly tapering. Plumage is usually black and white below with colored patches or spiky decorative plumes on the head. On land they walk, hop or slide on the belly. In water they swim fast and to considerable depths after fish, squid and crustaceans, breathing during porpoiselike leaps. They can swim at the surface with head raised. Highly gregarious, they have loud trumpeting and braying calls and breed by the sea in large noisy colonies. Nests are bare sites, heaps of stones or debris, or burrows, where 1–2 white eggs are incubated by both birds and the downy semialtricial young fed on regurgitated food taken from the adult's mouth. Larger young may form crêches. In King and Emperor Penguins the male incubates the single egg and small young on his feet under a flap of belly skin before relief by the female.

115. Divers or Loons (Gaviidae) 1 genus, 5 species, 21.2–36.4 in (53–91 cm). These large, streamlined underwater hunters occur on inland to coastal, subpolar to temperate waters of the Northern Hemisphere. The body is long with a short tail, short strong legs with webbed feet set toward its rear for propulsion and rather small tapering wings. A smooth head tapering to a strong dagger bill is set on a thick neck. They need to run to become airborne but flight is fast and direct with the neck a little drooped. They swim well and move fast under water, catching fish and other small water creatures. They have long pair bonds and are highly territorial when breeding on inland waters, with loud cackling, yodeling and wailing cries. The nest is a scrape near the water's edge or a low heap of material in shallow water with usually two dark patterned eggs, incubated by both birds. Dark downy young are precocial, swim and may rest on an adult's back. They are fed by the adults for a time after fledging. In winter they mostly move to seacoasts and may occur in small flocks. Movement on land is difficult.

116–18. Procellariidae has three subfamilies.
116. Shearwaters and Petrels (Procellariinae) 15 genera, 80 species, 4.4–34.8 in (11–87 cm). This family of typical tubenose seabirds, including Fulmars and Prions and found worldwide at sea and on coasts, embraces a large range of gliding seabirds with long narrow wings and fairly short tails. Their feet are webbed and their legs are often rather weak for movement on land but used for swimming. The head is rounded and the bill stout to slender, short to moderately long, with a hook tip and tubular nostril sheaths. The Giant Petrel is like a large albatross, can walk on land and uses a massive bill to scavenge beached carcasses. The Diving Petrel is tiny, with short bill and wings, and dives for crustaceans. More typical species are oceanic, slimly built, glide much of the time to conserve energy and take small sea creatures at or just below the surface, using the wings under water. Mostly migratory or nomadic, they return to breed colonially at island or coastal sites. The nest is an open scrape on a

cliff ledge, on the ground or in burrows with a single white egg incubated by both sexes. Young are downy and altricial, fed by regurgitation from the adult's bill and growing very fat.

117. Albatrosses (Diomedeinae) 2 genera, 14 species, 28.4–54 in (71–135 cm). These very large gliding seabirds of southern and Pacific Oceans have very long, narrow and pointed wings and a short tail. The feet are webbed and legs short, but strong enough to stand and walk on, and to run for a takeoff. Flight consists mainly of gliding using updrafts and currents with hardly any flapping and albatrosses tend to rest on the water when the wind drops. They can swim and dive shallowly and appear to feed mainly on squid and octopus, but will take fish and other sea animals, sometimes small birds, and scavenge around fishing boats. They breed at isolated island colonial sites, with elaborate noisy displays. The nest is a bare site or a

mound of plant debris on soil. A single white egg is incubated by both adults. The semialtricial young is fed on regurgitated food.

118. Storm-Petrels (Hydrobatinae) 7 genera, 21 species, 4.8–10 in (12–25 cm). These are very small, tubenosed seabirds, usually with a fluttering and swooping flight. The wings are shorter and more rounded than those of typical petrels, tails rounded, square or bluntly forked, legs long and slender with webbed feet and bills short and blunt with a hooked tip and prominent nostril tubes. They fly low over the sea with hanging legs, or patter along the surface, picking up small marine creatures. They nest in loose colonies on small islands or some inland sites, the nest usually in a burrow or rock crevice. A single white egg is incubated by both adults, the downy altricial young fed on regurgitated food. When not nesting they are widely migratory and nomadic and occur worldwide except in Arctic seas.

Above DIVERS OR LOONS: A Red-throated Loon (Diver) (Gavia stellata) about to scramble up onto its nest of peat and plant debris to incubate its typical two-egg clutch.

Left SHEARWATERS AND PETRELS: These birds scour the oceans for food. Like this Flesh-footed Shearwater (Puffinus carneipes) they can put down and swim on the sea, making shallow dives in pursuit of fish and squids.

Following pages ALBATROSSES: The tubenoses of these ocean wanderers are less prominent than in related groups. Scraped up soil and plant material makes the drum-shaped nests of this colony of Black-browed Albatross (Diomedea melanophris).

SONGBIRDS Passeriformes

119. New Zealand Wrens (Acanthisittidae) 2 genera, 4 species (possibly 2 species extinct), 3.2–4 in (8–10 cm). These are small birds of the New Zealand forest or high mountain vegetation with short rounded wings, short tail, small thin sharp-pointed bill and relatively large strong legs and feet. They eat insects and some small fruits, the Rifleman feeding mainly on beech forest tree trunks, the Rock Wren in thin alpine vegetation. They are furtive, infrequent fliers, and have short high-pitched calls. The nest is a loosely woven domed structure in a hole or crevice with 2–5 relatively large white eggs. Incubation and feeding of the young is by both parents with some evidence of additional helpers.

120. Pittas (Pittidae) 1 genus, 31 species, 6–11.2 in (15–28 cm). Round-bodied, short-necked and large-headed, with a stout and tapering bill, these ground-feeding birds occur in forest and scrub from India and Japan to Australia, with one in Africa. Their wings are rounded, tails short, legs long and strong, and they move in bounding hops. Food is all kinds of small creatures, taken from the ground or by shallow digging. Snails are broken on stones. Although mainly terrestrial, they roost in, and sing from trees, with loud whistling calls. The nest is a large domed structure in low vegetation or on a sheltered ground site. There are usually 3–5 rounded, spotted eggs. Incubation and care of young is by both parents. Some species are migratory.

121. Broadbills (Eurylaimidae) 8 genera, 14 species, 5.6–11.2 in (13–28 cm). Arboreal birds with stout bodies and largish heads, broadbills occur in pairs or small groups in lowland and montane forest, forest edges and scrub in Africa, India, southeastern Asia and Borneo. Legs are short and feet strong, tail short or long and graduated, wings rounded. The bill is short and stout, sometimes wide and swollen with a

hooked tip, and surmounted by a low crest in the Green Broadbill. Food varies from insects and other small creatures to fruit and buds, mostly taken from trees by searching. Plumage is dull or brightly colored and calls shrill double notes with whistles and churrs. The nest is a hanging, pear-shaped bag, stoutly built but hung with untidy trailing material, with a low, porched, side entrance and suspended from a branch, sometimes low down. Clutches vary from 2–8 white-to-pink spotted eggs. The Dusky Broadbill has a group of helpers at the nest.

122. Asities (Philepittidae) 2 genera, 4 species, 3.6–6.8 in (9–17 cm). Asities are small, stoutly built birds with short rounded wings and tail, which occur in the thick evergreen forest of Madagascar. Males are blue and yellow or black and yellow in breeding plumage with blue and green wattles around or above the eye. The two larger asities have a short, stout bill and are mainly fruit eating. Two smaller sunbird asities have long downcurved bills and appear to eat mainly insects, possibly some nectar. All are rather sluggish, usually solitary and quiet. The Velvet Asities' pear-shaped nest hangs from twigs, its porch-sheltered side entrance near the top. There are three white eggs.

123. Sapayoa (Sapayoidae) 1 genus, 1 species, 5.6 in (14 cm). The Broad-billed Sapayoa is a greenish bird of undergrowth near streams in lowland forests from the Pacific side of Panama to northwestern Ecuador. It has an uncertain affinity with the tyrants. Its round head has a broad flattened bill with a small hook at the tip, suited to its insectivorous diet. It is usually quiet with a soft trilling call. Males have a concealed yellow crown stripe. Nests and breeding behavior are not recorded.

124–29. Tyrants (Tyrannidae) comprise a family with five subfamilies, the Tityrinae being divided into two tribes.

124. Mionectine Flycatchers (Pipromorphinae) 8 genera, 53 species, 2.8–5.6 in (7–14 cm). This is a varied group of mostly dull-colored small birds of lower forest growth in forests, forest edges and open woodland in tropical Central and South America. Flycatcher types have longish wings and tails, with short thin bills. Pygmy-Tyrants, Tody-Tyrants and Tody-Flycatchers have more rounded wings, short to medium tails, bills short to fairly long and sometimes dorsally flattened. Most are insect-eaters but *Mionectes* flycatchers pick small fruits while hovering and Antpipits walk about gleaning from undersides of foliage. Calls are mostly low, sharp and abrupt. Antpipits have shrill whistles. Where nests are known they are hanging rounded structures with side entrances, or pendent and purse shaped. Antpipits make domed nests on the ground.

125. Tyrants (Tyranninae) 91 genera, 340 species, 2–20 in (5–50 cm). Varied small to medium-sized birds, adapted for many passerine niches, this family occurs in all habitats through

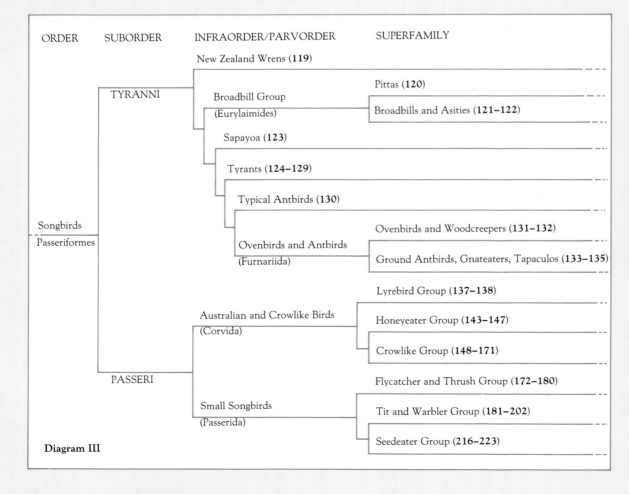

ORDER	SUBORDER	INFRAORDER/PARVORDER	SUPERFAMILY
		New Zealand Wrens (**119**)	
	TYRANNI	Broadbill Group (Eurylaimides)	Pittas (**120**)
			Broadbills and Asities (**121–122**)
		Sapayoa (**123**)	
		Tyrants (**124–129**)	
		Typical Antbirds (**130**)	
Songbirds Passeriformes		Ovenbirds and Antbirds (Furnariida)	Ovenbirds and Woodcreepers (**131–132**)
			Ground Antbirds, Gnateaters, Tapaculos (**133–135**)
	PASSERI	Australian and Crowlike Birds (Corvida)	Lyrebird Group (**137–138**)
			Honeyeater Group (**143–147**)
			Crowlike Group (**148–171**)
		Small Songbirds (Passerida)	Flycatcher and Thrush Group (**172–180**)
			Tit and Warbler Group (**181–202**)
			Seedeater Group (**216–223**)

Diagram III

Earlier Songbird classifications were confused by cases of evolutionary convergence: birds with similar life styles adapting so that they closely resemble each other, although derived from different groups, such as those loosely called flycatchers, robins or wrens. The DNA classification does not rely on such external characteristics, with interesting results.

The New Zealand Wrens and Old World Broadbills appear to have diverged early and not to be part of the pattern. With these exceptions the Tyranni contains the early passerines that have radiated and adapted to the available ecological niches in South America, from Tyrants to Tapaculos.

In the Passeri two divisions appear to show a general linkage with continental landmasses: a group that appears to have risen from adaptive radiation within Australasia and another more closely associated with Eurasia and Africa.

The final Seedeater superfamily shows some of the surprises produced by this classification in the apparently close affinities of Sparrows, Wagtails and Dunnocks.

The numbers on the right refer to the numbered bird groups in the text.

Opposite left *NEW ZEALAND WRENS: These four species of early songbirds have long been isolated. They are wrenlike in being small and round bodied. This Rock Wren* (Xenicus gilviventris) *is almost tailless.*

Right *PITTAS: A Noisy Pitta* (Pitta versicolor) *at the entrance to its untidy domed nest. Tails seem to be a disadvantage to such ground-living birds and long legs a necessity.*

Below right *TYRANTS: This family of mainly flycatcherlike birds has diversified to take advantage of many different songbird niches. The tail of the Scissor-tailed Flycatcher* (Tyrannus forficatus) *has developed into a long and exaggerated structure.*

Bottom right *TITYRAS AND BECARDS: The Masked Tityra* (Tityra semifasciata) *and other tityras are birds of open plains that advertise themselves with plumage and calls. The becards are inconspicuous in forest scrub.*

the Americas and their islands. It includes foliage and undergrowth gleaners, often rounded winged, short tailed and small billed, aerial feeders, often with long tails, many flycatching types, terrestrial birds of forest and open country and birds of marsh vegetation. In this subfamily are the American Flycatchers, Phoebes, Pewees, Kiskadees and Kingbirds. Bills are often broad, sometimes flattened, sometimes hook tipped, often broad based with bristles. A few have bright colors or patterns, mostly those of open country, and the Royal Flycatcher can spread an extraordinary transverse fan-shaped crest. Food includes insects and all kinds of small creatures, caught in various ways, and fruits. Calls and songs are simple and unexceptional. A few species have conspicuous displays. Most live in pairs, a few more sociable, and some have helpers when nesting. Most are cup nesters, a few make domed nests or use cavities. Eggs, usually 3–4, are whitish and incubation normally by the female, though both tend young. Species in colder regions are migratory.

126. Schiffornis (Schiffornithini) 1 genus, 3 species, 5.5–6.4 in (14–16 cm). These small, chatlike forest birds of the undergrowth in lowland forest, woodland and scrub from Mexico to northern Argentina, are blue, brown or cinnamon with more reddish wings and tail. Their wings are rounded, tail moderately long and the bill small and short. They feed on insects and fruit and are secretive, with shrill whistling calls. The nest is a stout open cup built by the female, usually on a broken branch or stump. Nestlings have long black down.

127. Tityras and Becards (Tityrini) 3 genera, 20 species, 4.8–8.4 in (12–21 cm). Becards are fairly large-headed and short-legged birds of lowland open woodland, forest edge, scrub, savanna and mangroves from southwestern U.S.A. to northern Argentina. The bill is short,

stout and broad based, wings rounded to long and tail moderately long and round tipped. Tityras are longer-bodied black and white birds with bare red facial skin and red bill base. The bill is deep, stout and blunt ended, the legs short. Becards forage through lower forest growth, tityras tend to perch on high open places and on dead branches and have noisy low calls. Both eat insects and fruit. Becards build a rounded woven pendent nest, hung near the end of a branch, with an entrance near the lower end and 3–6 spotted white eggs. Tityras build nests in tree cavities and holes.

128. Cotingas (Cotinginae) 28 genera, 69 species, 3.2–18.4 in (8–46 cm). This group includes the small conical billed Sharpbill and finchlike Plantcutters. A diversely shaped and sometimes vividly colored group of birds, they occur in scrub and forest, from lowland to high altitudes, from southern Mexico to southern Brazil.

In the main they are stoutly built with rounded wings, short legs and a short and broad-based bill with a slightly hooked tip. Plumage color includes deep reds, purples, blue or white and ornamentation of varied crests, feathered or unfeathered wattles, bare throats or bald heads. Smaller species are less strikingly ornamented. Most are fruit eaters, Bellbirds taking almost wholly fruit, others taking fruit and insects from perches or on the wing, but the Swallow-tailed Cotinga and martin-like Purpletufts hawk insects in the air. A few species occur in pairs but most are polygynous, the males having elaborate displays, often on display grounds, the display noisy in Bellbirds and Calfbirds and aerial in white-winged species. In most species incubation and possibly feeding of the young is by the female alone. In Fruitcrows a nest is attended by a social group. Cock-of-the-rock and other birds making bulky nest cups stuck to rock faces have 2–3 eggs but many species have tiny nests with single eggs. Nestlings are downy, differing in color between species, mossy looking in some.

129. Manakins (Piprinae) 15 genera, 52 species, 3.6–7.6 in (9–19 cm). Small birds of tropical lowland and montane forest and secondary growth from southern Mexico to northern Argentina, manakins are short and squat.They have short wings, tail and bill, which is rather broad based with a slightly hooked tip. Males tend to be black with areas of bright plumage, females dull olive. They feed mainly on small fruits taken on the wing and some insects. Males perform elaborate displays singly or with others, often with odd noises. The female nests alone, slinging a small woven cup in a twig fork, usually laying two colored and spotted eggs.

130. Typical Antbirds (Thamnophilidae) 45 genera, 188 species, 3.2–14 in (8–35 cm). These small to medium insect-eating foragers occur mainly in lowland tropical forest or scrub, but some in montane and swamp scrub, from northern Mexico to Argentina. They often present a slightly crouched or hunchbacked stance, with wings rounded, tail short to medium and legs and feet strong for clinging to stems. Bills hook tipped and flattish, or slender, and short to long. Some are ornamented with bare colored skin or a crest on the head, the plumage is otherwise dull. About one sixth of the species follow army ants, others forage in various ways at various levels, often as part of mixed-species forest flocks. Food includes insects, spiders and a range of small vertebrates, more rarely fruit. Some antshrikes are fly-catchers. Antbirds have simple whistling or harsh songs and odd notes accompanying threat displays. Pair bonds are usually long lasting, with both parents building cup or domed nests and incubating and caring for young. There are usually two patterned eggs and nestlings are naked.

131–32. Ovenbirds (Furnariidae) have two subfamilies.
131. Ovenbirds (Furnariinae) 53 genera, 231 species, 4–10 in (10–26 cm). A diverse group of small to medium songbirds, ovenbirds occur in all habitats from central Mexico to Tierra del Fuego. Their wings vary from short and rounded to long and narrow, tails from short to long, graduated or forked and with a tendency for spiny tips. The bill is often short, straight and pointed but may be short to long and straight to downcurved, more rarely short and upcurved. Legs are strong in terrestrial species. Food is mainly insects and other small creatures but some open country species take seeds and parts

Right COTINGAS: *The vivid male Lovely Cotinga (Cotinga amabilis); females are dull brown. His wing feathers make a loud rattle in flight. Members of this very diverse family often have beautiful display plumage.*

Opposite left WOODCREEPERS: *The Wedge-billed Woodcreeper (Glyphorhynchus spirurus) of the rainforests of Colombia has strong claws with which to move about tree trunks and branches or hang from them.*

of plants. Species may be specialized for gleaning insects in foliage, climbing trunks and branches, foraging in forest undergrowth or low scrub and scattered bushes, in grasses or swamp vegetation, in bare open country, by water or on beaches and at all altitudes. They are often reluctant to fly and may prefer to run. Pair bonds are strong. Nesting is diverse and poorly studied: some have cup nests, typical ovenbirds have domed clay nests with side entrances, many, particularly Spinetails, make roofed twig structures, huge in some cases, others have domed ground nests, make burrows or use holes and cavities. There are usually 3–5 eggs, sometimes more, and these are plain white or blue.

132. Woodcreepers (Dendrocolaptinae) 13 genera, 49 species, 6–14.8 in (15–37 cm). These are small to medium-sized brown-plumaged woodpeckerlike birds of trees in the forest, open forest, forest edge and mangroves from northern Mexico to northern Argentina. They have a narrow body, short legs and strong feet with sharp claws for clambering and rounded wings. The tail has stiffened quills and supports the body when climbing, as in woodpeckers. The bill is often strong and laterally compressed, sometimes longer and thinner and, in some, very long and downcurved. They feed like treecreepers, climbing trunks or branches, probing in crevices and epiphytic plants for insects and any small creatures. They may follow army ant swarms and some species feed on the ground. They usually occur singly or in pairs and have a variety of loud calls.

133. Ground Antbirds (Formicariidae) 7 genera, 56 species, 4.4–9.6 in (11–24 cm). These are specialized antbirds of mainly terrestrial habits and forms, occurring from southern Mexico to northern Argentina. Bills tend to be relatively slender, short to medium length, wings rounded, tail short and legs long with strong feet. Antthrushes have a superficially thrushlike appearance, but with longer legs and a short, at times cocked, tail. Antpittas have long and large legs and feet, very short tails and largish heads with big eyes. They are birds of the forest floors and undergrowth of rainforests, thick secondary forest and bamboo thickets. Hopping or walking they take insects and small creatures. Calls are mostly series of whistled notes. They have long pair bonds, both birds incubating and feeding young. Known nests are cups in vegetation on or near the ground or in ends of stumps, with plain white or blue eggs, usually

two. Nestlings may be downy and adults may each tend one fledged young.

134. Gnateaters (Conopophagidae) 1 genus, 8 species, 4.4–5.6 in (11–14 cm). These small squat birds of forest and scrub undergrowth from Colombia and Brazil to northern Argentina have long thin legs, short rounded wings and very short tails. The bill is short and slender. They usually occur in pairs, in low undergrowth, rather silent but with a short wheezy call and whistled songs. They are sluggish, dropping to take insects, but may hop and scratch on the ground. At least one species has a rattling display flight. The nest is a well-built cup in low vegetation with two patterned eggs, both birds incubating.

135. Tapaculos (Rhinocryptidae) 12 genera, 28 species, 4.4–10 in (11–25 cm). Small to medium-sized ground-living songbirds, tapaculos occur throughout South America and to Costa Rica, except in lowland rainforest. Legs and feet are long and strong, wings short and rounded, tail short to long, often held erect or tilted forwards, and the bill stout and short. They are usually furtive, tending to run rather than hop, and are reluctant to fly. They are dull colored and have repetitive monotonous calls used by both sexes. Food is mainly insects and other small creatures. Habitats range from forest undergrowth to low shrubby growth in open country. Nests may be in a burrow dug by the bird, a natural tree cavity or a rounded nest with a side entrance set in a low shrub. There are 2–4 white eggs. Both adults incubate and tend the young.

136. Australian Treecreepers (Climacteridae) 2 genera, 7 species, 4.8–7.6 in (12–19 cm). These small arboreal songbirds occur from rainforest to arid open country with scattered trees in Australia and New Guinea. Wings are rounded, tail rounded at the tip, but not strengthened or used in climbing, legs fairly long, feet strong and claws sharp. The bill is fairly slender and slightly downcurved. Food is insects, mainly ants, and the birds feed by hopping up tree trunks and branches slightly aslant, with one foot ahead of the other. They may probe under bark. They also perch across twigs in a typical songbird manner and feed on the ground. They have shrill whistling calls and occur in pairs or small groups. The *Climacteris* species may have additional helpers at the nest. Nests are a cup built deep down in a hollow branch or trunk with 2–3 whitish spotted eggs. Incubation is by the female.

LYREBIRDS: *The male Superb Lyrebird (Menura novaehollandiae) makes a display mound and spreads his tail to arch forward over him as a quivering canopy as he sings a loud and sustained musical song, full of mimicry of other species.*

Right *BOWERBIRDS: An Australian Greater Bowerbird (Chlamydera nuchalis) has built an avenue of upright twigs, ornamented and floored with shells, and spreads his nape feathers to reveal a normally-hidden magenta crest. Bowerbirds have varied plumages and build a bewildering variety of bowers.*

FAIRYWRENS: *The male Splendid Fairywren (Malurus splendens) is one of the brightest in a family of brightly colored males, most conspicuous in the dominant male of groups.*

137–38. Menuridae has two subfamilies.
137. Lyrebirds (Menurinae) 1 genus, 2 species, males 35.6–40 in (89–100 cm), females 30.4–34.4 in (76–86 cm). These pheasant-sized, mainly terrestrial songbirds of the montane forests of eastern Australia have long legs and large feet with long claws used for scratching and digging. Their wings are short and rounded and flight is very weak. High roosting perches in trees are reached by jumping and gliding. The neck is slender and the head rather small with a fine bill. The tail is long and in the male has some elaborate and filamentous plumes. Lyrebirds are furtive, living in forest undergrowth searching and digging for a range of small invertebrate prey. Males are territorial, displaying on small mounds, tree trunks or twig platforms with loud prolonged song and tail erected forwards or as a canopy over the bird and shaken. Males are polygamous or promiscuous. Females build large domed nests on low raised sites: banks, rocks or trees. There is a single patterned egg. Incubation and feeding of the downy nestling is by the female alone.
138. Scrub-birds (Atrichornithinae) 1 genus, 2 species, 6.4–8.4 in (16–21 cm). Smallish and undistinguished, these ground-living wren-like songbirds occur in a few localities in Australia. Wings are short and rounded, flight very poor and weak, the tail is relatively long, legs and feet large and strong, and the bill short, stout and slightly curved at the tip. They live in thick undergrowth where forest meets swamp and are now reduced to a few scattered sites. Food is mainly insects, taken from the ground, and occasional small frogs or lizards. Males maintain territories with loud song. Females, which appear to have their own preferred areas with strong site fidelity, build a domed nest with a side entrance in low vegetation, incubate one intensely white egg and rear the young.
139. Bowerbirds (Ptilonorhynchidae) 7 genera, 20 species, 8–16 in (20–40 cm). These medium-sized birds, which occur from rainforest to open dry bushy areas in Australia and New Guinea, are often stoutly built with usually short wing and tail, strong legs with short hind toe and short, stout bill, sometimes slightly curved and hook tipped. Females are dull but some males show bright color, or colored nape crests. Food is fruit and various small creatures. Catbirds form pairs and the males are involved in nesting but most males are polygynous or promiscuous and build bowers on display sites. These vary from a few leaves on a cleared patch to upright avenues of twigs and some are elaborate masses of twigs, built up saplings or cleared avenues walled and roofed with twigs. Bowers are decorated with objects and when females visit males display and mate. These females nest alone. The nest is a bulky cup in a tree or crevice with usually 1–2 plain or patterned eggs.
140–42. Maluridae has two subfamilies: Malurinae, which has two tribes, and Grasswrens (Amytornithinae).
140. Fairywrens (Malurini) 3 genera, 15 species, 4.8–6 in (12–15 cm). Small to very small songbirds of Australia and New Guinea, Fairywren habitat ranges from rainforest to arid semidesert. Their long narrow tail is usually carried erect, the head is proportionally large with small thin bill, wings are rounded and legs long and thin. They normally progress by rapid springs, hops and short flights. Food is mainly small insects. Breeding males have vivid plumage, often with glossy blue tints. They have simple trilling songs. They are usually found in small social groups that assist the nesting of a dominant pair. The nest is a domed structure

with a side entrance, usually placed in a low shrub. The female incubates 2–5 white, reddish-spotted eggs.

141. Emuwrens (Stipiturini) 1 genus, 3 species, 6.4–7.6 in (16–19 cm). These very small Australian birds occur in low bushes, grasses and spinifex of open swamp or arid country. They have a large thin tail of sparsely barbed, "decomposed" or heavily worn-looking feathers, forming just over half their length, and carried vertically. Plumage is loose looking, head large, bill slender, wings rounded and legs long. Very furtive and reluctant to fly, they skulk in ground vegetation. Food is insects. Call notes are thin and shrill. The domed nest is built in a low shrub or tussock. The female incubates the 2–5 white, reddish-spotted eggs.

142. Grasswrens (Amytornithinae) 1 genus, 8 species, 5.6–8 in (14–20 cm). These are long-tailed, streaky-plumaged, skulking birds of ground vegetation of plains or rocky outcrops in drier regions of Australia. Legs are thin and powerful, they run rather than hop and rarely fly, taking seeds, insects and other small invertebrates on the ground. They have short song trills or sharp notes. They nest in small social groups, the nest sometimes incompletely domed, in a low bush or grass tussock with 2–3 sparsely marked white eggs incubated by the female.

143. Honeyeaters (Meliphagidae) 42 genera, 182 species, 3.2–18 in (8–45 cm). These small to medium-sized, usually arboreal birds occur from Australia and New Guinea through western Pacific islands to Bali. They include the Friarbirds, Wattlebirds, Miners, Spinebills, the New Zealand Tui and Bellbird, occupying a variety of habitat and behavior niches but all with a brush-tipped tongue and primarily nectar feeding. Bills are mainly slender and slightly downcurved, longer in some small species. Some have bare facial skin or wattles and the larger Friarbirds have a bare face and forehead lump. Wings and tail are usually fairly long and feet strong. Food is mainly nectar and insects, with fruit in some species. They feed mainly in trees and shrubs from tropical forest to open heathland, with a few species such as Chats terrestrial in arid semidesert. Vocalizations vary from long and musical to short and harsh. Mainly gregarious and often nomadic. Nests are mainly cup shaped, sometimes slung between twigs. The two small Fasciated Honeyeaters build domed nests, the big Blue-faced Honeyeater uses domed babbler nests. The 1–4 spotted eggs are incubated by the female or by both birds, both feed young and some species have helpers.

144–47. Pardalotidae has three subfamilies, Acanthizinae having two tribes.

144. Pardalotes (Pardalotinae) 1 genus, 4 species, 3.6–4.4 in (9–11 cm). Small Australian birds of forest, open woodland or scattered trees, pardalotes have stout stubby bills, short tails and strong legs and feet. The crown, or plumage generally, is often pale spotted. They are leaf gleaners in trees, taking small insects, gregarious when not breeding. They have loud short call notes. The nest is a cup at the end of a sloping tunnel made in the ground by both birds, who also share incubation and care of the young, or a domed or cup nest in a tree cavity. There are 2–5 white eggs.

145. Bristlebirds (Dasyornithinae) 1 genus, 3 species, 7.2–10.8 in (18–27 cm). These are dull-colored, thrushlike birds, occurring in localized sites in heathland and forest of southern Australia, with longish tapering tails, short rounded wings and very weak and reluctant flight. Legs and feet are strong and the bill short and stout.

HONEYEATERS: *New Zealand Tuis* (Prosthemadera novaeseelandiae) *gathered around a container of sugar solution put out to attract them.*

Left THORNBILLS: *The Buff-rumped Thornbill* (Acanthiza reguloides) *is a bird of open eucalypt forest. It may build its untidy domed nest in sites from tree trunks to among tall ground grass clumps, like this one.*

They are extremely secretive in thick low shrubs and grasses, fast running and very rarely seen, with short harsh alarm calls and brief song phrases. Food is insects and other small creatures, berries and seeds. The nest is a domed structure in grass or thick shrubs near the ground with two patterned eggs. Activities of breeding birds are not known.

146. Scrubwrens (Sericornithini) 10 genera, 26 species, 4.4–6.8 in (11–17 cm). Small, thin-billed warblerlike birds of Australia and New Guinea, which include the Hylacolas, Calamanthus and Mouse-warblers, these are mostly ground feeders of low thick undergrowth and low vegetation from rainforest to heath and open arid land. The Origma or Rock Warbler is a bird of rock outcrops. The Pilotbird is longer tailed and a weak flier. Food is mainly insects taken in low vegetation or on the ground, the birds quiet and inconspicuous unless responding to disturbance. Some species have musical songs. The nest is domed with a side entrance, on or near the ground and hidden in vegetation. The Origma suspends a domed nest by spiders' webs

in a cave. Both parents incubate the 2–3 spotted, white or colored eggs and rear the young.

147. Thornbills (Acanthizini) 4 genera, 35 species, 8 in (20 cm). Small tit- and warblerlike birds of habitats from rainforest and mangrove to open woodland, dry scrub and semidesert, occurring from Australia to Indonesia and western Pacific islands, with one species in Malaysia. Gerygones are like small warblers, Thornbills are short tailed, strong footed and shorter billed, Whitefaces are mainly ground feeders, with very short stout little bills. Thornbills and Whitefaces have mostly short calls but Gerygones may have long musical songs. Food is mainly insects and other small creatures gleaned from foliage and some seeds. Birds tend to be gregarious when not breeding. The nest is domed, bound with spiders' webs and sometimes suspended from twigs in Gerygones, or built into a small cavity or crevice. The 2–5 spotted pale eggs are incubated by the female but both parents feed the young.

148. Australian Robins (Eopsaltriidae) 14 genera, 46 species, 4–6.8 in (10–17 cm). Small, plump, rather upright-perching arboreal birds, found in Australia, New Zealand and New Guinea with one into Malaysia and another up to the Himalayas and South China. These are mainly birds of lower shrubby vegetation, occurring from rainforest and mangroves to more open forest, heathland and thin arid scrub or wet montane growth, with one in mountain streams and another on high mountain rocks. They have large dark eyes, short broad-based and hook-tipped bills and strong feet for clinging to upright perches, and rapid flight. Some males have a bright red, pink or yellow breast. Food is mainly insects, taken from on or near the ground in a swift downward swoop from a low perch, or hawked, flycatcher-fashion, from a high vantage point, or in Scrub-Robins by terrestrial hunting. They usually have short weak songs and varied calls. Usually solitary or in pairs, they build a cup-shaped nest, very thin and shallow in some flycatcherlike species, with 2–3 colored and patterned eggs. Incubation is by the female alone, both parents feeding the young. A few species are locally migratory. Species include the Tomtit and the Jacky-winter.

149. Leafbirds and Fairy-bluebirds (Irenidae) 2 genera, 10 species, 7.8–10.8 in (19–27 cm). These medium-sized arboreal birds of forest and forest edge from northern India and China to the Philippines, have soft plumage, glossy blue and black in the male Fairy-bluebird, in Leafbirds mainly green. Wings and tail are moderately long and flight swift, legs are short and feet strong, bill tapering, shorter in the Bluebird, slender and slightly downcurved in Leafbirds, with a brush-tipped tongue. Food is mainly fruit and nectar, taken from trees, and some seeds, buds and insects, usually taken from the canopy where Leafbirds are aerobatic in search of it. The Bluebird nest is a cup of fine material on a twig base in a tree fork, the Leafbirds' cups of fine material bound with spiders' webs and suspended by the rim. There are 2–3 colored and patterned eggs that the female incubates. In Bluebirds both parents feed the young.

150. Logrunners (Orthonychidae) 1 genus, 2 species, 6.8–12.4 in (17–31 cm). These are medium-sized, mainly resident, ground-living birds of soft forest floors in eastern Australia. Their wings are rounded and they fly little. Legs are strong, feet large, bill short and strong, and the tail broad with feather-shafts ending in spiny tips. The bird tilts sideways with the tail tip pressed into the ground as a prop, digging with long scratching strokes for its food of insects and other small creatures. Occurring in pairs or family parties, the female building a domed nest on or near the ground, made of large twigs in the Chowchilla, with 1–2 white eggs. She incubates and tends the young.

151. Australasian Babblers (Pomatostomidae) 1 genus, 5 species, 8–10.4 in (20–26 cm). Medium-sized, highly sociable birds that usually live in small groups, these birds occur in lower growth of rainforest, tree savanna, open woodland and thin arid scrub of Australia and New Guinea. They tend to carry themselves more horizontally than most birds. Wings are rounded, tail is moderately long with rounded tip, bill strong, narrow, tapering and slightly curved and the legs and feet strong. They tend to fly low and for short distances, moving in a group over a territory, with soft low contact calls that can become noisy in alarm, and

AUSTRALIAN ROBINS: A Yellow Robin (Eopsaltria australis) feeds its mate, perhaps having to do so in flight because there is no space to perch on the occupied nest. Some of this family have red breasts, hence their name.

LEAFBIRDS AND FAIRY-BLUEBIRDS: A Blue-winged Leafbird (Chloropsis cochinchinensis) is typical of the leafbirds but the family also includes the glossy blue and black Fairy-bluebirds.

search the ground and low vegetation for insects, other small creatures including lizards and seeds. Nests are large domed structures of twigs, with side entrances, up in the branches of a tree, hanging from a vine in the Rufous Babbler, and built for roosting as well as nesting. Birds huddle together when perched, preen each other and roost together. The dominant pair nest, helped by the group. There are 3–5 colored and patterned eggs.

152. Typical Shrikes (Laniidae) 3 genera, 30 species, 6.8–10 in (17–25 cm), plus 10 in (25 cm) for two long-tailed species. These are small to medium-sized, plump-bodied and large-headed raptorial birds of open woodland, scrub and bush areas, tree savanna and open and cultivated areas. They occur in North America, Eurasia and south to Indonesia, the Philippines and New Guinea. Wings are rounded, tails medium to long and flight swift. The bill is short and deep with a hooked tip and notch on the cutting edge. Food is mainly larger insects but extends to small birds and mice. Some prey may be impaled on thorns. They are birds of open habitats, watching for prey from low vantage perches and mainly solitary or in pairs, though long-tailed shrikes are gregarious at all times. Calls are harsh, but some have musical songs. The nest is a cup in a tree or bush with 2–7 eggs that vary in color and markings. Incubation is by the female or both birds and both feed nestlings, with helpers in the long-tailed shrikes. Some northern species are migratory.

153. Vireos (Vireonidae) 4 genera, 51 species, 4.6–8 in (10–17 cm). Occurring from southern Canada to northern Argentina, these birds of forest and scrub are typically slim, thin billed, small and arboreal, with frequently repeated song phrases. The tropical Peppershrikes and Shrike-Vireos are heavier birds than the rest of the family, with stouter bills, finely hook-tipped in smaller species, more strongly hooked in larger birds. The legs are short and strong and food may be held down in the foot. Food is mainly insects taken by foraging in foliage and twigs, sometimes hovering or flycatching, and some small fruits. The nest is a cup suspended between forked twigs with 2–5 spotted or plain white eggs. The female or both parents incubate and both feed nestlings. Some species are migratory.

154–69. Crow Family (Corvidae) has many subdivisions so, to avoid confusion, individual headings have been inserted for subfamilies.
154. Quail-thrushes and Whipbirds (Cinclosomatinae) 6 genera, 15 species, 7.6–12 in (19–30 cm). These birds occur from forest to open stony places and in low scrub and bushes in Australia and New Guinea, with the Rail-babbler in southeastern Asia. Medium sized, slim built and mainly terrestrial, but varied, many are inconspicuous species with loud calls or songs. The Ifrit is a plump, chatlike bird of mountain forest, hunting moss-covered trees and branches for insects. The Whipbirds and Wedgebills are babblerlike secretive birds of low bushy cover, with short wings, longish tails,

spiky crests and short stout bills. Whipbirds scratch for food with strong feet. The Quail-thrushes and the bright blue and chestnut Jewel-babblers walk on the ground and tend to have longish tails, short wings and strong legs. Quail-thrushes crouch in alarm and their flight is abrupt and low. The Rail-babbler is similar but with an oddly slim head and neck. Food is mainly insects and possibly some fruit. Whipbirds, Wedgebills and the Ifrit build cup nests in bushes; others make nests in depressions on the ground, often at a tree or rock base. The Ifrit has one white egg, others have 2–4 colored and patterned eggs. In Whipbirds both parents incubate, in Quail-thrushes females only. Both feed young.

155. Australian Chough and Apostlebird (Corcoracinae) 2 genera, 2 species, 15.8 in (47 cm) and 12–13.4 in (30–33 cm). Highly sociable, these group-loving birds are mainly terrestrial in open woodlands and scrub in eastern Australia. Choughs are black with rounded white-patched wings, long tails and long strong legs. The bill is slender and downcurved. Apostlebirds are smaller, gray and with a very short stout bill. Both forage in dispersed social groups, mainly walking on the ground. They fly reluctantly but roost in trees and have various harsh and whistling calls. Food is insects, other small creatures and some seeds and plants. The nest is a big, communally-constructed mud bowl on a tree branch. More than one female may lay and care for eggs and young is communal with 2–5 pale and blotched eggs from each individual.

156–59. Pachycephalinae is a subfamily of the Crows with four tribes.

156. Sittellas (Neosittini) 1 genus, 2 species, 4–4.8 in (10–12 cm). Small Australasian counterparts of nuthatches, these birds occur in montane forest of New Guinea and areas with trees in Australia. They are short-tailed and round headed, with well-developed legs and feet for clambering up, down and sideways in nuthatch fashion. The slender tapering bill is laterally compressed and has a slightly upturned tip. Sittellas are sociable, usually in small flocks working over twigs and branches probing under bark flakes and eating any small invertebrates. They have thin high-pitched calls. The Varied Sittella has local subspecies varying in color of head, back and wing stripe. They nest in social groups. The cup nest in a fork is beautifully camouflaged with spiders' webs and bark flakes, like a broken branch end. The dominant female lays and incubates but the social group assist with nest building and rearing.

Above *TYPICAL SHRIKES: Red-backed Shrikes (Lanius collurio), the male in the foreground and the young already showing the development of the strong hook-tipped bill that can deal with small mice and fledgling birds as well as insects.*

Center *VIREOS: A Red-eyed Vireo (Vireo olivaceus), typical in shape and slender bill. The upper edge of the suspended nest cup is woven around thin twigs.*

Left *QUAIL-THRUSHES AND WHIPBIRDS: The Eastern Whipbird (Psophodes olivaceus) is named for the loud whipcrack note of the male in the duetting call that he shares with his mate.*

157. Mohouas (Mohouini) 1 genus, 3 species, 6 in (15 cm). This tribe of small New Zealand forest birds has short tapering bills, short legs with strong feet, and broad tails with spiny feather tips. Head and breast are white or yellow. They feed in pairs, parties or small flocks, mostly high in forest trees, occasionally at ground level, searching acrobatically in twigs and foliage and using the tail as a prop when clambering on branches and trunks. Food is insects and fruit. Frequent call notes are used. The Whitehead builds a cup nest in a fork, the Yellowhead in a tree cavity. Both birds incubate the 2–4 colored and patterned eggs and feed the young, but additional birds may be present.

158. Shrike-tits (Falcunculini) 3 genera, 3 species, 6–9.4 in (15–23 cm). This tribe includes three diverse species. The Mottled Whistler is a dull, whistlerlike bird of New Guinea forest, feeding mainly on fruit, rather sluggish and inconspicuous. The Crested Bellbird of Australia is another whistlerlike species, the male with an upright shaggy crest and dark vertical band through the eye. A bird of more open and arid woodland, it hops on the ground, eating insects. The Shrike-tit, found in Australian eucalypt forest and woodland, has a shaggy, helmetlike crest and a short stout and powerful bill with a hooked tip. It feeds acrobatically on branches, taking insects, and can prise up bark for hidden creatures. The last two species make cup nests in tree forks with 2–3 patterned white eggs.

159. Whistlers or Thick-heads (Pachycephalini) 9 genera, 51 species, 4.8–10 in (12–25 cm). These small to medium arboreal birds of forest, mangroves, open woodland and rocky or arid country with scattered trees are found from Australia to Indonesia and the Philippines, with the Mangrove Whistler to northeastern India. They are thrushlike birds, including the Shrike-thrushes and Pitohui, stoutly built with rounded head and often rather upright pose. The stout bill is of moderate length, sometimes with a small hooked tip, sometimes slightly downcurved. The Ploughbill has a stout parrotlike bill and pendent cheek wattles. Often they have loud (sometimes explosive) musical songs. Food is mainly insects, various small animals and sometimes fruit and is mostly taken from vegetation, or sometimes by pouncing. Ploughbills appear adapted to break into rotten wood. The nest is normally a cup in a tree or bush, in low vegetation, on a rock ledge, in a crevice or on the ground. Both parents incubate the colored and patterned eggs, usually 2–4.

160–63. Corvinae is a subfamily of the Crows with four tribes.

160. Crows and Magpies (Corvini) 25 genera, 117 species, 6–28.4 in (15–71 cm). Worldwide, except for the polar regions, in habitats ranging from forest to open semidesert or mountains and rocky shores, these large to small birds are mainly intelligent, opportunistic and often omnivorous. They include jays, choughs and nutcrackers and are strong fliers with long to rounded wings and strong legs and feed by hopping, walking and holding down food objects. Tails are short to medium, and long and decorative in a few species. Bills are generally strong, heavy and slightly curved, but vary from very short to long and from stout and deep to slender and curved. Plumage is mostly black, gray and white; bright blue or green in some species. Larger species are minor predators, scavengers and carrion eaters, smaller species eat more insects and fruits, nuts and seeds. Some species hide and store food, espe-

WHISTLERS or THICKHEADS: *The Little Shrike-thrush* (Colluricincla megarhyncha) *is a forest bird. The group is named because they look thrushlike but have a strong hooked bill tip like that of shrikes.*

cially nuts and acorns for winter use. Voices are usually loud and harsh. Birds may be solitary or gregarious, some living and breeding in small groups. Nests may be cups in trees or bushes, on ledges, in holes, or poorly domed tree nests. The 3–10 colored and patterned eggs are incubated by the female or both birds, both feed the young, sometimes with helpers.

161. Birds-of-paradise (Paradisaeini) 17 genera, 45 species, 6–44 in (15–110 cm). These medium-sized to large arboreal birds, occurring from New Guinea to northeastern Australia and the Moluccas, live in forest and wooded savannas. Males often have extraordinarily modified feathers producing areas of vivid color and unusual shape, used in display. In various species this may involve feathers of head, breast, nape, wings or tail. Some have only limited modified feathers or face wattles and are mainly dark colored. Females have dull plumage. In general these birds have rounded wings, varied tails and strong legs and feet. Bills vary from moderately stout and tapering to slender, and from short to long and curved. Food is fruit and plants, insects and other small creatures. Decorated males display with loud calls or noises, sometimes in group leks. Females visit the males for mating and nest alone, but in the dark-plumaged forms males may assist with nesting. The nest is a bulky or sparse shallow cup in a tree, usually with 1–2 eggs, heavily streaked longitudinally. Incubation and all care by the female.

162. Currawongs and Wood-swallows (Artamini) This tribe comprises two recognizable units: the crowlike Currawongs, Australian Butcherbirds and Magpies, 4 genera, 12 species, 7.6–20 in (19–50 cm); and the martinlike Wood-swallows 2 genera, 12 species, 4.8–8 in (12–20 cm).

Currawongs occur in Australia and New Guinea, Magpies now also in New Zealand and Fiji. Habitat ranges from rainforest to open scrub and grassland. They include longer-legged ground feeders and shorter-legged arboreal birds. Wings and tail are long and flight is strong, the bill long and thick with a hooked tip. Food is mainly insects and small animals, some are omnivorous. The New Guinea Peltops behave like flycatchers. Solitary or gregarious, Australian Magpies live in small close groups. Calls are loud and some songs are highly musical. Nest is a cup in a tree and incubation is mainly by the female. In Magpies males may help with feeding young and in Butcherbirds immature young may remain as helpers.

Wood-swallows occur over a wide range of habitats from northern India and south China to Australia and Fiji. They are stoutly built, big-headed birds with tapering wings, short tails, short legs and strong feet. The bill is stout, short and tapering. They catch flying insects by aerial hunting or watching from an open perch, occasionally taking prey from foliage or the ground. They huddle when resting and roost in communal masses. They have harsh and twittering calls, and are the only passerines possessing powder downs. The nest is a shallow cup on a branch or stump, or in a tree or rock crevice. They nest in colonies and adults may act as helpers. The Bornean Bristlehead appears to be an aberrant member of this group.

163. Orioles and Cuckoo-shrikes (Oriolini) This tribe comprises two recognizable units: the Orioles and Figbirds, 2 genera, 29 species, 8–12 in (20–30 cm); and the Cuckoo-shrikes, Trillers and Minivets, 6 genera, 82 species, 4.8–16 in (14–40 cm).

Orioles and **Figbirds** inhabit forest and woodland in Africa and from temperate Eurasia

to Australia. They are slender-built, wholly arboreal birds with long, pointed wings, moderately long tail, short legs and strong feet. The bill is strong, pointed and slightly curved. Food is mainly fruit and insects, calls are loud and sometimes musical. The nest is a cup slung between twigs in a tree. The 2–5 eggs are light-colored and patterned. Incubation and care of young appears to be by both adults. Some species are migratory.

Cuckoo-shrikes and Minivets occur in Africa and from northern India, China and Japan to Australia and the islands of the western Pacific, in forest, open forest, forest edge and more open and scattered trees. They are small to medium arboreal birds with long wings and tails and small legs and feet. The bill is fairly short and stout, slightly curved and hook tipped. Flight is fairly strong. The Ground Cuckoo-shrike is a longer-legged, semiterrestrial species of open country, its flight usually strong but short. Trillers are smaller and have shorter wings and tail and a more slender bill without a hook. They are more warblerlike in behavior. The Minivets are narrow-tailed, more active insect hunters with slender bills. All these birds have loud whistles or harsh calls. Males of some larger species have a wing-shuffling display. The nest is a cup, stout in Minivets, small and shallow in others, in a tree. The female or both birds incubate the 2–5 greenish and patterned eggs.

164–66. Dicrurinae is a subfamily with three tribes.

164. Fantails (Rhipidurini) 1 genus, 42 species, 5.6–10 in (14–20 cm). These small to medium-sized arboreal birds that occur in all types of woodland, scrub and mangrove from Pakistan, northern India and southern China to Aus-

tralia and islands of the western Pacific, have a large distinctive fanned and rounded tail that forms half their length. They are short necked with a rounded head, small stubby bill and tapering wings. Legs and feet are small, but the terrestrially adapted Willie Wagtail has longer legs and swings its tail laterally. Food is insects, taken by flycatching from a perch but more often using the erect fanned tail to flush insects when moving through foliage in a fussily active manner, using a foot to hold down prey. They have weak abrupt calls. The nest is a neat, deep

cup built mainly onto a horizontal twig, smoothed over with spiders' webs, tapering to a "tail," with 2–4 colored and patterned eggs. Both parents incubate and care for young.

165. Drongos (Dicrurini) 2 genera, 24 species, 7.4–15.2 in (18–38 cm) and up to 28.8 in (72 cm) with longest tail. Upright, alert and usually black birds of open woodland and forest edge, savanna and farmland, which occur in Africa and from Afghanistan, northern India and southern China to Australia. Legs and feet are short but strong, wings long and tapering, tail

Above ORIOLES AND CUCKOO-SHRIKES: A Varied Triller (Lalage leucomela), one of the cuckoo-shrikes, balanced on its tiny cup nest. The orioles suspend nests between twigs.

Top CURRAWONGS AND WOOD-SWALLOWS: This single tribe includes such disparate-seeming birds as Australian Magpies, Currawongs, Butcherbirds — and Wood-swallows. The White-breasted Wood-swallow (Artamus leucorynchus) is small and stout-billed but swallowlike in behavior, typical of the wood-swallows.

Left FANTAILS: A typical fantail, the Gray Fantail (Rhipidura fuliginosa). Most use their tail to flush insects out of foliage, though a few just perch and wait, and the mainly terrestrial Willie Wagtail wags its tail low over the ground.

long to very long, usually forked, the outer shafts sometimes with large rounded vanes. The head is often crested. Bills are stout and slightly curved, with hooked tip and bristles at the base. Flight is usually short but strong. Food is mainly insects, usually hawked from a low open perch, and they will follow grazing animals to hunt, but will take other creatures and some species take nectar. They are usually solitary, bold and aggressive (particularly in defense of the nest), with harsh and whistling calls. The nest is a small shallow saucer high in a tree fork, with 2–4 colored and patterned eggs. Incubation and care of young is by both birds.

166. Monarchs (Monarchini) 18 genera, 98 species, 4.8–12 in (12–30 cm), up to 18 in (45 cm) in long-tailed Paradise Flycatchers. Occurring in Africa and from Turkestan and northern China to Australia and western Pacific islands, these are birds of rainforest and open woodland to bushy savanna and open areas with trees and include the Australasian Flycatchers. Most are arboreal flycatchers, but the large terrestrially-adapted Magpie-larks are also assigned to this tribe. Typical birds have medium to long tapering wings, small legs and feet and a moderate to very long tail. The head is often slightly crested, the bill broad based, sometimes flattened, with a hooked tip. They are usually solitary or in pairs, with short harsh calls. Food is insects and other small creatures taken by hawking, pouncing or searching. Nest is a deep cup, sometimes finely shaped, elongated and bound with spiders' webs, on a twig or fork, sometimes suspended at the rim, with 2–4 pale patterned eggs. Both adults incubate and care for the young. The Magpie-larks are like pied passerine plovers with broad wings, usually found near water, who build a mud bowl nest on a bare horizontal branch.

167. Ioras (Aegithininae) 1 genus, 4 species, 5.2–6.8 in (13–17 cm). Small arboreal, warbler-like birds with slender bills that live in open forest, forest edge and scrub from Pakistan, northern India and southwestern China to Indonesia and the Philippines. Food is mainly insects, taken by leaf gleaning, and some nectar. They are active and acrobatic with whistling calls. They are usually in pairs. The nest is a

small cup bound into a twig fork with spiders' webs.

168–69. Malaconotinae is a subfamily with two tribes.

168. Bush-shrikes (Malaconotini) 8 genera, 48 species, 5.8–10.8 in (14–27 cm). Small to medium shrikes of Africa and southern Arabia, these birds occur in habitats from forest to sparse dry scrub or savanna. They often have some bright yellow, orange or red coloring. Wings and tail are fairly long and feet strong. The short hook-tipped bill varies from slender to stout. Mainly insect feeders, they sometimes take other small creatures. Unlike typical shrikes they more often search for prey among vegetation, sometimes near or on the ground. Usually found in pairs or small social groups, they have often musical and sometimes duetting calls. The nest is a shallow cup on a branch or in a fork, with 2–3 colored and patterned eggs. Incubation is usually by the female, both feeding the young. Species include Brubrus, Puffbacks, Tchagras, Boubous, Goneleks and Bokmakierie.

169. Helmet-shrikes and Vangas (Vangini) 19 genera, 58 species, 3.5–17 in (9–32 cm). In this tribe the Helmet-shrikes include the small flycatcherlike Batis and Wattle-eyes and the Woodshrikes. They occur in various types of

HELMET-SHRIKES AND VANGAS: A curly-crested form of the variable and widespread White Helmet-shrike (Prionops plumatus).

Above left *DRONGOS: The White-bellied Drongo (Dicrurus caerulescens) has a modestly forked tail; some are much more extreme or have racquet tails. This keen-eyed family sit and wait for food to catch but are bold in defense of territory.*

Left *NEW ZEALAND WATTLEBIRDS: The Saddleback (Creadion carunculatus) is starlinglike but has the bill wattle that gives the family its name. It often builds its cup nest in a tree cavity.*

thick or open forest, dry scrub and savanna in Africa and from northern India and southern China to Indonesia and Borneo. They are shrikes with bills a little more slender and flatter, their forehead crested and with an eye wattle. Arboreal, they systematically search vegetation for insects in titlike fashion and are found in social groups that act as helpers during nesting. The Batis and Wattle-eyes are small, short-tailed birds with thin hook-tipped bills. They feed in foliage like tits or warblers and Batis are active flycatchers. The Woodshrikes are similar in active insect searching and join mixed foraging groups. All have cup nests bound with spiders' webs set in trees, with 2–4 colored and patterned eggs.

Vangas are a Madagascan group with a strong hook-tipped bill, varying in some species to a massive casque structure or long, thin and curved. They are mainly insect feeders of forest, scrub or swamp. The nest is usually a twig cup with 2–3 pale, patterned eggs.

170. New Zealand Wattlebirds (Callaeatidae) 2 genera, 2 species (and 1 genus, 1 species extinct), 8.8–20 in (22–50 cm). This New Zealand family of thick forest birds includes the extinct Huia in which the male's bill was short and stout, the female's long and curved. Among extant species the Kokako or Wattled Crow has a short, very stout and slightly curved bill, the smaller Saddleback, known only on a few small islands, a tapering thin, starlinglike bill. There are fleshy pendent wattles at the bill base, blue orange in the first, red in the other. Wings are rounded and weak, and flight is usually short. Legs and feet are well developed and strong. Food is fruit, flowers, nectar and other parts of plants. The Saddleback eats more insects, searching and probing among branches, and has high-pitched notes. The Kokako has more musical song and calls and tends to hop up trees and branches, gliding between them. The nest is a lined twig cup in a tree hollow or dense vegetation (Saddleback) or finer cup of plant material (Kokako) on a twig base, fairly low in a tree, with 2–3 colored and patterned eggs incubated by the female. Both parents feed the nestlings.

171. Rock-jumpers and Rockfowl (Picathartidae) 2 genera, 4 species, 7.2–16 in (18–40 cm). Rock-jumpers occur in open rocky montane habitats of southern Africa and Rockfowl on the floor of rainforest in rocky areas of western Africa. Both are vigorous hoppers and reluctant fliers, with well-developed legs and feet and rounded wings, which feed on insects and small creatures. Rock-jumpers are boldly patterned in reddish brown, black and white. They have rather harsh calls and make a cup nest in a hole or crevice with four white or spotted eggs. Rockfowl are mainly gray but the bare head is yellow and black, or blue, red and black. They nest in colonies making a huge mud cup, stuck to vertical rock or a cave roof, with 1–2 patterned eggs. Both parents incubate and feed young.

172–74. Bombycillidae is divided into three tribes.

172. Palmchat (Dulini) 1 genus, 1 species, 7.2 in (18 cm). A medium-sized, dull-colored bird of Hispaniola in the Caribbean, with short rounded wings and a short strong bill. It is a noisy and sociable species, roosting in a huddle and feeding on berries, flowers and other parts of plants. Nests are large masses of twigs in trees, usually in palms and built into frond bases. The structure is a mass of nests with separate entrances built one against another, lined with finer materials, with usually 4 patterned white eggs.

173. Silky-flycatchers (Ptilogonatini) 3 genera, 4 species, 7.8–9.2 in (17–23 cm). Slender, long-tailed birds with rounded wings and short legs found in habitats ranging from montane forest to dry open scrub from the southwestern United States to Central America. The head is crested, except in the Black-and-yellow Silky-flycatcher, the bill short and rather broad. They flycatch, hawking insects from observation perches, and also eat many berries. They make frequent calls and have brief songs. The nest is a compact cup in a tree or bush, often high up, with 2–3 colored and patterned eggs. Females or both adults incubate and both feed young. Species include the Phainopepla.

174. Waxwings (Bombycillini) 1 genus, 3 species, 7.2–8 in (18–20 cm). Medium-sized arboreal birds occurring across the northern forest regions of Eurasia and North America, irrupting south when food supplies are poor, they have smooth plumage and a pointed crest. The wings are tapering with small red waxy blobs on the tips of secondary feathers. Tail and legs are short, the bill short and stubby, broad based and slightly hooked at the tip. Food is fruit, principally berries, and insects caught in flight during the nesting season. Flight is strong

ROCK-JUMPERS AND ROCKFOWL: The Gray-necked Rock Fowl (Picathartes oreas) shows the brightly colored bald head characteristic of this genus.

Left DIPPERS: A White-throated or Eurasian Dipper (Cinclus cinclus), typically perched on a half-submerged stone about to carry food to a nest. From such a spot they bob with a leg-flexing action that earns the name Dipper.

and birds are gregarious and nomadic. They have a soft trilling call. A cup nest is built in a tree. Both parents incubate 3–7 colored and patterned eggs and care for the young.

175. Dippers (Cinclidae) 1 genus, 5 species, 6–6.8 in (15–17 cm). These small, squat birds of running streams and rivers are found in Eurasia, north Africa, southeast Asia and the Americas, mainly in mountains but sometimes in estuaries in winter, when altitudinal movements may occur. They have a short neck, short tail and strong legs and feet. The bill is slender, straight and fairly short. They walk into and under water and swim using their wings. Food is

aquatic insects and small water creatures. Terrestrial on rocks, they have a typical bobbing movement when alert, short call notes and a long song. They build a large domed nest, with a low side entrance, on a ledge or support overlooking water. The female incubates usually 5 white eggs and both parents feed young.

176–78. Muscicapidae has two subfamilies, of which the Muscicapinae divides into two tribes.

176. Thrushes (Turdinae) 22 genera, 179 species, 6–13.2 in (15–33 cm). This thrush subfamily includes the Eurasian Blackbird, American Robin, Bluebirds, Shortwings, Solitaires and Alethes. They are small to medium-sized birds that occur almost world-wide, except in polar regions, habitats ranging from rainforest to open forest, scrub, savanna, rocky slopes and hills, rocky streams and rivers. Nests are a cup, often bulky, in a tree or bush, on a ledge, or in a tree or rock cavity, with 2–6 colored and patterned eggs. Incubation is by the female, both parents feeding young. Some species are migratory.

177. Old World Flycatchers (Muscicapini) 17 genera, 115 species, 4–8.2 in (10–21 cm). The habitats of these small arboreal birds range through all types of forest, open woodland, scattered trees and scrub in Africa and from temperate Eurasia south to Indonesia, the Moluccas and Philippines. They have a rather upright stance with wings usually long and tapering, flight strong and agile, the tail moderately long to short, legs short and feet small. The head is longish and rounded with big eyes and a flattened, broad-based bill with a slight hook tip and bristles at the base. Food is mainly insects caught in flight, sometimes taken from vegetation or the ground. The voice is usually rather weak. A cup nest is built in a tree, in a crevice, on a ledge or in a cavity, and a domed nest at ground level in the Black-and-rufous Flycatcher. The 2–6 colored and patterned eggs are incubated by the female or both birds and both feed the young.

178. Chats (Saxicolini) 30 genera, 155 species, 4.4–10.8 in (11–27 cm). Small to medium-sized thrushlike birds that occur in Africa and its islands, through Eurasia and south to Indonesia and the Philippines, the Pied Chat extending from Iran to New Guinea, a few reach Alaska, the Northern Wheatear almost Holarctic, from Alaska, via Eurasia to Eastern Canada. They have habitats ranging from various levels of forest to open woodland, savanna, heathland, waterside, arid scrub, semidesert and rocks. The tribe includes the Robins, Nightingales, Redstarts, Forktails, Scrub-Robins, Cochoas, Shamas and Akalats. They are usually plump bodied, round headed and short necked and tend to be slender legged with thin bills. Wings vary from rounded to tapering, tails from short to long and forked. Food is mainly insects and small creatures and many species watch and swoop from a perch. Many have sharp calls and musical songs. The nest is usually a cup in a tree, bush, ground vegetation, tree or rock cavity or on a ledge. The 2–6 colored, plain or patterned eggs are usually incubated by the female but both parents feed the young. Some species are migratory.

179–80. Sturnidae is a family that divides into two tribes.
179. Starlings (Sturnini) 27 genera, 114 species, 6.4–26 in (16–65 cm). These small to medium-sized, solidly built birds, which include the Mynas and the Oxpeckers, occur from forest and forest edge to grassland in Africa and from Eurasia to Australia and the islands of the west Pacific. Plumage is glossy and the head sometimes has a shaggy crest, bare skin or wattles. The bill is frequently tapering, sharp pointed and straight or slightly curved, though sometimes stouter or blunter and exceptionally may be very short. Their wings are tapering and flight strong and direct, tail often short, sometimes long. Legs and feet are strong and ground feeders walk and run. Posture is rather upright. Food is insects or other small creatures, taken often by probing the ground or crevices, or by chasing. Fruit, nectar, seeds and other parts of plants are also eaten. Many starlings are gregarious and often noisy, with whistling calls and songs. The nest is a lining in a cavity in a tree

or rocks, or a hole in a bank, grouped pendent stick nests or a domed nest in a bush. There are 2–6 colored eggs, plain or spotted, incubation and care of young being by both parents. Oxpeckers have sharp claws and tails as supports for climbing over the large grazing animals of Africa. Their blunt, flattened bill removes ticks and flies, scabs and damaged wound tissue. They roost communally in trees, a few on buildings, and nest communally in small groups. Some species migrate, and the Common Starling and Myna have been introduced from Eurasia and India to North America, Australia and New Zealand.

180. Mockingbirds (Mimini) 11 genera, 34 species, 8–13.2 in (20–33 cm). This tribe includes Mockingbirds, Thrashers and the Catbird. They occur from southern Canada southwards right through South America inhabiting forest edge, open woodland, scrub and bushy open country. They are medium-sized, thrushlike birds, with long tails, wings usually rounded and, in some species, weak flight. The medium to long bill is strong, fairly slender and sometimes curved. Most feed on the ground or in low cover, Thrashers probing and searching leaf litter. Food is insects and other small creatures, fruit and seed. Mockingbirds are noisy, with frequent loud song, other species are less obtrusive. The nest is a cup of twigs with a softer lining, built in a tree, bush or tree cavity. The 2–5 plain or patterned colored eggs are incubated by the female or both parents. Both tend the young, occasionally with helpers.

181–82. Sittidae is made up of two subfamilies.
181. Nuthatches (Sittinae) 1 genus, 24 species, 5.6–8 in (14–20 cm). Small, arboreal or rock-climbing birds of forest, open woodland and parkland or rocky areas, Nuthatches are found in North America and Eurasia south to North Africa and Indonesia. They have a compact body and head, short tail, short stout legs and strong feet with large claws. With the feet alone for support they move in any direction over tree trunks and branches (they are the only birds that habitually hunt by walking down tree trunks head first) and rock faces. The wings are tapering and flight strong. The head is large with a longish tapering bill with a sharp tip. Food is insects, seeds and nuts that are wedged in a crevice and hammered open. Food may be stored. Loud call notes are repeated as songs. The nest is a cup in a tree cavity, the entrance reduced with mud or smeared with resin, or a domed mud structure stuck into a rock hollow. The female incubates 2–4 white, spotted eggs and both parents feed the young.

182. Wallcreeper (Tichodrominae) 1 genus, 1 species, 5.2–6.4 in (13–16 cm). This is a small, nuthatchlike climber of inland cliffs and rocks that occurs in higher Eurasian mountains from the Pyrenees to the Himalayas, shifting to lower winter altitudes. The bill is long and slender and slightly curved, the wings are large, broad and rounded, the tail moderately long. Legs and feet are not particularly strong. It moves between small rock projections, hopping upwards with constant flicking open of the wings, showing red patches. Food is insects and spiders. It has rather quiet calls and song phrases used by both sexes. The nest is a cup in a crevice with 3–5 white, red brown speckled eggs incubated by the female. The male helps feed both female and young.

183–86. Certhiidae has three subfamilies, Certhiinae dividing into two tribes.
183. Northern Treecreepers (Certhiini) 1 genus, 6 species, 4–8.6 in (12–15 cm). These small, tree-climbing birds of forest and open

Above WALLCREEPER: *The Wallcreeper* (Tichodroma muraria) *looks dull gray when resting; only in flight does it display the color-patterned wings and tail.*

Above center MOCKINGBIRDS: *The Catbird* (Dumetella carolinensis) *is more furtive than others in the family and tends to keep to thickets where it betrays itself by its cat-like call.*

Left THRUSHES: *The Wood Thrush (Hypocichla mustelina) is a melodius songster of swamp and woodlands of North America.*

Right NORTHERN TREECREEPERS: *The Eurasian Treecreeper (Certhia familiaris). Treecreepers spend their lives climbing on tree bark, even nesting behind loose pieces. They move downwards by short backward hops.*

Below WRENS: *Wrens originated in the Americas, only one invading Eurasia. The Sedge Wren (Cistothorus platensis) is a summer visitor to eastern North America where it nests in sedge marshes.*

woodland from North America south to Nicaragua and across Eurasia and southeastern Asia have long, slender and slightly curved bills, short wings and long tails with stiffened spiny shafts that act as a support against the bark. Legs are short and toes long with large sharp claws. They climb tree trunks and branches, usually upwards, swooping down to the next tree trunk. Food is insects and small creatures found by probing into bark crevices. Calls and song are thin and high pitched. The nest is a cup behind loose bark or in a crevice, usually with 3–7 spotted, white eggs. Incubation is mainly by the female, both parents feeding the young.

184. African Treecreeper (Salpornithini) 1 genus, 1 species, 5.2 in (13 cm). Also known as the Spotted Creeper, this bird of *Acacia* woodland, dry scrub and savanna occurs in Afrotropical Africa and parts of India. It resembles other treecreepers but has longer wings and an unstiffened square tail. It feeds over tree trunks and branches, more like a nuthatch, with its tail clear of the bark and wings fluttered more often, and eats insects and small invertebrates. Its nest is a cup bound with spiders' webs on a horizontal branch, with 2–3 colored and patterned eggs incubated by the female. The male feeds the female and helps feed the young.

185. Wrens (Troglodytinae) 16 genera, 75 species, 3.2–6 in (8–15 cm). Small, stocky birds of thick vegetation from forest to scrub, and in marshland, wrens are found through the Americas and Eurasia. They have a thin, pointed, sometimes long bill, short and rounded wings and a short to moderately long tail that is often cocked. They are mainly birds of low cover, adapted to move through undergrowth, eating insects and small invertebrates. Pair nesters, such as Cactus Wrens, have simple calls, polygamous species have a loud, long advertisement song. The nest is domed with a side entrance, and sometimes an entrance tunnel. Polygamous males build a number of nests, the female lining the one she chooses and laying 2–10 spotted pale eggs. Both parents feed the young. Species include Donacobius.

186. Gnatcatchers (Polioptilinae) 4 genera, 15 species, 4–6 in (10–12 cm). This subfamily, which includes the Verdin and Gnatwrens, occurs in forest scrub, savanna and semidesert from temperate North America to northern Argentina. Gnatcatchers are slender warbler-like birds of higher vegetation with thin bills and long tails. Gnatwrens feed at lower levels and are wrenlike, with a short tail and a long thin bill, whereas the Verdin is like a desert tit with short thin bill. All eat insects and small invertebrates, taken by searching and fly-catching. They have short thin call notes. Nests are small neat cups bound with spiders' webs in a low tree or shrub, except in the Verdin that makes a domed twig structure with a side entrance, also used for roosting. There are usually 4–7 colored and patterned eggs, both adults incubating and feeding the young.

187–88. Paridae is a family with two subfamilies.

187. Penduline-Tits (Remizinae) 4 genera, 12 species, 2.8–4.4 in (7–11 cm). This subfamily includes the Fire-capped Tit and the African Tit-hylia. They are small acrobatic tits with short, thin, pointed bills and live in forest, scrub, marshes and reed beds in Africa and through Eurasia and southeast Asia, migrants wintering in Iraq and India. Food is insects and small seeds. Elaborate nests are made from downy plant seed, felted to form solid walls. The final nest is a pendent rounded structure with a downward-directed tubelike entrance, hung from the end of a twig. The Tit-hylia makes a rounded felt nest among twigs and the Fire-capped Tit a cup nest in a tree hole. The typical penduline-tits live in small social groups with extra individuals as helpers in nesting, laying 3–6 white or pale blue eggs, usually incubated by the female. Both of a pair tend the young.

188. Typical Tits (Parinae) 3 genera, 53 species, 4.4–5.6 in (11–14 cm). Small, active arboreal birds of forest, parkland and scrub in Africa, through Eurasia to India, southeast Asia and the Philippines, and North America south to Mexico, the typical tits include Titmice, Blue Tits, Great Tits and various other Tits and Chickadees. They are compact and short necked with strong legs and feet, and rounded to tapering wings, with strong flight. The head is usually boldly patterned and sometimes crested, the bill short, conical and strong. They are inquisitive, hunting and exploring through vegetation with agile acrobatic flight. Food is insects, seeds and nuts. They can hold food down in one foot to break or hammer it, and some hide and store food. Calls are short, loud and repetitive. They are sometimes sociable when not breeding. The nest is a cup in a cavity in a tree or rock, sometimes excavated by the bird. The female lays and incubates 4–12 spotted white eggs, both adults feeding the young.

189. Long-tailed Tits (Aegithalidae) 3 genera, 8 species, 3.6–5.6 in (9–14 cm). This family of forest and scrub, found across Eurasia, in Java

and in western North America from Canada to Mexico, includes the American Bushtits. Small arboreal birds with rounded bodies and large heads with bills very short, deep and laterally flattened. The wings are rounded, the tail distinctly long and narrow and the feet and legs small but strong. They are nervously active and acrobatic, searching twigs for insects and small invertebrates. They have small, frequent, shrill and explosive calls, usually move in a social group and roost in a tight huddle. There may be helpers at the nest, which is tall and domed with an entrance near the top, and built of moss and spiders' webs. The 4–14 speckled white eggs are incubated by the female, the male helping to feed the young.

190–91. Hirundinidae is a family of two sub-families.
190. River-Martins (Pseudochelidoninae) 1 genus, 2 species, 5.2–6 in (13–15 cm), plus 4 in (10 cm) for tail streamers. These two specialized martins differ from typical martins in their much heavier and broader bill and strong legs and feet. The short-tailed African River-Martin lives on the Congo and Ubangi rivers. The White-eyed River-Martin, known only from a few wintering individuals in reed beds in central Thailand, has a very short tail with two long filaments. They spend most of the time on the wing, catching insects. The African species nests in colonies of holes in sandbanks when rivers are low and migrates up and down larger rivers.

191. Swallows and Martins (Hirundininae) 13 genera, 87 species, 4–5 in (11–22 cm). These small, long-winged, aerial, feeding birds, which include the Sawwings, occur worldwide, except for cold areas, and particularly near water. The body is long, wings tapered, tail short to long and forked and the legs and feet very small but functional with an upright perching posture, the eyes large and the bill short, broad and flattened with bristles at the base. Flight is rapid with swift maneuvering, hawking flying insects. They have sharp and twittering calls and musical songs. The nest is a lined mud cup or enclosed structure, stuck to rock or a building, or a cup in a burrow in a bank. Either the female or both birds incubate the 3–8 spotted white eggs. Both feed the young. Many species are migratory.

192. Kinglets (Regulidae) 1 genus, 6 species, 3.6–4.8 in (9–12 cm). Very small arboreal birds of coniferous and mixed woodland, kinglets occur in North America south to Guatemala, through Eurasia and in the Canaries and Taiwan. They include the Goldcrests and Firecrests and have compact, rounded wings, a short tail, strong feet and short very fine bills. There is a concealed color stripe on the crown. They constantly hunt higher leaves and twigs for tiny insects, invertebrates and their eggs. They have rather quiet, thin high-pitched calls. The nest is a stout cup slung from the underside of conifer stems with spiders' webs.

193. Bulbuls (Pycnonotidae) 21 genera, 137 species, 5.2–9.2 in (13–22 cm). They include Finchbills, Tetrakas, Nicators and smaller species called Greenbuls and Leaf-loves. These small to medium-sized arboreal birds of Africa, Madagascar and Mascarene Islands, and from Turkey to northern India and southern China south to the Malaccas and Philippines, live mainly in forest, with some in scrub or cultivated areas. They have short wings, longish tails and legs often short. The head may be brightly colored, sometimes crested, the bill slender and sometimes slightly curved, often with bristles at the gape. Often gregarious, behavior varies from conspicuous and noisy to quiet and furtive, the voice from harsh babbling to musical calls and song. Food is fruit and insects. The nest is a shallow cup in a tree with 2–5 colored and patterned eggs incubated by both parents. Both feed the young and some have helpers. They have been introduced elsewhere.

194. Hypocolius (Hypocoliidae) 1 genus, 1 species, 9.2 in (23 cm). A shrikelike, gray bird of scrub, bushes and cultivation occurring from Iraq to southern Iran, wintering in Arabia, the Hypocolius has a long narrow tail, short wings, small legs and feet and a rather upright posture. The bill is short and broad with a slightly hooked tip, flight is strong and direct. Often found in sociable groups, it is fairly sluggish, feeding on dates, berries and some insects. The nest is a large untidy cup in a palm or small twiggy tree, with 4–5 colored and patterned eggs. Both birds are involved in nesting.

195. African Warblers (Cisticolidae) 14 genera, 119 species, 3.6–8 in (9–20 cm). Most numerous are the various Cisticolas, but the family also includes Prinias, Apalises, Cameropteras and Scrub-Warbler. Mostly small birds, usually streaky brown or plain species of low cover in open places, or more boldly marked arboreal birds, these warblers occur from forest to open grassland, swamp and semidesert in Africa, with the Scrub-Warbler to Iraq and Afghanistan and two Cisticolas to southern Eurasia and south to Australia. All have small thin bills, rather slender legs and short rounded wings. Tails vary from very short to long. Open country forms in grass or scrub tend to have repetitive loud call notes and often distinctive song flights. Arboreal birds have shorter warbled songs. Food is mainly insects, small invertebrates and some nectar. Nests are mostly pear-shaped structures in low vegetation, bound together and to vegetation with spiders' webs, with an entrance at the top; some are between hanging leaves. Others, such as those of the

Left GNATCATCHERS: *The range of the Blue-gray Gnatcatcher (Polioptila caerulea) extends well north in the United States. It uses its tail as a balancer in pursuit of insects, swinging it widely, and chasing in flycatcher fashion.*

Right TYPICAL TIT: *The Tufted Titmouse (Parus bicolor) is a winter visitor to birdfeeders in the more wooded regions of eastern North America.*

Right BULBULS: *A Red-eyed Bulbul (Pycnonotus nigricans). Some bulbuls are more brightly colored but most draw attention with their lively manner and noisy, often musical calls.*

Below SWALLOWS AND MARTINS: *An adult Barn Swallow (Hirundo rustica) and a younger bird, summer visitors in the Northern Hemisphere, wintering south, even meeting on migration the Welcome Swallow (H. neoxena) that replaces it in Australia.*

terrestrial, semidesert Scrub-Warbler and the forest Oriole Warbler, build domed nests, that of the latter hanging from a twig and a giant 10 in (20 cm). The 2–7 colored and patterned eggs are usually incubated by both birds, who also feed the young.

196. White-eyes (Zosteropidae) 13 genera, 96 species, 5–5.6 in (10–14 cm). Birds of forests, mangroves, scrub and cultivated areas occur in Africa and from Pakistan, southern Tibet and southern China to Australasia, the Indian Ocean and western Pacific islands. They are very small, greenish or yellowish, arboreal birds with a white eye rim, some island forms being larger or darker. Their wings are short and rounded, bill thin, pointed and slightly curved and the eyes close set for probing. They are active, usually gregarious, and have thin, shrill calls and song phrases. Food is small insects, nectar and fruit. Soft fruit is sometimes punctured and sucked. The nest is a fine small cup suspended in a twig fork of a tree. The 2–4 whitish eggs are incubated, and young fed, by both parents.

197–202. Sylviidae has four subfamilies of which Sylviinae is made up of three tribes.

197. Leaf-Warblers (Acrocephalinae) 36 genera, 221 species, 3.6–6.8 in (9–17 cm). Found in Africa, across Eurasia and south to New Guinea and the Solomon Islands, these birds include the genera of well-known warblers such as Reed, Grasshopper and Icterine Warblers, Cetti's and other bush-warblers, Willow Warbler, Chiffchaff, Tesias, Tailorbird and less known groups such as Eremomelas, Crombecs and Tit-Warblers as well as the typical Leaf-Warblers. Habitats range from forest or scattered trees or shrubs to grassland, swamps and reed beds. They are mostly slender birds with tapering wings and slender bills, capable of clinging to thin stems and searching among vegetation. Tails are sometimes very short, or bills long and slender. Food is mainly insects, small invertebrates and some nectar. Songs may be simple and repetitive, harsh or musical. Some males are polygamous. The nest is usually a deep cup, sometimes domed with a side entrance, built in a tree, bush, reeds, grasses or ground debris. Tailorbirds suspend cups in hanging leaves, bound together with fibers. Either the female or both parents incubate 2–6 colored and patterned eggs. Both feed the young.

198. Grass-Warblers (Megalurinae) 10 genera, 21 species, 5.2–10 in (13–25 cm). This subfamily includes the fernbirds, Spinifexbird, Thicketbird and songlarks. Typical grass-warblers are slender and short winged with long tails, sometimes broad or tapering, or with reduced feather structure guarding against wear, the legs usually long and strong. They are skulkers in tall grass or reeds, habitats ranging through forest, bamboos, grassland, swamp and semidesert in Africa, Madagascar and from Pakistan, India and China to the Philippines, Australasia, Solomon Islands and Fiji. Flight is poor. The two songlarks are birds of more open habitats, with display flights, having shorter tails and longer wings. The Rufous Songlark is associated with the presence of some trees. The big Brown Songlark, the male half as large again as the female, prefers open grassland and saltbush. It may be polygamous. All grass-warblers feed mainly on insects and small creatures, some seed taken by songlarks. The nest is a concealed deep cup in low vegetation, with 2–5 pale pink, spotted eggs.

199. Laughingthrushes (Garrulacinae) 2 genera, 54 species, 9.6–14 in (24–35 cm).

Medium-sized, thrushlike babblers, mainly of forest and scrub and occurring from northern Pakistan, southern Tibet and central China to Sumatra and Borneo, these birds have short wings, less rigid tails, strong legs and feet and a strong bill. They often have a short-necked, slightly crouching posture. Most are highly sociable, with contact calls that may rise to shrieking choruses. Food is all kinds of small creatures, fruits, seeds and sometimes nectar, mostly obtained by constant searching, on and above the ground. The nest is usually a cup, set in a fork or suspended by its rim, with pale plain or spotted eggs. Some nest in pairs, others in groups with helpers.

200. Babblers (Timaliini) 51 genera, 233 species, 4–12 in (10–30 cm). These are small to medium-sized birds of Africa, the Middle East and from India and northern China to Indonesia and the Philippines, their habitats ranging from forest and scrub to cultivated land and semidesert with sparse shrubs. The Bearded Reedling is found across Eurasia. They are warbler- or thrushlike, but with well-developed strong legs and feet, often with stouter bills and a heavier build. Wings are often rounded. Tails vary from very short to long. Bills are short to long and may be stout, parrotlike and blunt, wedge shaped, slender or long and downcurved, sometimes with basal bristles. Typically birds of vegetation from forest canopy to low scrub, they are often highly sociable in small groups, often with group territories, and noisy with short and often harsh calls, sometimes duetting. Some have musical songs. Food is mainly various small creatures, seed and fruit, occasionally nectar. Pair bonds are usually long. The nest is a cup in a tree, bush or low vegetation, or a domed nest near or on the ground. The 2–6 colored and patterned or plain eggs are incubated by the female or both birds. Both feed the young, with helpers in group species. Babblers also include Illadopsis, Barwings, Fulvettas, Sibias, Yuhinas and Parrotbills.

201. Wrentit (Chamaeini) 1 genus, 1 species, 6 in (15 cm). This babbler, isolated in North America and resembling some warblers, occurs in thick scrub and chaparral from Oregon to southern California. It has short round wings and a long narrow tail, often carried slightly cocked. The bill is short and pointed. It is a sedentary bird of areas with low bushes in which it skulks most of the time. The male has a loud trilling song phrase, the female a shorter one. Food is insects and other small creatures and berries. There is a long pair bond. The nest is a compact cup low in a bush or tree, the 3–5 colored eggs incubated, and the young tended, by both parents.

202. Typical Warblers (Sylviini) 1 genus, 22 species, 4.8–6 in (12–15 cm). These are the typical tree and bush warblers that occur in all types of wooded and shrubby habitat from forest to semidesert and in cultivated areas, breeding across Eurasia into Africa, Arabia and northern India and wintering in southern parts of that range, many species being migratory. They are slim, with tapering wings and short slender bills. They are less furtive than some other types of warblers and males have distinctive songs, often musical. They feed on insects, small invertebrates and soft fruits. They breed as separate pairs, building a cup nest in a tree or bush with usually 4–5 colored and patterned eggs. Incubation is by both birds or mainly by the female. Species include White-throats and Blackcap.

203. Larks (Alaudidae) 17 genera, 91 species, 4.8–9.6 in (12–24 cm). These are small, ground-living birds of open places, including desert, grassland, moorland and tundra, in Africa, and across Eurasia to southeastern Asia and the Philippines, with one species to Australia and one in North America south to Mexico and central Colombia. They are strong fliers with tapering broad wings, strong legs and feet, a fairly stout pointed bill, sometimes long slender and slightly curved or deep and blunt, and with the head sometimes crested. Usually living on bare soil or sparse vegetation, they have drab cryptic plumage, combined with loud, often musical and extended song flights. Food is insects, seeds and parts of plants. The nest is a cup, usually in a ground hollow sheltered by a plant tuft or stone, with 2–6 colored and patterned eggs incubated by the female or by both parents. Both feed the young.

204–6. Nectariniidae has two subfamilies, Nectariniinae dividing into two tribes.

204. Sugarbirds (Promeropinae) 1 genus, 2 species, 9.2–11.2 in (23–28 cm), male 17.2 in (43 cm) with tail in Cape Sugarbird. Found in the *Protea* stands of mountain slopes in South Africa, they are like large, drab-colored sunbirds with a long, slender downcurved bill and males having a very long tail, displayed from a high perch or in an aerial display flight. Food is mainly nectar and a few insects and they are dependent upon the large flowers of *Protea* shrubs. They are territorial, the nest a cup low in thick *Protea* bush. The female incubates the two colored and patterned eggs but both parents feed the young.

205. Flowerpeckers (Dicaeini) 2 genera, 44 species, 3.6–5.2 in (9–13 cm). Small, sometimes brightly-colored arboreal birds of habitats from forest to open scrub and cultivated land, these birds are found from the Himalayas and southwestern China to Australia, the Philippines and the Solomon Islands. Their tail and legs are short and the bill short and either tapering and pointed or stubby and blunt ended. Food includes nectar and small insects but is mainly berries, particularly mistletoes, of which they are an important disperser. Energetic and noisy, with small high-pitched calls, they tend to be in pairs or families. The nest is a pendent, untidy, pear-shaped structure, with an entrance high on one side. The female incubates 1–4 spotted white eggs, both parents feeding the young. The southernmost species, the Mistletoebird, is migratory.

206. Sunbirds (Nectariniini) 5 genera, 123 species, 3.2–6.4 in (8–16 cm) up to 12 in (30 cm) for some long-tailed males. This tribe includes the Spiderhunters. Sunbirds are small slender active birds with long, thin, curved bills, occurring in Africa, through the Middle East, from Pakistan, northern India and central China to Australia in habitats from forest to cultivated land and heathland. Their wings are rounded and tails vary from short and square to graduated with very long central tail feathers. Male plumage is often vividly colored. They are brush-tongued, feeding mainly on nectar, obtained by agile perching, and small insects. They are aggressively active, with sharp calls and rapid songs. The nest is a domed structure hung by spiders' webs from a twig or branch, elongated and with a side entrance that is often porched. The female incubates 2–3 pale patterned eggs and both parents feed the young. Spiderhunters are greenish with short tail and very long curved bill. Tubular or cup nests are bound under a large leaf with spiders' webs and both birds incubate.

207–8. Melanocharitidae divides directly into two tribes.

SUGARBIRDS: *The Cape Sugarbirds* (Promerops cafer) *are like larger versions of sunbirds but with dull plumage and very long tails.*

Above left GRASS WARBLERS: *The Fernbird* (Megalurus punctatus), *of swampy grassland and bracken in New Zealand is typically skulking and a weak flier. In many of the family the long tail has weak barbs that look as though they have been worn away.*

Top right LAUGHINGTHRUSHES: *The Red-tailed Laughingthrush* (Garrulax milnei) *has the low stance and tail that looks loosely attached, typical of these noisy, sociable oriental birds.*

Left FLOWERPECKER: *An Orange-bellied Flowerpecker* (Dicaeum trigonostigma) *has the dark back and colorful breast typical of the tribe.*

207. Melanocharis or Berrypeckers (Melanocharitini) 1 genus, 6 species, 4.4–6 in (11–15 cm). Small arboreal birds of the lowland and montane forest of New Guinea, Melanocharis are mostly blue black in males, olive green in females, with small light tufts at the sides of the breast. Bills are slender and of moderate length, in one species short, in another long. Tails are broad, short to long. They feed in shrubs and trees of middle forest vegetation and on forest edges, hovering to snatch small fruit and spiders. They are usually solitary. Flight is fast and agile. They have short unmusical song phrases. The nest is a cup in a shrub or low tree built in a fork or bound on to a branch.

208. Toxorhamphus or Longbills (Toxorhamphini) 2 genera, 4 species, 2.8–5.2 in (7–13 cm). Small drab sunbirdlike birds with shortish tails and long slender, slightly curved bills that occur in forests of New Guinea and nearby islands, are inconspicuous. They are nervously active, taking insects by hovering or searching leaves and branches, and also taking nectar from flowering shrubs. They feed in various forest vegetation levels but often up in the canopy. They have short unmusical calls. The Pygmy Longbill is usually in small parties. A cup nest is built in a sapling or bush, with a single white or spotted egg.

209. Paramythias (Paramythiidae) 2 genera, 2 species, 5.2–8 in (13–20 cm). These are birds of the mountain forests of New Guinea. The Crested Berrypecker is starling sized with a small, thin, pointed bill, and a black and white crest, whereas the Tit Berrypecker looks like a Great Tit, with bright yellow cheeks and orange-tinted underside. Both are active in various levels of forest vegetation, sociable and often in small groups. They have small shrill calls and

SUNBIRDS: The Malachite Sunbird (Nectarinia famosa). Sunbirds are the Old World equivalent of the hummingbirds. They share small size, bright plumage and nectar-seeking bills but lack their hovering flight, feeding when perched.

Right *SPARROWS: Less specialized and more adaptable relatives of the weavers, both House and Tree Sparrows have learned to use human settlement for their habitats. Though often nesting in building crannies, in a tree they make a domed nest like this House Sparrow (Passer domesticus).*

the Tit Berrypecker has a small repeated song. The nest of the Crested Berrypecker is a deep untidy cup in a shrubby tree. One patterned egg is incubated by the female, both parents tending the young.

210–15. Passeridae is made up of five sub-families of which the Estrildinae divide into two tribes.

210. Sparrows (Passerinae) 4 genera, 36 species, 4–8 in (10–20 cm). Small birds sometimes found in woodland, but more often of open savanna, grassland, cultivated ground or open rocky or mountain areas, they occur in Africa, throughout Eurasia, the Middle East, and India to Indonesia and have been widely introduced elsewhere. They have short, stout

seed-eating bills. They tend to occur in more open places, often feeding mainly on the ground. Food is seeds, parts of plants and insects. Most are sociable, living and sometimes breeding in loose colonies, and roosting communally. Their noisy calls are mainly unmusical and sometimes harsh. Snowfinches have a flight display and song. Nests are domed structures with a side entrance, in a bush, tree, rock or building crevice, or a cup in a crevice or hole in the case of Snowfinches. The 3–6 patterned eggs are incubated by the female or both parents and both tend the young. Species include the Petronias.

211. Wagtails and Pipits (Motacillinae) 5 genera, 65 species, 4.8–8.8 in (12–22 cm). Small, slender, mainly ground-feeding birds that occur worldwide except at the Poles and on remote islands, living in rocky or grassy areas near water, grassland and bare rocky or sandy areas in deserts and mountains. They have long legs and long tails, wings are tapering, flight strong and undulating and the bill thin. Wagtails are more brightly colored with black, white and yellow. Their long black and white tails are in motion during very active insect chasing, usually near water. Pipits and Longclaws are less obvious, brown and streaked terrestrial birds of grassland and open places. Food is insects and other small creatures. Wagtails have loud calls and songs, Pipits quieter calls and display song-flights when nesting. Nonbreeding birds are often gregarious. The nest is a cup on the ground, in low vegetation or in a crevice or bank. The 2–6 colored and patterned eggs are incubated by the female or by both parents and both feed the young.

212. Dunnocks (Prunellinae) 1 genus, 13 species, 5.2–7.2 in (13–18 cm). Rather drab and secretive birds of low vegetation, ranging from open forest to scrub, thickets in open areas and sparse rocky slopes, Dunnocks occur across Eurasia and to North Africa, Iraq, Iran and northern India. They have slender bills. Food is mainly insects in summer, seed in winter. Solitary or gregarious, they have small sharp calls and musical but monotonous short songs. They are furtive, tending to keep to cover. In the Common Dunnock at least, the mating systems vary with circumstances. The nest is a cup in a low bush, ground vegetation or rock crevice and 3–6 plain blue eggs are incubated by the female or by both parents. Both feed the young.

213. Weavers (Ploceinae) 17 genera, 117 species, 5.2–10.4 in (13–26 cm) plus some additional tails up to 20 in (50 cm) long. They include the Weavers, Widowbirds, Queleas, Foudias and Bishops and are small tree and grassland birds of warmer climates occurring in Africa, Madagascar and from northern India and southern China to Indonesia in habitats ranging from forest to scrub, grassland and open marshland. They have short, stout, seed-eater bills. Breeding males are often very brightly colored, some having long tails. Food is seeds, insects and parts of plants, exceptionally nectar or fruit. Forest weavers may live in pairs but most other species are highly gregarious, with noisy harsh call notes and displays. In open-country nesters displays may be aerial, or with dancing leaps in Jackson's Widowbird and wing flapping near the nest in most others. Many nest colonially. The nest may be domed and of twigs, singly or several in a mass, woven upright oval in tall grasses or a tree, or a finely woven hanging nest suspended from twig tips with a nest chamber and a side entrance often elongated into a hanging tube. Males, often polygamous, build nests and females line them. The 2–8 eggs are highly varied in color and markings. Incubation is by the female or both parents and both feed the young. The Cuckoo Weaver parasitizes small warblers' nests.

214. Grass or Estrildine Finches (Estrildini) 29 genera, 140 species, 3.6–5.6 in (9–14 cm). Small to tiny birds of Africa, Madagascar, southern Arabia, Pakistan, northern India and southern China to Indonesia, Australia and western Pacific islands, and introduced elsewhere, these occupy habitats varying from forest edge and clearings to scrub, cultivated land, grassland, swamp and semidesert with very little vegetation. They are mainly ground-feeding birds with short, stout, seed-eater bills, sometimes more slender or more massive. Male plumage is brightly colored and patterned. Some have

WAGTAILS AND PIPITS: A male Yellow-hooded Wagtail (Motacilla citreola) in full spring glory; it will lose its bright color in winter. Most pipits are cryptically colored to match the grassland or open areas in which they live.

Following pages GRASS FINCHES: *Chestnut-breasted Finches (Lonchura castaneothorax) are grassland birds, adapted to cling to stems when feeding; sociable, they occur in flocks on cultivated grain or rice. The young among this group have more speckled plumage.*

Below DUNNOCKS OR ACCENTORS: *The European Dunnock (Prunella modularis) has a monotonous song and a complicated pairing system. In display, the male waves one of his rounded wings above his head like a banner.*

tapering or long tails and legs and feet are often strong. They are mainly birds of low cover, or growing grasses and small bare areas. Food is small seeds and insects. Pair bonds tend to be long term but, whereas forest species may live in pairs or families, open-country birds may form large flocks and are social at most times. Calls and sometimes musical songs are fairly quiet. The nest is usually a domed structure in a low tree, a bush or ground vegetation, with a side entrance and sometimes an entrance tube; a few species nest in tree cavities or the old nests of other birds. Usually 4–6 white eggs are laid. Incubation and care of the young is by both parents. Species include Waxbills, Negrofinches, Olive-backs, Crimson-wings, Pytilia, Twinspots, Firefinches, Grenadiers, Avadavats, Firetails, Silverbills, Munias, Java Sparrow and Cutthroat.

215. Parasitic Whydahs (Viduini) 1 genus, 15 species, 4–4.4 in (10–11 cm), tails of breeding males add 7.6–10.4 in (19–26 cm). These small African birds with seed-eater bills occur in similar habitats to the Grass Finches (*above*), on

which they are brood parasites. The females are streaky brown, the males boldly patterned in dark blue or purple, black, white and buff, and with exaggeratedly long ornate tail feathers. Food is seeds, parts of plants and insects. Males perform conspicuous display flights and in singing may mimic host species, holding territories in dispersed leks, with the individuals more widely scattered. They are promiscuous. Females lay 1–4 white eggs in the nest or nests of particular host species. The young mimic the host nestlings and are reared with them.

216–24. Fringillidae has three subfamilies, of which the Fringillinae divide into three tribes: Chaffinches, Cardueline Finches and Hawaiian Honeycreepers; and Emberizinae into five: Buntings, Parulid Warblers, Tanagers, Cardinals and Troupials.

216. Olive Warbler (Peucedraminae) 1 genus, 1 species, 4.4–5.2 in (11–13 cm). Although previously considered to be a Parulid Warbler (*below*), this species is now separated. A bird of mountain forest from the extreme southwest of

the United States to Nicaragua, in general it resembles one of them, and has a small thin bill and notched tail. It hunts insects in the high foliage of mountain conifer forest and has a soft whistling call and a repetitive tit-like song. The nest is a cup high in a tree. It is a partial migrant in winter.

217. Chaffinches (Fringillini) 1 genus, 3 species, 5.6–6.4 in (14–16 cm). These are small, mainly ground-feeding finches occurring across Eurasia and in the Canary Islands in forest, forest edges and scrub to open country and cultivated areas with some trees. They have sharp conical bills. Males are more brightly colored and have a loud repetitive song phrase when breeding. Nonbreeding birds may form winter flocks. Food is mainly seed and also insects, especially when breeding. Bramblings feed extensively on beechnuts. They usually hop, but may partly walk when on the ground. Flight is strong and undulating. The nest is a thick cup, mainly of moss bound with spiders' webs, in which 1–7 colored and patterned eggs are incubated by the female. Both adults feed the young.

218. Cardueline Finches (Carduelini) 20 genera, 136 species, 4.4–7.6 in (11–19 cm). These small birds occur in Africa, through Eurasia, the Mediterranean and Middle East, into southeastern Asia and the Philippines and through the Americas and have been introduced elsewhere. Habitats range from open forest, scrub and cultivated land to weedy grassland and bare rocky lowland or montane areas. They have seed-eating bills, short but varying in depth, sometimes massive. Bill tips are sometimes crossed. Legs are sometimes short, feet strong and the tail short to medium length. Some are mainly ground feeders, others feed among twigs, sometimes aerobatically, or in herbage. Food is seeds, parts of plants and insects, sometimes fruit. Males are often brightly colored and calls and song musical and sometimes prolonged. Mostly gregarious or found in small parties, some nest near each other. They build a cup nest in a tree, bush, ground vegetation or crevice, laying 3–5 colored and patterned eggs, incubated by the female, both parents feeding the young. Species include Serins, Seedeaters, Canaries, Siskins, Goldfinch, Redpoll, Linnet, Twite, crossbills, grosbeaks and Hawfinches.

219. Hawaiian Honeycreepers (Drepanidini) 18 genera, 30 species (8 extinct, others vulnerable), 4–8 in (10–20 cm). Small and basically finchlike, with indigenous Hawaiian names, these birds of the mature montane forest and scrub of the Hawaiian Islands are strong footed and have bill shapes that show adaptive radiation for different types of food. They vary from almost parrotlike to finchtype seed-eater bills, long slender curved bills, and one with a long, curved upper mandible and short straight lower one. Food may be primarily insects, seed, nectar or fruit, and obtaining it may include bark-crevice probing and breaking rotten wood. Voice varies from high-pitched notes to short song phrases. Known nests are usually open cups in trees, shrubs, ground vegetation or a cavity. The female lays and incubates 2–4 colored and patterned eggs. Both parents feed the young.

220. Buntings (Emberizini) 32 genera, 156 species, 4.4–8.4 in (11–21 cm). Small, finchlike birds of the Americas, Africa and across Eurasia to the Middle East, India and central southeastern Asia, bunting habitats range from forest to swamp, desert edge, mountains and tundra. Their bills tend to have the lower mandible deeper than the upper. Feet may be strong, Old

World buntings walking and hopping, many New World species hopping and able to scratch the ground for food. Longspurs are purely terrestrial. Breeding males are often brightly colored and sometimes crested, with distinct repetitive songs. Food is mainly seeds and parts of plants, but with more insects and small creatures than most finches eat. Usually gregarious, they breed in pairs, are polygamous or, in at least one species, promiscuous. The nest is a cup in a low tree, bush, rock crevice or among ground vegetation, with 2–7 colored and patterned eggs incubated by the female or both parents. Usually both feed the young. Species include Longspurs, Juncos, Towhees, Brush-Finches, South American Cardinals and American Sparrows.

221. Parulid Warblers (American Wood Warblers) (Parulini) 25 genera, 115 species, 4–6.4 in (10–16 cm). Small, slim insectivorous birds of all types of forest and woodland, scrub, swamps and sparse desert vegetation, these birds occur through the Americas except at polar extremes. They include Yellowthroats, Waterthrushes, American Redstarts, Ovenbird and American Chats. They have pointed bills and resemble Old World Warblers but show a considerable variety of bright color and pattern. Most are insect-gleaning species of trees and shrubs, taking berries in some species. Some have more flycatcherlike habits, a few are terrestrial within woodland and one with nuthatchlike, tree bark-searching habits. The Wrenthrush is included as a terrestrial short-winged member of this tribe. Most species have distinct, loud songs. Usually living in pairs or family parties they build a cup nest in a tree, a bush or ground vegetation, or in a natural cavity or a domed ground nest. The female incubates 4–5 colored and patterned eggs but both parents feed the young. Some species are migratory.

222. Tanagers (Thraupini) 104 genera, 413 species, 4–11.2 in (10–28 cm). This tribe includes many bunting and finchlike seed eaters of South America and the Galapagos finches. Its members occur throughout the Americas,

except in polar and subpolar regions, in habitats ranging from forest to low growth in open places, grassland, swamps and sparse mountain vegetation. They include Conebills, Hemispingus, Euphonias, Chlorophonias, Dacnis, Inca-Finches, Warbling-Finches, Yellow-Finches, Grassquit, American Seedeaters, Flower-piercers and the Galapagos Finches. They have seed-eater type bills but, although very stout in some instances, these tend to be a little more slender and blunt tipped and they are principally fruit eaters. Food also includes insects and some seeds. Some of the smaller species are nectar feeders with slender curved bills and, in the Flower-piercers, slender and upcurved with a small hook tip. Plumage color and pattern is often vivid and varied, and shared by both sexes. Many species are sociable, occurring in parties or joining mixed flocks. Calls are varied but song is not well developed. The nest is a cup in a tree, bush or on the ground, or in a crevice, or a domed nest with a side entrance in a bush, cavity or hole. The aerial-feeding Swallow Tanager makes a nest-burrow. The 2–5 colored and patterned eggs are usually incubated by the female. Both parents feed the young and there are nest helpers in some species. Some species are migratory.

223. Cardinals (Cardinalini) 13 genera, 42 species, 4.4–10.8 in (11–27 cm). Small to medium-sized birds of the Americas from Canada to northern Argentina, Cardinals occur from rainforest, open woodland and woodland edge to scrub and thickets and rough grassland. They include American Grosbeaks, Dickcissels and Saltators. They have stout, heavy, seed-eater bills and breeding males are boldly and brightly colored, some having crests. Their songs are loud and musical. Food is seeds, buds, blossoms, insects and some fruits. They stay mainly in pairs or family parties and build cup nests in a tree or bush or in ground vegetations. Either the female or both parents incubate the 2–4 colored and patterned eggs, and both feed the young. The Dickcissel is a grassland species with the male polygamous and the female alone tending young. Some species are migratory.

224. Troupials (New World Blackbirds) (Icterini) 26 genera, 97 species, 6–22.8 in (15–57 cm). Found in forests, scrub, savannas, grasslands and marshes through the Americas, except on tundra and mountains, troupials are large to small, arboreal and ground-living birds. Their bills may be slender and sharp, tapering and pointed, sometimes long and extending back to a forehead shield or, at the other extreme, short, stout and conical. Breeding males are mainly black, often with bright yellow to red patterning. They are often gregarious and noisy with harsh, guttural, squawking or whistling calls. Habitats range from arboreal to terrestrial. Feeding birds often use open-bill probing and can hold food down with the foot and also scratch for food. They eat insects and other small creatures, fruit and seeds. Breeding is often colonial. Mating may be in pairs or polygynous. Nests vary from deep cups in ground or marsh vegetation, or in shrubs or low trees, to pendent nests suspended between twigs in trees or long baglike nests, suspended in high trees, which have an entrance at the upper end. The female usually incubates the 2–6 colored and patterned eggs but the young may be fed by the female or by both parents. Cowbirds are brood parasitic, laying up to 30 eggs in nests of a wide range of host species. Species include Oropendola, Cacique, American Orioles, American Blackbirds, Meadowlarks, Marshbirds, Grackles, Cowbirds and Bobolink.

Above CARDINALS: The vivid plumage of the male Northern Cardinal (Cardinalis cardinalis) earned this bird its name, and from it came the tribal name. It is a frequent park and garden resident in North America.

Left TANAGERS: A male Scarlet Tanager (Piranga olivacea) in breeding plumage, one of the many vividly colored members of the tribe, and one of the few that migrate to temperate North America.

Opposite inset CHAFFINCHES: A male Chaffinch (Fringilla coelebs) in breeding plumage. Unlike other finches the two Chaffinches and their northern counterpart, the Brambling, make thick moss nests bound with spiders' webs.

Below TROUPIALS (NEW WORLD BLACKBIRDS): Like this Yellow-billed Cacique (Amblycercus holosericeus) of South American marshes and reed beds, troupials often have glossy black plumage with areas of color.

BIRDS AND PEOPLE

BIRDS AS FOOD

Birds and birds' eggs must have been taken as human food from the earliest times by raiding nests and knocking birds down with stones or sticks or, later, by using arrows and ensnaring them in nets and traps. The ancient Egyptians used a throwing stick and the Australian aborigines had their own version, which they called a boomerang.

Small birds were often caught by "liming," using a sticky substance to trap birds that become immobilized when they perch upon it. This was usually spread on branches in a tree or bush where birds were known to roost at night, so that when the birds returned they became stuck to their perches and could be taken.

Like geese, ducklings are easily imprinted at hatching by a combination of movement and calls. A duckherd in Bali carries a cloth on a stick. As in China millennia ago, when a similar flag was used, the ducks have been imprinted on this and follow where it is carried or remain where it is stuck into the ground.

A painting in the tomb of the Egyptian sculptor Nebuman shows him wielding a throwing stick, used to knock birds out of the air or from their perches. The birds, which are not to scale, include egrets, a small crane and songbirds as well as waterfowl. Is the duck on the front of his boat a tame decoy, used to attract others and lure them into a sense of security? Other ancient Egyptian tomb paintings and carvings show clap nets baited with grain to trap birds.

One recipe for lime involved boiling up holly leaves and twigs and mixing in corn mush. The Romans certainly knew the technique and it was probably used centuries earlier. A variation, applicable in daytime, was to tether an owl inside a bush that had been limed so that small birds who came to mob it would be trapped.

As an alternative to liming, one medieval illustration shows a man hiding in a bush from which extend pairs of sticks: if a bird landed on one of them, the hunter tugged on a string to pull the sticks together and trap its feet.

A great variety of traps and nets was employed. Flegg nets, like huge scoops, were used by hunters lowered down on ropes to catch birds from the cliff-nesting colonies of seabirds in the Scottish Hebrides. Long poles carrying a noose

of rope were another way in which the inhabitants of these islands used to take a bird from the cliff. Simple traps operated by pulling away the supporting stick were used for birds as well as other animals; simply placing a mirror beneath them was said to be enough to attract and snare a pheasant.

By the seventeenth century, illustrated books were showing the many kinds of nets that could be used and explaining how to employ them. The crow net was placed by a barn door where corn was being winnowed, where it could be concealed by throwing chaff over it, or in stubble or even on greensward where birds gathered worms, to trap them by their feet. The day net was about 12 feet (3.6 m) deep and used in stubble fields a couple of hours before sunset or daybreak and drawn over the birds by cords operated from about 60 feet (20 m) away.

The sparrow net was a purse-like pouch mounted on cross pieces so that draw strings could snap the top edges together. It was recommended by Francis Willughby in his *Ornithology* in 1678, for use under the eaves of buildings, especially by falconers:

"With this Engine you may taken Evening and Morning so many birds as you please, and give them warm to your Hawk, which is the greatest nourishment that can be, raising a Hawk soon, and making her mew fast."

Spaniels were trained to drive birds into nets or to mark where birds were so that a net could be drawn or dropped over them, and various kinds of tunnels constructed into which birds could be lured or driven. Willughby suggests using a "stalking horse" — a real horse or cow to hide behind as you approach wildfowl — or building an "Engine made like an horse or Ox" as a disguise, then "having covered your head with some hood of green or dark blew stuff, stalk with your Horse or Engine towards the

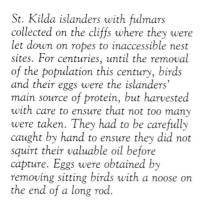

St. Kilda islanders with fulmars collected on the cliffs where they were let down on ropes to inaccessible nest sites. For centuries, until the removal of the population this century, birds and their eggs were the islanders' main source of protein, but harvested with care to ensure that not too many were taken. They had to be carefully caught by hand to ensure they did not squirt their valuable oil before capture. Eggs were obtained by removing sitting birds with a noose on the end of a long rod.

Birds by gentle and slow steps, and so raise them, and drive them before you (for it is their nature to run before a Horse or Beast out of fear lest it tread on them).

"Some stalk with dead Engines, as an artificial Tree, Shrub or Bush or a dead Hedge. But these are not so useful for the stalk as the stand. It being unnatural for dead things to move, the fowl will not only apprehend but eschew it. Therefore if you use them, you must either not move them at all, or only slowly, that their motion shall not be perceived."

How to take Crows and Rooks

Take some thick brown Paper and divide a sheet into eight parts, and make them up like Sugar-loaves [into cones]. Then lime the inside of the Paper a very little. Let them be limed three or four days before you set them, then put some Corn in them, and lay fifty or sixty of them up and down the ground, as much as you can under some clod of earth, and early in the Morning before they come to feed, then stand at a good distance, and you will see excellent sport. For as soon as Rook, Crow or Pigeon comes to pick out any of the Corn, it will hang upon his head, and he will immediately fly bold upright so high that he shall seem like a small bird, and when he is spent come tumbling down, as if he were shot in the Air.

Repeated from an earlier source in Francis Willughby's Ornithology, 1678.

Illustrations from Francis Willughby's Ornithology (1678) show a variety of techniques for trapping birds.

The pantiere net, recommended for taking larks, had rings along the upper edge and was hung between stakes two hours before sunset or before daybreak in stubble fields. Two men then walked toward the net, dragging a long rope across the field to raise the larks that did not fly but run into the net.

Quails and similar birds were driven into tunnel nets. On the left, lacking a real stalking horse, the bird catcher has disguised himself as a cow while on the right caged quails on poles are decoys and the fowlers, who have cast seed in front of the net, are driving the birds in alternately shaking a jingling instrument called a sonagiera.

The crow net was recommended for use near barn doors or again in stubble fields. With one end secured it was stretched over the ground and disguised by scattered chaff, then the free edge pulled forwards over the birds.

The Italian lanciotoia, mounted on a handle, was used at night. Birds were found by lamplight, which also helped to immobilize them, and the net brought down over them.

The day net was recommended for level surfaces: short barley stubbles, smooth green leys or level meadow from August to November, again set before dawn.

These nets were pulled over the birds from cover and ropes were also used to operate the turning gigs set with pieces of looking glass to attract inquisitive birds.

Spinning gigs of goose feathers twirling in the wind on long poles and live larks or buntings tethered to a peg in the ground acted as decoys for similar species and to draw birds of prey.

Trapping birds with limed cones set in the ground, a sixteenth-century engraving.

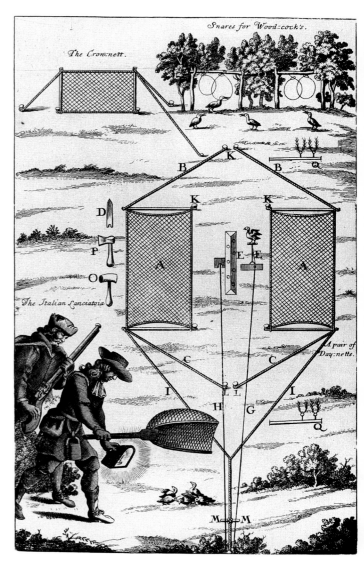

An owl tethered on top of a pole used to attract mobbing birds, which are caught if they perch on the limed posts on either side.

Foxes sometimes perform an intricate kind of "dance" to bring inquisitive ducks within reach of capture and on both sides of the Atlantic breeds of dog were developed — the Nova Scotia Duck Tolling Dog and the Dutch Kooikerhondje — and used in a similar way to act as decoys. A stick was thrown for the Toller to chase and play with to attract the birds within shooting distance, whereas the European dog was trained to dodge out around screens to lure inquisitive ducks into a "pipe" of netting.

The mist net, a very fine net that is almost invisible to the birds that fly straight into it, was produced by the Japanese, allegedly originally made from women's hair. Since the 1950s, these have been used extensively in southern Europe and on the Mediterranean islands to catch migratory birds when they come down to rest after flying across the sea from Africa.

Many of these methods of catching birds are now outlawed in North America, Australia, New Zealand and most European countries. Wild birds may not now be caught unless by special dispensation for research purposes.

When settled communities developed and people began to domesticate animals, it was much easier to rear birds for food than to have to go out catching them. The domestic goose had its origin in the Greylag Goose, the chicken in the Asian Red Junglefowl and the duck in the Mallard.

The Greylag Goose (Anser anser) was the origin of domesticated geese. It was easily tamed by imprinting newly hatched goslings. Domestication brought increased weight, a tendency to put on fat and white feathers, preferred for filling mattresses and pillows, and perhaps making farmed birds easier to see if they strayed.

The Junglefowl (Gallus gallus) was the origin of the domestic chicken. This cockerel with some young has the coloring of the wild bird but the full, raised tail is evidence of domestication. The true wild bird has fewer and downcurved tail feathers, as in Joseph Wolf and Joseph Smits' lithograph.

GALLUS FERRUGINEUS.

Egg production now uses "factory farming" techniques to maximize economic returns. Limited to minimal movement, birds effectively become eating and laying machines, eggs carried away by conveyor belt as soon as they are laid. So called "free range" methods leave birds free to move around, not usually in fields and farmyards but in sheds where they are still crowded together at high densities. Experiments have shown that under both conditions birds still retain all their instinctive behavior.

Geese were domesticated at least 4,000 years ago and the ancient Greeks already knew nine or more different breeds. The primary Iron Age role of the geese may have been as "watchdogs," for the noise they make when disturbed would have woken a whole settlement, and the ancient city of Rome was once saved from attack by the warning given by geese kept on the Capitoline Hill.

Poultry rearing has a long history: 3,000 years ago the Egyptians and Chinese were hatching eggs by artificial incubation. On the other side of the world, a subspecies of the wild turkey of Mexico was being raised by the Mayans and the Aztecs. How it gained its misleading English name is something of a mystery; though widely known as a "turkie-fowl" when served as a delicacy in the sixteenth century it was taken to Europe by the Conquistadors and had no connection with the Middle East.

In the wild, a Junglefowl lays an egg each day and, in common with many other species, will go on doing so until it can see the appropriate clutch of half a dozen. By taking eggs away it can be induced to go on laying indefinitely and provide a ready source of food. Selection for the birds that went on laying longest has produced modern hens that will lay as many as 340 eggs before they stop.

Domestic fowl are now found all over the world and an enormous variety of different kinds have been developed. The Junglefowl can still be recognized in the modern chicken, though many fancy breeds have also been created; in ducks and geese the changes have been greater. Large ducks, such as the Aylesbury breeds, may be four times as heavy as the original Mallard and most now have white plumage. Domestic geese now often carry so much weight that it would be quite impossible for them to make the Greylag's long migration flights.

Although some domestic poultry are still allowed to roam freely around the yard or farmstead, many are now intensely farmed by "factory" methods in row upon row of cages, where they have barely room to move and have either become egg-laying machines or are fattened up as rapidly as possible for slaughter.

Whereas factory farming is a comparatively recent development, pressured rearing has a very ancient history in the production of the French gourmet delicacy *pâté de foie gras*, made from the enlarged livers of geese that are force-fed. But those who criticize such treatment might look at what they do find acceptable, for animal exploitation always involved interference, if not obvious suffering.

The aggressiveness of the Junglefowl has been exploited by the selection of the most

A cock pit in eighteenth-century London. William Hogarth's engraving is satirical in intent but shows a typical scene of betting on a cockfight.

belligerent to face each other in cockfights. These have a very ancient history and still take place openly in many countries and clandestinely in some where they are against the law. The birds' natural weapons are sometimes supplemented by strapping sharp metal talons to their legs.

Pigeons are not now so widely eaten but they were once a very important food requiring little husbandry. Their domestication may be even older than that of the chicken and they were reared in large communities but usually free-flying, although the Romans adopted a kind of factory farming, shutting up the pigeons in towers called *columbaria* where they were fattened up on a diet of chewed bread. To make sure they did not lose weight through exercise, flight feathers were pulled out and sometimes even their legs broken.

The domestic pigeon is a form of the wild Rock Dove, which originally nested on rock ledges in caves and foraged for grain on the plains of Western Asia, around the Mediterranean and up the Atlantic coast as far as Scotland. It spread through the once forested regions of Europe as they fell to the plough, wherever local conditions or human activity provided cave-like nesting sites. It can usually find enough food for itself right through the winter or, if necessary, can be fed on a little stored grain, so it provided a useful source of fresh meat right through the year, whereas, because of the difficulty of finding fodder, most livestock were slaughtered in the autumn and dried or salted for the winter.

The ancient Egyptians, the civilizations of the Fertile Crescent and the Greeks all kept pigeons. The Arabs raised them in towers made up of stacks of tapering pipes, which simulated their natural cliff sites, sometimes built in groups to resemble a multi-turreted castle. Such structures could be found from Moorish Spain to Egypt. In northern Europe, where dove- and pigeon-keeping was restricted to feudal lords and those of higher rank, free-standing dovecotes were built along similar lines with thousands of nesting cavities in each. They were unpopular with other people because they fed on everybody's crops. When restrictions on who could keep them were relaxed, many a building would have rows of openings in a gable or wall end to allow access to pigeon nesting places.

A modern cockfight in Bangkok.

Pigeons may lay up to a dozen clutches of eggs each year, providing a plentiful supply of eggs or young squabs that could be taken from the nest while adults were out feeding. Culling to keep numbers in check provided more fresh meat.

Trained hunters

As well as domesticating birds to rear them for the table, people have exploited the birds' own hunting and fishing skills. Cormorants were trained to dive and bring back fish, first probably in Japan in the fifth century of our era, the custom then spreading to China and elsewhere. Galore Perrier, a sixteenth-century European traveler, described how

"At the hour appointed to fish, all the barges are brought together in a circle, where the river is shallow and the cormorants, tied together under the wings, are let leap down into the water, some under, some above, worth the looking upon. Each one as he hath filled his bag, goeth to his own barge and emptieth it, which done, he returneth to fish again. Thus having taken good store of fish, they set the cormorants at liberty, and do suffer them to fish for their own pleasure. There were in that city . . . twenty barges at the least of these aforesaid cormorants. I went almost every day to see them, yet I could never be thoroughly satisfied to see so strange a kind of fishing."

Perrier appears to be describing daytime fishing, but today cormorant fishing is usually a night occupation. The boats, poled like punts, each carry a lamp to attract the fish. The birds are tied to the boat by one leg and have another string or a soft leather collar around the neck, tight enough to prevent them swallowing any of the fish they catch. Forming a circle, the boats concentrate their lamps to form a pool of light in which fish soon shoal. Then the cormorants are released, each man urging on his bird with individual cries. They return, each to their boat, with any fish they

catch and, on releasing it, are fed mashed beans or pieces of fish small enough for them to swallow.

It seems likely that the idea was taken up in Europe by the sixteenth century, for Louis XIII of France kept cormorants at Fontainbleau and James I of England had an official Master of Cormorants. In Britain the practice still survived, or was reintroduced, in the mid-nineteenth century, but reports tell us little about it.

In modern Japan, cormorant fishing is now largely a tourist attraction, but in China fishermen on the Li River of Guangxi province still use the birds as a way of gathering their food. Each bird can catch enough to feed a fisherman and his family in addition to the bird's own needs.

Egyptian dovecotes made from Nile mud to house feral pigeons, are still used as a source of fertilizer.

Below *The interior of a circular medieval pigeon loft in England. The ladder pivots round the center post to give easy access to all the ledges and nesting holes. Droppings would accumulate on the floor.*

A Japanese woodblock print of night fishing with cormorants. Lines attach each bird to the boat.

Hunting for sport

Long before the Japanese began to use fishing cormorants, hawks were being set to kill other birds not just for the larder but in sport, in what became the art of the falconer. In China falconry may date back as early as 2000 B.C., though it possibly began even earlier, in India. The Persians were certainly using hawks by 1700 B.C. and may have learned how to train and handle them from the Indians.

Falconry was practiced by the Greeks and Romans and developed by the Franks and Visigoths to become a sport of kings. The Emperor Charlemagne banned serfs from hawking and even forbade abbots and abbesses from hawking on their own convent land. During the Middle Ages strict laws decreed what type of bird a person could or could not fly according to their rank or social status. Priests and gentlemen might fly a Goshawk or a sparrowhawk. Princes, dukes and earls could fly a Peregrine Falcon and their wives a Merlin. The flying of Gyrfalcons was reserved to royalty alone.

A sixth-century legal code, probably from Burgundy, gives some idea of the value placed on hawks in the punishment for stealing one. The Latin allows a variety of translations. One version requires that the thief should pay the hawk's owner six silver coins, plus a fine of two silver coins; read another way the punishment inflicted is to place six ounces of meat over the thief's testicles for the hawk to eat, or, more painfully, it could mean that the hawk should be placed on the offender's testicles and then allowed to eat six ounces of meat!

Hawking was usually undertaken on horseback, for hawks do not bring back their kill; the falconer must go to where the quarry falls. The hawk is carried on the wrist of a gloved hand, or sometimes, if there is a long distance

to ride to reach the hunting ground, it may be put in a cage. Its legs can be strapped to the wrist, or to a perch, by leather bands known as jesses and its head encased in a hood so that the bird sees nothing to disturb or distract it.

Before the use of the hood, the eyelids were sewn up with knotted threads passed through the lower lid just below the roots of the lashes, which when pulled drew them closed and were then tied over the head.

The hawk often wears a bell on the legs, or sometimes at the neck or top of the tail. Its tinkling helps to locate the bird. Two bells about a semitone apart in pitch are even better for they are easier to hear.

Falconry still has a strong following as a sport. Training a hawk requires skill and patience on the part of the falconer. Terence White's *The Goshawk* shows just how difficult it is for the novice. Barry Hines's book *A Kestrel for a Knave*, about a boy and his falcon in northern Britain, and *Kes*, Ken Loach's fine film based upon it, sadly prompted some people to try to catch falcons and train them, often with disastrous results for the birds. Taking wild birds is illegal in Britain.

In the Middle East, where falconry has long been practiced by the Bedouin for food, it remains a popular sport among wealthy sheiks. Birds are caught each year, trained and then released at the end of the season, despite the high prices that trained hawks fetch. Many medieval falconers probably did the same. A passage in a tenth-century schoolroom reader has a keeper complaining that the birds eat too much in the summer and require too much looking after. In the winter they catch enough to feed him and themselves but in spring he releases them in a wood and in the fall, since he is skilled at catching others — not just one but many — he catches young birds and trains them.

Modern falconry takes a toll of native birds in North Africa across to Pakistan and threatens the extinction of the Houbara Bustard. That bird has already become so scarce in Arabia

A falcon hooded and wearing jesses.

Left *A Mogul prince with his hooded falcon, painted about 1750.*

Right *A modern British falconer with a Peregrine Falcon (Falco peregrinus) on his wrist. Stout leather gauntlets are worn for the bird to perch on. The hood has just been removed ready for the bird to be sent hunting. The falconer must obtain a license and is limited to taking a set number of birds of particular species.*

that falconers travel to North Africa and Pakistan to hunt, going out into the desert in motoring parties with up to 90 falcons.

The demand for falcons, and the high prices they fetch, encourages an illegal trade in birds that are themselves seriously threatened.

Traditional Arab techniques for catching falcons range from using various snares and traps baited by pigeons to a man buried in the desert with his head camouflaged and holding a live pigeon in his hand. When a hawk comes down for the kill, the other hand grabs its legs!

Training and flying techniques vary according to the type of bird, type of prey and national traditions, but they are usually worked from the wrist, the way in which the falconer launches the bird helping it to attain speed.

Under fire

Portable firearms were already being used for hunting in the fifteenth century, although they were cumbersome and inaccurate. In the sixteenth and early seventeenth century "fowling pieces" were developed as long as 6 feet (1.8 m), because the long barrel gave a more accurate discharge. Long guns — some with barrels of even greater length — were later used for duck shooting from punts on lakes and marshes and gained the name punt guns. Instead of a single ball, they fired a number of small lead pellets (shot) that spread out as they left the barrel, giving a greater chance of hitting small moving targets such as birds.

It was not until improvements in firearm design and manufacture produced an accurate shorter and lighter weapon, making it possible to have a double-barreled gun, that firearms took a heavy toll on birds. By then, in Europe, the art of falconry had given place to sportsmen with a shotgun, though it continued as a sport in the Middle East and has seen a revival of interest in recent years.

Geese and ducks were heavily hunted and some goose wintering grounds almost completely cleared, removing a valuable resource that, before the days of refrigeration, supplied fresh winter meat when other kinds were unavailable.

Some of our ancestors were well aware of the need not to take too many birds; as early as 1534 the English Parliament had introduced a close season for wildfowl from June to August. Further legislation to prevent indiscriminate slaughter came in time to ensure there were birds for future sportsmen and wildfowling is now strictly controlled in both Europe and North America. Although firearms have become increasingly sophisticated, in Britain it is still considered unsporting for a pump gun or repeating action gun to be used. A double-barreled weapon is permitted but this limits the hunter to two shots before having to pause to reload or change guns, giving the quarry a chance to get out of range.

The pheasant, a bird originally from Asia and the Middle East and probably kept as an ornamental pet by the Romans, was widely introduced through most of Europe as a gamebird. A great many were taken to Britain from France after the Norman Conquest, and today's wild population is enormously boosted by the large numbers that are artificially reared and released in late summer just in time to be killed when the shooting season opens.

Landowners and gamekeepers eager to protect their birds have benefited wildlife in some ways but, by waging war against vermin and raptor species, they have seriously reduced the numbers of all birds of prey and scavengers. These birds have suffered further from habitat changes, which have removed their prey, and from the effects of agrochemicals.

The migration flights of numerous species from Africa to Europe take huge numbers of birds along set routes at easily predictable times. As ownership of firearms spread, increasing numbers of hunters lay in wait for migrants, both on the Mediterranean islands and on the mainland. It is not just the gamebird species regularly shot for sport that these hunters are after. Small songbirds, also destined for the gourmet table, often set in aspic or turned into pâté, form a large proportion of their quarry. On the island of Cyprus alone, between three and seven million birds were killed each year, with hunters in Portugal, Spain, France, Turkey and Malta taking millions more and an estimated 240 million or more in Italy. European legislation now protects all except the gamebirds, though these are now more widely defined to include not just the traditional species of pheasants, partridge, geese and duck, but also thrushes, Eurasian Blackbirds, Skylarks, Redwings and Fieldfares.

The Passenger Pigeon

The gun was largely responsible for the extinction of what was once America's most numerous bird species. Only two centuries ago there were probably several thousand million Pas-

Flocks of Passenger Pigeons were so dense that a single shot brought down many birds. When breech-loading guns became common in the 1880s the slaughter was even more efficient.

Martha, the last Passenger Pigeon, displayed stuffed in the National Museum in Washington D.C. The Passenger Pigeon (Ectopistes migratorius) was about 16 inches (40 cm) long with blue gray wings and back, reddish hazel on throat, breast and flanks, with the lower neck gold, purplish red or green, a black bill and bright orange eyes. Chief Pokagon of Michigan recorded that "it was proverbial with our fathers that if the Great Spirit in his wisdom could have created a more elegant bird in plumage, form and movement, he never did." But it was not its beauty that spelled out its doom but its edibility and the fact that it flocked in thousands.

swept close over the earth with inconceivable velocity, mounted perpendicularly so as to resemble a vast column and, when high, were seen wheeling and twisting within their continued lines, which then resembled the coils of a gigantic serpent."

Such huge numbers could strip an area so rapidly that the Bishop of Montreal once excommunicated the entire breed, but it was its taste rather than its depredations that encouraged people to strike them down with poles as they swept over hills, lay salt to attract them to nets or fire up into the tightly packed flocks and bring down a dozen or more birds with one shot. After dark, a shot fired up into the trees felled roosting birds. Just three hunters might bag 6,000 birds in a single night.

Native Americans did not hunt when adult pigeons were rearing young, but the incoming Europeans had no such qualms for there were so many that they believed with Audubon that

"The Passenger Pigeon needs no protection. Wonderfully prolific and having vast forests of the north as its breeding grounds, traveling hundreds of miles in search of food, it is here today and elsewhere tomorrow, and no ordinary destruction can lessen them or be missed from the myriads that were yearly produced."

He was wrong. As the forests were felled the pigeons' habitat was destroyed. Netting in New England was decimating populations. Railroad officials would telegraph sightings of a nesting flock so that hunters were alerted, the railroad profiting from the carriage of the birds to market. In 1878, five freight cars full of birds were dispatched each day for 30 days from a single flock. If birds were surplus or too mangled to be salable for human consumption, pigs might be fed on the carcasses.

When the pigeons became scarce most people believed that they had simply moved elsewhere. Although some states did pass legislation to protect nesting birds, these laws were usually ignored. Soon the big flocks were restricted to northern Michigan but the slaughter on the breeding grounds around Lake Superior continued.

There must have been some survivors and there were captive pigeons in zoos, but the zoo birds did not breed successfully; perhaps the community of the flock was an important aspect of their breeding behavior, and if so that would have affected the isolated birds still at liberty. So the bird that had once filled American skies became extinct.

senger Pigeons in North American skies; about half of the entire bird population of the United States. By 1914 only one was left, a bird called Martha, who died September 1 in Cincinnati Zoological Gardens.

The Passenger Pigeon was a woodland bird, living on beechnuts, acorns and chestnuts, though it would also take grain. It ranged over eastern North America from Canada south to the Gulf Coast and west to Montana and western Texas. John James Audubon described it gliding through the woods "like a thought," suddenly gone and searched for in vain, but it gathered in huge flocks and, as Audubon continued:

"when a hawk chanced to press upon the rear [of a flock], like a torrent, and with a noise like thunder . . . they darted forward in undulating and angular lines, descended and

Other extinctions

The disappearance of the Passenger Pigeon shocks because of its former huge numbers but there are many other bird species that have been made extinct by man. Overhunting was responsible for the demise of the Great Auk, once common in the Arctic, ranging south down Atlantic coasts to Spain and Florida. A fast swimmer, one of its original names was penguin — it was borrowed for Southern Hemisphere birds — and it too was flightless. On land it was awkward and slow, which made it easy to catch and kill. It was hunted by the Vikings and, during the breeding season especially, became a staple for later mariners and fishermen who, it is said, sometimes simply herded the birds into their boats using a sail stretched from shore. By 1829, the only known colony was on a small island off Iceland, which itself was then destroyed by volcanic activity. Expeditions did find a few survivors on the neighboring islet of Eldey but, instead of being protected and left to recolonize, as one would hope they would be today, even these were hunted down to provide specimens for museums and collectors. The last living pair were slaughtered and their egg destroyed in June 1844.

Flightless birds are particularly vulnerable when hunted. The Dodo, a native of Mauritius, was a huge member of the pigeon family, or closely related to it, and weighed about 50 pounds (22.7 kg). No one paid it any attention until one was brought back to Europe in the sixteenth century, when the Dutch who found them called them *walghvogels*, because they tasted so awful. Nonetheless, Mauritius and its neighboring islands, where two different but very similar kinds of birds were found, were far from other landfall and later sailors using them as a staging post killed many for food.

When a colony was established on Mauritius, the settlers found eggs and chicks better to eat than the adult birds, and the pigs and monkeys which they introduced ate them too. By 1638, an English traveler was mourning the disappearance of the birds that had intrigued him on a visit only four years earlier, but some did survive until about 1681, whereas the related species, the Solitaires, lasted on Réunion until about 1750 and those on Rodriguez almost to the end of the eighteenth century.

In New Zealand the lack of predators allowed the development of a number of flightless birds, kept safe by the islands' isolation. The Kiwi, now the country's national symbol, still survives but it once had more than 20 larger relatives, the Moas, which ranged from the size of a turkey to a towering 12 feet (3.7 m). Some were extinct even before the Maoris arrived in New Zealand 1,000 years ago. Although one or more species possibly survived into the eighteenth century, the majority are thought to have become extinct by the end of the seventeenth. It is probable that the clearing (by burning) of land for agriculture (particularly in the South Island where there were most species) played as important a part in their decline into extinction as did hunting by man (they were apparently good eating). However, the full story of their disappearance is not known.

Other New Zealand birds have been more affected by the dogs, rats and other predators introduced by Europeans. Unable to escape into the trees, and with no defensive behavior patterns against predators, the flightless, ground-nesting birds were, and are, particularly vulnerable. In 1894 on Stephens Island, for instance, the pet cat of the lighthouse keeper brought home specimens of a previously unknown species, the Stephens Island Wren, but having first served science, in the year that followed its hunting skills made this endemic species quite extinct. The appearance of another species, the Takahe, was known only from four specimens, the last taken in 1898. Brilliantly blue-green with a distinctive red frontal shield, it is as big as a small turkey. Then, in 1948, a small population was discovered surviving in a southern alpine valley. Now, with protection and a careful breeding program, the Takahe is beginning to be re-established.

No such possibility survives for the Elephant-bird of Madagascar, not so tall as some of the moas at 9 feet (2.7 m) but weighing almost half a ton (500 kg). Its huge, thick-shelled eggs with a volume of 2 gallons (9 L) are still occasionally found but the bird itself died out more than half a millennium ago. Although it could not fly, it is possible that this was the legendary Roc of the *Thousand and One Tales of the Arabian Nights* story of Sinbad the Sailor.

Extinction is part of the process of evolution, whether caused by environmental change, unbalanced predation or species competition. Human pressure and predations could be considered part of that natural balance. However, *Homo sapiens* is the only species that has achieved sufficient dominance over and control of others to upset and interfere with long-established patterns. It is impossible to accurately assess human impact in the distant past but over just the last 300–400 years at least 60 bird species have become extinct and humans — either by hunting, predation by species they introduced or by their destruction of habitat — have been responsible in most cases. We continue to destroy the global environment on such a scale that more are bound to disappear, though they are only a fraction of the losses of other creatures and the enormous number of plants, some as yet unknown, which are disappearing even as you read.

The Great Auk (Pinguinus impennis), *as illustrated in John Gould's* Birds of Great Britain *a quarter century after it became extinct. The Great Auk was about as large as a goose, standing about 2 feet (60 cm) tall. It had a white belly, a coal black head and back, with a white patch between the eye and bill, which was shaped like that of the Razorbill* (Alca torda). *It laid a pear-shaped egg, about 5 inches (12.5 cm) long.*

ALCA IMPENNIS.

STOLEN PLUMES

Clothing and decoration

It was not just the flesh of birds or the sport of killing that attracted hunters: skins could be used for clothing and colorful feathers used as decoration. The people of the Scottish island of St. Kilda made shoes from the skins of the gannets that they ate; nothing was wasted from their catch and their harvests were controlled to ensure future supplies, but it was when skins and feathers were frivolously used by people thousands of miles away from the birds' homes that the greatest slaughter ensued.

Many cultures used feathers as decoration. The people of Hawaii made beautiful cloaks from the feathers of native birds, including the yellow feathers of the O'o, which might take 500,000 feathers for a single cloak. The Maori also made feather cloaks, and the Aztecs tied feathers into fabric as it was made on the loom as well as making feather headdresses and decorating shields and panels worn on the back mounted on wicker frames with insignia and animals picked out in feathers. A fine round feather shield from Mexico, now in the Museum für Völkerkunde in Vienna, may have been presented to Hernando Cortez by the Aztec emperor Montezuma, and a magnificent headdress of green quetzal plumes shipped to Europe in the early years of the Conquistadors also survives.

In South America the people of Peru also made feather cloaks or ponchos and feather designs were used to decorate ceremonial standards. On the eastern side of the continent too, the brilliantly colored feathers of tropical birds were used, and are still, to make necklaces and body ornaments — a practice now often adopted by modern European and North American jewelry makers. In Brazil feathers can also be found glued to the surface of wooden "Cara Granda" masks, worn by the Tapirape people for the harvest festival of the Banana Fiesta.

The native peoples of what is now the United States and Canada also used feather adornment, sewn onto leather clothing or placed in the hair. The position of each feather and their number had a significance comparable to a badge of rank and the kind of feather, its trim or the dye applied to it might all be significant of achievement in battle or other attributes. The codes varied not only from tribe to tribe but were particular to societies within a tribe.

The "war bonnet," a headdress decorated with closely placed rows of feathers, seems to have been first worn by tribes to the east, spreading to the plains and westward. The Blackfoot used a feather crown with tall sides, the Californian tribes used raven and scarlet woodpecker feathers with which they incorporated long reeds tipped with poppy flowers and cotton balls, but the most elaborate were the headdress of the Sioux.

Native American feather decoration and symbolism has been continually developing.

MOHO NOBILIS, (MERREM) ♂ & ♀ AD.

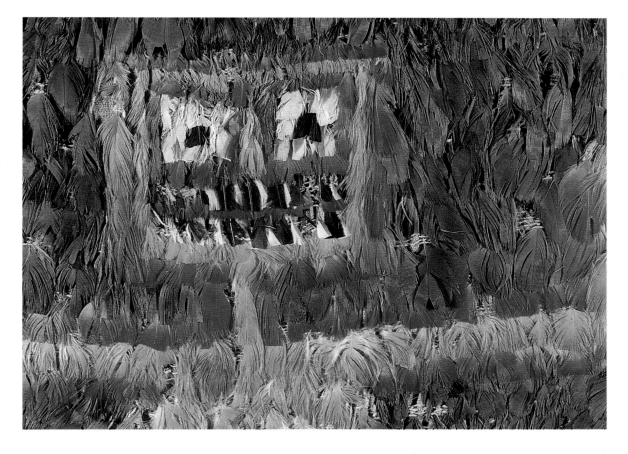

The rapid spread of the pheasant in North America, after its introduction into Oregon in 1880, soon saw both individual feathers and full pheasant skins being used in Plains Indian clothing. They were especially popular in the "Crow" or "Raven," a sort of circular bustle supported on a belt and worn on the back. The bustle was itself a relatively recent development worn by men of the Omaha and other Plains tribes who had gained high war honors. Its centerpiece was a rawhide frame covered with the entire skin of an eagle or a crow and only the feathers of the other birds that appeared after a battle were originally used in its construction.

Feathers are used by Native Americans to decorate fans and batons as well as for body and costume ornament and bird quills, dyed and softened for attachment to hide, were also often used by Native North Americans in the same way as porcupine quills to make a form of appliqué decoration.

In Europe, too, feathers were a popular decoration. The Egyptians used peacock feathers to make fans and they set a high value on beautiful and exotic plumage. Ancient Greek women dressed their hair with heron feathers and Roman soldiers decorated their helmets with plumes from the domestic cockerel.

Centuries later, Genoa, Florence and Pisa became centers for a trade in ostrich feathers imported from North Africa where they could still be hunted, and those of egret, heron, pheasant and colorfully plumaged indigenous birds. As European voyages of exploration made contact with other parts of the world, a trade developed in exotics such as the beautiful birds-of-paradise, whose skins were already being imported in considerable numbers by the end of the sixteenth century.

For centuries it was only the wealthy who decked themselves out in feather finery, usually on their hats or to embellish a coiffure but, as living standards began to rise and better communications expanded in the latter half of the nineteenth century, more and more people wanted to follow the fashions of society and there was a huge expansion in the demand for feathers for the millinery trade. Already the survival of the Ostrich was under threat and, though the development of Ostrich farming replenished the supply and saved that species, increasing demand and pressure for new exotic fancy feathers began to affect bird populations around the world.

Molted feathers tended to be dirty and lack sparkle, so, although fresh feathers could some-

PEHRISKA-RUHPA.

Hunters in Papua New Guinea used knob-headed arrows to stun birds-of-paradise that fell from their perches without damaging their plumage. They were then skinned and stretched on a frame to harden. Some European scientists were baffled by these birds that, when they reached Europe, had no bones or feet, deciding that they lived always in the air. An illustration from A. R. Wallace's The Malay Archipelago.

Below *Late nineteenth-century fashion demanded a lavish use of feathers in millinery and even to decorate dresses. Here Edith Evans, as Lady Bracknell in the film version of Oscar Wilde's* The Importance of Being Earnest *illustrates the trend.*

times be pulled from the living bird, collectors usually found it simpler to kill the bird to get them. This happened with the egrets, for instance, whose dorsal feathers were particularly sought. They nest high up in the trees and, to take the few feathers that were marketable, millions of birds were being killed; one year it was estimated that one and a half million egrets were killed in Venezuela alone! Nesting time found the birds both in finest plumage and at their most vulnerable, but instead of seeing the raising of a new generation, it ended with the parents slaughtered and the young dying of starvation in their nests.

The assault on the avian world was waged all around the world: from the quetzals of Mexico to the hummingbirds of South America, to the albatrosses of Hawaii, the Lyrebirds of Australia, the pheasants of India, the weaver birds of Africa, and even the kingfishers of Britain.

Hats were weighed down with whole flocks of birds; hummingbirds quivered over artificial flowers, severed wings pointed to the sky. Pieces of bird skins, with their feathers, were layered on collars, birds' heads decorated the hems of dresses and, as if the demands of fashion were not enough, carefully mounted displays of birds under glass domes became a desirable addition to the drawing room, though this was part of a vogue that saw every kind of animal from pike to domestic kittens stuffed and put on show.

Few of those who flaunted their stolen plumes gave any thought to the carnage and pain caused to get them, but the mindless destruction did not go unprotested. Laws against cruelty to animals were already on the statute book and organizations to protect them had already been formed. In Britain in 1869 an act was passed in Parliament that gave protection to seabirds, not so much on humanitarian grounds as

because the birds helped fishermen to locate their catch and aided farmers by eating soil and crop pests.

In 1880 a further act gave more general protection by establishing a close season for wild birds. Then, in 1885, the Rev. F. O. Morris, who had been involved in pressing for the parliamentary reforms, founded the Plumage League, its membership restricted to women, to campaign against the use of real birds as decoration and encourage the use of artificial plumage. Four years later, another body was formed by women who wanted to stop the trade in exotic bird feathers. This eventually became the Royal Society for the Protection of Birds, though it took more than 30 years — till 1921 — before they achieved their objective of stopping the trade.

In the United States, too, there was concern and in 1886 the first Audubon Society was founded, the National Association of Audubon Societies being created in 1905 and the prohibition of the import of birds' skins and plumage coming in 1913, some years before the European legislation. Ladies arriving at U.S. Customs were met by officers who snipped the feathers from the hats and gowns that they had purchased on their European trips!

There is still some demand for feathers, and a supply, mainly from the Far East. This is centered on domestic fowl and duck feathers, and feathers of wild ducks, but also includes kingfishers and owls and probably others. A few decades ago, following the Chinese occupation of Tibet, quantities of wing feathers of large birds of prey, apparently from this region, were offered for sale. Stuffed birds and pictures made from bird feathers are still offered from China.

The fashion for feathers could always flare up again. Whenever a market exists for live creatures or parts of their bodies, suppliers can be found.

Mattresses and comforters

Feathers are not only useful for decoration. The soft down feathers of the young and those from the breast that the adult uses to line the nest, can be enclosed in bags to make warm coverings and comfortable surfaces to sleep upon. Domesticated pigeons, geese and ducks were convenient sources of feathers, but it is those of the Eider Duck that have long been considered the most superior.

In England, eiderdown has given its name to the quilted bedcover that Americans call a comforter, though it may not be eider feathers that fill it. Goose feathers were the traditional filling for the deep feather beds that preceded modern sprung mattresses and waterbeds, and feathers remain the favored filling for the continental duvet, whose use is now so common, and for the best pillows.

No birds have to be killed in collecting eider down. In Iceland and Denmark, wild flocks have been farmed by giving them protection and they have been encouraged to nest in colonies that may exceed 10,000 birds. The eider's nest is a simple hollow lined with vegetation and a mass of down. The birds like to nest up against something or in a sheltered niche, so arranging groups of stones or sticks spaced across a site attracts them. Farmers also set up sticks from which they fly colored ribbons, which also seem to please the ducks, and even aeolian chimes. The attraction may be that they serve to scare off predators. The female not only lines the nest hollow with down but covers the eggs with it when she leaves them. She can line the equivalent of about one and a half nests, so has a surplus, of which farmers take some from the upper lining of the nest before the eggs hatch; this is best quality down. Later, when the chicks have been successfully reared the rest of the lining is collected. Poorer quality because it is matted and dirty, it has to be carefully cleaned.

There are still further uses for feathers. For centuries, until the development of the metal nib, bird quills were used as pens, feathers still fledge arrows and the shuttlecocks used to play badminton, and they are even tied together to make artificial flies and used as lures by fishermen.

Farmers' friends?

Birds take grain seeds and can raid fruit crops, as well as annoy gardeners when, for instance, they tear at the petals of the early crocus, but they also play an active role in controlling soil pests, eating snails and slugs and picking insects off plants.

All kinds of methods have been tried for keeping birds from stealing or damaging crops. The only really effective way is to cage them — not the birds, the crops — and a great deal of soft fruit is grown inside cages so that the birds cannot get at it. This is not so practical for large orchard trees and certainly not for grain.

In time past children were employed as bird scarers, but with changing social attitudes and opportunities other methods had to be developed. The scarecrow dressed to simulate a man or woman may work when it is first erected but is soon as likely to be a perch as a deterrent. Strings of metal foil, vibrating wires, cat faces with reflective eyes, even plastic snakes have been tried. Arranging a series of irregularly timed and placed detonations will at least make a flock of birds take to the air, though not ensure that they will not soon come back to feed. The only effective method is probably to go out into the fields and create a great deal of noise and movement, as Indian villagers do, banging their cooking pots, to keep birds off crops as they near readiness for harvest.

Some farmers and gardeners, however, will tolerate a modest level of loss and ignore the rooks or gulls following the plow, and gardeners may even welcome a friendly robin waiting for pickings as they turn the soil.

Birds not only help in pest control; their droppings have been used as a valued fertilizer. This was a by-product of dovecotes and pigeon lofts and could be harvested in quantity from the haunts of cliff-living birds, though it seems not to have been exploited in the case of the Passenger Pigeon flocks. There are many places where this forms an important economic resource. Herring Gull colonies in Massachusetts, for instance, produce a harvest of 100,000–200,000 tons of nitrate- and phosphate-rich droppings known as guano.

Extensive deposits of guano in the Gulf of California, on islands off the Cape of Good Hope in South Africa, in the southwestern Pacific on Nauru and Ocean Island (Banaba) in the Gilbert Islands (Kiribati), and on Christmas Island in the Indian Ocean, have all been commercially exploited. It is possible that much of the deep deposits on Christmas Island may be a build-up of marine fossils but on the Ballestas Islands, off the coast of Peru, the guano (which gets its name from the Guanay Cormorant of Chilean and Peruvian coasts) had been built up since the Pleistocene. Beginning early in the nineteenth century, a hundred years of digging removed most of the original deposits but the birds still produce sufficient quantity every year (about 35 pounds (16 kg) from each Guanay in a single season) to maintain the trade.

On the bare rock of the Peruvian islands removing the guano does no harm. Elsewhere it may remove vegetation and damage topsoil as well as interfering with the birds, though the guano itself produces a change in vegetation from, say, fine-leaved grasses to nettles, docks and grasses that thrive on nitrogen. In parts of Japan, straw is laid under the trees where cormorant colonies breed inland to aid the collection of guano for fertilizing paddy fields and in both South Africa and Florida commercial collectors have built offshore platforms to attract cormorants to roost and breed, and to create sites from which the guano is easily collected.

Collecting Eider Duck (Somateria mollissima) *eggs and down at a nesting colony in Iceland.*

A flock of Red-billed Quelea (Quelea quelea) *in Namibia. These birds can be a serious threat to farmers in the savanna grasslands of Africa. They make sudden irruptive migrations to follow the rains and coupled with a breeding pattern triggered by rainfall, appropriate conditions can suddenly create huge increases in numbers in already large flocks, making exceptional demands on food sources. They can strip a neighborhood like a plague of locusts and are an especial problem for rice growers.*

CAGE BIRDS AND ORNAMENTAL BIRDS

When humans first domesticated birds as a source of food probably they did not keep them shut in cages, but the pleasure to be had from birdsong or attractive plumage, together perhaps with an urge for dominion over other creatures, seems to have led to birds being captured and confined by the ancient civilizations of the Old World and the New. Modern jungle tribal peoples have pet birds, and it is likely that pet keeping has a very ancient history, but it is to the Ancient Egyptians that we must look for the first records of wild birds being kept and exotic species being introduced. Ancient China, India and the Middle Eastern cultures all kept birds and by the time of King Solomon peacocks and pheasants, like pigeons, were already being kept both as ornament and as a future meal. Pigeons might be retained by providing food and nesting places and fowl prevented from flying by clipping the wings, but small singing birds were kept in aviaries or shut in little cages.

Wing clipping

Bird keepers whose birds are not caged but want to stop them from flying away have to resort to reducing their ability to fly. However, especially with ornamental birds, they do not want to lose the flight feathers. Trimming the edges of the feathers reduces a bird's flying ability, though this has to be repeated after each molt. Trimming one wing throws the bird off balance. Trimming both gives the bird a limited dipping, woodpecker-style flight that limits its range but puts a strain on the bird and especially the wing muscles.

Various methods of surgery have been tried. Cutting muscle or ligaments is liable to produce a dragging wing. With mainly walking, running or swimming birds, cutting off the bone at the end of the wing, the carpometacarpus, complete with flight feathers has been the usual solution, although it leaves one wing permanently short. With waterfowl this is now usually done within a day or two of hatching when the bones are still soft and partly cartilaginous.

By the fifth century B.C., sparrows, starlings, blackbirds, magpies, jackdaws and nightingales were already favorite cagebirds. Parrots were

Mr. and Mrs. William Chase by Joseph Wright (1734–1797) shows this prosperous couple with their parrot.

Not in front of Polly!

Owning a talking bird can be fraught with problems, quite apart from looking after it! Some species' skills in mimicry are amazing, but unfortunately their taste in what to imitate may not be their owner's and tact is rarely an apparent characteristic.

The parrot or myna that imitates a road drill or next door's Siamese cat may be just an irritant, worse if it discovers a sound that prompts a reaction in a human or another animal. When it perfects the doorbell or the telephone it becomes a nuisance.

Your children may welcome the excuse that they thought it was the bird, not you, that was calling (and it usually will be). However, when it imitates you perfectly screaming your spouse's name and "where the expletive expletive have you put the expletive car keys?" you cannot pass it off as learned from the sailor who used to own it.

Bird mimics always seem to give their most outrageous performances in front of the wrong people. They may even imitate those people if they are regular visitors, or worse, repeat your comments about them!

Talking birds are marvelous, but never let them within earshot of anyone from whom you have *any* secrets.

A nineteenth-century Indian woodcut. Mynas can be as clever mimics as parrots.

tamed in India and Persia, where a Greek traveler saw a talking parakeet in 401 B.C., though it was nearly a century later before they were first taken back to Greece. These birds also found their way to Egypt, and became extremely popular among the wealthy patricians of ancient Rome, especially if they were good talkers.

At the time of his victory over Marc Antony, Octavius Caesar, the future Emperor Augustus, paid a high price for a raven that could greet him with *"Ave Caesar Victor Imperator."* No doubt he did not realize the dealer had also taught another bird to call out Antony's praises in case the other side won! Roman trainers hid behind a mirror to teach their birds to speak, hoping that their pupil would think it was another bird speaking to it, but birds mimic many sounds other than those of birds.

Exotic birds were highly valued and exchanged as gifts between the courts of medieval Europe, whereas more ordinary folk might have a native lark or Goldfinch in a cage hanging near a window or outside a door.

By the tenth century the Mute Swan had already been semi-domesticated in many parts of Europe, appreciated for its elegance but even more for its meat on the banqueting table. By the time of the Crusades, a variety of parrots could be found in the homes of the nobility and high clerics in much of Europe. Later the voyages to the New World, where Spanish Conquistadors discovered the well-stocked aviaries of the Aztec emperors, brought back the macaw to Europe.

Until the sixteenth century, though the fowl and other birds allowed to range freely might breed, cagebirds had to be caught in the wild, and most still were until the mid-twentieth century. Goldfinches were probably the most frequently kept in Europe, bulbuls in the Middle East and cardinals in America. Then a bird was found that could be tamed and would regularly breed in captivity. This was the Canary, from the Canary Islands off the west coast of Africa, which is first mentioned in a treatise of 1558.

Although these Dog Islands (from the Latin *Canis*; the bird takes its name from them) were known to the Phoenicians and other ancient seamen, the bird seems to have gone unremarked until the islands became part of Spain in 1479 but, once known, it soon became popular elsewhere. Canaries were already known in England and in Germany before the end of the sixteenth century, and it was in these countries that many of the numerous different modern breeds were evolved.

Canaries

The original Canary (*Serinus canaria*) is a small yellow and brown species of finch with a lively manner and a cheerful song. The familiar yellow bird of today is the result of controlled breeding usually suppressing the dark pigments in the plumage.

Breeding has also produced a wide range of colors in shades and mixtures of white, red (which needs a carotene-rich diet to maintain the color), green and brown, tufted headcaps and variations in body shape. Birds produced by crossbreeding with Red Hooded Siskins (to produce red) and Mules (hybrids with other finches such as the Goldfinch and Linnet), are not taxonomically true canaries but are exhibited as such. The Roller, Malinois and Spanish Timbrado are considered the most musical breeds.

For over 300 years, canaries were the most popular of cagebirds. The African Collared Dove also proved able to breed in a comparatively small cage and became quite popular, mainly for its sandy-colored or white variants known as Barbary Doves, but it was the Budgerigar, introduced to Europe by John Gould in 1840, which challenged and has now surpassed the popularity of the Canary.

Parrots are companionable birds but the clever mimicry of some can become a liability!

Right *An intensive red variegated canary, one of the many breeds developed by canary fanciers.*

The only birds most people could keep were those that could feed and breed on a diet of seed. A round head with short features, like a child's, elicits the parental instinct in people. Hence the popularity of the Canary in which these are combined. The parrots could supersede this and the Budgerigar, a desert parrot that could survive on a dry seed and water diet, was ideal. It is bred to have a still larger and rounder head, and the fact that some could be taught to talk confirmed its desirability for many people.

It was not until the present century that faster communications, improved aviculture and a popular demand for exotic species led to the development by the 1930s of a considerable international trade in other small birds. The expansion of air freight after World War II saw millions of birds being transported, often under very poor conditions. Quite apart from any humanitarian considerations, and although

*A detail from Elizabeth Gould's lithograph of Budgerigars (*Melopsittacus undulatus*) for John Gould's* Birds of Australia. *It was Gould who introduced the Budgerigar to Europe. The name is a corruption of the aboriginal "betcherrygah," whereas their scientific name of* undulatus *reflects their typical up and down flight pattern.*

Right *A Yellow-faced Sky-blue Budgerigar. One of the many color forms through blue, yellow, white and violet that have been bred from the light green and yellow wild grass parakeets seen in flocks in Australia. The development of new forms is one of the attractions of the bird to aviculturalists but its popularity as a pet is based more on its parrot family characteristics: it seems to have a lively intelligence, rather humanoid traits in the way it climbs around, looks in mirrors and will play with toys and it talks, or more accurately is a good mimic of all kinds of sounds.*

not on so huge a scale as bird hunting for the feather market, the increasing impact of this trade on individual species, with great numbers of birds dying in the process of capture and transportation, has made the imposition of bans and strict controls essential. The capture and keeping of native species and the importation of wild birds is now illegal in many countries.

Cages and aviaries

The first cages were probably made of twigs and strong stems. Wicker, bamboo and similar materials are still used to make cages in a variety of shapes, some traditional to particular areas. The development of metal rods and wire made it possible to make cages with secure sides that would give greater visibility but it was not until the development of the commercial production of wire mesh netting that large housing could be easily constructed. Yet aviaries not only formed part of the menagerie collections of emperors and kings but were a decorative feature of the gardens of wealthy Romans and Renaissance lords.

The Roman scholar Marcus Terentius Varro (116–27 B.C.), in a treatise on farming and gardening, describes the aviaries at his Casinum villa that were set in a quadrangle 48×72 feet (14.4×22.6 m) with a rounded extension. There were free-standing cages in the middle of a walk and open colonnades on either side, closed in at the top and between the columns with a hemp net. At the far end a circular building, again with netting between columns, formed a series of divided cages to house songbirds such as nightingales and blackbirds, and to provide space for a luxurious dining area. At a villa at Tusculum his contemporary Lucullus had an aviary-dining room where birds flew freely as his guests ate dishes of thrushes and ortolans.

Englishman Francis Bacon, in his essay *On Gardens*, published 1,650 years later, recommends cages of birds to be set about the main part of a garden and André Mollet's *Jardin de Plaisir* (1651), again reminds the reader that one should not neglect aviaries among the ornaments of a pleasure garden. As Philip II of Spain (1556–97) had not at his Palacio del Pardo near Madrid, where the empty moat was planted with flowers and the arches beneath two of its bridges turned into aviaries. At the Eremitage in Bayreuth, Germany, the Neues Schloss was originally built about 1750 as a bird house and an orangery, and at the Nyphenburg Schlosspark, Munich, an aviary was added in 1757. In Britain there is an elegant eighteenth-century rococo aviary at Waddesdon Manor and at Dropmore House one in nineteenth-century Chinese style.

Those are only just a few examples of some of the grander aviaries and bird rooms. Today all kinds of people have taken up aviculture with a small aviary in their backyard, but few can have indulged their hobby so far as the Marques de Marianco. In his gardens at the

Parque de Sama, west of Tarragona, Spain, laid out in 1881, not only were there aviaries but between each tree along an avenue of oriental planes he set a parrot on a perch.

In zoological collections, too, aviaries became an important feature. In 1829, Decimus Burton designed a beautiful parrot cage for the London Zoological Garden, later used for ravens but now only a decorative feature by the Fellows'

At the Villa Barbarigo, at Valsanzibio in the Italian Veneto, the domed aviary is on an island (originally used for breeding rabbits) in a pond.

Below *An aviary design by eighteenth-century English landscape designer Humphry Repton.*

The Snowdon Aviary at London Zoo was an exciting concept that aimed to give a more natural experience to the visitor while providing better conditions for the birds. Unfortunately its concept was flawed but its problems offer an object lesson to other designers.

it excited considerable enthusiasm as an architectural concept.

With hindsight it is an example of the problems such structures produce. The provision of a cliff for nesting seabirds was negated by a raised walkway above and in front of it that nesting birds would not tolerate. The enclosure gave more flying space than most cages but the angularity of the structure produced pockets into which birds could drive each other, putting more vulnerable species at the mercy of aggressive ones. The internal support structure was difficult to keep free of droppings and stresses on the outer cover necessitated frequent repair of splits high above. There was no way in which the upper space could be reached to catch birds or to retrieve injured ones, and the difficulty of providing resting perches and possibly design faults in relation to winds were perhaps why birds made little use of the upper half.

The "walk-through" bird room has also become a feature of tropical bird exhibits where hummingbirds and other species flit past the eye in exciting proximity, although given a choice, birds clearly prefer humans to be outside the enclosure — they feel safer.

Design problems apart, it is probably time that the concept of "walk-through" enclosures was reviewed. Such structures may give pleasure to the people using them, but they cause stress to the birds — and many other animals — who need areas of safe retreat and appear to be more at ease behind a wire barrier.

enclosure, for it does not meet modern standards for housing birds. Zoo specimens are still too often confined in small spaces but modern construction methods and materials have now been used to create aviaries with wide flying spaces for even larger birds, such as the one designed for London by Lord Snowdon with Cedric Price and Frank Newby.

Planned to house many species in a variety of environments, including water features, and so that visitors would not only view birds from outside but would walk through among them,

Bird therapy

A budgerigar or other small cagebird is one of the least demanding of pets. It does not have to be taken for walks, poses no problems with its toilet and does not cost much to feed. Yet it has been shown that keeping a budgerigar has a very beneficial effect, especially for the elderly or handicapped person living alone. It does not force you to go out or provide an excuse for contact with strangers as dogs often do, nor give the opportunity for affectionate physical contact that comes with a cat, but they can make people feel more secure and less lonely, give a sense of being needed and of interaction.

It is claimed that pets can improve the chances for and speed of recovery in postoperative and convalescent patients. They now also play a role in socializing those with psychiatric problems. Budgies became an integral part of a pet program at the Ohio State Hospital for the Criminally Insane. This was originally begun when one of the inmates found an injured wild bird and tried to nurse it and others began to get involved. Caring for budgies, fish and other small animals that were introduced, seemed to reduce violence in prisoners and produced

increased trust between patients and therapists. In a film made in the prison in 1979 one man, a multiple murderer, seen with his budgie, which he would turn and kiss while the budgie gently pecked him back, told the cameraman "This is my first friend. I love him and he loves me. I didn't know what love was until I was given this bird."

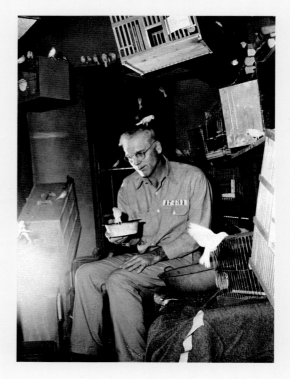

Right inset *Burt Lancaster as Robert Stroud in* The Bird Man of Alcatraz, *in John Frankenheimer's film about him. A convicted murder in the notorious California prison, he developed a deep interest in ornithology and his devotion to his birds helped him through half a century of incarceration.*

MESSAGE CARRIERS

A dove brings a green shoot back to Noah; a woodcut from a fifteenth-century German Bible.

The Hebrew authors of the book of Genesis describe how the 600-year-old Noah, after ten months afloat in the ark with the animals that were to restock the world, waited a further 40 days and then released a raven and a dove. The raven did not return but the dove, finding the earth still covered with water, came back. A week later Noah released the dove again and it came back with an olive branch in its beak, then after another seven days he let it out once more and this time it too failed to return. Since then, the dove and its olive branch have been a lasting symbol of reconciliation and peace, a messenger between God and man.

The Jewish faith is not the only one to envisage its god in the heavens and birds are a common messenger between sky gods and man. In the Classical world, the eagle was Zeus's messenger. For the Hopi Indians too, it was the eagle that was a messenger to and from the spirits, whereas among some North American tribes this role was assigned to the crow. It is the dove, however, in its domesticated form of the pigeon, that has long been used as a messenger between mortals.

Probably first raised as food, the pigeon's homing abilities are said to have been exploited by Persians, Assyrians and Phoenicians to send back military intelligence. A pigeon can fly faster and more directly than a person or a horse can run, so it made an ideal message carrier. The Ancient Egyptians took pigeons on their ships, releasing one when approaching port to give notice of arrival, and the Greeks and Romans used them to carry news of sporting events. Julius Caesar is reported using them during the conquest of Gaul and they were employed by Saracen armies at the time of the Crusades; the crusaders sent up Peregrine Falcons to intercept them. A pigeon post was in use in Baghdad in the twelfth century and under the Mamelukes in Egypt in the following century.

Peregrine Falcons have been under suspicion by pigeon owners right up to the present day because they fail to discriminate between wild and tame pigeons. It was the demand by British racing pigeon keepers for their control in the 1960s that led to the discovery that the continued existence of Peregrines was threatened by the use of toxic chemicals. In spite of many conservation schemes, they are only gradually reestablishing themselves, and this has led to pigeon keepers making fresh demands for their control.

Carrier pigeons were used to carry messages back into towns that were besieged: at Acre and Jerusalem in Palestine, Leyden in the Netherlands, Venice and, most famously perhaps, during the Siege of Paris in 1870.

They were used by Paul Julius von Reuter in 1850 to form a link between Aachen and Brussels, terminal points of the German and French/Belgian telegraph systems, speeding communications for his newly-founded news agency. In Britain they carried the results of race meetings at Ascot and Newmarket back to London sporting journals such as *Bell's Life*. Some Belgian financiers began to use pigeons to carry stock market reports from London and Paris (leading to competition to produce the fastest and most reliable birds and giving an impetus to pigeon racing as a sport) and various British business companies established private pigeon posts to communicate between their head offices and provincial branches.

In the later nineteenth century, the French, German, Russian and Italian governments all set up army pigeon lofts and, despite the development of telegraphy and radio, they continued to be used in both twentieth-century World Wars, especially for sending messages back from units deep within enemy territory. They were trained to fly at night and even to home back to mobile lofts.

Not all pigeons got through; eleventh-century crusaders chronicled one example of a pigeon killed by a hawk that fell near the tent of the Bishop of Apt and was found to be carrying a message from the governor of Acre to rouse the

Moslems of Palestine against the invaders. Messages were often duplicated to make it more certain that one reached its destination.

A once famous war hero was Cher Ami, a British-bred pigeon serving with a U.S. Battalion from New York at the front line during World War I. His head wounded, blind in one eye, and a leg shattered by gunfire almost as soon as he was released, he flew 25 miles (40 km) back to base in 25 minutes, his message carrier still strapped to a leg that was stripped to a few strands of sinew. The pigeons' importance was shown by a German order that, as their troops advanced into French and Belgian territory, they should destroy all Allied pigeons.

During World War II, an Army Pigeon Service, made up of experienced pigeon fanciers, was set up to control the use of pigeons by the British forces and a voluntary civilian National Pigeon Service created to supply pigeons, though the Army later also bred and trained its own. More than 200,000 birds were supplied by civilian lofts. Breeders received a supply of pigeon feed to supplement their rations but many had to go out collecting acorns to supplement what was available.

Royal Air Force Coastal Command aircraft carried pigeons for release if planes had to "ditch" at sea; minesweepers carried them to send back information on newly discovered mines at sea and more than 17,000 pigeons were dropped over occupied countries as a means of gathering intelligence. They were parachuted down in cardboard containers after bombing raids with a message carrier, message pad, pencil and instructions on how to attach the carrier to the bird's leg, together with a bag of corn to feed the pigeon for a couple of days. Many birds ended up as a meal for people short of food but of 17,000 dropped more than 10 per cent reached home with valuable information. German occupying forces announced the death penalty for anyone found harboring pigeons.

In India some birds were trained to fly back and forth between two points. This "boomerang" training was based on the behavior pattern of the wild Rock Dove that roosts in one place and feeds in another, but it is only possible over relatively short distances.

The U.S. Army established its own pigeon unit operating in the Mediterranean and Pacific theaters of war. Several of its birds gained military decorations, including Anzio Boy who completed 30 missions, many of them carrying messages during the initial stages of the Anzio beachhead in 1943.

Thirty-two pigeons were recipients of the Dickin Medal, instituted in 1943 to recognize the outstanding war services by British dogs, horses and pigeons and named after the founder of the People's Dispensary for Sick Animals, the charitable animal welfare organization that provides free veterinary care.

Pigeons were still being used by American agents dropped behind enemy lines in Korea, but in 1956 the U.S. military sold their last birds and now rely on electronics.

Although radio and electronic communications have largely superseded the pigeon as message carrier, there must still be many pigeon fanciers who send a message home by pigeon post. Telephone lines and optic cables cannot carry actual objects so pigeons can still have a role, especially if local terrain makes rapid communication difficult. In both northwestern France and the English West Country, for instance, they have been used to speed blood samples back to laboratories for urgent analysis.

Racing pigeons

Competitive pigeon racing began in a regular way in Belgium in the early part of the nineteenth century, being taken up somewhat later in Britain and America. Enthusiasm for the sport was greatly increased by reports of the use of homing pigeons during the Siege of Paris in 1870. The earliest record of a British race was from Spalding in Lincolnshire in 1872 and about that time Belgian birds were also being imported into the United States. Interest has since become worldwide and an International Federation was set up in 1948. Each member

Pigeons of Paris

In 1870, the citizens of Paris, surrounded by the Prussian army, used hot air balloons to carry men and messages above and beyond the enemy lines. With them traveled 381 carrier pigeons to bring messages back into the city. To increase the amount of information the birds could carry, a new technique was used: microphotography. Messages were reduced to minute size and then tightly inserted into the hollow quills of feathers that were then sealed and tied back onto a tail feather. It was claimed that a single bird could carry 40,000 messages, they were so light. On arrival the film was projected onto a screen by "magic lantern."

Of 302 birds dispatched back to Paris, only 59 managed to get through. Many of those that failed died of cold or were brought down by hawks that the Prussian army brought in specially to intercept them.

country has its own governing body: the American Racing Pigeon Union, for instance, in the United States and the Royal National Homing Union in the United Kingdom. The patron of the British Union is Queen Elizabeth II, who has her own flight of racing pigeons, as did her father and grandfather, pigeon fancier George V. It was he who established the first Royal Lofts, near the royal country house in Norfolk, in the garden of the Sandringham village schoolmaster, Ernest Steele.

Not all pigeons are homers, nor do all fly fast. Breeders have selected for these qualities and now Racing Homers that are able to cover 1,000 miles (16,000 km) over two days are not uncommon. The sport consists of taking birds to a place distant from their loft, releasing them and then timing their arrival home. This is done by fitting a rubber race ring to the leg that its owner removes on arrival and places in a special clock mechanism to register the time of its insertion. It is not the first bird home that wins but the one that makes the best speed, dividing the distance from the loft by the time it takes.

Birds must be carefully trained. They must get used to being in the kind of basket in which they travel to the release point, to avoid anxiety and stress. They must become familiar with their own loft and its neighborhood, get used to flying home over increasingly greater distances and be conditioned to "trap" (to enter the forepart of the loft where they can be deringed) immediately on arrival. Trap training is based upon getting them to respond to a call or whistle at feeding times.

Pigeons differ greatly in the distances over which they produce their best speeds and in

Above *A basket of pigeons is loaded into a balloon about to leave besieged Paris in 1870.*
When one of the Paris pigeons reached home, the microphotograph messages it carried were projected and transcribed.

Below *Racing pigeons being released from a carrier truck at the beginning of a race.*

what provides the strongest incentive to hurry home. What may seem to many to be morally objectionable methods, are sometimes used, but rarely mentioned, by enthusiasts. Over short distances, for instance, one bird may perform best because it is eager to get back to eggs, or an intensely jealous male may be eager to get back to a mate. Belgian breeders, in particular, exploit male jealousy, calling the technique "widowhood." To increase the cock's anxiety to return, they will give him a last glimpse of the hen in the company of another male before he goes in the traveling basket.

Highfliers

Highflying, or roof flying, is a sport that was already established in Modena, Italy, in the fourteenth century and until the 1950s was very popular in New York City. Since then, the disappearance of the old tenement blocks on the roofs of which many fanciers had their lofts, has led to its decline, but it is still practiced in Eastern Europe and in India.

The aim is to capture birds belonging to another flock by sending up your own birds, directing their flight by whistles and waving a flag on a long pole so that the other birds fly with them and come down along with your own when they are called. They are then caught and offered for ransom. Sometimes whole flocks are captured. Accounts tell of a Modena flier, or *Triganiere*, who would signal his flock to different parts of the city to mix with other flocks. The Modena breed is now a show pigeon with 150 different color varieties. The traditional New York highflier was the Domestic Flight, though there are a number of other breeds.

Modena's pigeon history goes back to Roman times when, besieged by Marc Antony in 44 B.C., Decimus Brutus sent out pigeons carrying messages.

Tumblers

An Asian pigeon breed became known for their habit of somersaulting or "tumbling" in flight and a variety of breeds have been devel-

oped with this characteristic, together with some related show varieties. The cause of their behavior is not known; it is possibly due to an inherited defect in the bird's inner ear, though a nineteenth-century theory was that it was a condition similar to epilepsy. The bird suffers a momentary failure of its balancing mechanism, starts to fall and then recovers itself. It is questionable whether an inherent physical defect of this kind should be perpetuated for human amusement.

A seventeenth-century Mogul painting shows a variety of fancy pigeons around a stylized dovecote. The pair upper left are "billing and cooing" replicating the typical action of courtship feeding. Two are fantail breeds, one is making the swollen-necked bowing courtship display and others are seen preening.

Show pigeons

Long before pigeon racing became an established sport, pigeons were being bred for their appearance and pigeon shows were held many years before the first dog and cat shows. Not only have a wide variety of colors and patterns of plumage been developed, but some extraordinarily bizarre appearances. The rapid evolution of physical differences was noted by Charles Darwin and was one of the ways in which he developed his theory of the origin of species.

GODS AND MYTHS

It is not surprising that the skyborne bird was often linked with the sky gods and sometimes given divine qualities itself. Able to soar above roofs and towers into the clouds, flying across water, mountain and man-built barriers, even the smallest songbird had a skill no human could achieve. The great birds of prey, fearsome in their ability to strike death from the sky, had a godlike power. Birds and bird-headed figures appear in ritualistic contexts in many cultures. Gods, angels and demons are often personified with wings, whereas the entrails of sacrificial birds became a source for priestly auguries.

In several cultures birds came right at the beginning of things. To the Native Americans of Alaska it was a swallow who showed the Crow Father Tulunguasaq the clay soil hardening at the bottom of an abyss that was to turn into Earth's other life forms. Tulunguasaq disguised himself with feathers and a beak and in one version of the story his descendants lost the power to remove them and have to stay on Earth as crows. Swallow and Crow create both light and time and the Crow taught humans how to build their houses, and how to hunt and fish before returning to the sky to create the stars. In a Siberian version of the story, Crow becomes a cheat, though one whose tricks seem to misfire and turn upon himself, a role reversal that is not unusual in religious myth.

Further south it is a jay that becomes the primal bird, whereas the Pueblos and Navajo tradition tells of a woodpecker, Iyatiku, who at the request of the Maize Mother, herself the primal mother of us all, pecks holes through the layers of rock that separate the worlds beneath the soil from the light of day. For the Hopi it is a dove that helps release people from the worlds beneath the earth, whereas a mockingbird, Yawapu, greets their emergence and bestows the gift of languages, and in a Bela-Coola myth an eagle is responsible for releasing the rivers of the world and their peoples by removing the rock from the cave in which they had been sealed.

It was a bird spirit, sometimes in the shape of a fulmar, sometimes a diving bird, who took the form of a handsome hunter to entice away the Eskimo girl Sedna who became goddess of the sea and sea animals, whereas Koodjanuk, a large bird with a black head, hooked beak and white body is the spirit that heals the sick.

Among the other birds important in North American mythology was Oshadagea, the Eagle of the Dew, carrying a lake of dew in a hollow of his back, who was rainbearer to the Iroquois and Huron peoples, but the chief responsibility for preventing the earth from drying and the vegetation from dying was the great Thunderbird, who was escorted by a flock of other spirits in the form of falcons or eagles, the beat of their wings making the sound of thunder. The ancient Chinese also had a thunder god with beak, wings and claws.

In the rainforest of South America it is the hummingbird that is sometimes said to have given people the gift of water, though to the Bororo it brought tobacco and to the Surura and Toba the gift of fire. In some other areas it is the pigeon that is the fire bringer.

Totem Poles at a Native American settlement at Alert Bay, British Columbia, topped by the Thunderbird.

Right *A stylized Raven hanging made by the Nakoatok tribe.*

*The falcon-headed Horus, Lord of the
Sky. The sky itself was sometimes
thought of as a falcon, the sun and
moon its eyes. The Egyptian
hieroglyph for god was a perched
falcon.*

To the Brazilian Bororo the macaw was one
resting place for the soul in a complex trans-
migration, and in many cultures bird forms, or
birds with human heads, are used to symbolize
the soul, especially on its passage to an afterlife.
In northwestern Manchuria, birds were painted
on coffins and birds on poles were placed
around the coffin of a shaman. Human-headed
birds are painted on the coffin cases of ancient
Egyptians and on the walls of their tombs.

Along with so many other animals, birds
were sacred creatures in ancient Egypt, perhaps
first as gods themselves and then as an earthly
incarnation or as symbols of the gods. The
goose was sacred to the goddess Isis; Thoth,
god of wisdom (and usually presented as a
baboon), might also take the form of the black
and white bird still known as the Sacred Ibis;
Horus, Lord of the Sky, was seen as a falcon or
as falcon-headed.

In early times it would probably have been
just one bird of a species, kept and cared for in
the temple of the god or goddess, which was
considered the incarnation of the divinity, but
later all members of the species came to be considered sacred. To honor the god or goddess,
devotees mummified the sacred birds and presented them at the temples of Thoth or Horus
as an offering to gain favor.

At the apex of the Nile delta is Saquarra, the
City of the Dead linked with Memphis. There,
beyond a catacomb where more than 400
mummified baboons were found, is a labyrinth
of galleries where hundreds of thousands of
falcons and millions of ibis lie mummified,
wrapped in bandages and placed in pottery
sarcophagi. At Hermopolis, an important
center for the cult of Thoth further up the Nile,
were other catacombs of ibis and baboons.
Although these mummies were the accumulated
offerings of hundreds of years they cannot have

A silver four-drachmae coin from Athens shows Athena's owl, the goddess's head on the other side.

Above right *A Roman fibula in the form of Leda and the Swan.*

A medieval image of the Phoenix rising from the flames in a bestiary of about 1200.

all been kept in the temple enclosures, nor even all have been pet birds offered by their owners.

Since to kill a sacred bird would have been punishable by death, no ordinary Egyptian would kill or capture the wild birds — so where could so many birds have come from?

In the same way as a worshipper in many Christian churches today may buy a candle to light before a shrine, archaeologists believe that the Egyptian priests sold mummies to those who came to the temples of Thoth and Horus for them to present as their offerings. The birds were probably reared specifically for this purpose by the temple priests. Indeed, at Saquarra there was a lake where ibis could have been bred as a ready source to be killed and embalmed for what must have been a very lucrative trade. This seems to be confirmed by the fact that many of the falcon wrappings do not contain falcons but the remains of other birds, or even a bundle of miscellaneous bird bones.

To the Egyptians the owl was a bird that represented cold, night and death; to most Native Americans it was also a death omen, though the Pawnees consider it a protection against the darkness; and for many African tribes it is linked with black magic. To the Romans its hooting was, again, a harbinger of death, as it still is to many European peoples, but to the Ancient Greeks it was the bird of Athena, a badge of wisdom, and this attribution has also persisted into modern times, probably because of its spectacle-like, bookish eyes.

Myths in which the gods turn themselves or others into animals or plants are frequently cited as evidence of early animistic beliefs before the deities were humanized. The Greek god Zeus had many such metamorphoses, usually assumed in pursuit of amorous conquest. It was as a swan that he seduced Leda, their love-making producing eggs from which hatched Castor and Pollox and Clytemnestra and Helen; as an eagle he swooped down on Ganymede when that beautiful boy caught his fancy, and is was as an eagle that he carried off the nymph Aegina. More surprisingly perhaps it was in the form of a pigeon that he seduced another nymph called Phthia and, according to Pausanius at least, as a cuckoo that he attempted to force himself upon Hera. He came to her in winter and he seemed so frozen that the goddess warmed the bird against her breast. When, thawed, he resumed his godly form but she resisted his advances until he promised marriage.

Asteria, another nymph whom Zeus pursued, turned herself into a quail to escape him and then threw herself into the sea, where she turned into the island of Delos. When his eye fell on Io, a priestess of Hera, Zeus took the form of a cloud and then, hoping to deceive his wife, turned Io into a cow. But Hera asked for the cow as a present and sent Argus Panoptes (the "all-seeing") of 100 eyes to guard her. Zeus instructed Hermes to set her free and he killed Argus whose eyes Hera transferred to the tail of the peacock. But for poor Io that was only the beginning of the story, though it involves no more birds, except that she ended up married to an Egyptian king and in later times became confused with Isis, to whom geese were sacred.

The Hindu god Vishnu had a great bird called Garuda as both companion and mount. Soma, in the Vedas a link between heaven and humans who takes many forms from a nectar, which confers immortality, to the prince of poets, was Ganymede-like, ravished by the god Indra and changed into a sparrowhawk.

In the northern European myths the Teutonic Odin or Wotan had two crows, Hugin (Thought) and Mugin (Memory), who were sent out each morning to question the living and the dead and bring back news of the entire world.

In the Judaic scriptures the prophet Isaiah has a raven messenger, whereas Noah's raven and dove in the story of the Flood have already been mentioned.

From China came the Phoenix, a mythological bird that may have had its origin in the pheasant, though in size more like an eagle. It was the emperor of birds and became the symbol of the sun. In Egypt and the Middle East, and later in European mythology, only one Phoenix was thought to exist at any one time. It lived in Paradise, where there was no death, and when it had reached an age of 500 years, or perhaps 1,000, burdened by its age, it flew to the ordinary world to die. In Arabia it gathered a bunch of herbs, then flew to the coast of ancient Phoenicia where it built a nest incorporating the dry herbs. As the sun rose it turned to face it and sang so thrillingly that even the sun god stopped to listen, halting his chariot in the sky. When he whipped his horses back into motion, a spark from one of their hooves would fall upon the nest, set fire to the tinder-dry herbs and make it burst into flame. Thus the Phoenix brought about its own immolation; then from the ashes a new Phoenix was born, perhaps the most vivid of all the symbols of regeneration.

King of the birds

The eagle was usually considered the King of the Birds but one ancient story tells how the wren won the crown. The birds decided that whoever flew the highest should rule over them and the eagle was so sure that would be him that he did not notice the wren climb onto his back as he soared upwards. When he reached the highest he could go, the wren flew just above his head and so flew higher and won the crown.

Not all the birds of mythology fulfill kindly roles. Zeus sent an eagle to daily tear at the liver of Prometheus where he was chained to a rock as punishment for stealing fire and giving it to the mortals. Heracles, as one of his labors, had to overcome a huge flock of monstrous birds who lived on the marshes of Stymphalis in Arcadia and were so numerous that when they took wing they blotted out the sun. They

Zeus's eagle pecks at the liver of the chained Prometheus while Atlas holds up the world on a Laconian kylx of about 550 B.C.

had beaks and claws of iron and fed on human flesh, but Heracles frightened them by clashing brass cymbals and brought them down with either slingshot or arrows. There was a demon bird that threatened India which the god Krishna overcame, and similar figures appear in other religions and mythologies.

Judaic law declared the owl to be an unclean bird, perhaps because it was associated with the Hittite goddess Lilith, for "unclean" appears to mean unsuitable for offering to the temple and the Judaic list is of birds and animals that were in some way sacred to other religions of the time. The raven, a carrion eater, is more understandably also declared unclean. Its form is sometimes said to have been taken by the Devil and represents the enemy in Russian legend. It is sometimes considered a carrier of plague and an omen of death and said to carry the souls of the damned to hell. However, it was also the cult bird of the god Mithras, worshipped by many Romans, and the frequency of the occurrence of raven bones in the remains of Roman villas suggests that they had a special status.

The Romans had religious officers, called Augurs, whose business was to predict the future from observation of the flight of birds, and it is perhaps a relic of this, together with the special status of birds such as the raven, crow and magpie in semi-religious beliefs that gave rise to the various rhymes that predict good and bad luck based, for instance, on the number of magpies seen at one time: "one for sorrow, two for mirth . . ."

The Roc, the giant bird of the Sinbad stories that could carry away an elephant, is usually considered pure fantasy, but research into extinct forms of island species in the Mediterranean has produced clear evidence of giant birds, including a huge vulture on Malta. These island forms also produced tiny dwarf elephants. Did the oral tradition on which the storytellers drew involve a memory of these creatures, since some seem to have survived until early humans reached the islands?

Christian symbolism

The early Christian Church adopted the Phoenix, already established as a symbol of renewal and resurrection, as a symbol that would remind the faithful of Christ's resurrection from the grave.

The farmyard cockerel too, herald of the dawn, already thought of as driving away the terrors of darkness, was adopted by the Christians as a symbol of the resurrection, and carried a reminder also of the need for constancy in faith because of the three times that the disciple Peter denied Christ at the time of his trial in the court of Ciaphas before cockcrow.

It is as a Christian emblem that it appears on the weathervanes of churches. The crowing cock was also associated with the birth of Christ, announcing Jesus' coming. A broadsheet printed in London in 1631 also assigns a vocal role to the raven and the crow, among the animals around the manger, interpreting

their natural voices, for, of course, they speak in Latin!

"The Cocke croweth, *Christus natus est.* (Christ is born.)
The Raven asked, *Quando?* (When?)
The Crow replyed, *Hic nocte.* (This night.)
The Oxe cryed out, *Ubi? Ubi?* (Where? Where?)
The Sheep bleated out, *Bethlem.* (Bethlehem.)"

The symbolic egg

Ancient Egyptian, Indian and Japanese civilizations were among the cultures that believed the world itself was hatched from an egg made by the Creator. An egg, painted above the figure of a mummy in Egyptian pictographs represented also "the seed of becoming," the hope for immortality, and clay egg shapes found even earlier in prehistoric tombs are thought to have been a symbol for immortality. Romans buried eggs with their dead, and among the Maori in New Zealand, before the Moa became extinct, it was the custom to place one of this bird's large eggs in the hand of the dead person.

The rebirth symbolism of the spring festivals of earlier beliefs and the celebration of the resurrected Christ are joined in the Christian Easter and the continuing custom of Easter eggs, whether the traditional dyed or painted hen's egg or the chocolate variety.

Eggs have been used for telling the future, the diviner cracking the egg into water and studying the shapes made by the albumen to form a prediction.

The pelican is another bird that found a place in Christian iconography. They became a symbol of motherly devotion because they were thought to feed their young by plucking at their own breast to feed them on their blood or, as one medieval bestiary writer told it,

"when [the young] begin to grow up, they flap their parents in the face with their wings, and the parents striking back, kill them. Three days afterwards the mother pierces her breast, opens her side, and lays herself across her young, pouring out her blood over the dead bodies. This brings them to life again."

This was seen as a parallel to the scorning of Christ and his subsequent self-sacrifice on humanity's behalf and so became a symbol of piety as well as mother love. It became a popular heraldic animal in armorial blazons. Although numerous species will pluck the downy feathers of their breast to line their nests it is more probable that what had been seen was a pelican dribbling the blood-like liquid food into the bills of recently-hatched young.

The little goldfinch, known in French as Chardonerette from its liking for thistles (chardons) is linked by them with Christ's crown of thorns and is used by some artists of the Renaissance as a symbol for Christ's Passion, often linked with its natural predator, a cat, which was frequently used as a symbol of the devil. Together they could represent the redemption of the faithful from sin.

The Peacock, often used as a lay image of pride, does not have that significance when it appears in paintings of the Madonna: since the flesh of the Peacock was reputed not to decay it was also used as a symbol of the purity and incorruptibility of the Virgin Mary.

Above left *In Christian symbolism the dove, linked with the end of the Flood and Jehovah's pact with man symbolized by the rainbow, becomes the emblem of the Holy Spirit, hovering over the baptism of Christ in this illumination from a Book of Hours of about 1500.*

The Goldfinch (Carduelis carduelis) became linked with Christ's Passion because of its close association with thistles.

The Holy Family by the seventeenth-century Spanish painter Bartolemé Esteban Murillo. The Goldfinch held by Jesus is a symbolic reminder of His Passion. Some painters also include a cat to represent the forces of the devil.

Below Though the idea of the wise old owl that persists today retains the ancient Greek association, this owl carved on a medieval misericorde in the Oude Kerk in Amsterdam was probably intended to remind monks of the evil powers of darkness. Neighboring carvings supporting these ledges on the underside of seats, intended to prop up tired monks during night time services, show a cat and a bat.

Popular symbolism

The use of the European robin as a Christmas symbol has no deep religious significance. The Robin Redbreast has long been a bold associate of people, waiting for the gardener to turn up a worm or feeding from scraps put out in winter. Its sprightly manner and colorful appearance have made it a cheery presence in the snows of winter and gained its popularity both in the garden and in the Christmas card tradition. However, its earlier name was Redbreast and the use of Robin suggests a connection with Robin Goodfellow, a polite name for the house-spirit or hobgoblin inherited from Norse mythology and otherwise known as Puck. It seems possible that the Robin, appearing suddenly around the house, was linked with that mischievous spirit that could assume other shapes.

Billing and cooing doves were linked with the goddess Aphrodite as her messengers but the demonstrative courtships of the pigeon family has ensured their association with love and lovers even more strongly than that of the lovebirds, whether budgerigars or African parakeets, that have been named for their displays of apparent affection.

The owl continues to be imagined as a "wise old bird," the swallow and its relations as a harbinger of summer when it returns after its winter migration, although in North America this role is sometimes taken over by the bluebird, and the peacock remains a symbol of the epitome of pride and display.

BIRDS IN THE ARTS

Literary birds

From their roles in religion, in myth and in fables like those of Aesop, birds have been widely used in the simile and metaphor of the world's writers. Even when a story or a poem appears to be about a bird itself some parallel with human experience will usually be found, and although a writer may include birds simply as part of the natural scene, they usually carry some echo beyond the mere descriptive.

With the flowering of dramatic poetry in Greece, Sophocles wrote a play based on the story of Philomela, who was raped by Tereus, the husband of her sister Procne. Tereus cut out her tongue so that she could not say who had violated her but she embroidered her account and in a rage Procne killed her son Itys and served him up as dinner for his father. To end this grisly vendetta, the gods turned all the protagonists into birds: a nightingale (Philomela, or in some versions Procne), a swallow (Procne, or Philomela), a hoopoe (Tereus), and a goldfinch (Itys, who was brought back to life). Aeschylus's nephew, Philocles, also dramatized the story and other versions include a modern treatment by Timberlake Wertenbaker, *Love of a Nightingale*.

Tereus the Hoopoe and Procne the Nightingale turn up again in happy domesticity in Aristophanes' comedy *The Birds*, first presented at the Athens Dionysia in 414 B.C. In this play, two citizens fleeing the taxes and litigation of the city convince the birds that they should build a city in the clouds where they can take power from the gods and claim dues both from Earth and heaven. There is a chorus of birds including partridge, francolin, mallard, halcyon (a seabird, not the kingfisher that bears the name today), sparrow, crested lark, reed warbler, wheatear, pigeon, stock dove, turtle dove, cuckoo, woodpecker, waxwing, firecrest, dabchick, rail, owl, kestrel, merlin, sparrowhawk and vulture, whereas dancers appear as flamingo, cockerel and another hoopoe. Hoopoe Tereus calls them all in a song, which in the original Greek creates an onomatopoeic rendering of bird calls in a manner that is rarely matched by later poets or by ornithologists who attempt transliterations in modern field guides, whereas the nightingale's song is interpreted by a flute.

Nearly 1,800 years later, when English was beginning to take its modern form in the verse of Geoffrey Chaucer, that poet presented a vision of a garden of the kind that is the setting for courtly romances such as the *Roman de la Rose* where the goddess Nature presides over the *The Parlement of Foules*. Aristophanes satirized his Athenian contemporaries, Chaucer rehearsed the medieval concepts of courtly love as three tiercel eagles argue the chances for the success of the knightly code in winning a lady against the more pragmatic methods proposed by a group of ducks. Chaucer's contemporary William Langland, as keen an observer of nature as he was of society, gave his plowman Piers the view of birds with which this book begins.

An Anglo-Saxon poem, *The Seafarer* written about A.D. 685, gives an example of birds used to build a vivid atmosphere as the unknown poet describes life at sea. This is how the ornithologist James Fisher translated some lines that probably describe the Bass Rock off the Scottish coast:

"There heard I naught but seething sea,
Ice-cold wave, awhile a song of swan,
There came to charm me gannets' pother
And whimbrels' trills for the laughter of men,
Kittiwake singing instead of mead.
Storms there the stacks thrashed, there
    answered them the tern
With icy feathers; full oft the erne [white-tailed
    eagle] wailed round
Spray feathered . . ."

The same quick conjuring of atmosphere occurs when William Shakespeare (a frequent user of bird images) makes Banquo notice the "temple haunting martlets" as he approaches Macbeth's castle, immediately giving the audience an image of the crag on which it is built.

The caged bird is a much used literary image to represent both physical imprisonment and spiritual confinement, for down the ages even those who have themselves caged birds recognize it as imprisonment, however much a bird may be cared for and loved.

"And I was filled with such delight
As prisoned birds must find in freedom"

wrote Siegfried Sassoon in his joyous poem *The Music Makers*, the lines somehow echoing the

Right *The Hoopoe* (Upupa epops), *whose distinctive call and characteristic crest make him easily recognizable in Aristophanes' The Birds.*

A parrot in Chinese paper cutout.

A Japanese woodblock print of geese by Bairei.

rush of birds as a cage is opened, rising into the sky in a way that few other simple similes can equal.

Birds often appear in moral fables, from Aesop onwards, and in fairy stories. In both traditional versions of the Babes in the Wood and in Walt Disney's 1930s animated cartoon movie of Snow White, woodland birds bring leaves to cover lost wanderers as they sleep, protecting them from cold (or in older versions burying dead children), and they often crop up as messengers or play another role. In the stories of Hans Christian Andersen they appear a number of times, among them the Ugly Duckling, who turns into a swan, the wild swans who are the enchanted brothers of Princess Elise, the storks who tell the tale of the Marsh King's daughter, the hens and owls who illustrate how gossip distorts and changes, and

the Emperor's nightingale, a story whose values seem particularly relevant today.

Oscar Wilde wrote a pair of touching stories in which birds sacrifice themselves for others. *The Happy Prince* has a little swallow, delaying its migration first because of unrequited love and then to help the statue of the prince bring happiness to others before dropping dead at his feet. In *The Nightingale and the Rose* he uses the old legend of the nightingale singing while her heart is pierced by a rose to show the sacrifice of a bird who places the beauty of love above all things to help a student provide a red rose, colored by her blood, as an offering for the object of his affections, who spurns it, so that he too throws it in the dust.

There are menacing birds too, in old stories and new, from Sinbad's Rocs to the raven of Edgar Allan Poe crying "Never More," and the

Right *The nightingale returns to the dying Emperor. Rex Whistler's illustration of Hans Andersen's tale of a real nightingale supplanted by a mechanical bird that inspired Igor Stravinsky's opera* The Nightingale.

Far right *David Bradley in Ken Loach's film* Kes *based on Barry Hines's novel about a young falconer* A Kestrel for a Knave.

A Robin Redbreast in a Cage
Puts all Heaven in a Rage. . .
A Skylark wounded in the wing,
A Cherubim does cease to sing.
The Game Cock clip'd & arm'd for fight
Does the Rising Sun affright . ..
He who shall hurt the little Wren
Shall never be belov'd by Men.

from William Blake's *Auguries of Innocence*.

Tippi Hedren in Alfred Hitchcock's film The Birds.

terrifying flocks of Daphne du Maurier's *The Birds*, so chillingly filmed by Alfred Hitchcock.

No bird has a more ominous presence than that of the albatross shot by the protagonist of Samuel Taylor Coleridge's *The Rime of the Ancient Mariner*, bringing a curse upon himself and his ship, in a poem that demanded respect for other species long before the modern ecological movement. Such respect is sadly lacking in the mariners who catch and taunt another albatross in a poem by Charles Baudelaire, who compares himself to the giant bird and its anguish.

Seabirds, gliding over the waters independent even of land for much of their lives, are a powerful image of freedom, but the real bird in Anton Chekhov's play *The Seagull* is shot by young Konstantin, who also threatens to kill himself for love of Nina. The dead bird gives the novelist Trigorin an idea for a story of a young girl, like the seagull living happy and free by a lake, until a man comes along and idly destroys her — and in real life that is exactly what Trigorin does to Nina, who later calls herself "the Seagull," though she in the end escapes, wounded but still flying, whereas it is Konstantin who, after her final rejection, shoots himself.

Turkish novelist Yashar Kemal's *Seagull* (known as *The Saga of a Seagull* in Britain) tells the story of a boy who rescues a bird with a broken wing and his attempts to find someone who can help to heal it, a parallel to the struggles of his own life and his dreams of the wide world and the freedom that the seagulls already know. The injured bird is often used by writers as a metaphor to echo the human handicaps and inadequacies that prevent us from soaring off into the sky to fulfill our hopes or match our ambitions.

Aviator Richard Bach's *Jonathan Livingston Seagull*, a best seller and cult book of the early 1970s, looks at learning to fly from the seagull's point of view. Aided by atmospheric flight photographs by Russell Munson — but completely anthropomorphic in concept — it echoed the feeling of liberation and self discovery that the sixties had generated with its message that

"To begin with . . . you've got to understand that a seagull is an unlimited idea of freedom, an image of the Great Gull, and your whole body, from wingtip to wingtip, is nothing more than your thought itself."

In *The Wild Duck* Henrik Ibsen used the story of the wild duck kept by young Hedwig

The heroes of the animated cartoon
have included numerous birds,
including Donald Duck, and range
from the crows of Dumbo to the
frenetic Roadrunner and Tweety Pie,
the canary seen here with his
perpetual antagonist the cat Sylvester.

Opposite *The two-note call of the*
Common Cuckoo (Cuculus canorus)
can be heard in many musical works.
As summer progresses the cu-cu gains
an extra syllable.

Hardy, W. H. Davies, and today, especially, Ted Hughes, though their "nature poetry" can have relevances far beyond the descriptive.

Bird music

It has been suggested that music has its origin in birdsong and attempts to imitate it. Certainly musicians have often sought to echo birdsong in their compositions. The cuckoo is perhaps the most easy voice to reproduce, its sound captured just in naming it. It can be heard in the anonymous medieval *Sumer is icumen in, Lhude sing cuccu!*, which probably dates from the thirteenth century and is thought to be the oldest surviving work written in canon form. Its call is easily distinguished in the second movement of Ludwig van Beethoven's *Pastoral Symphony*, where its voice (on the clarinet) is joined by the nightingale (flute) and the quail (oboe). Antonio Vivaldi's *The Four Seasons* is another work where the cuckoo is clearly heard in "Summer," the second concerto, and a lark, a turtle dove and other birds are heard elsewhere in the music. Vivaldi also wrote a whole concerto devoted to the goldfinch, the main voice given to a brilliant and fluttery flute, whereas strings suggest the busy pecking of this voracious little bird. Leopold Mozart has a cuckoo (and quails) in his *Toy Symphony*, the seventeenth-century German composer Johann Kerll, wrote a *Cuckoo Capriccio* and his Italian contemporary Bernardo Pasquini also wrote a cuckoo piece. The species attracted many other composers too, most notably perhaps England's Frederick Delius with his *On Hearing the First Cuckoo in Spring*.

The familiar cuckoo call has been presented musically in many ways and, in life, changes with the season. John Heywood, sixteenth-century English composer and dramatist, analyzed its voice in musical terms (a little oversimplified) as a minor third on arrival, then a major third, then a fourth, later a fifth, after which it breaks without attaining a sixth.

In his setting of songs from the German collection of folk poetry *Des Knaben Wunderhorn* (The Youth's Magic Horn) Gustav Mahler includes a retelling of the old medieval jest of a singing contest between the cuckoo and the nightingale, judged by a donkey, who can't stand the nightingale and makes cuckoo the winner. Cuckoo, nightingale and donkey are all there in the music.

The cuckoo often features in folk music too, from Polish songs to one from the Appalachians (where the parasitic species is not indigenous) that is a version of an old English song which must have been taken there by early settlers:

"The cuckoo is a pretty bird and sings as she
  flies,
She brings us good tidings and tells us no lies,
She sucks little birds' eggs to make her voice
  clear
And she never sings 'cuckoo' 'til the
  springtime is here."

Benjamin Britten included *Sumer is icumen in* and a setting of Edmund Spenser's *The Merry*

Ekdal as a central symbol that pervades the play. First the bird lives in a carefree wild state, like Hedwig at the beginning of the play, then, shot down and in pain, it dives to the bottom of the sea but is brought out by a dog. After failing to recover properly in the hunter's house, and still crippled, it is taken to the Ekdals where an artificial environment appears to keep it happy, until its life is finally offered as a sacrifice, as is that of young Hedwig herself.

Jean Anouilh's choice of *The Lark* as a title for his play about St. Joan calls on the image of the free, high-flying bird, trapped and imprisoned, whereas Maurice Maeterlinck symbolized the search for happiness in *The Bluebird*, which we risk losing the moment that we try to cage it.

The killing of birds by a domestic cat is a theme that has been taken up by many poets, from the sixth-century B.C. Greek Agathias to the ninth-century Ibn Alalaf Alnaharwany of Baghdad, fifteenth-century Englishman John Skelton and twentieth-century Edward Thomas. As for those poets whose verses have celebrated the natural bird, they pervade the history of poetry, as a few names from those writing in English demonstrate: William Langland, Michael Drayton, John Clare, John Keats, Thomas

Anna Pavlova, Russian ballerina famous for her portrayal of The Dying Swan, *in the garden of her London home with her pet swan Jack, whose movements she studied in developing the work.*

Tamara Karsavina and Adolphe Bohm in the Stravinsky-Fokine ballet The Firebird, *based on a Russian fairy tale.*

and hisses; the elegiac "swansong" of the dying bird is a figment of the romantic imagination. The music for the cygnets' *pas de trois* in *Swan Lake*, perhaps appropriately, has the perky jerkiness of a group of ducklings, but it is surprising that the musical bugling of the Whooper and Bewick Swans have not yet found their way into musical scores.

Igor Stravinsky's music and Michel Fokine's choreography give a flicker of flame and shivering feathers to the magical *Firebird* and the Bluebird *pas de deux* in Tchaikovsky's *The Sleeping Beauty* is a favorite with many balletomanes. There are waiter penguins in David Bintley's ballet *Penguin Cafe* to Simon Jeffes's score (and of course in Ralph Vaughan Williams's *Sinfonia Antartica*, developed from his music for a film about Captain Scott's ill-fated expedition). There is a whole dawn chorus, in the music at least, in the "Daybreak" scene of Maurice Ravel's *Daphnis and Chloe* but it is to opera and opera-ballet that one must look for most musical birds upon the stage.

Cuckoo in his *Spring Symphony* and one of Jane Taylor's *Cuckoo* in *Songs for Friday Afternoons*, but his most remarkable birds appear in *Noyes Fludde*, where there is not only the calling and twittering of all the birds as they approach Noah's ark but the departure of the raven and the delightful flight of the dove, written as a musical palindrome as the bird flies first out from and then back to the ark.

It is natural that themes of flight, and hence of birds, often occur in ballet, the essence of which is elevation from the ground, but though the music may soar and the dancers take to the air, neither Pyotr Tchaikovsky's score for *Swan Lake*, nor Camille Saint-Saëns's *The Dying Swan* has any opportunity to offer a rendering of birdsong, for both probably had in mind the Mute Swan that makes only guttural sounds

Mechanical birdsong

The watchmaker and the jeweler have often displayed their art in making mechanical birds, like the one in Hans Christian Andersen's story of the Emperor's nightingale which was the origin for Stravinsky's opera, putting them in cages or setting them on musical boxes.

Maurice Ravel owned one, which he called Zizi, that would flutter its feathers and warble when it was wound up.

There is Nikolai Rimsky-Korsakov's *Golden Cockerel*, Stravinsky's *Nightingale*, another nightingale and other woodland birds in Maurice Ravel's *The Child and the Spells*, in which the coloratura bird competes with a piccolo and, most crucially, the forest bird in Richard Wagner's *Siegfried* that tells the hero of the Nibelungen treasure, the Tarnhelm and the sleeping Brünhilde encircled by her ring of fire and then leads him to his meeting with Wotan. In Wolfgang Mozart's *The Magic Flute*, bird-catcher Papageno plays birdsong imitations on his panpipe and with his partner Papagena has a duet that itself is birdlike. Then there is Rossini's *Thieving Magpie* and, of course, the Swan in Wagner's *Lohengrin*, which draws the hero's boat and is in fact a man under a spell, whereas the White Dove of the Holy Grail appears at the end of the opera to draw the Grail Knight's boat away.

Orlando Gibbons set the madrigal *Silver Swan*, and another swan glides on the waters that surround the Finnish underworld in Jean Sibelius's *Swan of Tuolena*, which is virtually a horn concerto, but although this swan in the *Kalevala* epic poem could not be a Mute Swan — they do not go so far north — it does not use the Whooper's bugling call. The nightingale appears again in Alessandro Scarlatti's *Nightingale Cantata* and in Thomas Bateson's setting of Philip Sidney's sonnet on a nightingale, whereas a real bird (on a recording) is scored to sing among the trees of the Janiculum in Ottorino Respighi's *Pines of Rome*. There is also an instrument called a nightingale that can be heard in the *Clock Symphony* that used to be attributed to Joseph Haydn.

Mozart's starling

In 1784, composer Wolfgang Amadeus Mozart bought a starling for 34 kreuzer. He claimed that it could sing the first five bars of the variations in the finale of his Piano Concerto in G Major. When it died three years later, Mozart wrote a doggerel elegy for it (here given in an English version by Marcia Davenport):

"A little fool lies here
Whom I held dear —
A starling in the prime
Of his brief time,
Whose doom it was to drain
Death's bitter pain.
Thinking of this, my heart
Is riven apart.
Oh, reader! shed a tear,
You also, here.
He was not naughty, quite,
But gay and bright,
And under all his brag
A foolish wag.
This no one can gainsay
And I will lay
That he is now on high,
And from the sky,
Praises me without pay
In his friendly way.
Yet unaware that death
Has choked his breath,
And thoughtless of the one
Whose rhyme is thus well done."

The starling was replaced by a canary which Mozart kept in his room.

There are birds in other, genuine works of Haydn, in George Frederick Handel's operas and masques and in the music of Jean-Philippe Rameau, including a hen in one piece. Nightingales, warblers, canaries and linnets all appear in the harpsichord works of François Couperin, whereas part songs for four voices mirror birdsong in the vocal writing of early sixteenth-century French composer Clement Janequin.

Thomas Vautor's setting of *Sweet Suffolk Owl* is only one example of the easily imitated owls being used, the crowing cock in Johann Sebastian Bach's *St. Matthew Passion* just one use of the cockerel. There are a hen and chickens in Modest Mussorgsky's *Pictures at an Exhibition*, and in Sergei Prokoviev's *Peter and the Wolf* there are a cheeky bird in a tree and the poor duck who ends up in the stomach of the wolf.

Every music lover could instance other examples of birds in music but, for sheer heart-stopping beauty, it is difficult to match Vaughan Williams's romance for violin and orchestra in *The Lark Ascending*, which takes wing even more than the extract from the poem by George Meredith with which the composer inscribed the score:

"He rises and begins to round,
He drops the silver chain of sound,
Of many links without a break,
In chirrup, whistle, slur and shake . . .
For singing till his heaven fills,
'Tis love of earth that he instils,
And ever winging up and up,
Our valley is his golden cup
And he the wine which overflows
To lift us with him as he goes . . .
Till lost on his aerial rings
In light, and then the fancy sings."

However, the composer whose work owes most to birdsong must be Olivier Messiaen, who took great pains to transcribe birdsong in the field and used it directly as melodic material in works such as *The Awakening of the Birds*, *Exotic Birds*, *Catalogue of Birds* and *Chronomchromie*.

Birds often appear in popular music too, carrying their symbolism with them, though not so often in direct imitation of birdsong as in so much of the classical music already mentioned. However, the writer of the World War II hit that carried a message of hope and happiness through those dark years with the promise of a peace when

"There'll be bluebirds over,
The white cliffs of Dover . . ."

apparently may not have realized that this is an American species, not known in Europe.

Emanuel Schikander, who commissioned Mozart's The Magic Flute *and co-wrote its libretto, as birdcatcher Papageno.*

Below *The Skylark (Alauda arvensis) was inspiration for Vaughan Williams's gloriously soaring composition* The Lark Ascending, *but although it may not fly so high, its close relative, this humble Woodlark (Lullula arborea), has perhaps an even more beautifully phrased song as it circles in the air.*

BIRD ARTISTS

Birds are so ever present in life that they naturally appear throughout the world's art, in drawings, paintings, sculpture and as images in pottery, weaving and other decorative media. Since, in earlier times, most art was produced for religious, ritual or dynastic reasons, they often have an emblematic role and probably the birds' broad symbolism is so deep-rooted that it affects the viewer's response in almost every representation, whether part of an historic fresco or on a modern calendar or greetings card.

Birds can be found right through the history of Western art, from prehistoric cave paintings through Roman mosaics and medieval illuminations to proud falconers painted with their birds or children with their pets. Landowners might ask for ornamental and exotic fowls to embellish paintings of their great estates, emphasizing one more aspect of the patron's wealth and taste. More modest genre scenes might also feature birds, and their sometimes enigmatic presence continues in twentieth-century painting with images such as the strange bird in Paul Nash's *Landscape from a Dream* (actually painted from an Egyptian sculpture), the directness of Pablo Picasso's early 1901 *Child with a Dove* or the later dove image that became such a universal symbol of the movement for World Peace.

In most paintings, however, birds are incidental, unless used for a symbolic purpose. It was not until the development of a scientific interest in birds as birds during the Renaissance that birds themselves became a subject for the European artist, though bird subjects were common in Chinese art, in which nature painting has a long and continuous history, and at one period Chinese porcelain was decorated with very precise depictions of individual species.

As in European art, birds often featured in Indian miniatures as part of a general scene but, at the time of the Emperor Akbar and in the later Mogul period, the painting of colorful or spectacular birds, both real and imaginary, became a feature of court painting. In the reign of Jahangir, in the seventeenth century, the artist Mansur specialized in birds, animals and flowers. He recorded examples on the emperor's orders, including a turkey, an exotic from the Americas, brought to the court by Portuguese from Goa.

Early ornithological illustration

The western painters of bird studies were often themselves ornithologists and, as the production and dissemination of printed books developed, their work was often intended as illustration for ornithological publications. In the Middle Ages, falconers had the best knowledge of birds and the illustrations in their treatises already have a more scientific basis than those in the bestiaries, but it is the bird volume of Conrad

Prehistoric people painted these geese, ducks and other bird forms, including an Avocet picking up a worm, in a cave in Spain.

Left *Ostriches scratched into rock in the Sahara more than 10,000 years ago.*

Chinese porcelain often used bird forms, such as this "famille-rose" tureen and cover in the form of a colorful goose, produced for export to Europe during the Qianlong period (1736–1795). Like earlier Chinese porcelains, these show the Swan Goose (Anser cygnoides) with its straight bill, before it became domesticated as the Chinese Goose and bred with a knob on the forehead and a shortened bill.

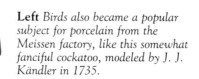

Left *Birds also became a popular subject for porcelain from the Meissen factory, like this somewhat fanciful cockatoo, modeled by J. J. Kändler in 1735.*

The Hiccory Tree. *Nux juglans Virginiana alba &c.*   The Pig-nut.   The red Bird. *Coccothraustes ruber.*

A Mogul-style painting of a Roller.

Above right *Mark Catesby's engraving of The Red Bird in* The Natural History of Carolina, Florida and the Bahama Islands *demonstrates the awkwardness and inaccuracy of some of the early work of this self-taught artist and ornithologist. For this is a study of what is now known as the Cardinal* (Cardinalis cardinalis), *a familiar bird to many Americans.*

Below *A Grebe preening, a woodcut from Conrad Gesner's* Historiae animalium, *1555.*

Gesner's *Historiae animalium*, published in 1551, that forms the first landmark in bird illustration. Its 800 pages present no less than 200 woodcut illustrations. In 1599 came Italian naturalist Ulisse Aldrovani's *Ornithologiae*, an attempt at a comprehensive natural history of birds for which the author took artists with him to watch birds and sketch them from nature. Among other books that followed was Francis Willughby's *Ornithology*, ranging over falconry and bird catching as well as individual species, published in 1678 with a section of bird illustrations at the end of the work.

Eleazar Albin (or Weiss, who is even better known for his insect pictures) issued his three-volume *A Natural History of Birds*, the first comprehensive book about British birds, between 1731 and 1738. It was one of the earliest such books to have colored illustrations, each tinted, rather haphazardly, by hand. They were often copied from other sources and some wrongly duplicate the same beak on several birds.

At the same period Mark Catesby published *The Natural History of Carolina, Florida and the Bahama Islands* (1731–43), based on his own detailed sketches and field observations, in which 113 of the plates are of birds. A self-taught artist, Catesby also learned to engrave so that he could produce the book; he then hand-colored every plate. He apologized for its inadequacies:

"As I was not born a painter, I hope some faults in perspective and other niceties may be more readily excused, for I humbly perceive . . . things done in a flat, though exact manner may serve the purpose of natural history better in some measure than in a bold and painter-like way."

Catesby taught his engraving skills to his friend George Edwards who, in the years that followed, brought out his own *A Natural History of Uncommon Birds* in 1743–51 and *Gleanings of Natural History* (1758–64). Edwards also worked from life whenever possible, though his sources included bird skins and sketches sent from America by John and William Bartram. He was a fine artist and good naturalist who had traveled extensively, before settling down in 1733 as Librarian to the Royal College of Physicians.

Bridging the middle of the century, 1734–65, came the four volumes of Albert Seba's *Thesaurus*, including numerous rather stiff bird engravings, many based on specimens in his own Amsterdam collection, and in 1770 Jan Christiaan Sepp produced his first pictures, placing the birds in natural surroundings, often with nest and eggs, for Cornelis Nozeman's *Nederlandische Vogelen*, though the complete book was not issued until 1829. In France, from 1749 onwards, the 36 volumes of George Buffon's *Histoire Naturelle* were published and the issue of a ten-volume edition of the bird material, with colored plates by François-

George Edwards's painting of the Blue-winged Goose (Cyanochen cyanopterus) for his A Natural History of Birds.

Right *A Eurasian Blackbird (Turdus merula), a woodcut by Thomas Bewick from his* History of British Birds, *1797.*

Top right *A Green-backed Heron (Butorides virescens) drawn by William Bartram, who sent sketches to George Edwards.*

Nicolas Martinet, was begun before the Comte de Buffon's death in 1788. Also in France, Jacques Barraband made the watercolors from which the engravings for François Levaillant's early nineteenth-century books were made, including one on the birds-of-paradise.

The great English wood engraver Thomas Bewick published his *History of British Birds* in 1797–1804, his cuts achieving a delicacy of image quite equal to that which others engraved on metal and, in most cases, beautifully observed.

Wilson and Audubon

In the newly independent United States, a weaver and poet who had emigrated from Scotland and become a schoolmaster had become fascinated by American birds and set about teaching himself to draw them. Alexander Wilson went on extensive journeys — 1,200 miles (1,920 km) from Philadelphia to Niagara

Falls in the fall of 1804, for instance — to study birds and collect specimens as part of his plan to produce an illustrated book of American birds. He gained the friendship of the Bartram family and of another Scottish emigrant, Alexander Lawson, who lent him engraving tools. Only three years after making his first faltering sketches of a stuffed owl Wilson wrote to President Thomas Jefferson that he had already completed "upwards of one hundred drawings . . . and two plates in folio already engraved."

Wilson left his teaching job and became editor of Rees's *Cyclopedia*, with a generous salary and time allowed to work on his own *Ornithology*, which Samuel Bradford, the encyclopedia publisher, also undertook to issue. But things did not go smoothly. Wilson had great difficulty in attracting sufficient subscribers to make his project viable. Eventually he produced eight volumes with 79 plates, mainly engraved by Lawson from Wilson's own drawings, but in the early stages there were problems in getting the coloring done and in getting subscriptions paid. The coloring problem was solved when they discovered Robert Leslie, who proved expert at subtly matching the colors in specimen skins; he later became a fashionable painter to Queen Victoria.

Volume I, with 40 birds on five plates and a meticulous text, was completed in 1808 and Wilson set off with a sample copy to find more subscribers and continue his field research. He covered more than 10,000 miles (16,100 km) plus a sea trip back from New Orleans to Philadelphia before he settled down to work on the third and remaining volumes, which occupied the rest of his life, the last two being published posthumously in 1814.

Despite his care to depict his subjects accurately, there is a certain stiffness and naivety about Wilson's pictures, but this does not detract from his magnificent achievement in so short a time.

One of the people on whom Wilson called on his selling trips was a storekeeper in Louisville, Kentucky. As he looked at the samples, this man's partner remarked (in French) "Your own drawings are far better!" The other artist was John James Audubon.

Audubon was born in the Caribbean but raised in France, where he claimed to have had some art tuition in Jacques-Louis David's atelier and to have studied birds with the naturalist Alcide d'Orbigny. He was sent over to America to check out some Pennsylvanian property that his father owned, which had a vein of lead on it, and to avoid being forced to join Napoleon's army. Eventually he became a storekeeper.

Some years after Wilson's visit, and after misguided business deals had eaten into the profits from his store, Audubon became bankrupt. He began to scratch a living from sketching portraits in black chalk, often commissioned as

memorial studies of the newly deceased. Later he found work preserving specimens in Dr. Drake's Western Museum in Cincinnati. Here it was that he decided to turn into reality a dream of producing an illustrated book of American birds. First he needed to collect bird sketches

Illustration from John James Audubon's Birds of America, produced from his paintings by the aquatint process.
Pinnated Grouse (Tetrao cupido). (Usually called the Greater Prairie Chicken).

Wilson's parakeet

When Alexander Wilson was collecting material for his *Ornithology* he often shot birds to provide himself with specimens. On one occasion he decided "to try the effects of education on one of those but slightly wounded in the wing." This was a parakeet, which he called Poll. She became his companion for his entire trip through the American West in 1809, traveling in his pocket, though she frequently escaped from her confinement.

When Wilson was staying as a guest of one subscriber to his work, Poll was put into a cage where she attracted flocks of other parakeets. Another parakeet that Wilson wounded became her companion for a time:

"She crept close up to it as it hung on the side of the cage; chattering to it in a low tone of voice as if sympathising in its misfortune; scratched about its head and neck with her bill; and both at night nestled as close as possible to each other, sometimes Poll's head being thrust among the plumage of the other. On the death of this companion, she appeared restless and inconsolable for several days. I placed a looking glass beside the place where she usually sat, and the instant she perceived her image, all her former fondness seemed to return, so that she could scarcely absent herself from it a moment. It was evident that she was

completely deceived. Always when evening drew on, and often during the day, she laid her head close to that of the image in the glass and began to doze with great composure and satisfaction."

Sadly, Poll got out of her cage during the sea voyage back to Philadelphia, flew overboard and perished in the waters of the Gulf of Mexico.

Alexander Wilson's study of a Carolina Parakeet (Conuropsis carolinensis), his companion on his travels in the West in 1809. The only parrot native to the United States, it is now extinct.

Opposite *Scarlet Macaw* (Macrocercus aracanga, *now* Ara macao) *by Edward Lear, from his* Illustrations of the Family of Psittacidae, or Parrots.

Iceland Falcon (Gyrfalcon) (Falco candicans, *now* F. rusticolus) *from James John Audubon's* Birds of America.

and specimens from further afield. He financed his expedition by working his passage on a boat to New Orleans by shooting and fishing to supply food for crew and passengers, and with his drawing.

Some people did not think very highly of Audubon's work. Alexander Lawson refused to engrave his pictures and he was unable to find a publisher for them in America so, in 1826, he set sail with 400 drawings to find one in Britain.

In Edinburgh an engraver called William Lizars — who was already engraving 218 life-size plates for Prideaux John Selby's *Illustrations of British Ornithology* (1821–34) — agreed to collaborate. A prospectus was drawn up and Audubon, like Wilson, set off to find subscribers, first in London, then in Paris. Before he completed *The Birds of America*, published 1827–38, he had changed engravers to Robert Havell who used a technique known as aquatint, traveled back and forth across the Atlantic

and undertaken more field trips, including one to Labrador.

Edward Lear and John Gould

In 1827, an English fifteen-year-old called Edward Lear began to earn money as a jobbing artist. As a sickly and neglected child he had developed his artistic skill by copying the birds in his father's copy of Buffon's *Histoire Naturelle*. Three years later he got permission to draw in the bird collection of the Zoological Society of London and began to invite subscriptions for his *Illustrations of the Family of Psittacidae, or Parrots*. He found 175 subscribers but the proceeds were not enough for him to produce as many plates as he had planned, though those issued in 1830–1832 were of a very high quality indeed. Lear had taught himself to use a new process: lithography, producing prints from drawings made in greasy materials directly onto stone, colors being applied by hand following the artist's original watercolors.

The curator of the Zoological Society's collection, John Gould, had an artistic wife and he persuaded her to learn the new lithographic process, as well as making delicate watercolors of birds, sometimes from his sketches. Gould then set up the publication of *A Century of Birds from the Himalayan Mountains*, choosing a similar format to Lear's book, and this became the first of many illustrated books that he published.

Lear probably helped Elizabeth Gould with her painting and himself painted plates for some of Gould's early books, especially *The Birds of Europe* (including some that the printing attributes to the Goulds); to research these he traveled to European zoos and museums. He went on to become even better known, first as a topographical painter and then for his nonsense verses and the sketches that accompany them — so different from his meticulously detailed bird pictures.

Gould used a number of other artists on his books, including the German Joseph Wolf who contributed the birds of prey to *The Birds of Great Britain. A Monograph of the Trochilidae, or Family of Humming Birds* (1849–61) is considered by many to be Gould's masterpiece, produced after Elizabeth's death with illustrations by Henry Constantine Richter. Wolf, who became an acclaimed animal painter, exhibiting at the Royal Academy, also produced lithographs for Daniel Giraud Elliot of Chicago.

Twentieth-century art

Until the beginning of the twentieth century, bird artists could be evaluated against the wider art of their contemporaries. The trends in modern art towards abstraction have produced a separation between the different schools that makes comparison invidious. Some modern critics view the representational with contempt, but bird art, as opposed to birds in art — and they still retain a symbolic role — is essentially the art of reality and *must* be representational.

MACROCERCUS ARACANGA.

Red and Yellow Maccaw.

2/3 Nat. Size.

Hummingbird (Cometes Sparganurus, *now* Sappho sparganura), *a plate from Gould's* Family of Hummingbirds, *drawn by Henry Richter. With over 300 plates, this book took 12 years to produce.*

At its best it shows birds in a way that is wholly accurate, while at the same time enhancing appreciation of what is shown and evoking a sympathetic recognition of what is familiar.

This is not easy. In trying to evaluate its success one encounters a dichotomy of availability. Much work, often of the highest quality, was commissioned, or dispersed rapidly among private enthusiasts and is not known or seen in public galleries. As a result bird artists are largely judged by what they have offered as book illustrations. In general this is of an extremely high standard, competing as it has had to do with color photography, and to offer something more to justify its use. At times anyone familiar with an artist's work will recognize when he or she has lacked enthusiasm for the subject requested. Nevertheless, even the more pedestrian of what is offered today will outshine most of what has been praised in the past.

Modern bird art may one day be recognized as a special "school," probably comparable with or better than past schools of flower or landscape painters. There are too many good artists for the subject to be covered here, beyond the mention of some of the best, uneasily aware that some are omitted and there are many others to whom credit is due.

The century's earlier artists tended to have special interests and illustration did not bring out the best in them. Archibald Thorburn was better in quick watercolors of birds of prey or gamebirds than in his formal works and George Lodge was essentially a painter of raptors. Both would seem to have been outshone at times by the Swedish artist Bruno Liljefors in his big bird canvases. Later Sir Peter Scott was some-

A peacock's head painted by William Mallord Turner, not usually thought of as a natural history painter although he did several studies of birds' heads.

one who managed to bridge the gap between canvases and illustration, and much of the appreciation of waterfowl today was aided by his art. There have been more fine bird artists in the last half century than in the ages before, including in Britain: Charles Tunnicliffe, Eric Ennion, R. A. Richardson, David Reid-Henry, Robert Gillmor, Keith Shackleton and, more recently possibly Philip Burton and Ian Lewington. In America, Roger Tory Peterson, Albert E. Gilbert, Don Eckleberry and Guy Tudor set high standards. John Busby deserves special mention as an artist who has brought his birds to life, and Lars Jonsson of Sweden for seeing birds from new angles. Australia has Peter Slater and in William T. Cooper has produced an exceptional artist whose consistent high standards put most nineteenth century work to shame.

Decoy ducks

Wildfowlers have often used wooden ducks to deceive the real birds, who they might also attract by imitating their calls, to bring them down to join them. These decoys, skillfully carved and painted and carefully balanced so that they would float realistically upon the water, have become an art form in themselves. Old ones are avidly collected and decorative forms made by craftsmen in Third World countries help earn much needed hard currency for them.

Following pages Wild Ducks by Sir Peter Scott. Already established as an artist, especially as a painter of wildfowl, Sir Peter became an important force in the conservation and ecology movement and instrumental in the creation of the World Wildlife Fund (or World Wide Fund for Nature as it is now known).

STUDYING THE BIRDS

For thousands of years the people who knew most about birds were those who hunted them, for by understanding the birds' habits hunters were able to make their trapping or shooting more successful. Later, it was hunters who became aware of declining populations and established the Flora and Fauna Preservation Society in 1903, while the first Audubon Society was launched through the pages of *Forest and Stream*.

Although birds are frequently seen, especially those species that nest in or near human habitations, until recently there was little known about their behavior. They were not easy to study when in a tree or high in the air, and even in a hedgerow were difficult to spot.

In the past, some very strange explanations were given as to why some of them disappeared in winter. Aristotle, who probably ranks as the first major naturalist — he was the tutor of Alexander the Great, who had specimens sent back to Aristotle from the countries that he conquered — seems to have realized that some birds, at least, migrated. He observed animals carefully and objectively, noting in his *Natural History* for example, that woodpeckers push nuts into crevices so that they can crack their shells. Unfortunately, when the Roman writer Pliny expanded Aristotle's book he introduced many fanciful ideas and it was this version that in turn formed the basis for the *Physiologus (Natural Historian)* from which the bestiary writers took their information — ideas such as that swallows hibernated through the winter, or that Barnacle Geese developed each year from a sort of worm or mollusk. For more than a thousand years most natural history, in Europe at least, was based on received ideas and not on observation.

Migration theories

"Where do the swallows go in winter?" was a question that baffled ancient peoples. They came up with some very strange solutions. One was that they rolled themselves into balls and slept the winter through at the bottom of ponds. Aristotle noted reports of swallows found torpid on the southern slopes of mountains during winter but he clearly knew about migration, for he saw that birds were fatter when they migrated.

It is often suggested that migration was not "discovered" until the eighteenth century, but the Hebrews must have known about it for the Old Testament story of Job mentions hawks flying to the south and this knowledge was not completely forgotten. A bestiary in Cambridge University library, copied (in Latin of course) in the twelfth century from earlier texts, clearly states that the swallow

"flies across the sea and there overseas it lives during the winter."

Of storks the same manuscript declares:

"these messengers of Spring . . . can migrate across the oceans and, having collected themselves into column of route, can go straight through to Asia. Crows fly in front of them as pathfinders and the storks follow like a squadron."

Bestiaries often contain quite fanciful notions and imaginary animals from legend, and whoever contributed these remarks got it wrong about the crows, but clearly they had observed migrating flocks and knew that they flew south. It would seem that some migration was accepted, and the main arguments in later centuries seem to have been about the swal-

In a typical songbird nest of a Dusky Flycatcher (Muscicapa adusta), *the helpless young stay low in the warmly lined cup.*

A flock of Barnacle Geese (Branta leucopsis) *wintering in Scotland.*

lows, but no one then appreciated the distances migration could take some birds or its true pattern; indeed, there are many aspects of migration that we still do not fully understand.

In the thirteenth century, the Holy Roman Emperor Frederick II, a scholar and mathematician who founded the University of Naples, was an exception who did study the world around him. Passionately keen on falconry, he observed both hawks and other birds. His *De Arte Venandi cum Avibus* shows that the migration of birds was no mystery to him, for he had seen their autumn (fall) and spring flights and noted that

"however terrible the weather, despite fatigue, the birds persist in their migration. Once they begin they press onward as though this was the most important thing in their lives."

Having heard that the "worms" of the Barnacle Goose were found on rotting timbers, Frederick sent north to obtain some, and his messenger brought back some wood with barnacles attached, but he decided that the true explanation was that geese migrated. He observed that cuckoos laid eggs in the nests of other species and in proof presented a hand-reared chick taken from a songbird's nest, which grew into a cuckoo. He even comments on the preen gland in aquatic birds. Although the Emperor put these things in his manuscript around 1250, it was centuries later before people gave up believing in the old stories.

The Renaissance brought a more scientific approach and the development of the telescope and later of binoculars made observation at a distance easier, while the increasing number of printed books speeded the dissemination of knowledge. Much effort went into the collection and identification of new species as explorers opened up fresh territories to Europeans. Specimens were usually collected by shooting them, a practice that continued right up to the mid-twentieth century and accounts for shot specimens being the only known examples of some rarities.

By the mid-seventeenth century men such as the English cleric John Ray were becoming careful observers, free of superstitious beliefs though seeing Nature as following some Divine Plan and their studies therefore as a way of understanding God's Will. With Francis Willughby, one of his students from Cambridge, Ray traveled the length and breadth of Britain and across Europe collecting plant specimens and studying wildlife. He rejected old ideas such as swallows spending the winter in the mud of ponds when he saw birds heading out to sea in autumn. Ray realized the connection between territory and aggressive behavior, and he demonstrated that a swallow would go on laying until its clutch was complete by daily removing eggs from a nest. When Willughby died in 1672, leaving him a small pension, Ray

Where do swallows go in winter?

Von Caub in his *Ortus Sanitatis* of 1485 thought they hibernated. Olaus Magnus, Archbishop of Uppsala acknowledged, in 1555, that some authors described how they flew to a warm climate for the winter months but claimed there were many others

"which are often pulled from the water in a large ball. They cling beak to beak, wing to wing, foot to foot, having bound themselves in the first days of autumn to hide among canes and reeds."

Francis Willughby strongly supported swallow migration and in 1703 an English naturalist called Morton claimed that they flew to the moon, though his pupil, novelist Daniel Defoe, perceptively saw that they followed their food, the insects, to warmer climes. Eighteenth-century English lexicographer Dr. Samuel Johnson, however, still declared that they

"certainly sleep all the winter. A number of them conglobulate together, by flying round and round, and then all in a heap throw themselves under water, and lie in the bed of a river."

The English naturalist Gilbert White favored hibernation for some individuals,

though his own brother had witnessed migrating birds flying across the Straits of Gibraltar, remarking that

"House swallows have some strange attachment to water, independent of the matter of food; and though they may not retire into that element, yet they may conceal themselves in the banks of pools and rivers during the uncomfortable months of winter."

One spring he set his gardeners to beat their way through bushes to flush out hibernating birds; of course, they did not find any.

Karl von Linné — the great Swedish botanist Linnaeus — and Cuvier the following century were others who favored the theory of the swallows' hibernation, though in 1758 anatomist John Hunter had shown that their respiratory system was not adapted to prolonged immersion in water.

John James Audubon, on the other hand, was a firm advocate of migration.

The old naturalists should not be judged too harshly; they did have some evidence for their beliefs. Swallows do tend to roost in large numbers among beds of water reeds and, if caught by a cold snap that eliminates their insect food supplies, may sometimes survive by reducing their metabolic rate and becoming torpid.

concentrated on writing about natural history, probably being responsible for most of what was published posthumously as Willughby's *Ornithology* as well as books under his own name.

John Ray was a friend of Mark Catesby, who became the first real ornithologist of America, and from the eighteenth century on the naturalists of different countries were often in contact, either by correspondence or through publications. Ray had originally set out with the idea of cataloging species and identification and classification was at the forefront of scientific interest, but behavior was also being more widely noted. Gilbert White, a parson in the south of England, rarely traveled far from his parish but his observations gave him an intimate knowledge of the local wildlife (recorded in letters that were later published as *The Natural History and Antiquities of Selborne*). He made a close study of birdsong and was probably the first person to use the difference in calls to identify species that are otherwise difficult to distinguish.

There was an explosion of interest and information gathering in the nineteenth century by inquiring natural historians such as Charles Darwin and ornithologists such as those already mentioned as bird artists. Scientific expeditions brought back countless specimens and John Gould, for instance, is known to have received detailed information from many of his sources, which, not being relevant he thought to a bird's appearance, he unfortunately discarded!

Increasingly, scientific disciplines became more precise. By the end of the nineteenth century most birds had been "described" (formally named and recorded scientifically) and some information about them gathered with specimens in museums for study. In the twentieth century photography and cinemaphotography, sound recording and other technical developments have made possible records of a different kind but it was not until well into the century that the study of the living bird and its behavior began to develop. Julian Huxley and Edmund Selous (both British), Konrad Lorenz (Austrian), Niko Tinnbergen (Dutch) and Margaret Nice (American) are only a few of the people who have contributed to the development of modern bird ethology. Attempts are now made to organize the collection and codification of information from ringing programs and carefully monitored observation on an international scale. Conservation has become an increasingly important concern and to be effective must be based on sound scientific knowledge.

From a subject for the amateur, ornithology has been largely taken over by the scientific professionals. For a time the body of information remained able to be understood by individuals, but now it has become so large that it is increasingly a matter of specialization. However, this does not invalidate the contribution that can still be made by the amateur bird watcher. What is necessary is that observations are made and recorded accurately.

BIRD-WATCHING

Birds have colonized almost every habitat and, because flight enables them to escape predators more easily than most other animals, those that do not live in a forest habitat can be easily observed flying and feeding, unless they have deliberately hidden themselves away, camouflaged among the leaves to escape danger or to disguise their eggs and brood.

There are locations where particular kinds of birds live in great numbers and places where migrating birds are seen *en masse* at particular times of year. They are well worth special visits, but birds can be seen each and every day without making a special expedition and irrespective of whether you live in town or country. A keen eye may catch sight of a soaring raptor among the high-rise blocks of a city financial district and spot a surprisingly wide range of visitors to a suburban garden.

Get yourself a field guide (a book illustrating and describing the identifying characteristics) for the birds in your geographical area so that you can put a name to those you see. Many people find identifying species quite absorbing and some like to notch up as many different sightings as possible, rushing off to places hundreds of miles away when a rare visitor has been reported. They have been given a special name — "twitchers" — and groups sometimes hold competitions to see who can see the greatest number of species over a set period. However, watching bird behavior and learning to understand it can be even more interesting, although you will need to be able to identify the species if this is to be of any scientific value.

Away from home you can bird-watch almost anywhere, while traveling to work, through the office window, around the factory site or out in the countryside. If you are going to a different area on holiday make sure that you take a field guide that covers the species you will find there.

A pair of binoculars or the modern type of telescope are a valuable asset in studying birds

for it is often difficult to get close to them. For extended study of a particular nest or location it may be worth building a "hide" from which you can watch the birds without disturbing them. A hide needs to be just that, something to hide you. It need not be elaborately disguised. After erection it should be left for the birds to get used to it and then, when you begin to visit it, you must stay quietly inside and wait for the birds to recover from the disturbance of your arrival. Some bird reserves have permanent hides from which visitors can watch.

Inconspicuous clothes that blend with the environment are best when bird-watching — remember that birds see in color. Dull greens, browns and grays will usually merge with the landscape and you might even wear something with a camouflage pattern, though in desert or dune country these will stand out against the sand. Wear a hat. It will break up the line of your head. Make use of bushes and other obstructions to disguise your presence further and, having chosen your place, stay there.

Birds are often active very early in the day so don't lie in bed; being in position before sunup may help you to see and the light will be continually improving. When birds come home to roost in the evening, visibility is rapidly going. If you plan to watch shorebirds, find out tide times; it is when the tide is out that most of them will be feeding. The solitary watcher may be less noticeable but going out with a couple of friends means more pairs of eyes to spot something that just one might miss.

The amateur bird-watcher can make a valuable contribution to scientific knowledge if he or she makes accurate identifications and observations and keeps careful records of them. Information on species distribution, understanding of behavior and monitoring of the effects of pollution and other environmental threats depend on the careful records of bird-

Left *The birds at this Ohio winter feeding table are mainly male and female Cardinals* (Cardinalis cardinalis) *with a Red-bellied Woodpecker* (Centaurus carolinus) *clinging to the tray and among the Cardinals on the ground a female Purple Finch* (Carpodacus purpureus), *Rufous-sided Towhee* (Pipilo erythrophthalmus) *and American Tree Sparrow* (Spizella arborea).

Right *The Eastern Bluebird* (Sialia sialis), *a summer visitor to the eastern and northern United States, a popular favorite that often made use of nesting boxes, has suffered heavily from pesticides and is now seldom seen. Introduced species such as European Starlings and House Sparrows have often evicted it from its nesting boxes and natural nesting holes. A major program of specially designed boxes is however meeting with some success.*

Birds outside your window

A bird table in your garden or yard, or fixed outside an apartment window, will attract birds, and in places with harsh winters may help birds get through who otherwise might starve. It may prove particularly valuable as a way to bring birds to where they can be easily seen by apartment dwellers and others lacking gardens. Careful choice of what foodstuffs you provide and how you make them available will attract particular breeds according to their diet and habits. Some bird table food may attract birds you might not want to encourage as well as those you do and may even become a focus for the attention of predatory species. A garden offers much better ways of attracting birds for you can organize it to offer the conditions they prefer. If you can encourage birds to nest, you will be able to watch their whole life cycles and natural behavior patterns, not just their table manners!

Developing your garden or yard to provide the diet of worms, insects, fruit and berries that indigenous birds prefer and creating areas of habitat where they can happily nest will be much more rewarding than a bird table — and creating a natural ecology probably will help to keep some of your garden pests under control. If local species are threatened by loss of habitat, by creating or preserving a small area of your own you will be doing a valuable job in helping them to survive.

Most birds like cover for their nests so low trees and bushes will often be preferred, and water should always be a feature both for drinking and for bathing, but make sure that it is not encroached by cover that could give predators a hidden approach (especially domestic cats). A lawn will provide a feeding ground for birds such as starlings and thrushes that peck for worms and ants, but they will happily hunt for worms and snails between your plants as well.

Leaving an area of meadow grass and flowers will provide natural food for some of the seed eaters: teazles, thistles, nettles and ragworts will attract finches to British gardens much more than their usual garden flowers, though sunflowers will provide welcome seeds. In other parts of the world, birds' needs may be different. Investigate the diets and habits of local and visitor species and make your plans accordingly.

Do not be too ready to disturb a stack of sticks or a pile of old pots in springtime; they may be just the place a robin or a wren decides will make a

An ornamental birdbath in an English garden finds ready users.

perfect nesting site. Creepers often provide a convenient nesting place and a hedge not only gives a place to nest but a useful source of insects and berries too.

Berry-bearing shrubs such as cotoneaster and pyracantha or trees such as hawthorn, rowan or holly will provide food for many birds, which will be drawn to them in winter. Making holes in tree trunks could bring in hole-nesting birds, but placing a nest box on a tree trunk or a wall can be just as effective. Position it at a height that predators cannot reach. If you are aiming to provide for a particular species, find out the optimum nesting space and the size of the entry hole so that is not taken over by a rival species.

Putting out food on a bird table or hanging up nuts and pieces of fat will attract birds and may provide much needed food in a harsh winter, but it may not be taken by the species for which you intend it. Squirrels, racoons and rats may get there first, and if you create an exposed place where small birds regularly congregate you may find hawks and other predators exploiting it as a source of prey.

Careful planning of your garden and of where you offer supplementary food can ensure that plenty of bird activity will be visible from indoors so that you can do your bird-watching in comfort, for once birds have discovered the facilities you offer they will come back to you.

Cannon nets shoot out over waders on an Australian beach to catch them for ringing and ring inspection. The nets are laid out upshore with one edge secured and poles attached to the opposite edge that are simultaneously fired from mortars to carry the net over the beach.

watchers. Contact local bird clubs or your national ornithological and bird protection organizations to find out more about what part you could play.

Studying bird movement

Some of the skills developed by bird trappers are employed today to capture wild birds so that they can be fitted with identifying rings and then released. They carry these rings for the rest of their lives and if they are found dead, trapped again, or when the identification code can be read through a bird-watcher's binoculars, valuable information is given on bird movement.

In a few cases, and with larger birds such as the Kakapo in New Zealand, radio monitoring has been employed, but for most small birds the weight of a transmitter would hamper their flight and could produce unnatural behavior (negating its purpose) as well as being an unjustifiable interference.

Techniques sometimes used in short-term studies include fixing numbered tags like artificial feathers to birds' wings so that the numbers can be read from a distance, using colored leg bands in combinations that identify individuals, or dyeing patches of plumage in bright colors to identify populations.

All such schemes rely on information getting back to the organizer. The last few mentioned tend to have limited publicity, but metal bands usually carry a return address and the information needed is the band number, date when found or when the bird died, and the place.

Banding (ringing) a Great Knot (Calidris tenuirostris). The pliers are used to gently close the ring around the leg; their graduated holes ensure a correct fit. The ring must not press on or chafe the leg. Light aluminum (aluminium) or alloy rings do not make extra demands on a bird or affect its balance. Plastic rings may be used in addition as short-term markers to identify individuals or populations. These are often split rings that can be easily put on or removed. Similar rings are often used in aviculture for captive birds.

Banding

The use of leg rings to identify individual birds goes back at least to Roman times; a guineafowl bone encircled by a metal ring was found on a Roman site in England and even earlier a string was sometimes tied around a bird's leg as a means of identification. Asian falconers often used bands too; Marco Polo saw them on his Asian travels in the thirteenth century. In the seventeenth and eighteenth centuries, some landed gentry put rings around the necks of swans.

In 1890, the Danish ornithologist Hans Christian Cornelius Mortenson pioneered modern scientific banding, though the zinc rings, labeled Viborg in ink, which he first used were unsatisfactory. Eight years later, using an aluminum band stamped with an individual serial number as well as a return address, he established the pattern used today.

BIRDS IN DANGER

The changing climate of the Earth and competition with other species have always been evolutionary forces affecting the survival of particular bird species and the days of any species were numbered if it could not find a way to outwit its enemies. Although the activities of human hunters could be seen as natural predation and just part of the process, the development of hunting and snaring weaponry and techniques and then the killing for sport and decoration as well as food has increasingly upset the natural balance. Appropriation of land for agriculture, and in more recent centuries for building and industry, the felling of forests and the destruction by pollution of much of what remained have all made inroads on the natural habitats of birds.

Many birds have exploited the environments created by humans, where these have offered conditions like those in which they originally flourished, and the mobility given by flight has helped birds to seek out new territories when their home environment is destroyed. However, migratory birds require not just one territory but two, and suitable resting and feeding places along the paths of their migration flights. Damage to any of these can affect their survival and, since destinations and routes appear to be part of the birds' heredity, the possibilities for modification and relocation are restricted.

The developing of single crop farming over large areas, theoretically easier to manage and harvest — especially for big landowners — has led to an increasing use of fertilizers and pesticides. To loss of habitat and hunting have been added chemical poisons, which may either be taken directly or via the food chain.

Plants produce their own deterrents and poisons against the insects and other predators that eat them and those predators in turn have developed resistance to them, aided by the speed and numbers of their reproduction. They continue to adapt to the chemicals that humans use against them, so new pesticides have to be continually developed. Birds and mammals do not adapt or reproduce so rapidly — nor do people. But this lesson has been learned too late to prevent enormous damage being done and frequently it is still ignored.

It was the discovery that the eggs of raptors and predatory seabirds in Europe and North America were showing an increasing number of breakages and malformations that alerted scientists to the danger of contamination by dichlorodiphenyltrichloroethane (DDT), a chemical that had been hailed as a great boon in eradicating insect parasites and disease vectors, from the malaria mosquito to the human flea. In fact, it builds up in animal tissue and is now banned in many parts of the world, though not in all, for in the poorer parts of the world its comparatively low cost outweighs the dangers that it poses.

The danger of poisonous metals, such as mercury, and of the chemicals known as polychlorinated biphenyls (PCBs) used in paints and plastics, have all been made clear by their effect on birds.

Pollution of inland waters not only directly poisons birds, plants and other wildlife but, by starving the water of oxygen, creates conditions in which a bacteria flourishes that produces botulism: poisoning that affects the nervous system, leading to paralysis of the respiratory system.

Toxicity in the air, contaminating distant areas in the form of acid rain, also takes its toll, destroying habitat and releasing metals from the soil that kill fish and in turn affect birds and other animals.

Hunters still take a considerable toll of birds, both of migrant species and of exotics that are trapped for the bird trade, many more dying in transit after capture. However, it is probably destruction of the environment that poses the greatest threat both now and in the future.

In 1985, the *Red Data Book of Birds*, a listing of endangered species published jointly by the International Union for the Conservation of Nature and the International Council for Bird Preservation, contained over 1,000 species — nearly 12 percent of all those known and it was predicted that, if present trends continue, by the end of the century one in twenty of known birds will have disappeared.

It is not only the possibility of total extinction that must concern everyone who cares about birds but the loss of species from any area — and, in addition to the most severely endangered species listed in the panel on page 278, there are many other birds that are locally endangered.

Bird conservation

The first bird protection organizations had their origins in the reaction against the depre-

The Nene or Hawaiian Goose (Branta sandvicensis) was first reduced to a very small population by hunting and, though captive breeding has raised their numbers, they have failed to reestablish themselves in the wild because their nests are heavily predated by introduced mammals.

Oiled seabirds

Oil used to be refined into gasoline or kerosene at plants near to the wells from which it came, but now it is considered more profitable to ship it in huge tankers in its crude state, aggravating the problem if a wreck or accident causes spillage or when unscrupulous shippers illegally wash out tanks at sea. The difference is that, quite apart from the quantities of oil involved, volatile petrol and kerosene evaporate fairly quickly — crude oil does not; it poisons the water, kills life in it and negates the water-repellent and insulating properties of bird feathers.

When the *Amaco Cadiz* supertanker went aground off the coast of Brittany, thousands of dead birds were found on French and Channel Island beaches. Many other sea and shore animals were affected too. In industrial and commercial spheres, insufficient notice was taken of what had happened and equally undesirable oil spills have occurred since, notably the Alaskan disaster with the tanker *Exon Valdez*.

There was an even greater toll of wildlife when crude oil was released into the sea during the Gulf War following the Iraqi invasion of Kuwait in 1990.

dations made by hunting for the plumage trade, but the concerns of those working for bird protection and conservation are now very much wider. Bodies such as the International Union for the Conservation of Nature (IUCN), the World Wide Fund for Nature (WWF) and national organizations play an important role in alerting people to the risk to the environment and the threat to all life forms and run programs to protect them; the Convention on International Trade in Endangered Species (CITES) provides a worldwide system of controls on international commerce in wild animals and plants — though it can only be as effective as its signatories make it — but these organizations are concerned with wildlife in general. There are also organizations which specifically concern themselves with birds, though working closely with the other conservationist groups for, as increasingly realized, the lives of all species in a particular habitat or biosphere are intimately interconnected.

Bodies of oiled seabirds litter the shore at Tanajib, Saudi Arabia. Destruction of oil wells in the conflict following the Iraqi invasion of Kuwait caused unprecedented pollution for hundreds of miles along the shores of the Arabian Gulf, but regular illegal oil-releases by tankers continually cause pollution quite apart from occasional accidents and disasters.

Birds as danger signals

Until 1992 miners used to take a caged canary underground to warn them of dangerous gases in the mine. The bird would react to poisons in the air before miners became aware of them.

Today, though other species may suffer first, it is often birds, their plumage fouled by oil, that alert us to the pollution of the seas and an analysis of bird tissues is now one of the ways in which scientists can monitor the contamination of the environment. Birds, whose entrails priests once consulted in divination, continue to offer warning of future dangers.

Canaries were used by rescue teams in coal mines to detect poisonous carbon monoxide gas. Reacting more rapidly than humans, their fluttering and other signs of distress gave warning when gas was present. Oxygen was also carried to help birds recover. No detecting apparatus was so reliable and canaries were used in British mines until 1992 when new electronic equipment, which can also meter the concentration of gas, was introduced.

The International Council for Bird Preservation forms a grouping to which most other bird organizations are affiliated. Developed from the International Committee for the Protection of Birds, which was set up in 1922, it is the world's oldest international conservation group. It acts as a propaganda and educational body but also collects and assesses data from scientists in more than 100 countries, advises on bird conservation and runs its own action programs, often in association with other bodies.

The first bird protection society was formed in the United States and now there is a network of State Audubon Societies, grouped from 1905 in the National Association of Audubon Societies. In 1940, the National Audubon Society was formed taking over much of the Association's work but there are still numerous State Societies that especially concentrate on local issues and are linked in the Audubon Alliance.

In Britain the Royal Society for the Protection of Birds is the major bird conservation body, and similar organizations now exist or are coming into being in most countries. Their common problem is to obtain the respect and cooperation of politicians and businessmen.

Conservation strategies

Conservation and protection measures must include preservation of habitat, the ending of environmental pollution, whether as a by-product of human activity or deliberate poisoning to control unwanted plants and animals, and a reduction in or cessation of hunting where this could reduce numbers below a viable breeding population. In all these areas conservationists are fighting against entrenched reactionary forces and even if they win out in the end the victory may be too late. Many more species will have been lost.

Below *The Seychelles Black Paradise Flycatcher* (Terpsiphone corvina) *is among the world's most endangered birds with wild populations now so small that survival is very doubtful.*

The world's most seriously endangered species

None of the birds in the following list has a wild population of more than 150 birds, many far less. The *Red Data Book of Birds*, published by the ICBP, lists more than 1,000 species that are threatened. Nearly half — 43 percent — are birds of tropical forests. There are many other birds that, though still holding their ground in some parts of the world, are in danger of disappearing in other places where they have formerly been well established.

Many of the birds in this short list occur on small islands. Such birds may be in less danger from the immediate activities of people but their natural populations are already so small and restricted in range that even very brief activity against them might bring about rapid extinction.

Islands are not only small pieces of land in oceans as far as birds are concerned. In many of the warmer areas of the world, forest or similar vegetation may be confined to a few hilltops or mountains within more open or developed regions. Such ecological islands sometimes contain one or more endemic subspecies or species. Tree felling for timber, firewood or extension of farmland, over a very short period could wipe out both vegetation and birds. Loss of habitat in this way is one of today's most serious conservation problems.

Aldabra Brush-Warbler (*Nesillas aldabrana*)
California Condor (*Gymnogyps californianus*)
Chatham Island Black Robin (*Petroica traversi*)
Chatham Island Oystercatcher (*Haematopus chathamensis*)
Chatham Island Plover (*Charadrius novaeseelandiae*)
Crested Ibis (*Nipponia nippon*)
Hawaiian Crow (*Corvus hawaiiensis*)
Imperial Woodpecker (*Campephilus imperialis*)
Ivory-billed Woodpecker (*Campephilus principalis*)
Kakapo (*Strigops habroptilus*)
Kauai O'o (*Moho braccatus*)
Lord Howe Island Woodhen (*Gallirallus sylvestris*)

Madagascar Sea-Eagle (*Haliaeetus vociferoides*)
Mauritius Kestrel (*Falco punctatus*)
Mauritius Parakeet (*Psittacula echo*)
Mauritius Pink Pigeon (*Columba mayeri*)
New Zealand Black Stilt (*Himantopus novaezelandiae*)
Noisy Scrub-bird (*Atrichornis clamosus*)
Okinawa Woodpecker (*Sapheopipo noguchii*)
Puerto Rican Parrot (*Amazona vittata*)
Rodriguez Brush-Warbler (*Bebrornis rodericanus*)
Seychelles Black Paradise Flycatcher (*Terpsiphone corvina*)
Seychelles Magpie-Robin (*Copsychus sechellarum*)
White-chested White-eye (*Zosterops albogularis*)

The Scots Pine at Loch Garten, which is the nesting site to which the Osprey (Pandion haliaetus) officially returned as a breeding bird in 1954, used annually ever since. With facilities for watching it from a public hide, it was a key site used by the Royal Society for the Protection of Birds for encouraging public interest in conservation. Decay and vandalism nearly destroyed it, but it was artificially rebuilt and has continued to be used by the birds.

In a world where damage to the environment is continuing at such a terrifying rate and most governments still seem unprepared to take action to match the urgency of the need, predictions for the future may seem gloomy, but there are very positive gains that have been made in recent years. In the case of a number of locally or globally threatened species, work by conservationists to save them has shown results. These birds are not yet out of danger but they show what can be achieved if the necessary understanding and will exist. Some examples show the kind of problems that exist and possible action to help the birds involved.

The California Condor is a species that by 1986 was down to three known birds in the wild. Once it ranged over the Rockies from British Colombia southwards and across to Florida. In the early 1940s, there were up to 100 in the wild but, by 1983, this was down to about 20 individuals and most of these did not survive the winter of 1984–1985.

They were not directly affected by hunting or habitat loss, though hunters' lead shot in the carcasses of birds they ate was one cause of their decline, along with toxins in other carrion — including poisoned bait that farmers put out to kill coyotes — and heavy levels of pesticide poisoning that also has the effect of seriously thinning eggshells and increasing the risk during incubation.

Condors raise only one chick at a time, and that involves so much time and energy that they produce a single chick every two years. In 1986, if the three known California Condors, which were all males, were the only survivors, this signaled the coming extinction of the species in the wild.

Proposals for action included tagging and radio tracking the remaining birds for an intensive study, trying to create an uncontaminated wild feeding range for the survivors and taking them into captivity to add to the gene pool of the 20 California Condors already in zoos to contribute to a captive breeding program. It was decided to capture the birds and add them to those in zoos.

In 1991, the first releases were made from the captive bred birds. They still face the same dangers. Each Condor pair requires a huge territory, so creating a safe zone is scarcely practicable, and only changes in human activity can free their food of poisons. Captive breeding still seems their only hope for survival.

In Britain the number of Barn Owls has been falling to the point where their survival as a native species is threatened. There is a considerable captive population, among which there has been a high level of successful breeding, but the change in agriculture and farm management has led to a loss not only of habitat for prey but of nesting sites as the barns and farm buildings that they use have been converted into homes and hedgerows uprooted. Unless new environmentally sensitive farming methods are adopted that will restore wildlife habitats, perhaps with payments to farmers to set aside land for wildlife, no amount of captive breeding will succeed in helping the species in the wild.

The Corncrake is a summer visitor to Britain, which farming methods also threaten. Earlier harvesting, rapid mechanical cutting and harvesting patterns that trap birds in the uncut section have aggravated already existing problems, which may include the increasing desertification of the Sahara.

A happier story is that of the Osprey, which, although not endangered elsewhere became rare if not extinct in Britain and has now been reestablished, though conservationists have had to protect it from egg collectors, vandals and overenthusiastic birders.

Reintroductions, from populations in other countries or from captive-bred birds appear to have shown signs of success in a number of cases. Red Kites, which now number only about 13,000 pairs worldwide, in 1992 bred successfully in England and Scotland for the first time in over a century, following a release program begun in 1989.

The Roseate Tern was one of the first species to benefit from the early campaigns against the plume trade but there has been a dramatic decline in both European and North American populations. Many of the European birds go to Ghana in the early autumn to exploit an abundance of small fish and many are still trapped there by small boys, although now illegally. However, it has now been discovered that the birds move on from Ghana to spend four months elsewhere, though where is not yet known. Conservation of such species requires much greater knowledge of their lives, though it is clear that the preservation of wetland environments, as the Ramsar Treaty sets out to promote, is an essential element for such migrants.

Endemic island species that have been threatened by the destruction of habitat and the introduction of predators have in some cases been saved by capturing them and transporting the remaining population to other islands where habitat survives and predators have been removed or excluded to make them bird reserves.

Whereas reports are all too often of species loss, there is also the rare occasion when a species considered extinct has been rediscovered. One such is the Kakapo of New Zealand. In the early 1970s, the only survivors were all males and the species thought to be doomed. Then, in 1976, a small colony was found in a remote part of Stewart Island. A program of translocation to safer sites has been in operation since 1985, including Little Barrier Island, a reserve without predators or competitors (in one area, in a single year, a quarter of all known Kakapos were killed by cats that can cause havoc among the endemic New Zealand species). Because the Kakapo is a slow developer and does not breed until five or six years old, it is not yet known whether Little Barrier will provide the conditions that will sustain a viable population of the species, but there is hope that this strange bird will survive.

GLOSSARY

Adaptive radiation The art of spreading to new areas and evolving differences in response to new environments.

Afrotropical Of the zoogeographical region of Africa south of the Sahara Desert.

Alar bar Bar on the wing.

Allopreening The preening of one individual by another.

Altricial (= Nidicolous) Describes a nestling that is helpless and wholly reliant on parents.

Anisodactyl Having three toes directed forward and one backward, as in most birds.

Axillaries Feathers in the "armpit" where the wing joins the body.

Bulla A hollow, rounded, bony structure.

Caecum (plural Caeca) A small branch of the gut with a closed end.

Calcite Calcium carbonate crystals.

Caruncle Hard or soft fleshy lump.

Casque A hollow, bony structure on head or bill.

Cere Area of bare skin around nostrils, as on falcons and some parrots.

Crepuscular Active at dusk.

Cryptic Describes plumage or structure aiding concealment.

Cursorial Moving by running and walking.

Decurved Curving downward.

Dimorphism Having two forms, differing in some noticeable respect.

DNA (Deoxyribonucleic Acid) A molecule of this material in each body cell contains two strands that carry all the genes that determine all the characteristics of an individual.

Eclipse Dull plumage assumed by a male through molt after breeding.

Facial disk A flattened circle of bristly feathers surrounding each eye.

Filoplumes Hairlike or bristlelike structures evolved from feathers.

Frontal plate A horny plate on the top of the bill extending up onto the forehead.

Furcula The wishbone of the breast, formed by the fusion of two clavicles.

Gape Inside of the mouth and bill.

Heterodactyl Having two toes directed forward and the inner and hind toes directed backward, as in trogons.

Holarctic Zoogeographic region including both Eurasia and North America.

Irruption A temporary and sometimes seasonal dispersal from the normal range, usually in response to food shortage.

Keratin A structural protein forming the horny parts of the skin, scales, feathers, and claw and bill sheaths.

Lek A communal display ground shared by a number of males simultaneously.

Mandible An upper or lower jaw.

Nidicolous see **Altricial**.

Nidifugous see **Precocial**.

Palaearctic The zoogeographical region including Eurasia, North Africa, and Arabia.

Pamprodactyl Having all four toes pointed forward, as in typical swifts.

Passerine Literally "sparrowlike," usually referring to the songbird order.

Pheromones Chemicals released into the air by an individual and attracting others of the opposite sex.

Polyandry The mating of a female with several males in one season.

Polygamy Having more than one mate during a season of breeding.

Polygyny The mating of a male with several females in one season.

Powder down Powder produced by steadily disintegrating down feathers, used in preening.

Precocial (= Nidifugous) Describes a nestling that is partly or wholly able to move and feed itself.

Raptor A bird of prey hunting other creatures for food.

Ratites A group of birds, including the very large flightless birds and the tinamous.

Rictal bristle A bristlelike feather growing from the base of a bird's bill.

Rostrum The bony projection of the front of the skull that forms the upper jaw.

Speciation The evolution of more than one separate species from a population that previously formed a single species.

Syrinx The voice box of the bird at the lower end of its windpipe.

Tubenose A seabird of the Procellariidae family, having a small tubular projection over each nostril on the bill.

Vibrissae Sensitive bristles.

Vitelline The name given to a membrane surrounding the yolk of an egg; vitellus being the Latin name for the yolk.

Warm-blooded Having the ability to maintain its own body temperature.

Wattle A projecting or hanging fleshy lump or appendage.

Zydodactyl Having two toes directed forward and the outer toe and hind toe backward, as in parrots and owls.

SCIENTIFIC NAMES

Scientific Names are not generally given in the text. This list gives the common name under which each bird appears in the main index. The numbers refer to the relevant paragraph in the "Birds of the World" section (pages 161–217).

INDEX

Numbers in parenthesis identify a bird's family by reference to that paragraph number in the "Birds of the World" section of this book (pages 161–217).

Figures in *italics* refer to illustrations.

ILLUSTRATION CREDITS

The publishers wish to thank the following for permission to reproduce photographs and other illustrations:

Alecto Editions 231b.
Brian Chudleigh 24(ar)(b), 25(a), 29(br), 32(b), 46(a), 53(r), 57(a), 62, 73(r), 75(b), 76(a), 78(bl), 84(b), 87, 97(a)(b), 101, 115(a)(cr), 116, 118(br), 131(a)(b), 132(c), 135(a), 139(b), 144, 155(c), 166(a)(b), 167(b), 181(ar), 183(b), 185(c), 191(b), 198(c), 275(a)(b).
Bridgeman Art Gallery 234/5, 250.
Bruce Coleman 112, 190(a).
E.T. Archive 226(a), 231(a), 239, 247(b), 249(a), 262 (al)(ar).
Fotopacific 2/3.
Frank Lane Picture Agency: R. Austin 201(c); Carvalhao 52(a); A. Christiansen 191(a); W.S. Clark 99(b), 118(a); P. Davey 19(a), 20, 21(b), 96(a), 185(b); E. Davis 121(cl)(cr); Z. Eichhorn 205(a); Ghani 117(ar); T. Gardner 167(a), 178 (al), 195(a), 199(b); T. & P. Gardner 133(a); M. Gore 44(ar), 171(b); D. Grewcock 45(ar); Hautala 83(b); V. Howes 78(br); D. Kinzler '10; A. Hamblin 36(a), 65(al), 75(ar), 110, 113(ar), 121(a), 141(a), 187(br), 207(a), 249(b); E. Hall 225(al); R. Hamblin 257; J. Hawkins 96(b), 117(al), 172 (ar) 181(c); P. Heard 211(c); E. & D. Hosking 6, 21(b), 22/23, 28, 31(b), 34, 35(b), 40(a), 47, 49(c), 50(a), 83(a), 91, 92(b), 102(b), 103(b), 117(b), 118(c), 119(a), 145, 164(b), 165(c), 167(cb), 169(a)(b), 170(a), 171(a), 172(al)(b), 177(a), 181(al), 182(a)(b)(c), 183(a), 184, 188(b), 190(b), 192/3, 204(al), 207(b), 213(a)(b)(c), 223(a), 227, 243; E. Hosking 29(al), 105(c); Karmali 93(c), 96(c); F. Lane 180(a), 180(b), 197, 198(b), 240(a); R. Langrish 174/5; L. Lee Rue 31(a), 105(a), 130(b), 209(b); S. Maslowski 35(a), 179(b), 195(c), 208(b), 259(b), 274; F. Merlet 48(bl); W. Miller 114(cl), 187(bl), 212(a); M. Newman 44(b), 198(a); A. Parker 99(a); P. Perry 80(a), 95(ar), 155(a), 168, 186(al); F. Polking 33, 39(bl), 67(b), 76(br), 187(a); A. Rile 173; L. Robinson 40(b), 44(al), 164(c); Silvestris 32(a), 147, 163, 201(a), 205(b), 206(b); R. Tidman 51(a), 84(a), 179(a), 188(a); B.S. Turner 29(ar),

135(c), 176; R. van Nostrand 30(b), 45(al), 165(a), 178(ar), 200(b), 211(ar); J. Watkins 60(a), 106, 185(a), 213(b); L. West 209(a); T. Whittaker 1; R. Wilmshurst 30(a), 69(b), 80(b), 104, 124(b), 128(a), 138, 141(b), 166(c); W. Wisniewski 4/5, 8, 27; M. Withers 129(b), 165(b), 179(c), 206(c); D. Zingel 189(a), 211(b); 173(a), 278, 281; **also** 19(c), 20, 51(b), 94, 109, 113(al), 122/3, 132(a), 136(b), 137(b), 146, 148, 156(a), 158, 159, 160, 204(ar), 206(a), 216, 217(ar)(al)(b), 246(r), 253, 270(a), 272, 273, 113(b).
Joel Findler Collection 232, 240(b), 255(r), 255(b), 256(a).
Guinness Brewing Worldwide Ltd. 25.
IKON 220(b), 245(l), 228(b).
A.F. Kersting 225(r).
Cyril Laubscher/C & L Nature World 237, 238(b).
Howard Loxton 251.
Mansell Collection 222(a), 246(l), 248, 258(b).
Moon, Geoff 19(b), 21(a), 26(a), 39(a1), 42/43, 59, 61, 65(r), 69(a), 76(bl), 77, 85(a)90(a), 92(a), 93(a)(b), 102(a), 115 (bl)(br), 124(a), 129(a), 134(b), 135(b), 152/3, 156(b), 167(ca), 172(b), 177(b), 194(a), 196, 199(a), 202(a), 203(b), 204(b), 205(a), 211(al), 212(b), 280(b).
Museum fur Naturkunde, Berlin 13.
Museum of London 258(a).
National Coal Board 277(b).
Reed Publishing Group 21(b), 222(b), 223(b).
Reflections Photo Library 54, 95(bl), 142, 218.
RSPB 25(b), 57(b), 60(b), 72, 75(a)(c), 98, 105(b), 130(a), 136(c), 270(b), 277(a), 279, 280(a).
South American Pictures 37(b), 64, 173(b).
Survival Anglia 12(b), 16, 17, 26(b), 29(bl), 30(c), 39(2)(3)(5), 45(b), 46(b), 48(br), 49(al), 52(bl)(br), 58, 67(a), 68, 70(b), 71, 73(l), 74, 75(al), 78(al), 79(a)(b), 81, 85(b), 86, 88/89, 95(al)(br), 100, 107(a)(b), 118(bl), 119(b), 120(a)(b)(c), 121(b), 126(b), 128(b), 132(b), 133(br), 134(a), 143(a)(b), 151, 195(b), 224(b);230(a), 233(a)(b), 276(b).
Cyril Webster 34(b), 66, 82, 127, 133(bl), 136(a), 137(a)(c), 139(a), 177(c), 186(r), 200(a), 201(b), 202(b), 203(ar)(c), 214/5.
(a) above; (c) center; (b) below/bottom; (t) top; (l) left; (r) right.